Mexico

Mexico

Political, Social and Economic Evolution

NORA HAMILTON
University of Southern California

New York   Oxford
OXFORD UNIVERSITY PRESS
2011

Oxford University Press, Inc., publishes works that further Oxford University's
objective of excellence in research, scholarship, and education.

Oxford New York
Auckland Cape Town Dar es Salaam Hong Kong Karachi
Kuala Lumpur Madrid Melbourne Mexico City Nairobi
New Delhi Shanghai Taipei Toronto

With offices in
Argentina Austria Brazil Chile Czech Republic France Greece
Guatemala Hungary Italy Japan Poland Portugal Singapore
South Korea Switzerland Thailand Turkey Ukraine Vietnam

For titles covered by Section 112 of the US Higher Education Opportunity
Act, please visit www.oup.com/us/he for the latest information about
pricing and alternate formats.

Published by Oxford University Press, Inc.
198 Madison Avenue, New York, New York 10016
http://www.oup.com

Oxford is a registered trademark of Oxford University Press

Library of Congress Cataloging-in-Publication Data
Hamilton, Nora, 1935-
    Mexico : political, social, and economic evolution / Nora Hamilton.
        p. cm.
    Includes bibliographical references and index.
    ISBN 978-0-19-974403-9
    1. Mexico—Social conditions. 2. Mexico—Politics and government. 3. Mexico—Economic conditions.
I. Title.
    HN113.H36 2011
    306.0972—dc22

                                                                    2010039882

BRIEF CONTENTS

CONTENTS

LIST OF FIGURES, MAPS AND TABLES

Figures

Maps

Tables

ACKNOWLEDGMENTS

This book has its origins in an abiding fascination with Mexico and a desire to understand its political, economic and social transformation over the past several decades. My goal in writing it is to present a multi-faceted approach to contemporary Mexico by analyzing the relationship between Mexico's past and present, the connections between its economic, political and social trajectories, and the interaction between domestic and international forces. The approach is to focus on different social and institutional actors—policy makers, business groups, social organizations, workers, indigenous groups, transnational corporations, and migrants, among others—and examine how their action and interaction have directly or indirectly influenced the changes that Mexico has experienced and continues to experience.

I have drawn on my experience in teaching a course on the Mexican political economy since the early 1980s, periodic research visits to Mexico and discussions with Mexican and U.S. scholars, as well as the extensive literature by both Mexican and non-Mexican authors that has emerged during this period and provided new information and insights into Mexico's history, politics, economy, culture and society. Over the years, I have benefited immensely from discussions with colleagues and friends in both the United States and Mexico. I also want to thank the students in my course on the Political Economy of Mexico whose comments on the class and feedback on an early version of the manuscript were very helpful in subsequent revisions.

Special thanks go to colleagues who read specific chapters and sections of the book: Judith Adler Hellman, Mark Kann, Manuel Pastor, Carol Thompson, Devra Weber and Irene Zea; their thoughtful comments and suggestions are deeply appreciated. And I am very thankful to the reviewers of Oxford University Press, whose detailed critiques and valuable insights into different aspects of Mexican history and contemporary Mexico were immensely helpful in the process of revision: Roderic Ai Camp, Claremont McKenna College; Carlos Alberto Contreras, Grossmont College; Maria Lorena Cook, Cornell University; Paul Hart, Texas State University; Claudio Holzner, University of Utah; Ava Lasseter, University of Florida; Gregory Love, University of Mississippi; Víctor M. Macías-González, University of Wisconsin, La Crosse; Suzanne Pasztor, Humboldt State University; Sergio Quesada, University of Georgia; Michael David Snodgrass, Indiana University-Purdue University Indianapolis; Strom Thacker, Boston University.

I am grateful to the University of California for research support. I am especially indebted to Barbara Robinson of the Boeckmann Library for her dedication in searching for data sources and illustrative materials. Thanks also to Lydia Brantley, who provided invaluable research assistance, and to Katherine Hill for her assistance in editing the manuscript. And I want to express my appreciation to Jennifer Carpenter, Maegan Sherlock, Erica Tucker Woods and Angela Riley of Oxford University Press for their patience, support and assistance throughout the editing and productive stages of the book.

Finally, I want to extend a special thanks to my friends for their support and encouragement throughout this process, and particularly to Eugenia, my sister and oldest friend, to whom this book is dedicated.

CHRONOLOGY OF MEXICAN HISTORY

1150–900 BC	Olmec culture (western Tabasco, Veracruz).
150 BC–900 AD	Classic period of ancient Meso-American culture; rise of major cities including Teotihuacán, Palenque, Monte Albán.
800–900	Decline of classic culture, rise of warrior tribes.
1250–1490	Aztecs gain control over substantial part of what is now Mexico. Building of Tenochtitlán, Aztec capital, now center of Mexico City.
1521	Conquest of Aztec empire by Spaniards under Hernán Cortés. Area incorporated in Spanish empire, including southwestern United States and Central America, as Viceroyalty of New Spain.
1521–1821	Spanish Colonial Period. Over time, Spanish and their descendants (Creoles) extend their control over indigenous communities, appropriating their land and labor.
1810–1815	Revolt against Spain led by Creole priest, Miguel Hidalgo. Put down by Spaniards, but date (September 15) commemorated as Mexican independence. Subsequent movement led by priest José Maria Morelos also defeated.
1821	Mexico wins independence under Gen. Agustín de Iturbide. Mexican territory at this point includes California, Texas, New Mexico, Arizona, and parts of Colorado, as well as Central America. Central American states secede.
1836	State of Texas declares independence; becomes part of the United States in 1845.
1847	Mexican-American War, culminating in Mexico's defeat. In the treaty of Guadalupe Hidalgo, Mexico loses half its territory to the United States.

1857	Beginning of the *Reforma*; Liberals come to power and a new constitution is adopted.
1862–1867	War of French intervention, supported by Conservatives against the Liberals. Initially defeated by Mexican Liberals at Puebla (May 5), but subsequently the French defeat the Liberal army. In 1864 Archduke Ferdinand Maximilian of Austria is appointed by Napoleon III as Emperor of Mexico.
1867	After the French withdraw their troops, Maximilian and the Conservatives are defeated by the Liberals under the leadership of Benito Juárez; the Liberal republic is re-established.
1876	Coup carried out by General Porfirio Díaz, who is subsequently elected president (1876-80). Following an interim term (1880-84) he is reelected, and continues to hold power, through successive (and frequently fraudulent) elections, until 1910.
1884–1910	Rule of Díaz (Porfiriato). Period of economic modernization and geographic and political centralization, growing foreign control of mining, petroleum, finance, and other sectors of the economy; growth of commercial agriculture leads to accelerated expropriation of peasant land.
1910	Following a promise by Díaz to permit free elections in 1910, the Anti-Re-electionist Party is formed, led by Francisco Madero. Díaz changes his mind, and Madero leads revolt against Pofirian regime. His followers include peasants in southern Mexico, led by Emiliano Zapata, who lost their land under the Porfirian regime. Marks the beginning of the Mexican revolution.
1911	Revolt succeeds; Díaz abdicates, and Madero is elected president.
1913	Madero assassinated by Victoriano Huerta who becomes president, dissolves Congress. Constitutionalist Army formed under leadership of Venustiano Carranza; Army of the South under Emiliano Zapata and Constitutionalist Army battle Huerta.
1914–1916	Huerta defeated. Victorious forces meet at convention of Aguascalientes, but different parties are unable to come to agreement, and there is a split between Constitutionalists and forces of Zapata and Pancho Villa, leading to conflict

	between two sides. In 1915 Carranza gains control of Mexico City, and in 1916 calls a constitutional convention.
1917	New constitution approved; is still in effect. Among other measures, establishes government control of education, national sovereignty over natural resources, and labor bill of rights. Permits expropriation of private property in the public interest, thus facilitating agrarian reform. Carranza president until 1920. In 1919 Zapata is assassinated.
1920	Carranza overthrown by Obregon who becomes president. Carranza later assassinated. Villa ends rebellion; he is assassinated in 1922.
1920–1934	Rule of Sonoran presidents, Alvaro Obregon (1920-24) and Plutarco Elias Calles (1920-24). Obregon is reelected in 1928 but assassinated before he can take office. Between 1928 and 1934 three presidents hold office, but Calles continues to control power (Maximato).
1927–1929	Cristero rebellion: uprising of pro-Catholic groups, especially rural populations in central Mexico, against anticlerical provisions of the government.
1929	Establishment of government party, National Revolutionary Party (PNR).
1934–1940	Election of Lázaro Cárdenas, who holds office until 1940. Period of substantial reforms including a major land reform and the formation of labor unions and central labor confederation (CTM).
1938	Cárdenas expropriates the U.S. and British owned oil companies, which come under government control. He also restructures the government party, which becomes the Party of the Mexican Revolution (PRM), on a corporatist model with four sectors: labor, peasant, popular and military.
1939	National Action Party (PAN) is formed; becomes major opposition party.
1940–1970	Under succeeding administrations, Mexican government shifts direction from emphasis on social reform to focus on economic development. In 1947, PRM becomes the Institutional Revolutionary Party (PRI); military sector is dropped. During this period five presidents govern Mexico: Manuel Avila Camacho (1940-46); Miguel Alemán (1946-52), Adolfo Ruís Cortines (1952-58), Adolfo López

Mateos (1958-64), and Gustavo Díaz Ordaz (1964-70). Period of Mexican economic "miracle."

1968 Student mobilization around issues of police brutality, freeing of political prisoners, poverty. On October 2, government forces surround student demonstration at Tlatelolco plaza, firing into the crowd and killing an estimated 200 to 400 students.

1970–1976 Luís Echeverría Alvarez becomes president. Initiates "democratic opening." Attempts to revive economy through increased state investing, resulting in massive growth of state sector. Term ends with economic crisis and peso devaluation.

1976–1982 José López Portillo president. Discovery and development of oil reserves result in economic boom based on development and export of oil, industrial expansion, foreign investment and heavy dependence on foreign loans. When oil prices drop in 1981, Mexican economy experiences a crisis.

1982 Mexico announces it is unable to service its foreign debt, the beginning of the debt crisis that within a few years affects nearly every country of Latin America. López Portillo nationalizes the banks which he blames for capital flight.

1982–1988 Under subsequent government of Miguel de la Madrid Hurtado, Mexico experiences a severe economic depression. Under pressure from international lending agencies (IMF) and creditor countries, especially the United States, Mexico launches a structural adjustment program that involves privatization of state assets, reduction or elimination of tariffs and other barriers to trade, removal of restrictions on foreign investment, and reorientation of economy to production for export.

1985 In September, two massive earthquakes in Mexico City result in extensive death and destruction, and the emergence of grassroots movements in reaction to insufficient government response.

1987–1988 Formation of democratic current within PRI under Cuauhtémoc Cárdenas. With selection of Carlos Salinas de Gortari as PRI presidential candidate, Cárdenas and democratic current abandon party. Cárdenas becomes candidate of coalition of parties and popular organizations,

	and obtains widespread popular support in electoral campaign.
1988–1994	After winning victory in clearly fraudulent elections, Carlos Salinas de Gortari becomes president. He accelerates the process of economic restructuring, including privatization of banks and Telmex, and begins negotiation with the United States and Canada to join the North American Free Trade Association. Cárdenas and followers form the Democratic Revolutionary Party (PRD).
1989	National Action Party (PAN) wins gubernatorial election in Baja California—the first time an opposition candidate becomes a state governor.
1993	Approval of North American Free Trade Agreement (NAFTA) by U.S. Congress, to go into effect on January 1, 1994.
1994	January 1. Uprising of Zapatista Army of National Liberation in Chiapas. After military effort to suppress the revolt, the government and Zapatistas begin negotiations, which continue, with extended interruptions, over the next several years.
1994	March. Assassination of PRI presidential candidate Luis Donoso Colosio, the first assassination of a high level PRI official since the 1928 assassination of Obregon in 1928. Ernesto Zedillo is selected as presidential candidate to replace him, and is elected in September in relatively open elections. Subsequently the secretary general of PRI, José Francisco Ruiz Mathieu, is assassinated.
1994	December. Foreign exchange crisis and peso devaluation, again plunging country into major recession.
1996	Emergence of another guerrilla group, ERP (Popular Revolutionary Army) in southern state of Guerrero.
1997	In midterm elections, Cárdenas becomes mayor of Mexico City, and the PRI loses control of Chamber of Deputies for the first time since the party was formed.
1999	On November 7, following first PRI primary in history, former Interior Minister and economist, Francisco Labastida, becomes presidential candidate.
2000	July 2. Vicente Fox, candidate of PAN, is elected president, defeating PRI candidate Labastida and Cuauhtémoc Cárdenas of the PRD, and ending 71 years of PRI dominance.

2006   Felipe Calderón of PAN elected president by narrow margin. Results contested by PRD candidate, Andrés Manuel López Obrador, but electoral tribunal confirms Calderón victory.

2006   December. Shortly after coming to office, Calderón launches a military offensive against the drug cartels, resulting in escalation of violence in Mexico. Estimated 15,000 killed in drug-related violence in following three years.

2009   Midterm elections result in significant victories for the PRI.

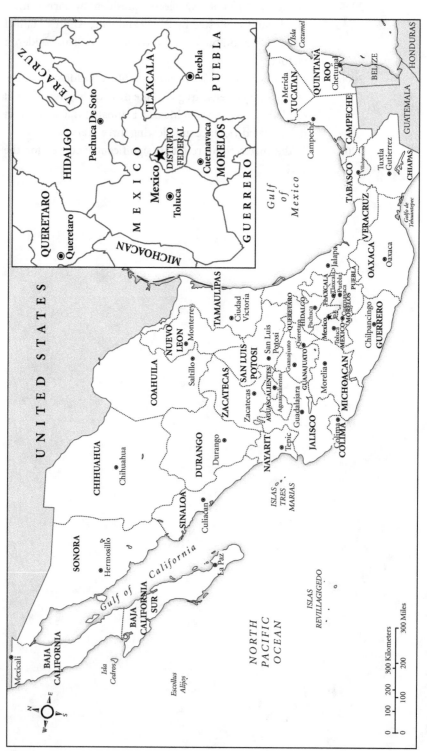

Map 1-1 Political Map of Mexico

CHAPTER 1

Introduction

The year 1910 was a pivotal one in Mexico's history. One hundred years before, a priest, Miguel Hidalgo, began the revolt that led to Mexico's independence from Spain. But while the nation was celebrating the centenary of its birth, a new revolution was about to begin, one that would have a significant impact on Mexico's trajectory over the following century. And in the last three decades, Mexico has again undergone important economic, political and social transitions, resulting in major challenges for Mexico as it enters its third century.

Mexico has experienced dramatic changes, but it is also characterized by enduring legacies. It is a country of pre-Columbian monuments and overbuilt modern cities, of indigenous communities governed by traditional customs in a nation governed by Harvard-educated technocrats, in which authoritarian practices coexist with the institutions of electoral democracy, and extraordinary wealth is juxtaposed with devastating poverty. In the early 1990s, Mexico negotiated a free trade agreement with the United States and Canada that cemented its economic transition from a state-guided, nationalist economic model to an open market economy focusing on export and closely integrated with the U.S. economy, a process that was projected to result in rapid economic modernization. But while there has indeed been substantial modernization in Mexico, poverty and lack of opportunity have continued to be the fate of substantial sectors of the population, and for many the situation has worsened in the years since the North American Free Trade Agreement (NAFTA) went into effect.

During the 1980s and 1990s, social groups, protest movements, and civic organizations mobilized and exerted pressure on Mexico's political system, which led to its gradual transition from a hegemonic party system to a more pluralistic system of competing parties. In 2000, Mexicans elected an opposition candidate for president for the first time in over 70 years, an event that was widely celebrated as Mexico's definitive transition from authoritarianism to democracy. In contrast to the euphoria that accompanied the elections of 2000, however, the 2006 presidential contest was surrounded by controversy, with a substantial portion of the population believing that the election results were fraudulent. In short, economic modernization has not ameliorated Mexico's long-term problems of poverty and inequality, while the ghosts of Mexico's authoritarian past continue to haunt its new democracy.

This book examines the elements of continuity and change in contemporary Mexico. Its goal is to explain the origins, development and implications of Mexico's economic, political and social transitions over the past 25 years—what happened, why it happened, and what its consequences have been. Recognizing that different population groups, or social actors, have different interests, pursue different goals, and are variously affected by change, it is particularly concerned with the ways in which the action and interaction of these groups have influenced events and how they have been affected by and responded to the process of transition. At the same time, this examination of Mexico will incorporate some of the theoretical concepts and debates that have developed around such issues as economic transition, democratization and the emergence of civil society, social movements and protest, and migration.

MEXICO IN THE LATIN AMERICAN CONTEXT

Mexico shares with other Latin American countries a similar position in the world economy, generally involving unequal relations with more powerful countries. Colonizing powers, particularly Spain and Portugal, dominated the region to a greater or lesser extent throughout the colonial period—roughly from the 1520s to the 1820s. Following political independence in the early 19thcentury, several of the new Latin American countries came under the influence of other European powers, especially England, as well as the United States, which became the dominant political and economic power in the region during the twentieth century. More recently, the process of globalization and the growing significance of new international actors, including global corporations and international lending agencies, as well as emerging economies, notably China, have exerted a major influence in Latin America as well as other parts of the world.

In addition, the populations of most countries consist of different racial and ethnic groups, resulting from the imposition of European settlement on indigenous regions and/or the import of Africans as slaves during the colonial period. While racial and ethnic mixing has occurred, to a greater or lesser degree, over the centuries, social inequality between racial and ethnic groups continues to exist. In recent years, indigenous populations in Mexico and other countries have strongly asserted their identity and called for the recognition of the multicultural nature of the respective societies and for greater political autonomy.

Some African-ancestry groups as well have pointed out the racism that often underlies official claims of racial equality and pushed initiatives to end racial discrimination.

Throughout much of their histories, the Latin American political systems have been authoritarian or characterized by an uneasy alternation of authoritarian with more open systems. There have also been certain parallels in post-independence economic models. While the majority of the Latin American populations engaged in subsistence farming into the twentieth century, during much of the nineteenth and twentieth centuries, economic growth in several countries was based on the production and export of one or a limited number of primary commodities, generally agricultural and/or mineral products. Following the depression of the 1930s, the larger countries, including Mexico, shifted to a model of state-guided industrialization for the internal market, which resulted in the growth of a substantial middle class. As noted above, there has been another shift beginning in the late twentieth century, again toward open market economies oriented to export. Recent years have also seen a transition from authoritarian to more democratic regimes.

Finally, the Latin American countries have been characterized by chronic problems of poverty and inequality, manifested historically in the concentration of land and agricultural resources, and more recently in vast inequalities of wealth and income. Today these countries confront the challenge of bringing modernization into conformity with the needs of their populations.

At the same time, Mexico is unique. While other Latin American countries have been influenced by external forces, Mexico is distinguished by its long geographic border with the United States, which has resulted in a special and often troubled relationship with its more powerful northern neighbor. During the colonial period Spanish settlements extended into much of what is now the southwest United States. In the mid-19th century the United States annexed half of Mexico's territory as a result of the Mexican-American war. Mexico's unique relation with the United States also includes a dynamic border culture along the 2000-mile U.S. Mexico border and the historic presence of Mexican communities in the United States since annexation, augmented by massive Mexico-U.S. migration. At 11.5 million, the number of foreign-born Mexicans in the United States exceeds by far that of any other country.

Their shared border is also a significant factor in major issues and problems in U.S.-Mexico relations, including questions of water rights between the border states, the role of Mexico in supplying the U.S. drug market (as well as the role of the United States in supplying arms to Mexico), and U.S. policy toward immigration and the treatment of Mexican migrants in the United States. In addition, although countries throughout Latin America as well as other parts of the world have to a greater or lesser degree implemented market-oriented economic models, Mexico differs from most developing countries in terms of its degree of economic integration with the United States, which is now responsible for over 80 percent of its trade.

Second, while the European conquest and colonization involved the subjugation of indigenous populations throughout the Americas, when the Spaniards arrived in the region that is now Mexico, they found a vast empire centered in what is now Mexico City.[1] The wealth of the empire, the density of the population, and the diversity of indigenous cultures distinguished the region from most other parts of the Americas, and influenced the complex patterns of interaction between the settlers and inhabitants that evolved, involving harsh exploitation of the indigenous populations on the one hand and the emergence of a mestizo population and culture on the other.

Mexico's historical trajectory also distinguishes it from other Latin American countries. In the first years of the twentieth century Mexico experienced a major social revolution[2] which had a profound effect on its subsequent socioeconomic and political development, its culture, and ideology. Ironically, one of the consequences of the revolution was the emergence of a stable political system based on a hegemonic but inclusive governing party. Mexico's stability—resting on what could be called a form of "flexible authoritarianism"—was in marked contrast to the political instability that characterized much of Latin America during the twentieth century. Its unique historical legacies continue to shape contemporary Mexico's economic, political and social development.

ANALYTICAL APPROACH

As indicated above, the focus of the analysis is on the ways in which different social actors (as distinguished from individuals) have acted and interacted to shape processes of economic, political and social change. It begins with the identification of key actors, their initiatives, goals, and strategies, with the goal of determining how they act and interact within historically-defined contexts that generally constrain their actions within given possibilities and options. These actors vary over different periods and across issues, but can be divided into three basic types. Socio-economic actors exercise power and influence either on the basis of their economic and/or social position or as a result of numbers, social mobilization and organization. Political actors include both state actors (e.g., the federal government, the military) whose power is based on control over formal institutions of policy-making and implementation, and political parties and factions, whose capacity lies in their base of support among different sectors of the population. Socio-economic actors may act politically (e.g., to seek to influence government officials, promote specific legislation), but their source of power resides in their socio-economic position. External actors, which may also be divided into socio-economic and political actors, are categorized separately given their importance for Latin American countries and include foreign states, foreign economic interests such as corporations, and international institutions, whose influence stems in large part from their economic and political leverage with respect to a particular country or groups within that country. Although generally less powerful, foreign and international NGOs (non-government organizations) and advocacy groups can provide certain kinds of resources, ranging from moral authority to monetary support, to specific groups and interests in a given country.

Social actors are affected by change in a variety of ways; they are also protagonists that seek to bring about (or resist) change. They may or may not act collectively. In some cases, such as unions, peasant organizations, social movements, or NGOs, they mobilize and organize for particular ends. In other cases, a sufficient number of individual actions by specific social actors may be effective: examples would be capital export by business firms, or the migration of a large number of individuals.

As noted above, actions of social actors take place within a given context, which includes the international and domestic structures and institutions that have evolved over the years, as well as external conditions. Structures refer to relationships among different groups within a particular system that endure over a long period of time, e.g., a capitalist economic system, an authoritarian political system. Institutions are formalized practices and patterns of behavior that tend to reinforce these structures, such as markets (including international markets), military regimes, or electoral systems.

These historically evolved institutions and structures influence the options and constraints within which socio-economic, political, and external actors operate. At the same time, the action and interaction of different actors may also modify or transform existing institutions, and even result in structural change over time. The new structures and institutions in turn form the context in which subsequent actors and groups act and interact, in the process challenging, modifying and/or reinforcing existing economic, political and social conditions.

The analysis is informed by three basic principles:

• The importance of understanding the past for understanding the present. What are the legacies from Mexico's past that have endured into the present? How has Mexico's contemporary structural and institutional context been shaped by its history? How are contemporary groups influenced by what has gone before?

• The interdependence of economic, political and social actors, conditions and events in explaining continuity and change. How do different social actors affect economic conditions and policies? How are they affected by these policies? How do they translate their needs and demands into political action? How are political decision-makers influenced by economic conditions and pressures by specific social actors?

- External conditions and foreign influences and how they interact with internal conditions and social and political actors to produce certain outcomes. To what extent, and how, do changes in the international context constrain developments in Mexico? How have the interests of key external actors, such as the United States, changed over time, and how do they relate to Mexican policy makers and other domestic groups and interests? To what extent, and how, do Mexico's social actors accept, moderate, or resist influences and pressures from abroad?

Finally, it is important to recognize the heterogeneity of Mexico in terms of the particularity of local and regional conditions and events. Mexico consists of several different regions each with a distinct economic, social and cultural profile. The process of creating a nation out of different regions jealously protecting their independence and autonomy was a protracted one, and throughout Mexico's history, local and regional actors have initiated events of national import, modified or resisted directives from the center, and been variously affected by national and international developments. While out of necessity focusing on events at the national level, this analysis will draw on significant examples of local initiatives and reactions to illustrate this complexity.

SETTING THE STAGE:
AN INTRODUCTION TO MEXICO

Mexico is the second largest country in Latin America in both size and population, with approximately 111 million people as of 2009 in an area of 761,601 square miles. Geographically, it is part of North America, sharing a 2,000-mile border with the United States. The semi-arid desert region of northern Mexico extends into the southwestern United States, while the chain of mountains that form the Sierra Nevada in the United States extends into the Sierra Madre of Mexico. Much of Mexico, like western Canada and the United States, is part of the Pacific earthquake zone. Aside from the semi-arid and desert region of the north, Mexico's terrain is characterized by temperate valleys in the mountain areas of central Mexico and tropical and semi-tropical zones in the east and southeast.

Brief Overview of Mexico's 20th Century Trajectory
The 20th century has been one of dramatic demographic change. The population has increased from approximately 10 to 15 million in 1900 to over 110 million today and continues to grow rapidly although the rate of growth has

declined, from 2.8 percent in the 1970s to 1.2 percent in the 2000s, in part the result of population control programs introduced in the 1970s. Like most Latin American countries, Mexico has also made the transition from a predominantly rural country, with approximately 90 percent of the population in the country-side at the beginning of the 20th century, to a predominantly urban country today, with over 75 percent of the total population in the cities, 30 percent in cities of over one million, and 20 percent in greater Mexico City. The concentra-tion of population in the capital city, again a characteristic of several other Latin American countries, reflects the historical centralization of political administra-tion and of economic, social and cultural life in Mexico City. Although some decentralization has occurred in recent decades, Mexico City is one of the larg-est cities in the world, and population pressures have led to extreme problems of smog and traffic congestion as well as shortages of basic services such as water and electricity.

The Mexican economy has also changed dramatically. In the late 19th and early 20th centuries, the Mexican economy was largely based on subsistence farm-ing, on the one hand, and commercial agriculture and mining production, much of it under foreign control and largely for export, on the other. Partly as a result of the depression of the 1930s, Mexico, like other Latin American countries, adopted an inwardly oriented development strategy under the guidance of the state and focused on industrialization for the domestic market. Mexico was among the most successful of the Latin American industrializing countries, achieving an annual growth rate of 6 percent and an industrial growth rate of 8 percent from the 1940s through the 1970s and creating an important manufacturing sector.

But despite some improvements in health, education and other services, growth was uneven, and Mexico—similar to Brazil, another important industri-alizing country—was characterized by extremes of wealth and poverty, with one of the most unequal distributions of wealth and income in the world. Economic inequality also has a regional dimension, with dramatic contrasts between the relatively wealthy northern states and the impoverished states of southern Mexico where much of the indigenous population is concentrated. Beginning in the 1980s, reflecting the process of economic globalization as well as the economic crisis Mexico and other Latin American countries were confronting, the economy again shifted to a more open, export-oriented system in which exports of industrial goods, often produced in collaboration with foreign, especially U.S., corporations and oriented to the U.S. market, predominated.

The agricultural sector has also undergone change. Reforms following the Mexican revolution, which broke up many of the landed estates and redistributed land to peasants and small farmers, reduced land concentration, and rural-urban migration lessened the proportion of the population in the rural sector. The rural sector has also become more complex, but again there is a sharp contrast between the efficient, irrigated farms of the north producing for export and the small farms and communities of southern Mexico dependent on annual rainfall and producing largely for subsistence and the domestic market. The failure of modernization to improve conditions for many in the rural sector, a constitutional amendment ending the distribution of land to the peasantry in 1992, and the implications of the pending NAFTA agreement for small farmers and indigenous groups were all factors in the uprising of the guerrilla army of the Zapatistas in 1994.

Political Mexico has changed as well. The Mexican revolution ended the highly authoritarian regime that characterized Mexico in the late 19th and early 20th centuries, and the 1917 constitution provided for a democratic, federal system with separation of powers and regular elections. In fact, what emerged was another authoritarian system, although considerably more flexible than before, dominated by a hegemonic political party and characterized by a highly centralized government with a strong executive, claiming to represent the principles and goals of the revolution, including national control of resources and the pursuit of social justice, as well as promoting economic growth. As noted above, today Mexico is experiencing a transition to a formal democracy based on a pluralistic party system and characterized by an increasing decentralization of power, although this process is far from complete.

Identification of Major Social Actors

It goes without saying that the demographic, socio-economic and political developments of the 20th century have resulted in significant changes in Mexico's social groups and classes. As noted above, at the beginning of the 20th century, the vast majority of the population was rural, consisting of peasants and indigenous communities producing largely for their own subsistence and agricultural workers on large traditional landholdings, mostly in central and southern Mexico, and on commercial estates producing for domestic and foreign markets. The major economic interests consisted of landowners, ranchers, mine owners, and commercial groups, particularly those of northern Mexico. There was a small manufacturing sector concentrated in Mexico City and Puebla and the northern city of Monterrey; and an industrial proletariat was emerging in mines, railroads and manufacturing industries. Politics was dominated by a small elite surrounding the long-term president, Porfirio Díaz, who had maintained himself in the presidency from the 1880s into the 20th century. The major external actors consisted of foreign investors, particularly U.S. companies in mining and petroleum as well as agriculture.

Today, the identification of groups and classes is much more complex. One of the most important changes resulting from the 20th century processes of industrialization, urbanization, and increased education has been the expansion of a significant middle class and working class. These groups are not monolithic. The working class incorporates those in formal, blue collar or white collar occupations, many of whom are organized, and a much larger number in small firms and informal enterprises who are not part of the formal labor sector. This distinction is currently breaking down, as many formal occupations, once full-time and relatively permanent, become part-time and/or temporary, and formal workers are forced to supplement their income through informal activities such as vending. The so-called middle class consists of a range of groups including professionals, small- and middle-level business owners, state employees, middle-level managers and administrators, and small- and medium-level farmers, who rarely act in concert.

Large business groups, along with foreign corporations, play the major role in the economy. These may also have different interests, e.g., export enterprises, including commercial farmers, vs. those oriented to domestic markets; manufacturers vs. bankers; but the most significant business groups tend to be multi-sectoral, including banks, manufacturing firms, real estate and insurance agencies, and other interests, dominated by a small number of investors (or in some cases individual families), often in collaboration with foreign enterprises.

Non-class based actors, i.e., those pursuing interests other than economic interests, are also important. The late 20th century has seen the emergence of new social movements and grassroots organizations as well as the consolidation and/or transformation of existing groups, including women's organizations, LGBT (Lesbian, Gay, Bisexual and Transsexual) organizations, community and neighborhood based groups, civic associations, environmental groups, and indigenous organizations, among others. The Catholic Church, a major institutional actor since the colonial period, continues to exercise influence, while other religious groups, including Pentecostal groups, have become increasingly important in some areas.

Foreign and international actors and institutions also have an impact in Mexico. Among the most important in the contemporary period are international lending agencies, foreign governments, especially the United States, and foreign corporations and banks. While many of these operate to defend their particular interests today, they are also likely to collaborate with specific Mexican nationals, such as certain business groups and/or Mexican government officials. Other foreign actors—less powerful but increasingly important—include foreign or international human rights, environmental, labor, and women's organizations, among others, that work with counterpart organizations in Mexico. As noted above, emerging economies such as China are having a growing impact in Mexico as well as other countries.

Mexican emigrants to the United States may be seen as "foreign" or binational social actors that have had an increasingly significant direct and indirect impact in Mexico. Their direct impact is most evident in the individual and collective remittances sent back to Mexico that help to sustain families, communities, and the Mexican economy as a whole; in some cases migrants have exercised social influence and played a political role as well.

Finally, the identification of political actors presents particular challenges. There is general debate as to whether the state itself can be considered an actor—one with its own agenda, or that represents national interests above those of particular parties, classes or groups, as well as in relation to foreign interests. If one considers the state as consisting of relatively permanent institutions and agencies (the Supreme Court, the armed forces), on the one hand, and the government, which may itself be divided, on the other, it is clear that the state cannot be considered monolithic but consists of a number of actors and agencies whose interests may or may not coincide and whose significance may vary over time or according to particular circumstances. In the following, reference will be made to particular state actors, or agencies, where possible; reference to the state will refer to it as an institutional actor, generally incorporating the central government and certain key agencies, responsible for the development and implementation of policies.

In the case of Mexico, the control of the state by a hegemonic government party, the PRI (Institutional Revolutionary Party), for most of the 20th century has also made it difficult to separate state and party; some have, in fact, referred to Mexico's political system during this period as a state-party system. This was also a period in which political power within the state tended to be centralized in the federal government and concentrated in the executive, especially the president and his cabinet. Even so, there were divisions within the government, e.g., between different ministries, which often involved alliances or links with specific classes or interests outside the state. In the current era of political pluralism and jurisdictional decentralization, the problem of identifying state or government actors is even more complex, as conflicts emerge between the president and congress, the Supreme Court acts with increasing autonomy, and particular state governments (and in some cases municipal governments) develop an independent agenda.

The shift from a hegemonic to a pluralist party system has also meant the increased importance of opposition parties, and today three major and several smaller parties contest power. Even during the period of PRI hegemony there were divisions within the government party, notably between the more traditional wing of the party (*políticos*) and the technical wing (*técnicos*), and different issues continue to divide the PRI as well as the other major parties.

To summarize, the principal social actors in contemporary Mexico may be defined as follows:

- Socio-economic actors, including peasants and small farmers, commercial landowners, business interests, and urban workers, indigenous communities, women's groups, social movements and civic associations, as well as institutions such as the Catholic Church and other religious denominations, among others. These groups obviously contain many subdivisions and subsectors, often with distinct and sometimes opposing interests, and the initiatives, alliances and conflicts among these groups and sectors will vary over time. Recently, drug cartels have emerged as significant and often powerful actors.
- Political actors, including, on the one hand, government policy makers and state agencies at different levels, and on the other major political parties, which may be further divided into different groups and factions.
- External/international actors, including foreign governments, especially the United States, foreign corporations and banks, and international lending agencies, as well as international agencies such as human rights organizations and labor confederations.

This book is an effort to understand how the action of these social, political and external actors, and the collaboration and conflicts among them, have affected the economic and political transitions of the past quarter century, and how these economic and political changes have in turn affected different population groups. The rest of the book is divided into three sections.

The next two chapters examine Mexico's historical trajectory in order to understand the context of developments in the late 20th and early 21st centuries. Chapter 2 examines Mexico's historical legacies, from the pre-Colombian period through the Mexican revolution. It will identify the social groups and classes whose emergence, development and action have shaped or been shaped by historical events; and examine the origins of particular structures and institutions that have continued to characterize Mexico's subsequent development.

Chapter 3 is concerned with understanding Mexico's development in the post-revolutionary period, between 1940 and 1982. On the one hand, this was a period characterized by substantial economic growth and a relatively stable, if authoritarian, political regime. On the other hand, it is one in which the limitations of Mexico's economic model, based on state-guided development for an expanding domestic market, and the contradictions of its "flexible authoritarian" political system became increasingly evident, ushering in the dramatic changes of the late 20th century. The last years of this period were characterized by efforts, ultimately unsuccessful, to cope with economic problems and respond to challenges to the political regime.

Chapters 4, 5 and 6 focus specifically on the trajectory of economic and political changes in the period from 1982 until the present. Chapter 4 examines efforts to resolve Mexico's economic crisis of 1982 and the subsequent establishment of a new economic model, based on an open market economy with minimal state intervention and oriented to production for export, which reversed many of the characteristics of Mexico's previous economic system. It examines external and internal factors that help to explain Mexico's shift to a new economic model and identifies the characteristics of this model and traces the trajectory of its implementation. Finally, the Chapter attempts to assess its implications for the Mexican economy and for different groups within Mexican society and examines its impact on Mexico's long-term problems of poverty and inequality.

Chapter 5 focuses on the process of political transition, beginning with a brief examination of conceptualizations of democracy; distinguishing between formal, or procedural, democracy, and participatory democracy, and analyses of regime change and democratization. It then introduces a model that examines the interaction of different processes to explain the political transition in Mexico: the socio-economic crisis and restructuring of the 1980s and 1990s; the emergence and mobilization of different organizations, protest movements, and opposition parties; the increase in Mexico's international exposure; and government responses—resulting in the increased salience of the opposition, shifts in electoral procedures, and changes in government institutions. It traces the influence of these factors in political change during the presidential administrations of Carlos Salinas (1988–1994), Ernesto Zedillo (1994–2000), and Vicente Fox (2000–2006). It concludes by addressing two questions: To what extent can Mexico be said to have the characteristics of a formal and/or a participatory democracy? What are the obstacles that remain to democratic consolidation in Mexico?

Chapters 6 and 7 shift the focus to those individuals and groups who have borne the brunt of recent changes and long-term economic, political and/or social exploitation, and the ways in which they have individually and collectively coped with and/or resisted these conditions and struggled for change. The sixth Chapter examines the development of social movements and the emergence of cycles of protest in Mexico. While previous chapters briefly address the role of these groups and organizations in Mexico's political and economic transitions, this Chapter examines more closely the origin, development, goals and achievements of specific groups.

Chapter 7 is specifically concerned with Mexican migration to the United States, the experience of Mexican immigrants, and the increasingly significant economic and political role that Mexican migrants are playing in their home country and their communities of origin. It examines Mexican migration in historical perspective, factors explaining Mexican integration in the United States and how Mexicans and Mexican Americans have coped with conditions in the United States, and the trajectories of two specific groups of immigrants: those from Zacatecas, a traditional state of out-migration to the United States, and indigenous groups from the state of Oaxaca.

Although U.S.-Mexican relations are discussed throughout the book, Chapter 8 specifically addresses these relations focusing on three specific issues: the impact of NAFTA and Mexico's economic ties with the United States, the drug issue, and U.S. migration policy.

In 2010 it will be 200 years since the revolt of Hidalgo signaled the birth of the Mexican nation and 100 years since the beginning of the revolution that would shape its historical development during much of the 20th century. The final Chapter will review the ways in which Mexico has changed over this period and the challenges that it confronts in the future.

CHAPTER 2

Legacies

These great towns and pyramids and buildings rising from the
water, all made of stone, seemed like an enchanted vision . . . It
was all so wonderful I do not know how to describe this first
glimpse of things never heard of, seen, or dreamed of before.
　　　　　　　　　　　—BERNAL DÍAZ DEL CASTILLO, 1963

When the Spaniards arrived in what is now Mexico they found a densely populated region with a diversity of groups, ranging from relatively nomadic hunting
societies in the north to highly complex civilizations in central and southern
Mexico. The encounter between the Spaniards and the indigenous populations
of the region would have a profound impact on shaping Mexico's subsequent
history.[1]

This Chapter traces the historical development of Mexico from the pre-
Colombian period through the early 20th century. Its purpose is to identify the
legacies of Mexico's history—how each period has introduced changes that
shaped Mexico's future trajectory and formed many of the characteristics of
Mexico today. It examines the emergence, development and interaction of different social actors; how the context in which these actors found themselves
constrained or facilitated their options; and how their actions and interaction in
turn changed or reinforced the context, shaping the subsequent options of social
actors.

Following a brief discussion of pre-Colombian Mexico and the Spanish conquest, the Chapter examines the period of Spanish colonization, from 1521 until
Mexico's independence in the early 19th century; the chaotic early years of the
new republic; the regime of Porfirio Díaz (1884–1910), which in certain respects
represented the culmination of the early republican period as well as the prelude
to the Mexican Revolution; and the revolution and immediate post-revolutionary
period (1910 to 1940), which had a decisive impact on the political and economic order of 20th century Mexico.

PRE-COLOMBIAN MEXICO

The "New World" was in fact not new.[2] Numerous civilizations had emerged, flourished and declined for over 3,000 years prior to the Spanish conquest; the oldest known civilizations going back to 2000 BC. During the classical period (approximately 150–900 AD) great city-states were constructed; their remnants are seen today in the pyramids and temples of Teotihuacán in Mexico's central valley, the Zapotec ruins of Monte Alban in the southern state of Oaxaca, and numerous Mayan sites in Mexico's south and southeast as well as Central America.

Several of these civilizations were highly advanced artistically, evident in their pottery and ceramics, sculpture, architecture, jewelry and other crafts, as well as in mathematics and astronomy. Trade among different regions flourished, and they developed a highly complex system of religious beliefs and practices. The indigenous population continues to constitute a substantial minority—estimated at 15 percent—in contemporary Mexico, including the Maya in the Southeast and in Central America; the Zapotec, Mixteca, and Mixe, among others, in the southern state of Oaxaca; the Tarascans in Michoacán; and the Yaqui and Mayo in the northwestern states of Sonora and Sinaloa.

In the middle of the 13th century, a group of warriors, the *Mexica*, or Aztecs, migrated to the central valley and settled on an island in a lake where, according to their legend, they had seen an eagle devouring a snake. From here they subjugated other peoples of the central valley, their empire eventually extending from the Caribbean to the Pacific Ocean and from Mexico's central valley south into what is now Central America. They extracted tribute and conscripted labor from the subject populations, and those conquered in war were sacrificed in elaborate rituals to provide blood for their voracious deities. The Aztecs believed that time was cyclical, with each epoch ending with the destruction of the sun, that the epoch they lived in was the fifth, and that sacrifice was necessary to keep the fifth sun alive.

By 1500, the wealth and power of the Aztecs was reflected in the temples and pyramids of Tenochtitlán, which in 200 years had emerged from a village of mud huts to a magnificent capital encompassing cities built on islands in the lake and on the mainland, which were connected by a series of broad causeways and bridges. Plants were cultivated on *chinampas*, rafts woven with seaweed with roots extending down into the lake bed, where they eventually became embedded. It is no wonder that when the Spanish forces, led by Hernán Cortés, reached Tenochtitlán they were astonished at what they saw, speaking of it in terms of dreams and visions, as evident in the chronicles of Bernal Díaz del Castillo, one of Cortés' lieutenants.

The great market of Tenochtitlán was a further source of amazement: As described by Díaz del Castillo, "On reaching the marketplace, we were astounded by the great number of people and quantities of merchandise . . . Let us begin with the dealers of gold, silver and special stones, feathered cloaks and embroidered goods, and male and female slaves who are sold there . . ." He goes on to describe cotton goods and fabrics, "chocolate merchants with their chocolate . . . sisal cloth and ropes and sandals they wear on their feet, which are made from the same plant." In other parts of the market there were skins of tigers and lions and other wild animals, vegetables, domestic animals, fruits, cooked food, pottery of all kinds, timbers and wood products, ointments, herbs, and cochineal (a red dye made from insects). The bounty described here indicates not only the wealth of the empire but also the importance of trade and industry, with many of the products having been brought from distant regions.

The Spanish conquest of Tenochtitlán was facilitated in part by the ambiguity with which the Aztec emperor, Moctezuma, regarded the arrival of Cortés due to a myth that the Aztec god Quetzacoatl, the legendary founder of the

Image 2-1 José Clemente Orozco, *Cortés y Malinche.*

Toltecs from whom the Aztecs claimed descent, would return to Mexico in a human form, and the belief that Cortés might in fact be Quetzacoatl. Another factor was the support from indigenous groups that Cortés and his army encountered during their two-year journey from the coast to Mexico, many of them resentful of their Aztec overlords. Among them was a young noblewoman, Marina, who became an interpreter for the Spanish forces and Cortés' mistress, bearing a son who was named Martin. From this union came two of Mexico's enduring cultural legacies: The first is that of the mestizo, born of the mixture of the Indian and the European, as the origins of a cosmic race, representing the positive melding of ethnicities and cultures. The second is that of La Malinche, the name given Marina, which has come to signify traitor to her people and of her union with Cortés as symbolic of the Spanish rape of indigenous Mexico.

A third interpretation argues that in fact there continues to be two separate and antagonistic cultures "with different projects . . . built on different ways of conceiving the world nature, society and humankind," and that the European-oriented civilization has never recognized the authenticity and value of the indigenous and rural Mesoamerican culture but sought to either isolate it or to assimilate it within a hegemonic Western framework. "The . . . history . . . of the last five hundred years is the story of a permanent confrontation between those attempting to direct the country toward the path of Western civilization and those, rooted in the Mesoamerican ways of life, who resist."[3]

Following the conquest, the temples and pyramids of Tenochtitlán were destroyed and a cathedral built over the site, a pattern that was followed in other areas taken over by the Spanish. In the late 20th century, remnants of the Aztec site in Mexico City were discovered and excavated and the Museum of the Templo Mayor built to house many of the artifacts. The older Museum of Anthropology houses a magnificent collection of sculpture, pottery and other artifacts from the Aztec, Mayan and other civilizations. The giant causeways linking Tenochtitlán to other cities on the lake are now major traffic arteries in modern Mexico City. Elements of the Aztec culture are evident in the food and language of modern Mexico. The Aztecs, or Mexica, also bequeathed to Mexico its name and symbol, the eagle devouring a serpent. As we will see, the interaction of the Spaniards and their descendants with indigenous groups throughout the three centuries of the colonial era has also left its mark on Mexican economic, social and political life.

THE COLONIAL PERIOD: 1521–1821

The era of the Spanish empire can be seen as one of conflict and accommodation among four major actors: the Spanish crown, the descendants of the Spanish conquerors (Creoles) born in the colonies, the indigenous populations, and the

Catholic Church. These actors were far from monolithic; their interests and goals, and their relations with each other, varied within each group or entity and shifted over time.[4]

Throughout most of this period two royal dynasties controlled the Spanish crown: the Hapsburgs, who ruled from 1516 to 1700, and the Bourbons who replaced them when the last Hapsburg king died without an heir. The Hapsburg regime sought to impose a corporate order in the colonies, in which cities, communities, and other institutions maintained their own jurisdictions, mediated by the crown. In contrast, the Bourbons promoted a centralized state that would foster a mining and commercial economy based on private property as a source of revenue for the crown. The shifting relationship between corporatism—with rights and responsibilities based on group membership—and liberalism, which is based on individual rights and responsibilities, continues to characterize Mexico's history to the present.[5]

For the Spanish crown, the colonies were a source of wealth and power. Mexico became the capital of the Viceroyalty of New Spain, one of two major centers of the empire, which by the end of the 17th century not only encompassed the areas controlled by the Aztecs but also extended into what is today the southwestern United States and south to encompass most of Central America. The crown controlled the political administration of the colonies through the appointment of viceroys and other officials. Authority was centralized in the Viceroy, who, although answerable to the crown, exercised considerable discretionary power. Bullion from the colonies shipped to Spain financed its wars and was traded with other parts of the world.

A major concern of the Spanish crown was to prevent the emergence of a rival power in the colonies, particularly a landed aristocracy that could contest Spanish domination. The crown sought to inhibit the acquisition of large tracts of land and passed laws prohibiting the enslavement of the indigenous populations. Eventually, the Creoles succeeded in disregarding the former and circumventing the latter, in part through the import of Africans as slaves, notably in the Caribbean regions, and particularly through various forms of coerced labor of indigenous groups. The crown also restricted foreign trade, initially to export to a single port in Spain, that of Seville, and attempted to prevent the development of an important manufacturing industry, although the production of textiles, shoes, and other products as well as crafts for local markets flourished.

The Spanish conquerors and settlers saw the colonies as a means of accruing personal wealth, initially with the purpose of returning to Spain with increased status. As they began to settle, the Spaniards, and eventually the Creoles, sought to expand their control over the land and populations of the colony, a process that, at various times and in diverse ways, pitted them against the crown, on the one hand, and the indigenous groups on the other. Although the fall of Tenochtitlán in 1821 is seen as the beginning of the Spanish empire in New Spain, the conquest of different indigenous groups was a much more protracted affair. Many resisted the Spaniards, their Creole descendants, and, following independence, the new Mexican state, asserting regional or local autonomy against the centralizing efforts of successive regimes. The Maya in Yucatan and the Yaqui and Mayo in what is now northern Mexico were not subdued until the 19th century or early 20th century.

Initially, the Spanish settlers took over the administrative structure of the Aztec empire, extracting tribute and labor from subject populations through their respective chiefs, or *caciques*.[6] The crown granted control over certain territories and the indigenous communities within them to individual colonists in the form of *encomiendas*, or trusts, with the trustee responsible for collecting taxes for the empire and converting the subject populations to Catholicism. The colonists also conscripted labor from these groups for building roads, houses and public buildings through a system of *repartimiento*, whereby indigenous communities were each responsible for providing a certain number of workers for a stipulated period. In other respects, however, these communities were to retain their autonomy and their customary laws and forms of government.

The discovery of silver mines in the mid-16th century resulted in another source of wealth for Spain as well as the colonists. The export of silver was a factor in incorporating Mexico into the world market as an exporter of commodities, particularly minerals, and the wealth of the Spanish and Creole mine owners financed the baroque cathedrals, handsome buildings, and expansive plazas of colonial cities such as Taxco, Guanajuato and Zacatecas.

Eventually many of the encomiendas were transformed into the private property of individual landowners, who over time usurped much of the land of the indigenous communities. The inhabitants of these communities were forced to provide labor through various mechanisms, such as debt peonage, whereby the landowners advanced loans to the indigenous groups, which could only be paid off through work on their estates. Debts could rarely be paid in full and were often passed on to the next generation.

The indigenous communities resisted the Spanish encroachment on their lands in various ways. Some appealed to the Spanish authorities representing the crown, which, as noted above, opposed the extensive private land ownership and the enslavement of the Indians. Indigenous villages brought numerous lawsuits against encroachment on their lands, orchards, water and forests. In other cases, often as a last resort, they rose up against the usurpers. With some exceptions, particularly in the northern regions and the Yucatán peninsula, these revolts were generally small and localized and were eventually crushed.

Ultimately, for many of the indigenous population, the conquest was an unmitigated disaster. Even those who had supported the Spaniards against the

Aztecs found that they had substituted one group of overlords for another. Labor conditions were exploitative and often brutal, especially in the mines, and many lost their lives due to harsh treatment and overwork. Even more lethal were the diseases, such as smallpox, that the Spaniards brought with them and for which the indigenous population had no resistance. In less than a century, the population of the region, estimated at 10 million at the time of the conquest, had been reduced to one million.

With the decline of the indigenous population the crown relocated the survivors into reconstituted communities, *repúblicas de indios*, indigenous republics, where they would continue to exercise autonomy in their communities while providing taxes for the crown and labor for colonial projects.

Within this context, the role of the Catholic Church was ambiguous. Visions of the New World as a place of unlimited opportunity included a messianic concept of the conversion of the inhabitants to Christianity. Clerics had accompanied the forces of Cortés, and the crown sent members of religious orders to Mexico shortly after the conquest of Tenochtitlán. In 1571, the Office of the Inquisition, which had emerged in Europe to root out heresy and had especially targeted Christianized Jews and Muslims suspected of backsliding, established tribunals in the colonies; among its concerns were those indigenous groups who resisted conversion or whose Christianity was mixed with indigenous religions and practices.

Although some religious officials decried the heathen practices of the indigenous populations, and religious zeal was a major motivation for the persecution of indigenous groups as well as the destruction of temples and other places of worship, other members of the clergy were impressed with the high level of scientific learning and artistic skills they found among the indigenous groups and played a major role in efforts to record and preserve their languages and culture. The Franciscans in particular also sought to modify the often harsh behavior of the Spaniards toward the indigenous populations and urged the crown to take measures to prevent their enslavement.

The Catholic clergy played an important role in the process of colonization, with religious conversion having the function of re-socializing the population into the norms and practices of a Christian society. Their efforts extended to the establishment of missions throughout the colonies, and their missions were the major outposts of the colonial empire in the northern regions, including what is now the U.S. southwest. Their attitudes toward the indigenous population were often protective but also paternalistic. In some cases they incorporated indigenous populations into institutions, such as haciendas, where they worked in the fields and were given lessons in reading and writing as well as catechism. Many of these haciendas were self-sufficient, producing textiles and clothing, leather products, and other needs as well as food. While paternalistic and sometimes exploitative, these institutions could also provide some protection against repression by the Spaniards and Creoles. In some cases, priests and religious orders sought to preserve indigenous practices, encouraging communal work and the retention of traditional authorities and customs.[7]

In attempting to convert the Indians, the clergy drew on similarities in ritual and customs between indigenous culture and those of Christianity. Although some indigenous groups resisted incorporation in the new institutions and the imposition of a foreign ideology, many Indians embraced Christianity, simply adding Christian saints to the deities they worshiped traditionally. One of the most enduring legacies of this syncretism is devotion to the Virgin of Guadalupe, who allegedly appeared to a peasant, Juan Diego, and asked him to build a church at the site. To attest to the miracle she told him to gather roses growing nearby to take back to authorities. When he opened his cloak to show the roses, the cloak was imprinted with the image of the Virgin of Guadalupe, which has become one of the most potent symbols of Mexico. During the 17th and 18th centuries, as the Creoles were increasingly asserting their autonomy from Spain, the Virgin of Guadalupe became the symbol of their links with the mestizo and indigenous populations; in 1754 she became the official patron of Mexico. In the early 19th century the Creole priest, Miguel Hidalgo, would raise the banner of the Virgin in declaring Mexico's independence, and during the Mexican Revolution in the early 20th century the troops of the peasant leader Emiliano Zapata would carry it into battle.[8] The annual celebrations of Mexico's independence still incorporate Hidalgo's famous call to arms: "Viva Mexico! Viva la Virgin de Guadalupe!"

Over time, the religious orders became among the wealthiest landlords in the region, their wealth derived not only from their large landholdings but also through their control of lending. Bishops and other high-level officials generally lived in luxury and identified with the interests of the landowners. While some priests at local levels worked with and continued to identify with the indigenous population, the Church in general was a conservative force, its educational efforts focused on the elite while its message to the poorer inhabitants was to accept their lot in this life in the expectation of happiness in the next. Fees were charged for services, such as burial; poor hacienda workers often had to borrow the money for such fees from the landowners, thus reinforcing the vicious circle of debt servitude.

Many of the social, political and economic developments that emerged during the three centuries of colonization endured well into the 19th century and some are still relevant today. First, the colonies were tied into the world market primarily as exporters of commodities, notably agricultural and mineral products, particularly with the establishment of free trade following the ascent of the Bourbon dynasty in Spain. Exports included cochineal and indigo (used in dyes), sugar, cacao, hemp, and especially silver.

Second, the social structures that emerged during the colonial period were characterized by a high degree of inequality that has continued to be a characteristic of Mexico. A small elite of wealthy landowners, merchants and mine owners controlled most of the wealth. The majority of the population consisted of the members of indigenous communities or small peasant families. By the end of the colonial period a small urban middle class of artisans, small merchants, and professionals had emerged, but the population continued to be predominantly rural and strongly polarized between a small elite and those lacking political and economic power. Some of the indigenous communities, however, were able to retain their autonomy until well into the 19th century.

The class system was reinforced by racial distinctions; for the most part the elite was comprised of Europeans or Creoles, while the majority of the population was indigenous, or mixed. Africans, including both slaves and free, were about 10 percent of the total. As racial mixtures among these three groups became more complex, the Creoles, obsessed with "purity of blood" (an initially religious concept originating in medieval Spain to distinguish "old Christians" from Jews and Moors who had converted and were considered "new Christians"—and therefore suspect) developed an elaborate system of *castas* (castes) to distinguish among the gradations of blood proportions between Europeans, Indians and Africans over several generations.[9] The offspring of white and Indian were *mestizo*; the child of a *mestizo* and white was a *castiza*. Through marriage to Spanish descendants, those with indigenous blood could be "whitened" after three or four generations. In contrast, the blood of Africans and their descendants (*mulattos*, the offspring of whites and blacks, and *zambargos*, the children of blacks and Indians) was considered "impure" and could not be diluted. Since purity of blood was essential for access to certain rights, positions, and privileges, the casta system was an important mechanism for racial exclusion. And since women were central in reproduction, not only biologically but also culturally— in that women imparted spiritual values and practices in the family—controlling the sexuality of the "pure woman" became an obsession in both Spanish and colonial society.

The casta system was never absolute, and over time the mestizos grew in number, eventually becoming the dominant population group. They often filled middle positions in society—small farmers, shopkeepers, or foremen on agricultural estates—but some indigenous and even African descendants achieved significant positions in colonial society. Nevertheless, racial exclusion was the norm, reinforcing the class differences that continue to characterize contemporary Mexico.

Another characteristic that emerged during the colonial period was the centralization of wealth, political power, education and culture in Mexico City. Even the landowners often had homes in the capital city, leaving the supervision of agricultural labor to their foremen. During the colonial era, Spanish officials continued the supervision of construction started under the Aztecs, drawing on indigenous or African labor to expand roads and construct drainage works. Hundreds of new towns and cities were constructed, many of them, like Mexico City, built around a central plaza dominated by a church or cathedral and surrounded by government buildings. Finally, as noted above, the Catholic Church became the predominant ideological and cultural force as well as an important economic force during the colonial period, and continued to be significant economically and culturally well into the 19th and early 20th centuries.

Over time, the Creole elites became increasingly frustrated with the economic and political control exercised by Spain. Bourbon reforms freed trade and expanded economic production, but the benefits of trade went primarily to Spain, and political power became increasingly centralized and authoritarian. Agricultural exporters wanted to trade directly with Europe, without the cumbersome and costly system of trading through the Spanish ports. The high taxes imposed by Spain were a further source of discontent. Creole elites also wished to exert more political power. The Bourbon monarchy expanded the Spanish military forces, which ruthlessly repressed rebellion and dissent. Some Creole elites and intellectuals, influenced by ideas of the European Enlightenment and the American and French revolutions, were also ideologically opposed to the traditional hierarchical and authoritarian character of colonial rule and wanted an egalitarian, secular republic.

Events in Spain brought these contradictions to a head. In 1808, Napoleon Bonaparte invaded Spain and put his brother, Joseph, on the throne. This weakened the authority of the Spanish crown in the Americas and increased the opposition of pro-independence groups. But while the Spaniards were opposed by both the Creoles and the indigenous populations, these groups were themselves divided. The indigenous population had been exploited by the Creoles and saw little difference between them and the Spaniards, while the Creoles themselves feared a movement that might go beyond a revolt against Spain to include a social revolution of the indigenous population against the Creoles.

The initial revolt was led by a Creole priest, Miguel Hidalgo, who sympathized with the indigenous populations and wanted to end the unjust social order as well as to free the Creoles from Spanish domination. His forces included indigenous groups and mestizos as well as Creoles. However, Hidalgo's forces were defeated and Hidalgo himself captured, tried and executed in 1811.

The command passed to another priest, José Maria Morelos, a mulatto, whose troops included individuals of African descent as well as indigenous and mixed castes. Perhaps even more than Hidalgo, Morelos was an advocate of social and economic justice, whose views challenged not only the Spanish crown but also the elitist and hierarchical system of the Creoles.

I would like to make the declaration that there is no nobility but that of virtue, knowledge, patriotism and charity; that we are all equal, since we all came from the same origin; that there are no privileges or ancestral rights; that there is no . . . reason for slavery since the color of the face does not change the color of the heart or of one's thoughts; that the children of the peasant and the sweeper should have the same education as the children of the rich hacendado; that every just claimant should have access to a court which listens, protects, and defends him against the strong and the arbitrary . . .[10]

Although a brilliant general, who won numerous battles, Morelos, too, was finally defeated, captured and executed in 1815.

It was only after a decade of violence and chaos, in 1821, that Mexico finally won independence under a former royalist general, Agustín de Iturbide, who had fought against Hidalgo but changed his allegiances following a conflict with the Spanish crown. But Hidalgo and Morelos—not Iturbide—are recognized as the heroes of Mexican independence, and the day that Hidalgo issued his famous call to arms, September 16, 1810, is celebrated as Mexico's independence day.

The legacies of the colonial period can be seen in Mexico today. They include the mixing of various racial and ethnic groups, notably European and indigenous, resulting in the predominant mestizo population of Mexico. At the same time, indigenous communities continue to struggle for their autonomy, notably in southern states, and the African presence is particularly notable in the Caribbean coastal areas. The Catholic Church became a dominant spiritual and economic power, and Catholicism a major cultural influence, although transformed by elements of indigenous beliefs. Parts of the colony were incorporated into the world market, at that time dominated by Europe, as an exporter of mineral and agricultural commodities.

The Spaniards introduced new landowning systems, both feudal and capitalist, characterized by large haciendas and commercial farms, in a region in which indigenous communities had been the predominant form of land tenure. The expropriation of many of these communities and the institution of debt servitude resulted in highly inegalitarian land structures which, in turn, became the basis of an unequal class structure, reinforced by racial and ethnic differences, at that time dominated by wealthy landowners, merchants, and mine owners. While the nature of the economic actors has shifted over time, class inequality persists. An authoritarian form of government reinforced the hierarchical structure that had characterized the Aztec empire, while efforts to introduce liberal reforms became the foundation for the conflict between conservative and liberal principles, on the one hand, and between corporatist views of communal rights and liberal concepts of individual rights, on the other, that would characterize Mexican politics long after independence.

INDEPENDENCE AND
THE EARLY REPUBLIC: 1821–1910

The Early Republic and the Liberal Reform: 1821–1876

The war for independence failed to bring about the economic and social changes that Hidalgo, Morelos, and their followers had hoped for. Although the mestizos had grown in number and some held intermediate positions in society, many of the indigenous communities remained under the control of the haciendas, and their inhabitants continued to be tied to the estates through debt peonage, in some cases into the 20th century.[11]

The Creoles, particularly the Creole elite, succeeded the Spanish crown as rulers of Mexico. But they were unable to establish a stable political and economic order. Differences between republicans and monarchists, federalists and centralists, pro-Church and anti-clerical positions played themselves out in various ways in the early post-independence period. Eventually they were consolidated in two major parties. The Conservatives—supported by the landowners, the Catholic Church, and much of the military—adhered to the ideology of traditional Spain, favoring a highly centralized government with a strong role for the Catholic Church and a hierarchical social order. The Liberals, including professionals and intellectuals, farmers, journalists, teachers, and lawyers, as well as frontiersmen of the north—ranchers and traders— similar to their counterparts on the U.S. frontier, were influenced by the European Enlightenment, adhered to values of freedom and individual liberty, and sought to emulate the political system and practices in the United States. Some were anti-clerical, strongly opposed to the privileges exercised by the Catholic Church and its exploitation of the poor, and promoted the separation of church and state.

These differences initially took the form of conflicts over what type of government Mexico should adopt, with the Conservatives favoring a centralized government with a strong executive, and the Liberals favoring a federal republic modeled on the United States. The constitution of 1824, for the most part, reflected the values of the Liberals and was partly modeled on that of the United States. Mexico would be a federal republic with 19 states and four territories, with federal authority divided between the executive, legislative and judiciary branches. The individual states would have substantial authority, including the election of the president and vice-president by state legislatures. At the same time, the president was given strong emergency powers, and Catholicism was the official religion. One of the major legacies of the wars for independence period had been an oversized military, and both the Catholic Church and the armed forces retained their own courts, placing them beyond the reach of civil authority.

The first decades following independence were a period of anarchy and conflict; the central government changed hands over 50 times and most of the country consisted of isolated towns and villages controlled by local strongmen, or caciques. The new Mexican government also proved unable to hold onto the territory won from the Spaniards. The Central American provinces seceded, initially forming a federation and eventually dividing into individual countries.

The United States, fearful of the expansion of other European countries into Latin America after it had won independence from Spain, issued the Monroe Doctrine in 1823, declaring that any attempt by foreign powers to control the newly independent Latin American countries would be seen as an unfriendly act toward the United States. But Latin America soon became a target of U.S. expansionism. Because of the sparse population of the northern territory of Texas—at that time part of the state of Coahuila y Tejas—the Mexican government encouraged settlement by U.S. citizens provided they were Catholic, conducted official transactions in Spanish, and agreed to abide by Mexican laws. Soon, U.S. settlers outnumbered Mexicans, resulting in increasing tensions between the two groups and their respective governments and culminating in a war between the U.S. Texans and Mexico, the secession of Texas, and its annexation by the United States. But in negotiations over the boundaries of Texas, the U.S. sought to incorporate an area twice its size, including what was then much of Mexico's territory of New Mexico (and today half of New Mexico and Colorado), and it became clear that the United States in fact wanted all of Mexico's northern territories.

In June 1846, U.S. troops entered Mexican territory, winning a succession of victories against the Mexican army, and by September 1847 had gained control of Mexico City, thus ending the war. A major factor in the Mexican defeat was the factionalism that dominated Mexican politics as well as the ineptitude displayed by some of its leaders, notably Santa Ana, a charismatic and opportunistic general, who during the wars for independence had fought against both the Hidalgo rebellion and the Spaniards and had controlled the presidency in much of the subsequent period, shifting allegiance from the Liberals to the Conservatives. In the treaty of Guadalupe Hidalgo, signed between Mexico and the United States in 1848, the United States gained the large territories of New Mexico and California. In the quarter century following independence, Mexico saw itself reduced to approximately half of its former size. (See Map 2-1, p. 27.)

This loss was profoundly demoralizing and the source of an enduring fear and resentment of the United States. But it also led to the emergence of a group of young liberal intellectuals and political activists who overthrew the discredited dictatorship of Santa Ana and established a liberal republic. Benito Juárez emerged as the leader of this movement. Juárez was a Zapotec, one of the largest of more than twenty indigenous nations in the state of Oaxaca. A shepherd in his

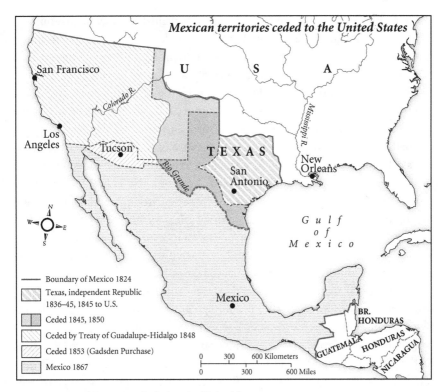

Map 2-1 Map of Territories Ceded to the United States

youth, he moved to the city of Oaxaca at the age of 12 where he learned Spanish and studied law, philosophy, and theology. He entered local and state politics, eventually becoming governor of the state of Oaxaca, where he gave special attention to education, building some 50 local schools and encouraging the education of women.

The Liberals overthrew the government of Santa Ana in 1855 and established a provisional government, initiating what has become known as the Reform, an effort to eliminate all vestiges of the colonial state. They approved several laws as well as a new constitution in 1857, calling for a liberal democracy, including equality before the law; freedom of speech, the press, and assembly; the elimination of slavery; and several measures challenging the power of the Catholic Church and the landowners. Among other provisions, Liberal legislation prohibited Church ownership of property other than that used in its daily operations, such as churches and monasteries; shifted responsibility for the registration of births, marriages, and deaths from the Church to civic officials; and prohibited the Church from charging high fees for administration of the sacraments; these fees were eliminated for the poor. It also eliminated previous references to Catholicism as the official religion.

The landowners and the Church revolted against the Juárez government, resulting in the War of the Reform, but they were defeated by the Liberals under the leadership of Juárez, who was elected president in 1861. When Juárez, confronted by a bankrupt treasury, temporarily suspended payment of Mexico's debt to several European countries, the French empire, taking advantage of the fact that the United States was embroiled in the Civil War, intervened in Mexico with the support of the Conservatives. A Mexican victory over French troops in the Battle of Puebla on May 5, 1862, was a cause of celebration after the disastrous defeat at the hands of the United States and continues to be commemorated in Cinco de Mayo celebrations. In 1864, however, the French defeated the Liberals and set up a government headed by the Austrian Archduke Ferdinand Maximilian, who was declared Emperor of Mexico. Juárez, who had fled to northern Mexico, was able to obtain U.S. assistance after the defeat of the confederacy, and in 1867, after a brutal and protracted war, the Liberals defeated the forces of the Empire and Juárez again became president.

The Liberal victory greatly reduced the influence of the Conservatives, widely condemned for selling out to a foreign power, and established the definitive separation of church and state. The Juárez government reinstated the 1857 constitution and carried out a major agrarian reform that expropriated the lands of the Church, thus eliminating its economic power. Although the Church retained religious and ideological influence, it never regained the type of economic and political power it had exercised during the colonial and early post-independence periods. The government also awarded large tracts of land in northern Mexico to the victorious generals of the Liberal Army.

The attack on corporate property targeted not only the Church, but also the holdings of the indigenous communities. The land was divided among the inhabitants of the community, who were given individual titles. The intention behind the division of communal lands was to turn Mexico into a country of small- and middle-sized farmers, which was seen as the key element in U.S. prosperity. But private property was an alien concept to many of the indigenous groups for whom the community generally provided security. Individual peasants also lacked access to many of the necessities for modern farming such as credit and technology. Although some were able to make a viable living on their own properties, others were forced to sell their lands; in many cases landowners took over the land by force. Much of the land ended up in the hands of wealthy landowners as well as members of an emerging agrarian middle class.

Decades of war and economic devastation had left the country destitute. Hundreds of armed bands and bandits roamed the countryside. Juárez created a rural police force, which restored order. He and his successor, Sebastian Lerdo de Tejada (1872–1876), lay the bases for modernizing the country, secured U.S.

and British as well as Mexican investment to extend railroad lines, increased telegraph communications, and doubled the number of schools.

But the Liberal government failed to achieve a lasting peace. Conflicts between different Liberal factions and revolts by peasants and indigenous groups, who had generally not benefited from the Reform—and in some respects found their situation worse than before—continued throughout the remaining years of the Juárez administration as well as the subsequent government of Lerdo de Tejada. It was only in the long regime of Porfirio Díaz, who overthrew the Lerdo government and held on to power either indirectly or for most part directly until 1910, that the long-sought peace and prosperity was achieved, and it would be at a high cost.

The Porfiriato: 1876–1910

Porfirio Díaz, like Juárez a native of Oaxaca, had been a general in the Liberal army and had distinguished himself in the War of the Reform. After two unsuccessful campaigns for the presidency, he led a successful revolt against the Lerdo government in 1876 and was subsequently elected president in 1877. Having campaigned on the platform of "effective suffrage, no re-election," Díaz did not run in the subsequent election of 1880, which was won by his chosen candidate, but was again elected in 1884 and, despite his earlier campaign slogan, held onto power, through regular but increasingly fraudulent elections, until 1910.

Díaz succeeded in establishing order and unifying the country under his control. He neutralized regional and local opponents through eliminating regional taxes, replacing regional leaders with commanders loyal to himself, playing off different cliques against each other, and providing opportunities for local and state officials to enrich themselves through foreign concessions. To maintain the loyalty of the military he increased the military budget, and to prevent it from obtaining too much power he formed or strengthened other military forces such as the rural police. He continued the programs of railroad construction of his predecessors, facilitating the physical unification of the country and enabling him to quickly send troops to suppress revolts wherever these appeared. The elimination of regional tariffs and the expansion of railroads in effect created a national market, facilitating the transport of goods throughout Mexico as well as to ports, providing a major impetus to production for the internal market and for export.

The regime, which became known as the *Porfiriato*,[12] coincided with the economic and industrial expansion of Europe and the United States in the late 19th and early 20th centuries. For European and U.S. companies, Latin America was a source of industrial minerals, for example, copper, zinc, and lead, and a market for their manufactured products. It was during this period that the United States became increasingly involved economically, politically, and often militarily in the Caribbean region, culminating in the Spanish American war and the occupation of Cuba and Puerto Rico as well as the Philippines, and in U.S.

support for the secession of Panama from Colombia to facilitate construction of the Panama Canal. In 1904, U.S. President Theodore Roosevelt added the Roosevelt Corollary to the Monroe Doctrine, asserting the U.S. right to intervene in Latin America to protect U.S. lives and property, which was drawn on repeatedly to justify U.S. involvement in the region.

This increase in U.S. interventionism in the region was, for a country that had lost half of its territory to the United States, a source of major concern to the government. At the same time, Díaz, like his predecessors, wished to modernize Mexico, and was convinced that, given Mexico's limited economic resources, foreign capital was necessary for Mexico's development. The Porfirian government gave generous concessions to U.S. companies to invest in Mexico, at the same time encouraging European investment and attempting in other ways— e.g., the encouragement of European immigration—to offset the power of the United States. The result, however, was foreign control of major sectors of Mexico's economy. A substantial proportion of Mexico's mines came under the control of U.S. conglomerates. U.S. companies were given concessions to build railroads, many of them serving to transport minerals from Mexican mining regions to the United States. European companies financed electric power, tramways, and communications systems. French banks controlled much of Mexico's finance. Concessions were given to U.S. and British companies to petroleum fields on the gulf coast. Even in agriculture, which remained largely in Mexican hands, large U.S. companies owned vast tracts of land in northern Mexico, and foreign investors controlled the production of rubber and much of coffee in southeastern states of Chiapas and Tabasco.

At the same time, the Mexican entrepreneurial sector was also growing, including middle class Mexican farmers and large landowners, some of whose families had benefited from the agrarian reform of the Juárez government. While the traditional latifundia based on the exploitation of cheap, often coerced, labor prevailed in the west central and central region near Mexico City, commercial farms also flourished, producing for export (henequen, tobacco, coffee), the domestic market (sugar), and industry (cotton). The establishment of a national market benefited manufacturing in areas like textiles, paper, glass, shoes, beer, and food processing, which was further promoted through tax concessions from the government.

The Porfiriato saw the emergence of what would become some of the most powerful economic groups in Mexico. Several of these were founded by immigrants, particularly from Spain and France, whose investments expanded from commerce into manufacturing, finance, and other interests. One example was immigrants from the French province of Barcelonette who came to Mexico in the late 19th and early 20th centuries and established manufacturing firms in beer, paper, and textiles, as well as two major commercial houses, El Puerto de Liverpool and Palacio de Hierro. This pattern of ownership, in which a particular investor or small group of investors, in some cases a single family, controlled interests in a broad range of economic firms, such as manufacturing, commerce, banking and finance, insurance, real estate, etc., became typical of the so-called economic groups that predominate in Mexico and other Latin American countries.

In 1890, three inter-related families established the Cuauhtémoc brewery in the northern city of Monterrey, a commercial city that had benefited from relations with the United States during the 19th century and would become Mexico's pre-eminent industrial city in the 20th century. This was the beginning of the Garza Sada family group, which was to become one of the most powerful economic groups in Mexico. Over the next few decades the family would create additional breweries and expand into industries to service the beer industry, such as glass bottles and packaging, and ultimately into steel and chemicals as well as finance, insurance, commerce, and construction. The initial Cuauhtémoc group has expanded into dozens of groups and subgroups in which descendants of the original founders continue to be active, and family members have been a source of leadership of the powerful Monterrey business interests.[13]

Mexico's economy grew dramatically during the Porfiriato, averaging 8 percent annually. Mexico was also increasingly integrated into the world economy as a producer of mineral and agricultural commodities and increasingly dependent on the United States as a market and source of investment. Between 1877 and 1911, the value of Mexico's exports increased 700 percent and the percentage going to the United States grew from 36 percent in 1872 to between 55 and 65 percent in the first decade of the 20th century. The growth in foreign investment was particularly dramatic during the first decade of the 20th century, when it tripled to over $3 billion.

But there was another side to Mexico's dramatic growth. The increase in agricultural exports led to the rapid expansion of agricultural estates into indigenous communities and the small holdings of Mexican villagers, accelerating a process that had begun during the colonial period. One result was the expulsion of peasants, small farmers, and villagers, driving up the number of rural families without access to land. Most of the cultivable land in the south-central state of Morelos was taken over by 17 sugar haciendas. In Yucatan, on estates cultivating henequen—the source of sisal for export—contracted workers were subject to brutal exploitation, living in conditions akin to slavery. In the northern states, commercial estates expanded into the lands of indigenous groups and independent farmers.

The growth of industries in such areas as textiles and leather resulted in displacing small artisan producers in many cities and towns in west central Mexico. At the same time, the expansion of mining, railroads, and manufacturing resulted in the growth of a new industrial proletariat. Conditions were particularly harsh in many of the new factories established in Mexico City, Puebla and Veracruz, where employers rejected—often violently—efforts of workers to organize as provided for in the Liberal constitution of 1857. In the foreign-owned mining companies and railroads conditions were somewhat better, although Mexicans frequently received lower wages than Americans doing similar work. The efforts of workers to organize these industries were supported by the Industrial Workers of the World (IWW), an anarchist group that was active on both sides of the U.S.-Mexican border. Many of the proletariat suffered from the economic cycle of the late 1890s and early years of the new century, when an economic boom led to inflation and lowered real wages, followed by a recession in which many workers lost their jobs.

In 1910, when the government staged elaborate celebrations to commemorate the centennial of Mexico's independence, it undoubtedly seemed to many that Mexico was a substantially different country than it had been some 30 or 40 years before. The government of Porfirio Díaz achieved what no previous government had been able to accomplish: the physical integration of the nation, the consolidation of the Mexican state, and the modernization of the Mexican economy. But underlying the *Pax Porfirista*—the Porfirian peace of order and progress—was that most of the population had suffered from the aggravations and disruptions of modernization which, added to the long-standing grievances of economic exploitation and political repression, would soon erupt into one of the bloodiest confrontations on the continent.

THE REVOLUTION: 1910–1940

Forces in Conflict: The Trajectory of Revolution (1910–1920)

What eventually erupted as the Mexican Revolution had its origins in thousands of local grievances throughout Mexico—against fraudulent elections and the imposition of state and local authorities by the central government; against corrupt, inefficient, and often repressive local officials; against hacienda takeovers of the land of villages and indigenous communities; against the exploitation of workers in mines and factories.[14]

There were broad groups that wanted change, but they wanted different types of change for different reasons. One group that coalesced during the pre-revolutionary period was composed for most part of middle and upper class groups who opposed the monopoly of political power by Porfirio Díaz and his supporters and pushed for a return to the democratic principles of the Liberal constitution of 1857. Liberal clubs were formed throughout the northeast, particularly in the states of Hidalgo and San Luis Potosí, and in 1906 the Liberal party was formed. The Liberals eventually split into a radical and more moderate faction. Among the leaders of the former were the brothers Ricardo and

Enrique Flores Magón, who were forced into exile, where they published the journal *Regeneración* and supported labor struggles in both the United States and Mexico.[15]

Francisco Madero, a privileged but relatively progressive member of one of the wealthiest families in Mexico, emerged as a leader of the moderate group. When Porfirio Díaz indicated in a 1908 interview with a U.S. reporter that he would not run for re-election in 1910, Madero formed the Anti-Re-electionist party, and, in April 1910 was nominated as its presidential candidate, campaigning with Díaz's former slogan: "effective suffrage—no re-election." By this time, the Díaz government had given numerous indications that it was not interested in either. In several electoral campaigns for state governor, candidates imposed by the federal government claimed victory over more popular opposition candidates through fraudulent elections, thereby increasing popular support for Madero. When a presidential campaign trip throughout the country revealed the extent of support for Madero, Díaz had him jailed until after the election, in which Díaz was again declared winner. Following his release Madero skipped bail and escaped to the United States, where he promulgated the Plan de San Luis Potosí, denouncing the dictatorship and issuing a call to revolt.

In the meantime, in the southern state of Morelos, the sugar haciendas had been taking over the lands of small farms and traditional villages for decades, but the process accelerated with the expansion of commercial production and the extension of sugar planters into processing and marketing in the late 19th and early 20th centuries. Federal legislation favored planters at the cost of the land and water rights of the villages. Over the years, as small farms disappeared and villages were taken over, leaders of the affected communities petitioned local, state and federal officials to recognize their legal titles, end the illegal take-overs of their holdings, and restore their land, but to no avail. In May 1910, when legal appeals failed to stop the takeover of the lands of the village of Anenecuilco, its young leader Emiliano Zapata (who had been involved in efforts to obtain official recognition of the village land titles) led a group of armed villagers into the fields and physically took them over, allocating the land to the villagers—an act that won admiration among villagers throughout the state. Zapata's followers expanded during the subsequent months as recruits from different parts of the state joined his forces. Based on a promise within the Plan of San Luis Potosí to return lands acquired illegally, Zapata joined the Madero revolt.

Other groups in various parts of the country, with their own frustrations against the long Díaz dictatorship, joined the Madero rebellion. Venustiano Carranza was a northern landowner from the state of Coahuila, which at independence had been the state of Coahuila y Tejas. The loss of the northern part of its territory with the secession of Texas in 1836 was a painful one for the state and an important factor in Carranza's concern for national sovereignty and resistance to foreign, and particularly U.S., intervention. Like many others he was frustrated by the concessions given by the Díaz regime to foreign interests and by the increase in foreign control over large sectors of the economy. When Díaz rejected Carrranza as candidate for governor of Coahuila in 1909 in favor of an official candidate, Carranza shifted his support to Madero.

To those fighting for a return to liberal democracy in opposition to the dictatorship, the restoration of land expropriated by landowners, and the assertion of Mexico's sovereignty in relation to the United States, could be added hundreds of thousands of others with different grievances and goals. All of them united momentarily around opposition to the Díaz regime and support for Madero.

The struggle between the Díaz government and supporters of Madero was relatively brief. Madero had chosen November 20, 1910, as the date of revolt. In the following months, there were uprisings throughout the country, although there was little coordination among them. By April of 1911, however, most of the Mexican countryside was controlled by the revolutionaries, and following negotiations, Díaz resigned from the presidency and went into exile to Paris. Elections were held which Madero won, and he assumed the presidency in November 1911.

But it soon became clear that this was only the first phase in a prolonged struggle. For Madero, the revolution was a political one: the restoration of democracy and of rights guaranteed under the 1857 constitution that had been usurped by the Porfirian regime. He legalized labor unions and the right to strike and also legitimated the concept of the expropriation and return of illegally seized land to agricultural villages. But when it came to acting directly, he vacillated. He failed to respond to Zapata's repeated requests that he honor his pledge to restore expropriated lands to peasants and small land holders, and Madero supported the sending of troops into Morelos to repel peasants who occupied the property of the landowners. Zapata responded by issuing the Plan de Ayala, in which he declared war on Madero and expanded the scope of his program to include not only the return of peasant holdings expropriated by the landowners but also the expropriation of one-third of land held by the large landowners and their distribution to landless rural workers.

In addition, much of the Porfirian bureaucracy remained in place. In an effort to maintain stability, Madero had the revolutionary army disarmed and discharged, retaining the federal army under the leadership of Victoriano Huerta, apparently against the advice of his own mother who told him that the federal troops should be dismantled and that Huerta could not be trusted. The Madero administration confronted numerous intrigues and revolts by Porfiristas as well as by some of Madero's former supporters. One such plot, involving the nephew of Porfirio Díaz, was joined by Victoriano Huerta, who on February 18, 1913 had Madero, his Vice President Pino Suárez, and several of their closest followers arrested. The coup was supported by the U.S. ambassador to Mexico,

Henry Lane Wilson, who was forewarned about the plot and refused to intervene to save Madero's life in spite of requests by Madero's wife and many others. Madero and Pino Suárez were killed on February 22, and Huerta became president with the support of the army.

This led to a second phase of the revolution, the revolt against the counterrevolutionary government of Huerta. The Constitutionalist Army was formed under the leadership of Venustiano Carranza, who like Madero was guided by the principles of the 1857 constitution. Carranza had supported Madero's revolt despite his misgivings about Madero himself, whom he saw as naive. His Army, which was divided into three divisions (North, Northeast, and Northwest), consisted largely of urban and rural workers in agriculture, ranching, mining, and other fields—many of them mobile workers who moved from one job to another, although the leadership was for most part composed of members of the provincial middle class—school teachers, government officials, farmers and ranchers.

Part of the success of the Constitutionalist Army against the forces of Huerta was attributed to the leadership of Pancho Villa, an uneducated ranch worker who had become a bandit after a conflict with the authorities.[16] Banditry was not uncommon in the northern sierra region, where haciendas, with government support, had surrounded and enclosed the land and cattle of local ranchers. Brutal and violent, Villa also had a keen sense of social justice; like many of the bandits, he was motivated by the desire for revenge against the hacendados and their accomplices. When the Constitutionalist Army was formed, Villa led the Division of the North, leading his troops to a series of impressive victories. Zapata did not join the army of Carranza, whom he did not trust, but led the Army of the South against Huerta. The Zapata-led forces regained control in several southern states, enabling villagers to recover the lands they had lost.

The British government, which at that time was involved in a struggle between British and U.S. petroleum interests in Mexico, supported Huerta. The United States, after some vacillation, supported the Constitutionalists. In April 1914 the U.S. government sent a naval fleet to Veracruz in an effort to force the resignation of Huerta and bring an end to the conflict, an intervention that not only mobilized the opposition of Huerta but also antagonized significant sectors of the population and the revolutionary leadership. Carranza denounced the intervention as a violation of Mexican sovereignty and Zapata promised to fight any U.S. troops that moved into Mexico. The United States shifted to negotiation, mediated by Argentina, Brazil, and Chile. In the meantime, the struggle of the revolutionary forces against Huerta continued, resulting in Huerta's defeat in August 1914.

Almost immediately following the defeat of Huerta, however, the revolutionary armies split, with Villa's Northern Division joining with the Zapata forces against those Constitutionalists remaining loyal to Carranza. This resulted in the third phase of the revolution, in which the armies of Villa and Zapata struggled against the Constitutionalists under Carranza. The United States, increasingly concerned about instability in Mexico in the context of the First World War, shifted its support among the different factions and used a combination of threats and promises in efforts to end the conflict, reconcile the conflicting forces, and restore order in a way that would favor U.S. interests. But victories on the battle-field reinforced Carranza's determination to win a military victory, and as it became clear that Carranza represented the only possibility of leading a viable government, the United States officially recognized it as the de facto government of Mexico in October 1915.

After the Constitutionalist forces had gained control of Mexico City, Car-ranza called for a constitutional convention to draft a new constitution. Car-ranza envisioned a document reflecting the values of the Liberal Reform that would rectify what were seen as some of the defects of the 1857 constitution. But many of the delegates had a more radical agenda, and the document that emerged incorporated the goals of the different protagonists in the struggle. Like the 1857 constitution it called for a federal system and separation of powers, banned re-election, and provided for individual rights. In contrast to the 1857 constitution, however, it called for a centralized government with a strong executive, includ-ing the right to legislate by decree, and a relatively weak legislature.

This was in keeping with Carranza's agenda, since he believed that a decen-tralized state had been one of the weaknesses of the 1857 constitution. But the 1917 document went further, calling for an interventionist state that would ensure national sovereignty and actively promote social justice. In certain respects it would replicate certain principles of the colonial era as described at the time by sociologist Andrés Molina Enríquez, who lamented that the Liberal state's promotion of individual private property rights had left the indigenous population without the protection they had received (in principle) under the Spanish crown, and called for the nation—like the Spanish sovereign during the colonial period—to have full rights over property and "to retain within its power everything necessary for its development."[17]

This principle was incorporated in Article 27 of the constitution, which vested ownership of all land and resources in the nation as represented by the Mexican state, enabling it to expropriate private property in the public interest, restore confiscated land to villages and communities, and take over hacienda land (with compensation) for distribution to villages lacking sufficient land. The constitution would also end concessions for foreign ownership of natural resources, which would be leased by the state to foreign companies for specific periods of time rather than "in perpetuity." In order to obtain such concessions, foreigners would have to "agree to consider themselves national with respect to such property, and bind themselves not to invoke the protection of their governments."[18] Foreigners could not own land along the coast or next to the border.

Other important measures included Article 123, which provided a range of rights for workers, including a minimum wage, an eight-hour day and a six-day week, equal pay for men and women and regardless of nationality, and the right to organize, bargain collectively, and strike. Article 3 called for state control of education, stating that primary education should be free, obligatory and secular. Its anti-clerical provisions went much further than those of the 1857 constitution, banning public worship outside the church, requiring priests to register with civil authorities, enabling state legislatures to determine their number, and requiring that any new church buildings be government approved.

The constitution thus combined principles of the Liberal Reform with elements of the corporatist order of the colonial period. It provided, at least in theory, for the political and economic incorporation of the peasantry and indigenous populations as well as the emerging proletariat. But at this point the constitution was a document; its implementation was another matter. Over the following decades peasants and workers would strive to make agrarian reform and labor rights a reality; church and state would struggle for ideological supremacy; and government officials would confront foreign interests in efforts to assert national sovereignty.

Elections were held and Carranza was elected president to serve until 1920, but the country was far from united. The Constitutionalist forces continued to attack the Zapatistas in Morelos and continued the war against the Villa forces in the north. It was not until 1919 that the Zapatistas were defeated with the assassination of Zapata. The Villista forces were also defeated in 1919; Villa retired to a hacienda in Chihuahua but was assassinated in 1922. Localized revolts continued. The government did little to implement the land distribution and labor provisions of the constitution, attempting to reverse the agrarian reform in Morelos and sending troops to crush a strike by workers in Veracruz.

Growing discontent with the Carranza administration was further exacerbated when Carranza tried to impose a virtually unknown candidate as nominee for the presidential elections of 1920. This was a signal for revolt, led by General Alvaro Obregon, who as leader of the Division of the Northwest of the Constitutionalist Army had distinguished himself in the struggles against the counter-revolutionary government of Huerta and subsequently against the army of Villa, and who was a leader of the radical faction of the Constitutionalists. Leading an army from the north, Obregon defeated the Carranza forces and Carranza was assassinated or, according to some accounts, committed suicide when facing capture. Elections were subsequently held following an interim government and Obregon was elected president.

The Establishment of the Post-Revolutionary Order:
I. The Sonoran Dynasty (1920–1934)

The election of Obregon marked the beginning of what became known as the Sonoran dynasty, with generals from the northwestern border state of Sonora dominating the Mexican government for the next 14 years. Obregon was succeeded by General Plutarco Elias Calles, another general from Sonora, in the elections of 1924. In 1928, Obregon was re-elected after the constitution was amended to permit re-election following an intervening term. However, Obregon was assassinated before he could take office. The Calles government called for a convention of revolutionary generals and regional leaders to establish a national party, the National Revolutionary Party (PNR), which would formalize the process of nomination. The amendment permitting the re-election of a previous president after an interim term was rescinded, and the presidential term was extended to six years. Over the next six years the presidential office passed from an interim president to an elected president who resigned after two years, at which point a new president was chosen to serve out the rest of his term. But it was Calles who oversaw the government, becoming known as the *Jefe Máximo* (Top Boss), and this period was known as the *Maximato*.

Obregon and his successors confronted immense challenges. An estimated 10 percent of the population—1 to 1.5 million—had died in the revolution and the immediate post-revolutionary conflicts. Many had died of starvation as a result of occupation of villages and towns by federal and/or revolutionary forces; the requisition of food supplies, destruction of crops, and theft of animals left farms and villages destitute. The country was in ruins: railroads, communications, mines had been destroyed, crops failed, the use of government resources for munitions left it bereft of funds and heavily in debt. There was no national currency; private banks and in some cases revolutionary generals and local officials issued their own currency, most of it worthless. Division commanders exercised considerable autonomy in their respective regions, including many of the revolutionary generals who had supported Obregon's revolt. Some were potential rivals for the presidency, as were some state governors and local caciques, some of whom sought to establish a rival political support base among labor and peasant organizations.

Government efforts to implement certain provisions of the constitution also led to confrontations with foreign companies, the United States government as well as the Church. The 1920s was also a period of mobilization by peasants and workers for land and labor rights. Landless peasants and indigenous communities called for the restoration of their farms and the distribution of land through the promised agrarian reform. Some state governors encouraged peasant mobilization and instituted land distribution programs, which led to conflicts with landowners, often supported by regional military commanders; land reforms were sometimes reversed by subsequent, more conservative governors. Industrial workers who organized unions and federations to claim their rights to decent wages and working conditions encountered fierce resistance by business interests, both national and foreign. Some companies fired and blacklisted labor organizers and formed their own militias, which were responsible for the assassination of more militant workers.

The dissatisfaction of the military was aggravated when the Obregon government cut military expenditures. In 1924, over half of the revolutionary generals joined a revolt led by another Sonoran general, Adolfo de la Huerta, against the central government. The government forces defeated them, with the help of the peasants and workers, and purged the leaders of the revolt. To further establish control over ambitious generals, the post-revolutionary governments utilized some of the same tactics as Porfirio Díaz—transferring generals to regions without their troops and taking steps to professionalize the military. A particularly effective tactic was to encourage revolutionary generals to take advantage of opportunities for entrepreneurship in commercial agriculture, real estate, and industry. Members of the government also took advantage of these opportunities. Calles also sought to neutralize political rivals among state governors and other local officials by uniting different factions and regional interests in a single government party, the National Revolutionary Party.

The most serious conflict during this period resulted from fierce opposition of the Church to Articles 3 and 130 of the constitution. Catholic resistance to the government was centered in the center-west states of Mexico, where traditional landholders and members of the clergy were united in their opposition to the new order. Priests denounced the agrarian reform from their pulpits and forbade the peasants from accepting land under its auspices. Many peasants resisted the new education programs of the government. Although some government officials were hesitant to push the more draconian anti-clerical provisions, this changed during the administration of Calles, who—as a teacher in Sonora prior to the revolution had witnessed the fierce debates around church versus government control of education in the state—viewed the role of the Church as completely reactionary. In 1926 he called for full implementation of the anti-clerical provisions of the constitution. Catholic schools, convents and monasteries were closed; priests were required to register with civil authorities; and foreign priests were expelled. Fiercely anti-clerical officials led attacks on churches, looting them and burning images of saints.

The official Church responded by suspending masses and religious services. Catholic leaders in several states called for a revolt against the government and organized the peasants into guerrilla forces. According to the government version, landlords and the clergy manipulated the peasants. But the anti-clericalism of the revolutionary leadership was not shared by many sectors of the peasantry, for whom religion was part of their way of life and who willingly fought to defend it. The result was a three-year conflict that pitted peasant armies supporting the revolution against those that sided with the Church. The pro-Church forces became known as the *cristeros,* reflecting their slogan "Viva Cristo Rey" (Long live Christ the King). The war between Church and state was characterized by atrocities on both sides and cost an estimated 70,000 to 80,000 lives. It finally ended in 1929 in a truce, but tensions between Catholics and anti-clerical groups continued through the 1930s, and peasants continued to resist the anti-clerical elements of the education program.[19]

The government also confronted serious obstacles in attempting to implement constitutional provisions for national sovereignty, which brought it into conflict with foreign, especially U.S. companies, and the U.S. government. The United States had emerged from the First World War as a world power, and many U.S. officials saw Latin America as a market for the expansion of U.S. trade and investment. The war had also interrupted European economic relations with Latin America, to the benefit of U.S. companies, and the United States was anxious to prevent a resurgence of European economic penetration in the region. The Mexican Revolution, and particularly the nationalist thrust of the revolutionary leaders and the Mexican constitution, was of particular concern. During the revolution the primary U.S. goal had been the protection of U.S. property and bringing the conflict to a close as quickly as possible. The United States shifted its support among different factions during different phases of the conflict and had intervened militarily twice: once in 1914, when President Woodrow Wilson sent a naval force to Veracruz to block an arms shipment to the counter-revolutionary government of Victoriano Huerta, and again in 1916 in response to an incursion of the troops of Villa into the United States, when the U.S. government sent an expedition to chase them back to Mexico.

U.S. officials had been particularly wary of the nationalist thrust of the Carranza forces and were concerned about Article 27 of the new constitution. The United States was also anxious to obtain compensation for U.S. citizens whose property had been destroyed or damaged during the conflict. In addition, Mexico was deeply in debt to U.S. and European banks, and in 1918 the International Bankers Committee was formed under the leadership of Thomas Lamont, a banker with J.P. Morgan, to negotiate with Mexico regarding debt repayment. Mexico's critical economic situation and need for foreign loans was an important source of leverage in these negotiations.[20] In addition, during the revolution, U.S. support for specific belligerent groups had been critical to their ability to obtain arms through the United States and to close off U.S. access to other forces, and recognition or non-recognition of the Mexican government continued to be an important source of U.S. pressure.

Following Obregon's revolt and subsequent election, the United States initially refused to recognize the new government in the absence of guarantees to U.S. petroleum and mining interests.[21] In 1921 when Obregon attempted to raise taxes on oil exports, the petroleum companies, supported by the U.S. State Department, halted production, leading to the unemployment of 20,000 workers. Obregon reduced the tax, and in 1923 reached an agreement with the United States, declaring that Article 27 would not be retroactive, in return for which the United States finally recognized the government.

But tensions flared again in 1925 when President Calles passed the Alien Land Act, declaring that foreigners could not own property along the Mexican border areas, and the Petroleum Law, requiring foreign mining and petroleum companies to renegotiate the contracts granted by Porfirio Díaz, which would be reduced to a maximum of 50 years. The U.S. government threatened retaliation, including possible military intervention. The issue was resolved when the Mexican Supreme Court declared the 1925 Petroleum Law unconstitutional.

Relations improved during the latter half of the Calles administration, in part due to the diplomatic efforts of Thomas Lamont and the Morgan bankers as well as a shift of the Mexican government toward a more conservative position. This could be explained by several factors. The government's need for financial support to repay its debts and promote economic recovery made it dependent on private sector groups as well as foreign investors. In addition, one of the mechanisms by which the Calles government had "domesticated" ambitious generals was by encouraging opportunities for enrichment. Calles himself, as well as members of his government and local government and military officials, took advantage of their positions to set up enterprises of various types: establishing construction companies that secured generous government contracts, obtaining loans from government banks, taking over expropriated properties, and obtaining kickbacks from private interests in return for promises to limit reforms. Some of the "revolutionary capitalists" were able to expand their interests to incorporate commercial farms, banks, processing industries, real estate, and other enterprises, forming new economic groups. They thus had a vested interest in maintaining stable conditions for themselves and for the private sector.

The government also worked closely with the private sector to restore Mexico's monetary and fiscal stability. While Carranza and other revolutionary leaders had regarded the Porfirian banks as centers of reaction, financial officials of the Obregon and Calles governments worked with the Porfirian bankers to reconstruct the Mexican banking system and created a government controlled central bank, the Banco de Mexico, which would have sole responsibility for issuing currency, thus ending the right of private banks to issue banknotes. Private banks would be regulated by the central bank and the National Banking Commission of the Finance Ministry, which would also exercise budgetary control over other government agencies. The peso would be pegged to the dollar. The establishment of an income tax was an important step in consolidating the fiscal system, although as late as 1937 it represented only 9 percent of government revenue, most of which came from taxes on imports and industry. Private bankers also collaborated with government financial officials and the International Bankers Committee to reschedule debt payments, and the new Banco de Mexico received loans from J.P. Morgan. In 1928 domestic bankers formed the Mexican Bankers' Association (ABM), which collaborated closely with government financial officials.

The goal of the government was to utilize the banking system to promote economic development through increased production for export, the substitution of imports, and the promotion of domestic industry. The government provided loans to establish banks oriented to specific commodities—coffee, sugar and cotton—and created several institutions to facilitate government intervention in major sectors of the economy, such as electricity, and facilitate the building of infrastructure, including roads and irrigation works. It also established the National Bank for Agricultural Credit to provide loans to local and regional agrarian societies.

While wary of foreign control over the Mexican economy, the Mexican government encouraged foreign investment in manufacturing, and several U.S. companies began to invest in Mexico, including the Ford Motor Company (which opened an assembly plant in 1926), Simmons, Dupont and B.F. Goodrich. By the end of the 1920s, the United States was the market for 65 to 85 percent of Mexico's exports, chiefly minerals and agricultural products, and provided 75 percent of Mexico's imports, for most part industrial goods.

In short, by the end of the 1920s the Sonoran leaders had reached an accommodation with the domestic private sector and foreign interests, notably the United States. They had instituted a new model for Mexico's economic recovery and reconstruction in which the state would have a critical role, which included promoting and guiding private investment, both domestic and foreign. According to U.S. banker Thomas Lamont, U.S. business leaders in Mexico felt that Calles was the best president Mexico had had since Porfirio Díaz.

But the Mexico of the 1920s was not the Mexico of the Porfiriato. A revolution had been fought for land and labor rights, and these goals had been institutionalized in the constitution. The peasants and workers who had been protagonists of that revolution were newly mobilized political actors whose demands had to be taken into account. The governments of Obregon and Calles recognized the necessity to respond to the demands of the peasantry and workers for agrarian reform, the right to organize, and better wages and working conditions in order to secure the legitimacy of the state as representative of the goals of the revolution. They also depended on peasant and worker support in suppressing military revolts and the Cristero rebellion. At the same time, they were increasingly concerned with containing labor and peasant mobilization and controlling labor and peasant organizations in the interests of establishing and maintaining economic recovery and development.

A pattern emerged that would characterize state relations with labor and peasant organizations throughout the following decades: the emergence of independent organizations and efforts by the state to co-opt these organizations and maintain them within its sphere of influence. Where it succeeded, the union leadership became beholden to the state, sometimes to the benefit but often to the detriment of the workers it supposedly represented. In the 1920s, this pattern intersected with efforts to establish and maintain the hegemony of the federal government relative to state and regional authorities whose encouragement of labor and/or peasant mobilization and organization in their respective areas could be seen as a means of establishing rival bases of support.

An early example of the pattern of co-opting was CROM, the Regional Confederation of Mexican Workers, established as an independent confederation in 1918, and composed chiefly of workers in manufacturing industries, for example textiles, which were concentrated in the states of Puebla, Tlaxcala and Veracruz. The CROM supported the Obregon revolt against Carranza and subsequently collaborated closely with the Obregon government, which CROM leader Luis Morones justified on the basis of the weakness of labor and its need for state support in its conflict with capital. This relationship was beneficial for the government and the CROM leaders, who were given cabinet posts and legislative positions, and initially for the workers as well, who were supported in their conflicts with management for higher wages and benefits. As the government became increasingly conservative in the late 1920s, however, CROM discouraged strikes in the interest of business-labor harmony and economic progress, a shift that was facilitated by the authoritarian structure of the organization.

Several other labor confederations and industry-based federations were formed during this period, often by anarchists and/or the Mexican Communist party, which had been created at the instigation of the Comintern[22] in 1918 in the wake of the Russian revolution. The CROM sought to undermine rival confederations, sometimes in collaboration with local government officials and employers. It frequently resorted to violent tactics, and by the end of the decade the independent confederations had been severely weakened. The industry based federations, including the railroad workers' union and the union of electric power workers as well as the individual oil workers' unions, remained independent, however, and were often fiercely militant. Some of these federations and unions dated to the anarchist and socialist unions formed under the Porfiriato. Among the most important labor disputes during the 1920s were those between the oil workers and foreign petroleum companies, which blocked unionization, fired and blacklisted labor organizers, and hired mercenaries whose tactics included assassination of union organizers and militants. Although the government had its own conflicts with the oil companies during this period, it generally did not support the oil workers.

In 1931, the Mexican government passed the Federal Labor Law in an effort to end the confusion resulting from conflicting norms prevailing in different states by moving jurisdiction over labor from the state to the federal level, a further element in centralizing government authority. The new law permitted strikes, forbade employer lockouts, and limited the ability of employers to fire workers. At the same time, it established state control over the labor movement by requiring unions to register with government authorities in order to be recognized and required the arbitration of labor-management conflicts by labor boards composed of representatives of labor, employers, and the government, thus giving the government veto power. In 1934, responding to labor demands, the government passed the exclusion clause which stated that workers had to belong to the relevant union in order to be hired by a particular firm and to keep their jobs. This would prevent management from forming company unions to undermine an independent union, but the clause also became a mechanism for union control of the workforce. Pro-labor legislation was strongly opposed by business groups, notably industrialists in Monterrey, who formed COPARMEX (Employers' Confederation of the Mexican Republic) in 1928 to ensure input into the new law and defend the business sector.

By the end of this period the CROM had lost favor with the government, and in 1933 a new confederation, the CGOCM (the General Labor and Peasant Confederation of Mexico) was formed, grouping the followers of Vicente Lombardo Toledano, a prominent Marxist intellectual and labor leader, and those of Fidel Velazquez, a pragmatic and opportunistic organizer who had played a role in controlling workers on behalf of local employers and government officials as a leader in CROM during the 1920s. At the same time, workers in independent unions continued to struggle to maintain their autonomy vis-à-vis the government and in relation to government unions, resulting in a division and often fierce conflict between independent and state-dominated unions.[23]

The mobilization of the rural sector was more diffuse, reflecting both the heterogeneity of this sector, which included peasants, small farmers, as well as landless workers on commercial estates, indigenous communities, tenant laborers and debt peons on traditional haciendas, and local conditions and leadership. Some of the most dramatic programs of peasant organizing and agrarian reform occurred at the state level, notably Michoacán, Tamaulipas, Veracruz, and Yucatán where governors encouraged peasant mobilization and carried out extensive land distribution programs, in some cases arming the peasants and forming them into militia to defend their holdings. They also promoted labor rights, established co-education programs, and encouraged the organization of women.[24]

The most successful case was that of Veracruz, where Governor Adalberto Tejeda supported independent peasant leagues organized by tenant organizations, labor unions, and the Communist Party. Peasant leagues also formed in other states, and in 1926 under the auspices of the Veracruz league they joined forces in the National Peasant League. But for the most part regional commanders, governors and local caciques sided with landowners in land disputes, and in some cases, such as Michoacán and Yucatán, reversed the land reforms of more progressive governors. In the meantime, the federal government was increasingly concerned regarding the support base of Veracruz governor Tejeda. In 1929, the new government party, the PNR, attempted to co-opt the National Peasant League, resulting in a three-way split, with one group joining the PNR, a second the Communist Party, while the largest group remained independent.

Despite the centrality of agrarian reform to the revolutionary agenda, land distribution during this period was limited to traditional landowners. The Sonoran reformers made a sharp distinction between these, which they regarded as backward, inefficient and oppressive, and commercial landowners who they saw as making an important contribution to agricultural production and export, a perspective that was undoubtedly reinforced as government officials themselves joined the ranks of the latter. Land distribution programs therefore targeted the land of traditional landowners, while that of commercial estates, such as the henequen plantations of Yucatán, the coffee estates of Tabasco, and cotton plantations of the Laguna region in Durango and Coahuila, were declared off limits.

Most of the land distributed in this period was in the form of *ejidos*, through which ownership is vested in the community and could be worked collectively or more often allocated to individual families for cultivation. The land could not be rented, sold or mortgaged, which was designed as means to prevent the takeover of land, as occurred during the Porfiriato, leaving much of the rural population landless. But the ejido was generally seen as a temporary expedient until the rural population acquired the necessary skills and techniques for modern farming.

Government initiatives toward the rural population during this period were based on a perception that they were ignorant, backward and superstitious, degraded by centuries of oppression and religious fanaticism. Education, an important project in a country that was still largely illiterate, was seen as a means of attacking their superstitious mentality, elevating their mental and moral capacities, and imparting the skills and techniques necessary to function in a market economy. It would have an important role in integrating isolated villages and communities into a modern nation. During the administration of Obregon,

José Vasconcelos, the energetic Secretary of Education, oversaw the construction of thousands of rural schools, set up cultural missions to train teachers, established libraries and published textbooks, and dispatched thousands of teachers to bring education to remote rural areas.[25]

The 1920s had brought substantial change to Mexico, although many of the issues raised in the revolution and the constitution had not been addressed. In certain respects, the achievements of the governments of the 1920s mirrored those of Porfirio Díaz. Order had been restored following a period of violence and chaos; authority was again concentrated in the central government, the military had been brought under control, and the conditions for economic modernization based on private enterprise and foreign investment reconstituted. But in contrast to the Porfiriato, the post-revolutionary government had resolved the problem of political succession (although elections continued to be fraudulent), reduced the threat of rebellion by dissident elites, strengthened the capacity of the state to intervene actively in the economy, and launched a major attack on the ideological authority exercised by the Catholic church.

These changes were achieved in part through the creation of new institutions: the electoral system, the PNR, state banks and other government agencies, and state schools. The prohibition against re-election under any circumstances mandated a turnover in all major offices of government, including the presidency, in effect opening the possibility of electoral office to anyone with political ambitions. The PNR further reduced the likelihood of rebellion by political dissidents by bringing different factions of the revolutionary elite together in a party which claimed the mantle of the revolution but in fact was essentially pragmatic, containing as it did radical reformers, political opportunists, and conservative beneficiaries of the new status quo. The post-revolutionary governments also established much of the machinery for active state intervention to promote and channel economic development and to support the evolution of the domestic private sector, through the creation of a central bank, various development banks as well as commissions for electric power and roads.

Finally, the post-revolutionary governments aimed to replace the educational and socialization functions of the Catholic Church through the establishment of the Ministry of Education, the construction of schools (particularly in rural areas), and the elaboration of curricula designed to replace religious superstition with rational thought, to teach practical skills, and to transform the "backward" sectors of the peasants and indigenous populations into modern citizens. However, as the Cristero rebellion and subsequent opposition to "socialist education" indicate, this goal was only partially achieved.

During this period the government also sponsored artistic production, notably the muralist movement. Rejecting the European models in which they had been schooled and following the mandate of art for the people, artists, notably Diego Rivera, José Clemente Orozco, and David Siquieres, painted their vast murals in public places such as the Government Palace and the Ministry of Education. Their work celebrated the pre-Colombian indigenous civilization and culture, extolled the leaders of the Independence movement and the Reforma, and commemorated the battles and achievements of the revolution. They honored the worker and *campesino* (peasant) and caricatured fanatical clergy, corrupt officials, and the ostentatiously wealthy.

The state had also begun to address the mobilization of new actors as a result of the revolution. The Federal Labor Law of 1931 implemented several provisions of Article 123 of the 1917 constitution favoring labor; at the same time, along with the labor boards which gave the government veto power with respect to labor disputes, it was a means of both channeling and containing labor demands. The government also succeeded in controlling the new labor confederation, CROM, through co-opting its leadership. This pattern of close collaboration between the state and the major labor confederation, at the cost of the independence of the workers, would be renewed in subsequent decades.

The government response to the mobilization of the rural population, which was much larger and more heterogeneous than the still small industrial labor movement, was more limited; with the most important initiatives both in land distribution and peasant organization occurring at the sub-national level in several states. In 1930, responding to the prompting of private domestic and foreign bankers as well as government financial officials, Calles proposed that the agrarian reform be brought to an end. He also called for an end to labor mobilization and strikes in the interests of economic development.

By the early 1930s, disillusion with the revolutionary leaders and government leadership was widespread. Corruption had reached unprecedented levels. The National Bank of Agrarian Credit, created to provide loans to agrarian reform beneficiaries, had become a source of enrichment for generals and government officials. In the fraudulent presidential elections of 1929, an unknown candidate handpicked by Calles won over the popular José Vasconcelos, the previous education minister, demonstrating that in spite of the non-succession principle, the new revolutionary order was no democracy. Labor militants and workers were frustrated at the corruption of labor leaders, while peasant activists and their supporters were angered at the decision to end agrarian reform. The latter in particular were supported by groups in the government and state bureaucracy as well as among the state governors—the so-called agrarians—who continued to support agrarian reform and to oppose the more conservative groups within the state.

In the meantime, Mexico was affected by significant international events. The world depression, beginning in 1929, led to a reduction in Mexico's exports, resulting in production cutbacks, the dismissal of workers, and wage reductions in Mexico's export industries, affecting mineral workers as well as rural workers on commercial agricultural estates. This in turn reduced the internal market for agricultural products and manufactured goods, again increasing unemployment, which was further impacted by the forced repatriation of thousands of Mexicans who had migrated to the United States during the revolution and the Cristero revolt. In Mexico and other Latin American countries, the depression called into question the viability of depending on an economy based on commodity exports, which were subject to fluctuations in world markets and international prices.

In the United States and Europe, the depression demonstrated the vulnerabilities of a capitalist market economy and led to broad acceptance of the ideas of British economist John Maynard Keynes, who proposed strong state intervention in the market, including substantial state investment in productive activities that would stimulate industrial and agricultural production and, through the creation of jobs, expand the consumer market. Keynesian ideas were implemented by several European governments as well as the government of U.S. President Franklin D. Roosevelt, whose "New Deal" promoted vast public works projects that would put unemployed workers back to work. In the meantime, in the Soviet Union, where the state had replaced the private sector, the apparent success of the first five-year plan in achieving the rapid industrialization of a relatively "backward" country seemed to offer an additional demonstration of the effectiveness of state economic intervention.

In Mexico, these events reinforced state-centric elements in the constitution and post-revolutionary government as well as socialist ideas that had been circulating among Mexican intellectual and policy circles since the victory of the Russian Revolution in 1917. Several officials in the Mexican government studied economics in England and continental Europe where they were influenced by the theories of Keynes as well as European models of direct state involvement in economic development. Many of them were also involved in establishing the first economics program in Mexico in 1929, which had the explicit purpose of training government officials and where the initial programs were strongly influenced by the works of Keynes and Marx.[26]

As noted above, the Communist Party had played an important role in labor organizing, notably among the railroad workers and mine workers, in the 1920s, and had its own confederation, the CSUM (the United Union Confederation of Mexico). Concepts of socialism were particularly evident in the field of education. Approximately one in eight teachers was a member of the Communist party and it is estimated that half were sympathizers. Toward the end of the 1920s, education became more explicitly popular and radical, in part reflecting the radicalization of teachers and educators through interaction with rural villages, in part due to the initiatives of the new Marxist Education Minister,

Narciso Bassols. In 1932, a congress of educators was held which established the Bases for Rural Education, calling for education to promote a shift to collective systems of production and distribution.

The Establishment of the Post-Revolutionary Order:
II. The Government of Lázaro Cárdenas (1934–1940)

The PNR convention held in December 1934 to nominate the candidate for president was dominated by the agrarians.[27] Influenced by international events and socialist ideas and ideology, they drew up a six-year plan that reflected the principles of the 1917 constitution as well as international influences. It committed the government to continue land distribution under agrarian reform, thus countervailing Calles' request to bring it to an end; reaffirmed the active and interventionist role of the state, e.g., through government control of the generation and distribution of electricity and the establishment of a government petroleum company; reasserted the principle of national sovereignty over subsoil rights through such measures as increased taxes on mineral exports; and called for strengthening union organization.

The presidential candidate, Lázaro Cárdenas, was an agrarian, but also a protégé of Calles, whom he served under in the Constitutionalist Army. Cárdenas had joined the revolutionary forces in 1913 at the age of 18, eventually rising to the rank of division commander. Between 1925 and 1928 he served as zone commander of Tampico, where he was able to observe firsthand the mistreatment of oil workers by the foreign-owned petroleum companies, which had created a virtual enclave in the region. Subsequently, as governor of his home state of Michoacán, he had carried out extensive land distribution programs, armed the women to protect their husbands as they tilled the land, and promoted the organization of rural and urban workers. He subsequently served as president of the Executive Committee of the PNR and secretary of government.

Cárdenas' candidacy was supported by agrarians within the government, peasant leagues, some military groups, and Calles himself, who probably assumed that he would be able to manage his young protégé as he had managed other executives, an assumption shared by Mexican and U.S. business groups. The U.S. Ambassador, Josephus Daniels, called Cárdenas a "loyal soldier" who would follow the guidance of a "superior authority."

However Cárdenas was a loyal soldier not of Calles but of the revolution— and by extension the new revolutionary state—and was perceived as representing its goals and principles. He envisioned an active role for workers and peasants in pushing for reform, and given the social injustices that characterized Mexico, he believed that the state had a special obligation to support "the weaker party" against more powerful interests. The state was "above classes" and only the state could arbitrate class conflict. In his own words, "[T]he state alone embodies the general interest, and for this reason only the state has a vision of the whole. The state must constantly broaden, increase, and deepen its intervention."[28] In short, like Calles, Cárdenas supported a strong state, but it was a state that was explicitly committed to carrying out the goals of the revolution.

Cárdenas launched an unprecedented campaign tour throughout Mexico, calling for the mobilization and organization of peasants and workers to make their demands heard and to support government reforms; for the physical integration of the country through the construction of roads, highways, dams and irrigation works; and for the expansion of education. Most of all, he observed and listened, gaining a firsthand understanding of conditions in different regions of the country and the needs of demands of their inhabitants. Direct personal contact with the people and efforts to respond to their needs were maintained throughout his administration; he traveled frequently to different parts of the country, opened the telegraph office for an hour each day to receive messages from the population, and encouraged others in his administration to increase their direct interaction with the people they served.

Although Cárdenas was anti-clerical, he was not an extremist on the subject, and did not want "socialist" education or anti-clerical campaigns to derail what he saw as the more fundamental goals of agrarian reform and land distribution. He sought to contain anti-clericalism in schools and reduced religious persecution. At the same time, teachers were seen as agents of the revolution; they had promoted the mobilization of peasants to petition for land in Michocán when he was governor, and he encouraged them to do similar acts during his presidency.

The evidence of a shift in the government orientation led to a resurgence of labor mobilization, which began prior to the Cárdenas administration and continued into the first months of his presidency. In contrast to previous practice, the labor boards began to recognize the legality of strike movements and Cárdenas publicly endorsed the rights of the workers to struggle for better wages and working conditions. This brought a sharp rejoinder by Calles, who accused the workers of being unpatriotic and acting against the national interests. At this point, Callistas were in control of the Senate and Chamber of Deputies as well as much of the federal bureaucracy and state and local governments. Labor leaders defended their rights, forming the Committee for the Defense of the Proletariat, and Cárdenas responded to the Calles challenge by forcefully defending the workers. He also acted promptly to fortify his own position, verifying the support of military commanders and substituting those he could not count on. It turned out that Callista support was weak among many government officials who did not want to lose their positions and many shifted their allegiance to Cárdenas. Calles backed down and eventually was forced into exile.

Cárdenas' defeat of Calles signaled the end of the Maximato and the exercise of power by a strongman. It institutionalized the concentration of authority not in an individual but in the office of the presidency itself. It thus represented an important step in the process of institutionalization following the revolution. But while Cárdenas and his supporters had gained the upper hand, the conservative forces within the government did not disappear, and the contradictions between the radical and conservative factions would eventually re-emerge.

In the meantime the Cárdenas government continued to support the workers in their conflicts with employers, in some cases directly confronting employers who attempted to prevent unionization or strikes. In February 1936 he confronted the Monterrey industrialists when they staged a lockout in response to a labor strike. As noted above, Monterrey industrialists had been leaders in the formation of a private sector confederation COPARMEX (Employers' Confederation of the Mexican Republic) to represent business interests in debates on the labor law, and many had attempted to undermine labor organization through the formation of company unions. Cárdenas denounced the refusal of Monterrey businessmen to follow the labor laws and used the occasion to encourage the workers to organize into a single national confederation to strengthen their position.

Cárdenas' goal of unifying the workers coincided with the desire for unity among Mexico's labor leadership and in 1936 the CTM (Confederation of Mexican Workers) was formed, which included local unions, regional federations, and industrial unions. The CGOCM, led by Lombardo Toledano, and the CSUM of the Communist party were disbanded and their constituent unions brought into the new confederation. The prevailing ideology was Marxist, reflecting that of its leader Vicente Lombardo Toledano and the Communist Party, which at that time was influenced by the Popular Front strategy calling for unity of all progressive forces against fascism. The assumption was that socialism was not yet possible in the conditions existing in the Latin American countries; the goal was to improve the conditions for labor within the framework of a capitalist economy.

The CTM was active in forming unions where these did not exist and involved in most of the major strikes of this period. For the most part, strikes were supported by the Cárdenas government, which used the criterion of the companies' ability to pay what the workers requested, and on occasion government commissions would examine the financial condition of affected companies to ascertain whether they could indeed meet the demands of the workers. Aside from better wages and working conditions, strikes also called for union recognition, the elimination of company unions, and collective contracts that would unify wages and other benefits across a given industry.

Despite the tensions between the Cárdenas government and the private sector, this period was one of substantial economic growth in which many business groups flourished. The gross domestic product (GDP) grew by over 30 percent between 1934 and 1940, and manufacturing output increased from 11 percent of GDP in 1925 to 16.7 percent in 1940. Even during the periods of major government-private sector confrontation, the private sector had access to the government, particularly the bankers, who were organized in the Association of Mexican Bankers and maintained close relations with the director of the Banco de Mexico, who was instrumental in representing their interests within the government.

Like its predecessors, the Cárdenas government invested in infrastructure, oriented to creating conditions for the economic expansion of domestic private firms relative to foreign firms, but it departed from them in its emphasis on small and medium producers and the agrarian reform sector. Several new government banks were set up, among them the National Ejidal Bank to provide credit to the ejidos, and the Foreign Trade Bank to encourage agricultural exports (which, in contrast to mineral exports, would benefit Mexican producers). The existing government banks also expanded their services, particularly the Public Works Bank, through investment in roads (including the expansion of the Pan American Highway), railroads, and irrigation systems; and Nacional Financiera, the development bank, which extended loans to private firms and invested in new private banks.

A new banking law passed in 1932 had required all banks to associate with the Banco de Mexico and invest in Mexico, and in 1935 the government passed an insurance law establishing control of the insurance companies by the Ministry of Finance and requiring them to restrict investments to Mexican goods and securities. In both cases, foreign financial companies left the country, opening the field to the formation of domestic banks and insurance companies to replace them. Several of the private banks and insurance companies established during this period became central institutions in the private economic groups, which, as noted above, incorporated companies in various sectors linked through ownership by a small number of investors and in some cases a single family. These groups were divided into those that continued to work closely with the government, generally concentrated in Mexico City, and more independent groups led by businessmen in Monterrey, which adamantly opposed the Cárdenas government.

A major distinction between the Cárdenas government and those of the 1920s was the approach to agrarian reform. While Calles and his supporters had attempted to end land distribution, arguing that neither small family farms nor ejidos were efficient, and that only commercial farms, which could exercise economies of scale (e.g., through mechanization) would permit higher levels of production and productivity, for agrarians within the Cárdenas government as well as Cárdenas himself, agrarian reform was a major goal. The reform carried out by the Cárdenas government also reflected a shift in the conception of the indigenous and peasant populations, previously perceived as shiftless, ignorant and superstitious to "energetic workers who created wealth under oppressive conditions and active subjects who sought justice through social struggle."[29]

In the six years of his administration, Cárdenas distributed more land to more peasant farmers than all of his predecessors combined. Since commercial estates were exempt from expropriation, the government initially concentrated on traditional estates, at the same time encouraging the establishment of unions for workers on large commercial farms. As he had in Michoacán, Cárdenas enlisted the help of rural teachers to mobilize the peasants to petition for land. In contrast to his predecessors, Cárdenas envisioned the ejido as not just a temporary expedient but as a viable form of production and a permanent element of rural Mexico.

The most controversial and innovative phase of Cárdenas' agrarian reform demonstrates the significance of peasant and labor mobilization and organization in supporting his reform efforts. It began with a general strike by unions in the Camarca Lagunera, an irrigated region in the states of Coahuila and Durango, where 70 percent of Mexico's cotton production was concentrated. Although the plantations in the region used modern forms of production, labor relations were semi-feudal. During the 19th century, many of the commercial estates had expanded into peasant lands, and prior to the revolution the major form of peasant protest was land invasions, which were repressed by the landowners.

Following the revolution, peasant and worker mobilization on these estates took the form of official petitions under Article 27 of the constitution and demands for better working conditions through Article 123. With few exceptions, these were rejected outright or subjected to interminable delays by local and state officials in league with the landowners. Landowners also engaged in such tactics as flooding the villages of peasants who requested land and destroying the houses of workers who belonged to the unions. Similar to patterns in other areas, a peasant league was formed in 1923 under the auspices of the state governor but was subsequently neutralized, and later peasant mobilization was repressed.

With the support of the Communist Party and the rural teachers, peasants and workers of the Camarca Lagunera declared a general strike on August 18, 1936. As in the past, the landowners appealed to the state labor board, which ruled in their favor. The union appealed to the Federal Labor Board. In the meantime, the Cárdenas government passed an Expropriation Law allowing the expropriation of all private property in the public interest, including the commercial estates previously declared off limits. Furthermore, Cárdenas decided to form collective ejidos on these estates, which would be farmed cooperatively by the ejidatarios.

The concept of the collective ejido combined historical influences of the pre-Colombian tradition of communal farming with socialist ideas current in the 1930s, as well as the experiments in collective farming in the Soviet Union. There had also been some experiments during the 1930s under progressive governors and the National Agrarian League, notably in Veracruz. For the Cárdenas government, the collective ejido would combine the goals of social justice with the need to maintain the productive efficiency of the privately owned commercial estates.

The Laguna expropriation was followed by the expropriation of henequen estates in Yucatán, wheat estates in Sonora, rice and livestock estates in Michoacán, and sugar plantations in several states, which affected both Mexican owners and foreign companies. Expropriations often followed peasant mobilization and land invasions, which the Cárdenas government used to justify the expropriation, claiming that failure to respond to these protests would result in even greater instability. By 1940, over 47 percent of the cultivated land, and 57 percent of irrigated land, was held in ejidos, compared to 15 percent in 1930. The Cárdenas government also established an Ejidal Bank to provide credit and technical assistance; it would also supervise the new collective ejidos.

Needless to say, landowners and their supporters fiercely opposed the reform. Mercenaries hired by the landowners attacked the new ejidos, leading the Cárdenas government to arm the *ejidatarios* to defend their land, as he had done in Michoacán. The landowners, who, according to law, were able to retain 150 hectares of expropriated land, often controlled financial resources, commercial firms, and in some cases processing plants such as sugar refineries, enabling them to exercise considerable leverage over the new ejidatarios.

In addition to the hostility of the landlords, the ejidatarios also faced other problems, including technical problems of insufficient water for irrigation, crop disease, and extensive debt due to purchase of new machinery and other inputs. The Ejidal Bank officials worked with the ejidatarios to solve these and other difficulties. But sometimes the bank itself, having been established with the somewhat paternalistic assumption that the new ejidatarios lacked the knowledge and skills for commercial farming, was part of the problem. The officials of the Ejidal Bank and its local branches often exercised their mandate with excessive authoritarianism and bureaucratic detail. In the worst cases, they were also corrupt, siphoning off funds that should have gone to the ejidatarios.

Complaints by the ejidatarios to the central government generally elicited a response and efforts to correct the situation, but also demonstrated the level of dependence of the new agrarian reform beneficiaries on a sympathetic voice in the central government. Given the agrarian sympathies of the Cárdenas government, the ejidos were able to survive despite the many difficulties they encountered, and some even managed to improve levels of productivity.

As in the case of labor, the Cárdenas government promoted the organization of peasants into a single organization. Following the formation of peasant leagues at the state level, their representatives came together in a convention in 1938 and formed the National Peasant Confederation (CNC), grouping some three million peasants, ejidatarios, organized rural workers, and small farmers. Although this achieved the desired unity among the peasantry and rural workers, the fact that the CNC was established by the state, from above, facilitated authoritarian tendencies in the organization as well as dependence on the state.

By this time the Cárdenas government had embarked on an even more ambitious and controversial project, the expropriation of the foreign-owned petroleum companies.[30] Similar to the launching of the agrarian experiment in collective ejidos, it began with a labor strike. The 21 independent oil workers' unions had united in an industry-wide federation, the Union of Petroleum Workers of the Mexican Republic, in December 1935. In July 1936, the Union began negotiations with the companies calling for a collective contract, an increase in wages and benefits, a 40-hour work week, and union control of most positions within the industry. When negotiations failed, the Union called a strike. The conflict was referred to the Federal Labor Board, which appointed a panel of experts to examine the financial condition of the companies in order to determine their ability to pay what the workers were requesting. The report submitted by the panel documented extensive financial irregularities and market manipulation, including the practice of overcharging Mexican consumers while charging prices well below market rates to its U.S. based branches, thus reducing the taxes paid to the Mexican government. In the meantime, real wages of workers had declined.

The companies rejected the findings and the dispute was returned to the Labor Board, which in December 1937 supported the union's demands for higher wages, improved working conditions, and a 40-hour week. The companies appealed the decision to Mexico's Supreme Court. At this point, the Cárdenas government was under substantial pressure. After several years of dramatic growth, the economy had begun to weaken in 1937, in part because a renewed recession in the United States resulted in a decline in Mexico's export earnings, which in turn led to reduction in the government's tax revenues. At the same time, expenditures were accelerating due to the growth in economic and social expenditures, among them those resulting from the agrarian reform and need to provide credit and other services to the new ejidatarios and small farmers.

The government became increasingly dependent on loans from the central bank and was also able to secure loans from the private sector, although this had the effect of increasing private sector leverage over the government. As the petroleum crisis continued, U.S. companies began to withdraw funds from banks, exporting all but what they needed for operating expenses. This led to a crisis of confidence and capital export by other U.S. and some Mexican companies. In the United States, the petroleum companies launched a press campaign against the Mexican government, and congress pressured the State Department to retaliate.

But the U.S. government was divided. While the State Department favored retaliation, the Treasury Secretary was more cautious, recognizing that U.S. investors had extensive interests in Mexico that could be negatively affected if the U.S. government took an intransigent attitude. U.S. Ambassador Josephus Daniels, a strong supporter of Roosevelt's New Deal and the Good Neighbor policy, tended to side with Mexico in the conflict and also pushed for a more conciliatory policy. However, the United States stipulated that the silver purchase agreement—a special arrangement whereby the U.S. government purchased a certain percentage of Mexico's silver, Mexico's major mineral export—would have to be renewed on a monthly basis. It also secured an agreement from Mexico to withdraw from a proposed mining law that it opposed. In return, the Treasury Department promised Mexico a substantial loan.

The conflict entered its final phase on March 1, 1938, when the Supreme Court issued its verdict upholding the decision of the Labor Board. When the companies failed to meet the deadline to put the decision into effect, the Labor Board declared them "in rebellion," and Cárdenas decided to apply the Expropriation Law. Denouncing the companies for their flagrant disregard of Mexico's laws, Cárdenas announced their expropriation on the evening of March 18. The companies were turned over to PEMEX (*Petroleos Mexicanos*), the government petroleum company.

There was an immediate and massive outpouring of support for the government's decision in Mexico. For many, the oil companies epitomized the arrogance of foreign-owned companies toward Mexico: their consistent defiance of Mexico's sovereignty, their mistreatment of workers, and their refusal to abide by the law. Through the expropriation of the companies Mexico had asserted its sovereignty, and the annual anniversary of the expropriation became a national holiday.

The oil companies pressured their respective governments to end diplomatic relations with Mexico and Britain immediately broke off relations. Despite considerable pressure from the U.S. oil companies, however, the United States maintained relations but discontinued the silver purchase agreement, causing a further decline in Mexico's export earnings, and canceled the proposed loan. Mexico's oil exports were boycotted by the United States and several European companies, forcing Mexico, much against the preferences of the Cárdenas government, to sell to the fascist powers—which at that point were threatening a war in Europe and Asia; the outbreak of war in 1939 cut off this market. The oil companies also persuaded U.S. manufacturers of refinery equipment to refuse to sell supplies and equipment to the Mexican oil industry. The State Department attempted to prevent Latin American countries from buying oil from Mexico and discouraged loans to the Mexican private sector.

The oil companies and the State Department pressured the Cárdenas government for "immediate and just" compensation. Cárdenas responded that Mexico's financial situation did not permit immediate compensation but pledged to pay they companies what they were owed over a 10-year period. Negotiations continued for several years over the amount of a "just" compensation, and an accord was finally reached in 1942. In the meantime, a study by the U.S. Department of the Interior found that in their requests for compensation the companies had greatly exaggerated their value.

Restoring and maintaining production of the oil fields in the absence of technical and managerial personnel, most of whom left the country when the companies were expropriated, was a major challenge. The oil workers themselves had primary responsibility and rose to the occasion. Accepting wage cuts ranging from 8 to 25 percent and working overtime without pay, they pooled their knowledge in different areas of expertise, restored old and rundown equipment, and innovated with new technologies.

The oil expropriation was significant for several reasons. First, it firmly established Mexico's right to demand compliance with its laws in its own territory and its sovereignty as a nation in a community of nations. One effect was to place U.S.-Mexican relations on a different plane. Although these relations continued to be unequal, and the United States continued to exert an undue influence in Mexico as well as other Latin American countries, Mexico had given notice that the kind of arrogance that had characterized the attitudes and actions of certain foreign companies would no longer be tolerated. In keeping with its defense of national sovereignty—as well as its concern regarding possible U.S. retaliation for Mexico's expropriation policies—the Cárdenas government also took the lead in pushing for a resolution at the Pan American conferences during the mid 1930s that committed member countries, including the United States, to uphold a policy of non-intervention in the internal and external affairs of the member states. Although this policy would be contravened by subsequent U.S. governments on numerous occasions over the next several decades, Mexico would continue to take the lead in upholding the principles of self-determination and non-intervention, opposing U.S. intervention in the region, and maintaining an independent foreign policy that often conflicted with that of the United States.[31]

The nationalization of the oil industry was also significant in bringing a major resource under the control of the state. The Cárdenas government had already brought the railroads under state control by nationalizing the remaining minority shares, and subsequent governments would buy out foreign interests in telecommunications and electric power. Control over these industries, which were critical for production in other sectors such as industry, agriculture and construction, as well as individual consumption, would enable the state to intervene more effectively in the economy. Costs to consumers and the private sector could be subsidized, and services provided on the basis of individual need and developmental priorities rather than the criteria of maximizing profit.

The three-year period between 1935 and March 1938 was one of remarkable achievement. Agrarian reform had transformed the countryside, weakening traditional haciendas and ending debt peonage. Much of the land was now in the hands of small farmers, peasants, and ejidatarios. Workers had won the right to organize and had achieved a somewhat tenuous labor unity in the new CTM; many had obtained significant increases in wages and other benefits. The petroleum expropriation had reaffirmed Mexico's sovereignty, and the state had been fortified as a promoter of economic development and legitimated as an agent for social justice. It was an exciting period of innovation and experimentation, exemplified in the collective ejido and in experiments in worker management.

But it was also a period of growing tension and confrontation. The mobilization of urban and rural workers, the Expropriation Law and the subsequent expropriation of commercial agricultural estates, the nationalization of the foreign-owned petroleum companies, and the allusions to socialism by more radical Cardenistas, had led to investment cutbacks and capital export by both foreign and domestic investors. Combined with growing inflation, the decline in exports following the petroleum expropriation, and the end of the silver purchase agreement, all of this resulted in a sharp reduction in Mexico's foreign reserves and pressures on the peso, which was devalued in 1938, reducing its value from 3.5 to five pesos to the dollar.

Conservative and right wing groups had also begun to mobilize. The most extreme were influenced by fascism and may have been financed by German or Spanish agents in Mexico; they were able to take advantage of anti-U.S. and anti-British sentiment in the wake of the petroleum expropriation and the fact that it had been the Axis countries that purchased Mexico's petroleum when it was boycotted by the United States and many of the European countries. In 1939, concerned about the expansion of "socialist education," a group of conservative intellectuals, professionals and businessmen, many of them centered in Monterrey, formed a new political party, the National Action Party. The party rejected the radical ideas of the revolution in favor of Hispanic traditions, and espoused a pro-Church and pro-business perspective. There was also substantial and growing opposition within the government itself and the PNR, particularly among state governors and sectors of the military.

Partly as a result of these pressures, the petroleum expropriation marked a turning point for the Cárdenas government, from actively promoting reform and innovation to a more defensive position of limiting further reforms in the interests of protecting existing achievements against the threats of growing instability and hostility. International events—the pending war in Europe and the concern for hemispheric defense in the event of attacks from the Axis countries in Europe and Asia—also influenced this shift. One result was a cutback in reforms, including a reduction in land expropriations, limited approval for labor strikes, and Labor Board decisions less favorable to workers. Control of education was shifted to state governments, many of them conservatives who repressed the radical teachers' movement.

At the same time, Cárdenas moved to strengthen and further unify progressive elements of the revolution, enabling them to effectively counter conservative forces and opposition groups by incorporating them into a restructured government party. The party, now called the Party of the Mexican Revolution (PRM) would include four sectors: labor, incorporating the CTM and other labor confederations as well as the large industrial unions; peasant, including the peasant leagues subsequently incorporated in the CNC, which was formed later in the year; popular, including groups such as organizations of small farmers, students, teachers, and women's groups, and the confederations of state employees and teachers, which would eventually become the most powerful group within the section, later organized in the CNOP (National Confederation of Popular Organizations); and the military, formed of representatives of different military zones of the country (and later dropped). This structure would provide an institutional channel for the constituent groups to articulate their needs and interests; at the same time it would enable the party and government to more closely monitor and control these groups. Some groups within the labor movement as well as the peasantry were opposed to this move, fearing the loss of organizational autonomy and excessive dependence on the government. However, most were persuaded to join, influenced by the progressive reforms of the Cárdenas government and the critical situation the government was facing.

DISCUSSION

One hundred years after Mexico's independence movement, Mexico continued to exhibit many of the trends that had emerged during the colonial period: unequal social structures with a stratified class system reinforced by racial distinctions, an economy tied into the international market and primarily oriented to the export of agricultural and mineral products, asymmetrical relations with dominant foreign powers, and tensions between the central government on the one hand and local and regional groups on the other. These, of course, took new and different forms; new social elites, among them industrial and commercial interests, had emerged, and there was an increase in urban middle class groups, and the beginning of an industrial working class—although the majority of the population continued to be rural with a growing number of landless rural workers. The Industrial Revolution in Europe and the United States had brought an increase in foreign investment involving control of key sectors of the economy, and the United States had become a major foreign economic as well as political force. The Liberal governments of the late 19th century, culminating with the Porfiriato, had succeeded in centralizing political power and in creating a modern, though ultimately authoritarian, state.

The Mexican Revolution challenged the status quo, and the 30-year period between the outbreak of the revolution in 1910 and the last year of the Cárdenas administration in 1940 had indeed brought profound changes to Mexico. At the same time, there were important elements of continuity between the Mexico of 1910 and that of 1940.

The Porfirian state, governed by a personal dictator and his entourage, had been replaced by a state governed by institutions. As before, periodic elections would be held, and as before, they would not be democratic, but the principle of no re-election had been institutionalized; the selection of candidates would be overseen by the governing party, and authority would reside in the institution of the presidency rather than an individual. Political power would again be concentrated in the national government; although state governors could exercise considerable authority within their respective domains.

Mexico would continue to be strongly influenced by international forces, particularly the United States, which remained the major source of foreign investment and Mexico's predominant trade partner, but Mexico had succeeded in establishing its sovereignty through the petroleum expropriation and controls on foreign finance; legislation by subsequent governments would reinforce state control of strategic industries and the exclusion of certain economic sectors from foreign ownership. U.S.-Mexican relations would continue to be unequal, but Mexico would exercise its political independence through its foreign policy, which on occasion contradicted that of the United States.

The concept of an interventionist state as a major economic actor as well as an agent of social reform and arbiter of class conflict was affirmed in the constitution of 1917, which in certain respects incorporated the corporatist concept of the state from the colonial period as well as 19th century liberalism, reinforced by the market failures evident in the Great Depression and the influence of Keynesianism in the 1930s. The governments of the 1920s and 1930s had developed much of the legal and institutional framework for the state's economic role—e.g., through banking and insurance laws subjecting financial institutions to state regulation and control; the establishment of government banks to promote economic development, encourage foreign trade, finance the construction of infrastructure, and provide credit to agrarian reform beneficiaries; and the extension of government loans and equity to new private firms and financial institutions.

In the meantime, private sector groups that had survived the revolution were joined by "revolutionary capitalists" recruited from military leaders and government officials. The private sector also benefited from government efforts to promote national investments to replace foreign interests. By the end of the 1930s, economic groups—combining investments in several different sectors such as financial institutions, manufacturing firms, commercial ventures, and real estate, and controlled by a small number of individuals or families—were taking shape and would dominate the private sector for much of the 20th century. The government was largely dependent on resources generated by the private sector, which, as demonstrated in the wake of the petroleum expropriation, could exercise considerable economic leverage by increasing or withholding investment, or exporting capital. Some of the more powerful groups had direct access to government officials, particularly through the Treasury Ministry and the Banco de Mexico, and more indirectly through business associations.

As a result of the revolution, formerly powerful groups had seen their influence reduced, while new political actors, urban and rural, had emerged. Among the former were traditional landowners, some of whom had lost most of their holdings while others faced the possibility of expropriation, and the Catholic Church, which had lost a significant instrument of influence through state control of education and secularization of the schools, although Catholicism continued to be the religion of the majority of Mexicans and to exercise considerable influence in certain areas, particularly in the west central states which had been the scene of Cristero rebellion. Among the new economic actors were workers in strategic industries and manufacturing firms, now organized in industrial unions and labor confederations, and peasants and rural workers, many of them formerly landless, who through agrarian reform had become small farmers and ejidatarios and were organized in peasant leagues and the CNC.

The social reforms carried out by the Cárdenas government in response to the mobilization of labor and the peasantry had legitimated the state as an agent of the social goals of the revolution. This was particularly true of the peasantry, and although not all rural families had benefited from the land distribution programs of the Cárdenas government, their faith in government had been restored. At the same time, although it was not immediately evident, the newly restructured government party was a powerful instrument for social control of newly mobilized groups. In effect, from the chaos of the revolution, a new foundation for "order and progress" had emerged—one that was more inclusive and more complex than the "Porfirian peace,"—which would characterize Mexico's economic and political trajectory over the next 40 years.

CHAPTER 3

The "Pax Priista" and the "Mexican Miracle"

Mexico's "revolutionary" period in effect ended in 1940 at the close of the Cárdenas administration. Although Mexico continued to be characterized by class divisions between the wealthy and the poor, an authoritarian political system, and asymmetric relations with the United States, the struggles of the previous three decades had brought new social and political actors onto the national scene and had transformed Mexico's social, economic and political structures. Population groups, such as peasants and workers that had been politically inactive, or whose initiatives and struggles had been localized or relatively isolated, had become national actors and could no longer be ignored or simply repressed. The reforms of the revolutionary period had provided definite benefits to these groups, particularly in the areas of land distribution and labor rights, at the same time establishing institutions, for example the tripartite labor boards, as well as labor and peasant confederations and their incorporation within the respective sectors of the reconstituted government party, that facilitated their subordination to state and party control.

There were also changes within elite groups. State control of education undermined the traditional ideological role of the Catholic Church, and land distribution programs had weakened traditional landowners. Other business groups, including commercial landowners, bankers, and industrialists, had survived, however, and were joined by the "revolutionary capitalists" drawn from military and civilian leaders of the new regime.

The reconstituted political system in effect modernized Mexico's authoritarian state. It included the creation of a "revolutionary" government party (the PRM), the institution of an electoral system that provided for a regular turnover of leadership (albeit within a single party), the centralization of political control and the subordination of regional powers, and a powerful presidency within a system ostensibly characterized by political pluralism and the separation of powers. The 1917 constitution established the basis for an important state role in the areas of education, social justice, and defense of national sovereignty. Initiatives of the 1920s and 1930s expanded the state's economic role with the creation of the central bank as well as state development banks and with state control of particular industries and sectors, notably the railroads and petroleum industry.

Finally, the Second World War had ushered in a new period of cooperation between the United States and Mexico. During the war, Mexico collaborated closely with the United States, forming a Joint Defense Committee, providing extensive rights to the U.S. military in Mexico, and sending an air force squadron to the Pacific Front, although the war itself was not popular among Mexicans. The United States and Mexico also established the *bracero* program, through which Mexicans were recruited for temporary work in U.S. agriculture to replace U.S. workers who had joined the armed services. Initiated in 1942, it was subsequently extended until 1964 and ultimately involved over four million workers.[1] In addition, the United States provided financial and technical assistance to Mexico and other Latin American countries to develop strategic raw materials and, in the case of Mexico and Brazil, to promote important industries; Mexican industrial output grew substantially during the war period, and the number of workers in manufacturing grew from 568,000 to 922,000 between 1940 and 1945.

U.S. policy toward Latin America in the post-war period was shaped by its new position as leader of the Western world and its confrontation with the Soviet Union in the Cold War. By the end of the war, the United States had emerged as the pre-eminent economic power, a position that was confirmed by the Bretton Woods agreements (named for a resort in New Hampshire where the meetings took place) signed by 44 countries in 1944 to create an international monetary and payments system that would prevent economic crises such as the world depression of the 1930s. Among other initiatives, the agreements made the dollar the standard currency for international transactions and created two institutions, the International Monetary Fund (IMF) to provide short-term loans to member countries confronting payments problems, and the International Bank for Reconstruction and Development (the World Bank), initially to provide reconstruction aid to European countries that had been devastated by the war.

Following the war, the United States briefly encouraged democratic openings in several Latin American countries, but with the inauguration of the Cold War in 1948, U.S. priorities in Latin America changed to promoting security and combating communism. This orientation was congruent with those of business groups and policy makers in several Latin American countries who were concerned about disruptions resulting from labor mobilization and in some cases by the advances of leftist political groups in the immediate post-war period; anti-communism became a convenient justification for repression not only of Communist parties but also labor militants and progressive groups perceived to threaten the status quo.[2]

In the case of Mexico, collaboration with the United States continued as the post-Cárdenas administrations moved to the right. Conservative governments generally adhered to the United States' Cold War policies and anti-communist ideology and instituted various policies to neutralize the left. Although some Mexican leaders continued their nationalist rhetoric and frequently challenged U.S. foreign policy, the United States benefited from having a stable government on its southern border, and the relationship shifted from one of political conflict to one largely based on negotiation and cooperation, in spite of occasional tensions.

These developments established the context for approximately 40 years of economic growth, which became known as the "Mexican Miracle," and relative political stability, sometimes referred to as the "Pax Priista."[3] This Chapter examines the characteristics of Mexico's political and economic models and how they help to explain why Mexico, in contrast to most other Latin American countries, experienced a long period of stability. It also focuses on conditions and events that challenged Mexico's economic model and political system, ultimately leading to economic crisis and restructuring and a gradual transformation of Mexico's political regime during the 1980s and 1990s.

THE 1940 ELECTIONS AND THE POST-CÁRDENAS ADMINISTRATIONS

The reforms of the Cárdenas government culminated with the petroleum expropriation. The U.S. government, as well as business groups within Mexico—led by the Monterrey group—and conservative groups within his own party and government were concerned about the nature of the Cárdenas reforms, the mobilization of peasants and workers, and what was viewed as the radical direction of the administration, and they began to exert direct and indirect pressures on Cárdenas and his associates. The petroleum conflict had taken a toll on Mexico's exports, and the export of capital by foreign and domestic investors led to a critical reduction in Mexico's foreign reserves, resulting in a devaluation in 1939 that reduced the peso by 50 percent. In 1939, a group of middle-class professionals, alienated by the Cárdenas reforms and opposed to the governing party, particularly its attacks on the Catholic Church, formed a new opposition party, the National Action Party, or PAN. Of more immediate concern, political stability was threatened by a regional military revolt led by a conservative general; the emergence of a quasi-fascist movement, the *Sinarquistas*, that carried out armed attacks against peasant petitioners and recipients of land grants; and even rumors of a military coup. Although the Cárdenas government succeeded in crushing the military revolt and in arming peasant militias so they could defend themselves against right-wing violence, the government also cut back on reforms in the agrarian sector and reduced support for labor strikes. In addition, Cárdenas supported a moderate candidate, General Manuel Avila Camacho, his minister of defense, for the party nomination in the upcoming presidential election over the more radical General Francisco Múgica, a close associate of Cárdenas and also a member of his cabinet, who would have continued and deepened the reforms of the Cárdenas period.[4]

Although this choice was disappointing to many Cárdenas supporters, it can be explained by several factors. First, given the critical economic and political situation, there was fear on the part of some progressive groups within the government of losing everything that had been gained, particularly if the nomination of Múgica split the government party, as seemed likely. Second, Cárdenas saw fascism as a major threat in the late 1930s, and his government had established the basis for cooperation with the United States in the likely event that it would be drawn into a two-front war involving Europe and Asia. The assumption was that both international and domestic conditions called for a temporary hiatus in the reform programs, and that following the war Mexico could again resume its progressive agenda. The moderate and conciliatory Avila Camacho could be trusted to maintain order and govern the country in the challenging period ahead.

The 1940 elections revealed the non-democratic character of the reconstructed government party and reaffirmed the lack of electoral democracy. Although the different sectors of the PRM were supposed to nominate the party candidate in their respective conventions, the candidacy of Avila Camacho was imposed by the leadership of the sectors, leading some within the rank and file of the labor and peasant sectors to abandon their respective institutions.

In the meantime, a conservative general, Juan Andreu Almazán, announced his candidacy in opposition to the PRM. A charismatic candidate, Almazán attracted support from both conservative groups that opposed the domination of the government party and progressive groups within the ranks of labor and the peasantry who had supported Múgica. The election was marred by considerable fraud as well as violence, and many believed that Almazán was the real winner, but Avila Camacho was declared victor by an outlandish margin, assuring the continued dominance of the government party.

Church-state relations continued to improve with the admission of Avila Camacho that he was a practicing Catholic. Over the following years, a modus vivendi was established between Church and state whereby each would respect the autonomy of the other. However, the Church continued to exercise extensive influence over public opinion and was particularly influential among members of the new PAN.

The administrations of Avila Camacho and subsequent presidents focused on economic growth rather than social reforms. This shift of emphasis was facilitated by the substantial reforms carried out under the Cárdenas administration which, although incomplete, had brought relative social stability and strengthened the popular perception of the state and government party as progressive— a perception which subsequent administrations sought to reinforce through revolutionary rhetoric. Over the following several decades, the government party maintained and increased its control not only through electoral fraud but also by co-optation of dissidents (repressing those who could not be co-opted), limited reforms, and the extension of its penetration into key sectors of society, including labor, the peasantry, and the urban poor.

Avila Camacho was succeeded by a pro-business president, Miguel Alemán (1946–1952), the first civilian president since the revolution and the most conservative president since Díaz.[5] Alemán brought into government a new generation of industrialists and lawyers "for whom the revolution was less a personal experience than a convenient myth."[6] Similar to the Porfiriato, the Alemán administration was one of remarkable economic expansion, including the construction of dams, roads and highways; the protection and promotion of domestic private investment; the expansion of tourism, notably the development of Acapulco (state of Guerrero) as a major tourist destination; and encouragement of foreign investment. The government also financed extensive irrigation systems, which benefited farmers in northern Mexico, and promoted the "Green Revolution," a program designed to dramatically increase productivity, resulting in significant increases in agricultural production.

At the same time, the Alemán government sought to dismantle agrarian reform and to tighten controls on workers and peasants. Wages dropped precipitously between 1940 and 1952, and the administration cut off government credit to the collective ejidos, undermining their viability since they lacked access to private bank loans. It collaborated with the cold war policy of the United States in marginalizing Marxist leaders, particularly in the labor movement, and instituted the practice of *charrismo*,[7] imposing labor and peasant leaders in unions and peasant confederations when the government opposed those elected. The economic expansion provided numerous opportunities for personal enrichment, and the Alemán administration was one of unprecedented corruption in which Alemán, other government officials, and their associates benefited from generous concessions to their businesses, in the process creating a nouveaux riche that is scathingly satirized in Carlos Fuentes' novels, *The Death of Artemio Cruz* and *Where the Air Is Clear*.[8]

The promotion of a national culture that accompanied the state-building processes during the 1920s and 1930s continued during the subsequent administrations and involved education, art, music, archeology, radio, newspapers, comic books, film and later television. Various media disseminated the government's messages and interpretations of events and publicized the actions of the president. The content of educational curricula shifted from an emphasis on class struggle and the revolutionary role of peasants and workers to promote identification with the government's modernization and development efforts. The goal was to promote the conception of Mexico for both domestic and international audiences as a modern, cosmopolitan country that at the same time retained its historical and cultural uniqueness, "a nation full of cosmopolitan splendor and folkloric charm."[9]

THE MEXICAN POLITICAL SYSTEM: THE INSTITUTIONAL REVOLUTION

In 1947 the Party of the Mexican Revolution was renamed the Institutional Revolutionary Party, in effect incorporating the contradictions that characterized the Mexican political system over the next several decades: the aspirations of government leaders to modernization and cosmopolitanism were combined with references to a revolution with strong indigenous and rural roots; in a context of corruption and personal enrichment they spoke of social justice; while promoting foreign investment they defended national sovereignty.[10]

At the same time, Mexico was unusual among Latin American countries during this period, when instability and frequent regime change was the norm, in its ability to maintain relative political stability through a system that combined authoritarianism with flexibility.[11] A key element distinguishing Mexico's system from that of most other Latin American countries was the subordination of the military to civilian rule. In other countries, the armed forces (or in some cases groups of military officers) held veto power: intervening in the political process or overthrowing elected civilian governments judged to be incapable of maintaining internal order or acting in the national interest. Mexico had in effect "resolved" the military issue through the defeat of regional uprisings led by revolutionary generals, and their subsequent incorporation into the party system and the economy during the 1920s and 1930s. Cárdenas incorporated the military into the governing party structure in order to reduce its influence by balancing it with the other three sectors. Interestingly, Avila Camacho, the last general to become president, had subsequently eliminated the military sector to further reduce its influence.

During the Calles presidency (1924–1928) the military had received 30 percent of the budget; this was reduced to 19 percent under Cárdenas, 14 percent under Avila Camacho, and eventually 2 percent under subsequent presidents. The hegemony of the governing party prior to the late 1990s also eliminated the ability of competing parties to draw on military support for any potential challenge to the party or government. Subordination to civilian rule, particularly the president as commander in chief, was instilled through officers' training in military schools. Throughout the 20th century, the major function of the military was the protection of national security; it has been called up to suppress labor revolts, peasant uprisings, student strikes and other alleged threats to the internal order.

The principle of "no re-election" also distinguished Mexican authoritarianism from many Latin American dictatorships led by a single individual or family, as well as from Mexico's pre-revolutionary period, the Porfiriato, when power was concentrated by a small clique—an important factor in the opposition to the regime by excluded groups. The principle of "no re-election" entailed a complete turnover of office at the upper and middle levels of government every six years. It meant there was "room at the top"; although the options of politically ambitious individuals were limited, those willing to work within the government party could eventually aspire to high level office.

Mexico's political system has been variously described as a hegemonic, or dominant, party system, or in some cases a state-party system. In contrast to pluralist systems in which two or more political parties contest political power, in Mexico the dominant party controlled the government at all levels; regular elections were held and opposition parties were tolerated and even allowed to field candidates, but prior to the 1980s, were prevented through various mechanisms from obtaining government office, with the occasional exception of municipal elections and a few seats in the Chamber of Deputies.

Fraud and intimidation were partly responsible for consistent PRI electoral victories. Fraudulent practices ranged from graveyard votes to stolen ballot boxes to manipulated voter registration lists, and resistance was often neutralized through intimidation, particularly in remote rural areas. At the same time, the corporatist structure of the party enabled it to penetrate broad sectors of the population, and the clientelism that characterized the corporatist relations within the party sectors enabled party leaders to provide protection and certain benefits to various constituencies in return for support to the government and/or PRI candidates in the form of votes, participation in political rallies, and assistance in political campaigns.

The case of Miguel Ramírez, a street vendor interviewed by Judith Hellman, demonstrates the functioning of the corporatist party system at various levels. As a child living in a rural area Miguel saw leaders of the CNC (the leading organization of the peasant sector) truck peasants to PRI rallies, paying them 10 pesos and providing lunch; on election day they returned to the area, were paid another 10 or 15 pesos in return for a vote for the PRI candidate. (In some cases, peasants were presented with marked ballots en route to polling places.) Later, as a worker in a plastics factory and member of a CTM-affiliated union, Miguel was periodically required to participate in rallies and demonstrations in the main government plaza, the Zócalo. When Miguel subsequently became a street vendor, he paid a fee to a political leader, becoming a member of the Union of Market Merchants, one of the organizations of the CNOP, the National Confederation of Popular Organizations, which incorporated groups in the popular sector. His fee guaranteed him a specific space in the vending area and protection from police harassment; his political leader in turn paid part of his receipts to local officials responsible for overseeing vending in the city; part went to bribe police to release vendors that were jailed and to help compensate them for losses. Again, he was expected to attend PRI rallies and vote for the PRI candidates in elections.[12]

As the term state-party system implies, there was a close integration between the state and the dominant party. Access to government funds enabled leaders of sectors and member organizations to provide certain benefits and payoffs to their respective constituencies. Leaders received various benefits in turn, including nomination and election to local office or Congress. The portion of federal deputies who were part of the labor sector increased steadily from 4.1 percent (7 deputies) in the 1937–1940 Congress to 21 percent (37 deputies) in that of 1967–1970 Congress, most of them from the CTM.

The Mexican political system was highly centralized. Authority was concentrated in the federal executive, with a legislature that functioned as a "rubber stamp" approving initiatives from the president, and a weak judiciary. During his six years in office (sexenio), the president exercised extraordinary power. Although he could not succeed himself, he did choose his successor, generally in consultation with key individuals in the party and government as well as other groups, especially business groups and leaders.[13] The national government and the PRI exercised strong control at the state and local level. Although members of Congress, governors and municipal officers were formally elected, the president often had a role in the selection of candidates, and, less frequently, the removal and/or replacement of incumbent officials. The national government also exercised budgetary control; 85 percent of public funds, and 80 percent of the funds to state and local governments came from the federal government, which has been known to withhold funds from opposition or dissident officials.

Nevertheless, the Mexican state was not autonomous, nor was it monolithic. Direct and indirect pressures from powerful business groups constrained the possibilities for government action. State governors and local officials, including caciques or political bosses, could exercise considerable and even arbitrary power at the regional and municipal levels, which was generally tolerated by the central government. Efforts by national level officials to implement reforms often found their efforts stymied at the local level by caciques and bureaucrats answerable to local interests. There were also differences and sometimes contradictions among different government agencies and officials, which could undermine the possibility of efficient government action.

Traditionally, government officials were divided between career politicians, or *políticos*, those groups who came up through the party and/or government bureaucracy and were linked in various ways to popular groups (particularly through the sectoral structure of the party), and economic specialists, or *técnicos*, whose careers were in the national government bureaucracy. Políticos were important in party positions, in government offices at the state and local levels, in the legislature, and in certain cabinet posts, for example, the Ministry of Interior and the presidency. Técnicos were important in economic institutions such as the Banco de Mexico (Mexico's central bank), government development banks, particularly Nacional Financiera (NAFINSA) and cabinet posts, for example, the Treasury. Historically the president had held an elected position in the past (such as state governor) and come from a government position such as the Interior Ministry.

Political recruitment occurred through *camarillas*, or cliques, consisting of groups that formed around an individual in a leadership position. At a given point, a political aspirant would attach himself or herself to the camarilla of a specific leader as a means of getting ahead. Career patterns generally involved moving up together through the state-party hierarchy: when the individual was selected for a post in government, he (occasionally she) brought his/her camarilla along. For example, members of a president's cabinet often included members of his camarilla. The camarilla is based partly on personal friendship, and partly on an unequal patron-client relationship, in which the leader or patron provides certain favors, such as jobs, in return for loyalty. Camarillas were frequently family based: political aspirants were often the relatives of established politicians, who helped in setting up contacts. University friendships were also important in the establishment of camarillas. Beginning with Miguel Alemán, whose presidency marked a shift from administrations led by former revolutionary generals to civilian-led governments, the major public university, UNAM, became a primary source of political recruitment (particularly from the Law faculty).

While the Mexican system was authoritarian, it was also flexible. The PRI itself incorporated a variety of ideologies and perspectives within its ranks and included sincere reformers as well as political opportunists, honest as well as corrupt politicians. Aside from the principle of no re-election, which permitted turnover in government (albeit within the dominant party), opposition parties existed and were even permitted to field candidates, although their candidates were rarely permitted to be elected to office. The major opposition party during this period was the National Action Party, or PAN, a conservative party established in 1939. Politically marginalized, PAN leadership focused on recruiting adherents at the state and local level, a practice that would eventually bear fruit in the 1980s and 1990s. The Communist Party, which had played an important role in the organization and leadership of independent unions such as the railroad workers' union as well as the formation of the CTM, continued to exist but was weakened by internal divisions as well as government persecution. A number of smaller leftist parties existed or emerged in the following decades, but for the most part, they were co-opted into the loyal opposition, and none were able to offer a serious challenge to the PRI.

In addition, the Mexican system was skilled at co-opting dissident leaders and opposition groups through mechanisms ranging from efforts to bribe the leadership or incorporate leaders into the state-party system, to partial reforms in response to demands of dissident groups in return for their support of the government. Even the most conservative governments carried out some social and/or nationalist reforms. While retaining the posture of a revolutionary government, pragmatism rather than ideology guided successive presidents, who often shaped the tenor and rhetoric of their administrations depending on the direction of opposition. For example, popular demonstrations and other manifestations of widespread popular discontent might lead to a relatively progressive orientation by a given administration; complaints by business sectors might result in a shift to a more pro-business stance by the subsequent government.

However, the government did not hesitate to resort to repression if dissident groups could not be co-opted. When the railroad workers' union carried out a series of strikes for increased wages and against charrismo in the late 1950s, the leadership was imprisoned. Laws protecting the rights of citizens were frequently ignored at the local level, particularly in impoverished rural areas, where governors, party leaders and police forces were generally able to operate with relative impunity, and the disappearance and assassination of peasant leaders or other dissidents were often unreported. Despite its flexibility and skills in neutralizing dissent, Mexico's "perfect dictatorship," like authoritarian regimes elsewhere, ultimately depended on a repressive infrastructure.

MEXICO'S ECONOMIC MIRACLE

Conceptualizing Development

While economic growth refers to an expansion of the economy, measured by indicators—such as an increase in gross domestic product (GDP), i.e., the amount of goods and services produced in a given country in a given year—the concept of development is a highly contested one. At a strictly economic level, it can be defined as growth that is self-generated and self-sustained, as opposed to growth that fluctuates and/or is primarily dependent on outside forces. Self-generated growth is the result of the constant reinvestment of the surplus, or profits, resulting from growth and is characterized by the increased complexity of the economy, indicated by the differentiation and flexibility of the productive structure. In this sense, development may be characterized as the production of an increasing *number* of products and services and of increasingly *complex* products, and the ability to shift into new products and services.

During much of the 20th century, economic development was associated with the process of industrialization, based on the Western and, to a certain degree, the Soviet models, as opposed to an economic strategy focused on trade in commodities, which could result in significant growth but could also lead to economic loss due to dependence on commodity prices in the international market. One mechanism through which industrialization leads to growth is through *backward* and *forward* linkages, e.g., the production of a particular product generates the production of the inputs that go into the making of that product, and/or becomes an input for the production of other products. An example is the steel industry, which can promote the increased production of mineral products, for example iron ore and coal, that go into the making of steel, while steel products in turn are used in building construction and in many manufacturing industries such as metal products and automobiles.

A second concept of development is based on the argument that development does not occur unless it results in a relatively equitable distribution of wealth and income and in higher standards of living for the entire population, which can be measured by such indicators as increases in literacy and education, health services, and life span, and by declines in infant mortality rates and in the deaths of children under five years of age, among others. More recently, partly as a result of the increasing evidence of the negative by-products of industrialization and concerns regarding the permanent loss of basic resources, the concept of sustainable development is becoming widespread. Sustainable development refers to the judicious use of resources in a way that increases the well-being of the current population without jeopardizing that of future generations.

At least as controversial as the meaning of the concept of development is the question of how it is achieved. Various models have been proposed, each with its defenders and detractors. The following discussion will concentrate primarily on Mexico's economic development, i.e., economic growth and self-generated development, particularly industrialization. At the same time, it is concerned with the implications of economic development for social development, involving higher standards of living and more equitable income distribution.

The Economic Model

The economic model that came to characterize Mexico as well as other industrializing Latin American countries during much of the 20th century was known as import substitution industrialization, or ISI.[14] As noted above, industrialization was widely understood as the means to development, and the idea was to domestically produce manufactured goods that had previously been imported. Production would be primarily oriented to the domestic market, which would be protected by high tariffs and other measures, such as import quotas, to enable new manufactured goods to compete with the products of more advanced countries. At the same time, the expansion of the industrial labor force, and wage increases, would expand the market for domestically manufactured goods. In several countries, this process was accompanied by the emergence of populist governments, which involved state alliances with labor, the middle class, and private industrial firms that would benefit from increased production, profits and wages.[15]

The state-guided ISI strategy can be explained by several factors. As noted in Chapter 2, the world depression of the 1930s reduced European and U.S. markets for commodities produced by Mexico and other countries, leading to a sharp reduction in export earnings and demonstrating the inherent weakness of an economy dependent on the export of a small number of commodities. This was followed by the interruption of European trade during World War II and the shift of U.S. production to a war economy, which reduced the import of manufactured products from Europe and the United States. Also, the fact that the domestic private sector was relatively weak left the state as the only domestic force with sufficient access to resources to promote growth and development.

During the post-war period, the rationale for the ISI model was articulated by a group of Latin American economists associated with the Economic Commission for Latin America (ECLA, today the Economic Commission for Latin America and the Caribbean, or ECLAC), one of several regional commissions created by the United Nations. According to the leading proponent of ISI, the Argentine economist Raul Prebisch, Latin American commodity exports were characterized by declining terms of trade relative to manufactured exports from the more industrialized countries, that is, the price of commodities fluctuate but tend to decline over time, while those of manufactured goods tend to rise steadily. This means, for instance, that a commodity exporter might have to produce and export twice as much in order to import the same amount of manufactured goods it was able to purchase in a previous period. Industrialization would solve this problem by reducing dependence on manufactured imports; export earnings could be used instead to invest in inputs to industry. While tariffs would be necessary initially to protect new industries from being undersold by more competitive foreign industries, over time Latin American industries would become more efficient and would be able to export their own products on the international market.

A second major characteristic of the economies during this period was the economic role of the state. In virtually all industrializing countries the state establishes and maintains certain conditions to facilitate the growth of industry, for example, the protection of new manufacturing industries through tariffs and the promotion or construction of the infrastructure—roads, railroads, ports—necessary to move products to internal and foreign markets. In "late industrializing" economies, the state often takes on additional functions, in part because the domestic private sector often lacks the financial and technological resources for certain types of investment and/or because certain sectors are not profitable except in the long run, and in part due to a desire by government policy makers to steer economic development in certain directions.[16] As discussed in the previous Chapter, the economic role of the state was reinforced by the Mexican revolution and the training of many of the leading economic officials in the government in continental Europe, where several countries had adopted a state-centric model.

In Mexico and other Latin American countries, an added factor was the concern for national control of resources and the desire to avoid foreign control of strategic industries, including the major export industries and those that provided the necessary infrastructure for a functioning market economy, including transportation, electric power, and communications. A further consideration was that many of these industries were considered "natural monopolies" in that one or a limited number of companies could control the entire domestic market, which meant that a private company motivated by profit could charge prices well above costs without fear of competition, whereas a state-controlled company would presumably be motivated by other nonprofit objectives, such as meeting public needs for certain services.

As noted previously, the administration of Avila Camacho began a shift in the focus of government policy toward an emphasis on growth and development, which was reinforced in the pro-business government of Miguel Alemán. But although the 1940s was characterized by a shift in emphasis toward economic goals, the previous post-revolutionary governments had established many of the conditions for subsequent growth and economic development. These included investment in infrastructure, the expansion of the domestic market through reforms, increasing wages, the formation of development banks that provided loans to private and public sector firms, and initiatives to help new enterprises through tax breaks and the establishment of protective tariffs.[17] The first steps had been taken toward substantial state intervention in the economy, and as of 1940 the Mexican government controlled the railroads and the petroleum industry. Subsequently it bought out foreign interests in public transport, communications, and electric energy. These government-controlled industries often provided services to private companies, as well as the general population, at subsidized prices, sometimes below costs.

In the post-war period, the state development bank, Nacional Financiera, moved aggressively to promote industrialization in such areas as steel, cement and paper. Its initiatives included the establishment of an integrated steel industry, the manufacture of railroad cars, and the expansion of a truck-manufacturing firm. In several of these industries, Nacional Financiera was a partial or majority owner, generally due to the inability of the domestic private sector to marshal the funds necessary for the initial investment or expansion of these industries or in order to save existing firms from bankruptcy. As of 1961, Nacional Financiera was a shareholder in 60 industrial firms and majority owner in 13 of these; in addition, it had provided funding for over 500 private enterprises.

Although state ownership and regulation were important, the Mexican economy was not a state-controlled system comparable to the Soviet Union or East Europe prior to the late 1980s. It could be considered a mixed economy, i.e., a market system regulated by the state with both state and private ownership. Through its control of strategic industries and its regulatory functions the state promoted private enterprise in various ways. In addition to subsidized prices for inputs and services, it provided tax breaks and tariff protection for new manufacturing industries. Nacional Financiera provided loans to private financial institutions and industries, and the government secured foreign loans for private firms and encouraged joint ventures between private foreign and domestic industries.

While certain sectors were closed to foreign investment, both the government and private sector leaders encouraged foreign investment in manufacturing. As noted previously, during the 1920s and 1930s Ford, General Motors and Chrysler opened auto-assembly plants, and several other industries such as B.F. Goodrich, Simmons, and DuPont opened branches in Mexico. Following World War II, economic growth and the size of the market also began to attract U.S. and in some cases European companies to invest in Mexico. Between 1940 and 1973, U.S. direct investment in Mexico increased from $358 million to $2.4 billion, and in manufacturing from $10 million to $1.8 billion. As of 1972, foreign assets in manufacturing were over half of total manufacturing assets; U.S. assets were 36 percent of the total and were particularly important in rubber (100 percent of the total), transportation equipment (70 percent), and chemicals (54 percent).[18]

Beginning in the 1960s, the Mexican government began negotiations with foreign automobile companies in an effort to establish an integrated automobile industry.[19] At this point, automobiles accounted for 11 percent of Mexico's imports, a major drain on the balance of trade. The initial aim was to create a domestic industry centered on a cheap, non-luxury model for domestic consumption. But foreign companies imposed their own conditions and in the end auto corporations manufactured their own models, although the number of makes and models was limited. The Mexican government established performance criteria for automobiles produced in Mexico by foreign companies, requiring them to obtain an increasing percentage of their inputs from domestic firms. By the mid-1970s, seven firms dominated Mexico's auto industry, for most part owned by foreign companies—Ford, GM, Chrysler, Nissan, Volkswagen, and Renault. Another company, DINA, was Mexican owned, and Vehiculos Automotores Mexicanas (VAM), which was jointly owned by a US company and the Mexican state, was later purchased by Renault.

The "Economic Miracle" and Its Implications

The implementation of Mexico's economic model brought impressive results in terms of growth.[20] Between 1940 and 1980, the Mexican economy grew at a rate of 6 percent a year. This was higher than the Latin American average and higher than the growth rates of the United States and England during their periods of major expansion. Government investment in agriculture, particularly in irrigation in northern Mexico, resulted in the development of a significant agricultural export sector, with an annual growth rate of 6 percent between 1935 and the mid-1960s. Industry grew even more dramatically, at a rate of 8 percent a year, increasing from an average of 25 percent of GDP in 1940 to 34 percent in 1970. At the same time, agriculture declined from 21 percent to 11 percent of GDP. Mexico had shifted from a primarily rural, agrarian country to a predominantly urban, semi-industrial one, with a growing middle class. The industrial labor force also increased, fed by migration from the countryside; the agricultural labor force declined from two-thirds to one-third of the total labor force.

As indicated previously, an important element in Mexico's growth was the economic role of the state. Between 1941 and 1970, the public sector was responsible for 40 percent of the capital formation in Mexico. Investment

Image 3-1 Juan O'Gorman, *La Ciudad de Mexico.*

priorities shifted over this period, with a reduction of the portion of investment in agriculture, from 16 to 11 percent, and in infrastructure, from 52 to 22 percent, and an increase in the percentage going to industry from 10 percent to 40 percent. Infrastructure investment went primarily to transportation, including roads, airports, railroads and ports, and communications. A major goal of public investment in agriculture was expansion of irrigation facilities, particularly in the arid regions of northern Mexico, where they benefitted commercial farmers largely oriented to export. Industrial investments were primarily dedicated to building and expanding key economic sectors such as oil, electricity and steel.

How did the government finance its expenditures? It should be noted that the Mexican government had one advantage over many Latin American countries: expenditures on the military, which counted for a substantial percentage of government expenses in many Latin American countries, were quite low, approximately 2 percent of the government budget during the 1941-1970 period. At the same time, low taxes and subsidized prices for government-owned industries reduced government revenues relative to what they might have been. Partly as a result of substantial tax breaks given to investors, Mexico had one of the lowest tax rates in the world—approximately 10 percent at the end of the 1960s. In the early part of this period the government compensated by printing money, which resulted in growing inflation. In 1952, the government devalued the peso to 12.5 to the dollar and maintained that rate for 24 years until 1976. This reduced Mexico's inflation to approximately 5 percent a year, another factor distinguishing it from many other Latin American countries, which had to deal with much higher rates of inflation and frequent devaluations. However, maintaining the peso-dollar exchange rate as well as obtaining the resources necessary for government investment, required increasing dependence on borrowing, particularly from foreign sources. Mexico's public debt increased from $485 million in 1946 to over $4 billion in 1970.[21]

This period was one of substantial growth for the private sector. Fixed capital investment grew from 8.2 percent of GDP to19 percent between 1940 and 1970, and the percentage of investment by the private sector increased from 45 to 66 percent of the total. Although most of the private firms were small or medium enterprises (SMEs), by 1970 the Mexican private sector was dominated by a small number of economic groups, or *grupos:*[22] a small group of investors or sometimes a single family, who exercised control over the economy and much of the wealth of the country; the grupos included major private industrial firms, banks, real estate and insurance companies, commercial ventures, and in some cases agricultural or mining interests. Members of the economic groups benefitted from having their own banks, which often gave preference to their own firms; easier access to foreign capital and technology, including joint ventures with transnational corporations; and often privileged access to government ministries and agencies.

The economic groups were in turn divided between those closely linked to and/or dependent on the state, generally centered in Mexico City, and more independent firms and groups centered in Monterrey, referred to as the Monterrey group and consisting of some 200 interrelated families. Some of these groups dated back to the Porfiriato. As noted in Chapter 2, the Garza-Sada groups of Monterrey began with the establishment of a brewery, Cervercería Cuauhtemoc, in the late 19th century. In 1901, a glass factory, Vidriera Monterrey, was established to supply bottles for the brewery and eventually other glass products, and in 1929 a separate firm, FAMSA, produced bottle tops, subsequently expanding into other metal products. Over the following years the investors established additional manufacturing companies as well as banks, insurance companies, and construction companies. By the late 1970s their holdings consisted of four major groups—the brewery, glass, steel and chemical groups, each consisting of about 20 to 30 firms, as well as several smaller groups. The glass group controlled most glass produced in Mexico. The steel group was a vertically integrated group that included its own mines and steel producing factories as well as metal products. Several firms in the chemical group consisted in joint ventures with U.S. or other foreign companies. By this time the grandchildren of the original founders were managing the firms.

Other groups were formed by "revolutionary capitalists" in the period after the revolution, or were promoted or formed directly by government officials who "retired" into the private sector following their tenure in government. Aaron Saenz, who had been an officer in the Constitutionalist Army and held several cabinet and sub-cabinet posts in the 1920s and early 1930s, established a sugar refinery with the help of loans from the Banco de Mexico; he as well as sugar refinery owners who had survived the revolution also benefitted from government initiatives to restore the sugar industry in the post-revolutionary period, including a provision exempting sugar properties from agrarian reform. Saenz subsequently expanded his sugar properties (assisted by loans from Nacional Financiera); gained controlling interest in a major commercial bank; and expanded into other industries, including hotels, airlines, steel and paper. A pattern whereby government officials obtained important positions in the private sector on their retirement from public office characterized subsequent administrations, notably that of Alemán (1946–1952), which, as indicated, was also noted for the high level of corruption of top officials as well as Alemán himself.[23]

The private sector was represented by several sectoral organizations established with support from the state, such as the National Confederation of Chambers of Commerce (CONCANACO), formed in 1917, and the National Confederation of Chambers of Industry (CONCAMIN), formed the following year. Although officially under state control, they became increasingly autonomous. In 1941, the National Chamber of Manufacturing Industries (CANACINTRA) was established to represent the interests of new manufacturing groups that were beneficiaries of government efforts to promote manufacturing. Over time, CANACINTRA became dominated by larger firms and became less dependent on the state.

Other sectoral groups, such as the Mexican Bankers' Association (ABM), formed independently and were generally more suspicious of government policies, although they maintained close relations with the Ministry of Finance. As discussed earlier, in 1928, private businessmen centered in the northern industrial city of Monterrey formed the Mexican Employers' Confederation (COPARMEX), which continued to maintain a highly critical stance toward the government, particularly government involvement in the economy. The most influential business group was (and continues to be) the CMHN, the Mexican Council of Businessmen, which groups the dominant 35–40 businessmen in Mexico. Its members collaborate in formulating their collective business interests, enjoy access to cabinet members and the president, and have direct input into major policy decisions. Powerful business groups also had recourse to investment strikes, production cutbacks, and capital flight when governments instituted policies perceived as contrary to their interests.

Business groups were in fact the major beneficiaries of Mexico's economic model, often to the detriment of other sectors of the population. Pressures by business groups were a factor in low levels of taxation, which limited the resources available to the government for social programs. The modification of a proposed tax reform in the mid-1960s, originally meant to close loopholes benefiting the private sector, instead resulted in increasing the income tax on labor income, which grew from 58 percent of government revenue (from the income tax) to nearly 80 percent between 1960 and 1966.[24] Business groups also pressured for the extension of tariffs and other forms of trade protection beyond the period it should have taken firms to become internationally competitive. The absence of competition enabled firms to continue to charge high prices for manufactured products, particularly in cases in which a small number of firms enjoyed control of the market.

As noted, urbanization and industrialization also led to the growth of the middle class as well as the urban working class. In the early part of this period, inflation cut into the earnings of workers; the real minimum wage in Mexico City in 1951 was only 44 percent of its 1939 value and did not again reach its pre-World War II level until the 1960s.[25] The implementation of the government stabilization program in 1955 resulted in an immediate increase in inflation, but inflation was reduced in the long term and real wages began to rise, continuing to increase through the 1970s.[26]

Table 3-1. Mexico: Social Indicators 1940–1980

	1940	1970	1980
Life Expectancy, years (men/women)	38/40	58/63	63/69
Infant Mortality (1000 births)	138.6	76.8	53.1
Literacy (percent)	41.8	76.3	83.0
Average years of schooling	2.6	3.4	4.6

Source: "Mexico: Social Indicators," from *Development and Growth in the Mexican Economy* by Juan Carlos Moreno-Brid and Jaime Ros (Oxford University Press, 2009): 262. By permission of Oxford University Press, Inc.

Government initiatives such as the staple foods program CONASUPO (the National Company for Subsistence Products), the government marketing board charged with administering price supports for basic products and stabilizing consumer prices, also benefited both urban workers and rural producers by providing price supports to farmers and subsidies of basic foods for consumers. Workers also benefitted from the increase in jobs, although the number of industrial jobs did not match the growth of the labor force due to natural population increase and rural-urban migration. Economic growth also enabled the government to obtain resources to expand health and education and other services, which also had the effect of expanding state employment.[27] Although the benefits of growth were very unevenly distributed, the welfare of the population in general improved significantly in the period 1940–1980, as table 3-1 shows.

Flaws in the Model

Despite its obvious success in promoting economic growth and industrial development, there were problems with Mexico's model and particularly its implementation. First, while the government promoted agricultural development, particularly during the first decades of this period, the focus of government programs tended to be on the large- and medium-sized farms in the north, which were supported though large-scale irrigation projects, to the neglect of small producers and ejidos in the central and southern regions of the country that produced food for themselves and the internal market. As noted earlier, the Alemán government had withdrawn support for the ejidal banks, which was the major source of credit for the ejidos since their land could not be mortgaged.

Favoritism toward the commercial agricultural enterprises of the north was also indicated by the Green Revolution, introduced in Mexico during this period. While the technology of the Green revolution could be used to expand the production of corn—the staple crop of small farmers and peasants—at relatively low cost, the program focused on technology leading to much more dramatic increases in wheat and cotton production, generally on large estates, at much higher costs in terms of inputs such as fertilizer, chemicals and machinery. This and similar policies assumed (incorrectly, according to some studies) that the large commercial holdings were more efficient than small farms, and they tended to widen the disparity between the large- and middle-level holdings and the small holdings and ejidos.[28] Beginning in the 1960s, the prices of food crops declined, which benefitted urban workers and their employers, but at the expense of farmers and peasants producing for the domestic market.

One effect of these imbalances was that while agricultural production (particularly of fruits and vegetables) for export increased, Mexico ceased to be self-sufficient in food production by the 1970s, and became increasingly dependent on food imports—importing half of its basic grains by 1983. Lack of government support for small holdings and ejidos, declining prices for basic food crops, as well as increased pressures on the land led to significant rural-urban migration. In 20 years, between 1950 and 1970, Mexico had shifted from a predominantly rural country to a predominantly urban one. While the proportion of the economically active population in agriculture declined from approximately two-thirds to just over a third of the EAP (economically active population) between 1940 and 1980, the absolute number of people working in agriculture increased. And while the number of people working in manufacturing in 1980 was seven times higher than in 1940, industries were unable to absorb the increased migrant population, and many were forced to find work in the informal sector, such as street vending, or poorly paid jobs in manufacturing workshops. Another consequence was the growth of the inner cities and particularly squatter settlements around the major cities, most strikingly in Mexico City, the major destination of migrants. (See Table 3-2)

A second problem was that although one of the goals of Mexico's industrialization was to make the economy less dependent on external factors, developments during this period tended to modify rather than eliminate Mexico's external dependence. Most of Mexico's trade was with the United States, with the result that it was heavily dependent on the health of the U.S. economy. Mexico also depended on the United States for foreign investment, and, as indicated in the case of the automobile industry, foreign investors in general were guided by priorities that did not necessarily coincide with those of Mexican development.

Third, much of Mexico's industrialization was concentrated in Mexico City, increasing the attraction of the capital for migrants and adding to population pressures on basic services, such as water and housing. Unable to find housing in the crowded inner city areas, most new arrivals established settlements in the areas surrounding Mexico City, which have grown to the extent that some are now satellite cities. The largest of these, Nezahyacoyotl, east of the airport, is now a major city of six million. Traffic congestion choked major arteries, and

Table 3-2. Mexico: Population 1940–1980

YEAR	POPULATION (1,000)	ECONOMICALLY ACTIVE POPULATION (EAP) (% OF TOTAL POPULATION)	EAP IN AGRICULTURE (% OF TOTAL EAP)	EAP IN MANUFACTURING (% OF TOTAL EAP)	URBAN POPULATION (% OF TOTAL POPULATION)
1940	19,650	5,858 (30)	3,831 (65)	502 (8.5)	
1950	25,790	8,272 (32)	5,465 (66)	950 (11.5)	10,976 (43)
1960	36,060	11,080 (30.7)	6,107 (55)	1,648 (14.9)	18,313 (50)
1970	50,690	14,926 (29.4)	6,541 (43.8)	2,544 (17)	29,907 (58.9)
1980	69,660	22,041 (31.6)	7,993 (36.3)	3,671 (16.7)	46,185 (67.2)

Source: Calculations based on Astorga, Pablo; Bergés, Ame R.; Fitzgerald, Edmund V.K. "The Oxford Latin American Economic Histroy Database (OxLAD)." The Latin American Centre, Oxford University, 2003. URL: http://oxlad.qeh.ox.ac.uk/.

pollution from factories and car exhaust grew to the extent that breathing in Mexico City was compared to smoking three packs of cigarettes a day. Migration from the rural area to Mexico City and the resulting urban problems can be attributed to a number of factors, including the long-term centralization of political and economic life in the city, the inadequacy of government efforts at decentralization, and the lack of attention to the rural area, particularly the more impoverished central and southern regions.

Finally, Mexico's period of dramatic growth was accompanied by increasing inequality.[29] Wealth continued to be highly concentrated, with the 20 percent of the population earning 64 percent of the income in 1969, compared to 59 percent in 1950. There had been some redistribution *within* the wealthiest group, which included urban middle sectors and some organized groups within the industrial working class, indicating that economic growth had benefitted some sectors. But the remaining 80 percent had lost out in relative terms, and the income of the lowest 20 percent of the population had been reduced from 4.7 to 4 percent of the total. Some of those in the lowest 10 percent probably lost out in absolute terms as well. Many of those living in urban ghettos and particularly many of the small farmers and peasants in the southern states were characterized by extreme poverty.

In part, skewed income distribution and continued poverty in the midst of growing wealth reflected government policies and priorities, which promoted economic growth above social reform and benefitted large business groups, often at the expense of other sectors of society. Low tax levels and extensive subsidies limited the availability of government resources for social services, while agricultural policies favored commercial export agriculture at the expense of small farmers producing for the domestic market, and industrial policies tended to favor large, technologically sophisticated industry at the expense of small firms. At the same time, the extension of tariff protection beyond the point it should have taken for firms to become internationally competitive meant that both small and large firms were often inefficient, charging high prices to consumers to offset high costs.

RESISTANCE, CO-OPTATION AND REPRESSION

Labor and Peasant Resistance

Throughout this period various groups mobilized in response to denial of their rights or to deteriorating conditions. Several unions and peasant organizations, and/or factions within them, attempted to assert their independence relative to the state-party system and to establish or re-establish democratic structures within their respective organizations, against efforts of successive administrations to maintain and extend government control. In some cases, dissident groups formed opposition parties, labor confederations, and peasant associations, challenging the hegemony of the government party.

As in other Latin American countries, workers in Mexico had experienced a sharp decline in real wages during World War II as a result of restrictions on wage increases during the war as well as inflation. In Mexico, real wages had declined to half their 1938 rate by 1946, resulting in a series of strikes by rank and file workers between 1946 and 1948. The labor movement at this point was divided between a large number of small and relatively weak unions in manufacturing firms such as textiles and food processing and in construction, and a small number of large industrial unions in strategic sectors such as railroads, petroleum, electric power generation, and telecommunications. While the former were part of the CTM, several of the industrial unions had left the CTM following a series of struggles in the late 1930s and 1940s. Within the labor movement, the large industrial unions were the most militant and the most active in efforts to improve wages and benefits in the post-war period.[30] Leaders of the railroad workers' union took the initiative to organize dissident unions, including those of telephone, electric power, tramway, aviation and cement workers, into a rival confederation, the CUT (Unitary Labor Confederation) in 1947, which in 1948 joined other unions (those of petroleum, mining, and textile workers) to form the Coalition of Worker and Peasant Organizations. The goals of the coalition, which rivaled the CTM in size, went beyond wage demands to include demands for autonomy and union democracy.

This movement was ultimately defeated by the Alemán government through a series of maneuvers to undermine pro-autonomy groups within the respective industrial unions by taking advantage of intra-union rivalries to support pro-government factions; utilizing government control over decisions recognizing or denying certification to unions and their leadership; and approving measures to centralize labor control, reduce union autonomy, and eliminate possibilities for rank and file protest. The departure of the industrial unions from the CTM had enabled a faction that was more accommodating to the PRI and the government to consolidate its control of the organization, which benefitted from the government success in weakening the industrial unions. The leader of this faction, Fidel Velazquez, became the leader of the confederation (a position he retained until his death in 1997) and the most powerful figure in the official labor sector during the second half of the 20th century.

At the same time, the Alemán government and succeeding administrations also sought to prevent the CTM from accruing too much power, recognizing rival confederations and playing them against each other.[31] In 1966, the government formed an umbrella organization, the CT (Congreso de Trabajo, or Labor Congress) to group all confederations and unions linked to the PRI. In addition to the CTM, the CT included other labor confederations, the major industrial unions that were not attached to the CTM, and the Federation of Public Service Workers Unions (FSTSE), which belonged to the popular sector of the PRI and was dominated by the National Union of Education Workers (SNTE). By the late 1970s, the CT incorporated most of organized labor, over 2.2 million workers. Many workers, however, particularly those in small firms or in the informal sector as well as many rural workers, remained outside the organized labor sector.

The CTM continued to be the dominant confederation within the official labor sector, and Fidel Velazquez became the first president of the CT. The close relationship of the CTM, and later the CT, with the government was the basis for the government-labor pact that underlay the political stability of much of this period. Workers organized in unions that were controlled by the official labor sector benefitted to some extent from the ability of labor leaders to deliver higher wages and substantial benefits in return for political support of the government and the PRI. Membership on governing boards for housing, financial credit and social security enabled labor leaders to provide these resources on a preferential basis to their own constituents.

At the same time, labor militancy continued. In the late 1950s several independent unions mobilized against the CTM, forming opposition coalitions, and the railroad workers union again took the lead in a series of strikes for higher wages and union autonomy which was joined by workers in other public sector unions, including petroleum and communications workers as well as teachers. The union won a number of concessions, including higher wages and recognition of independent union leadership, but the movement was eventually crushed when the government sent military forces to break up strikes and work stoppages throughout the country, resulting in the arrest and dismissal of thousands of railroad workers and the imprisonment of the leaders for the next 11 years.[32]

Independent movements also emerged within the peasantry.[33] As noted, the post-Cárdenas governments had shifted the focus of agrarian policy from the ejidal and small peasant sectors to large-scale and middle-level farmers producing for export in the northern states, who benefitted from government resources for irrigation and other inputs as well as the Green Revolution. Many of the ejidal leaders had succumbed to corruption; increasing amounts of ejidal land were lost to urbanization and tourism; and the CNC was even less likely to challenge the government than the CTM. Frustrated with the inadequacy of response from the official peasant sector, peasants, indigenous communities, small producers and ejiditarios formed alternative organizations, staged land invasions, and in some cases took up arms in an ongoing struggle for agrarian reform and against government corruption and repression at various levels. Again, the government responded with a combination of coercion and a broad array of co-optive measures, among them buying off leadership, partial concessions in return for "loyal opposition," and neutralizing dissident movements by splitting off "moderate" groups from the more "radical" factions.

These tactics were evident in the government response to two dissident movements that formed in northwest Mexico, the UGOCM (General Union of Workers and Peasants of Mexico) and the CCI (Independent Peasant Confederation). Both were linked to larger movements. The UGOCM, formed in 1949, was affiliated with the PP (Popular Party), led by charismatic Marxist leader Vicente Lombardo Toledano, who had played a major role in the labor movement in the 1920s and 1930s. Lombardo Toledano was one of the founders of the CTM but was later expelled from the confederation in 1947, partly in response to anti-Communist pressures from the United States. When, in 1958, the UGOCM staged a series of land invasions, the government responded by jailing the leadership. Lombardo Toledano, however, hoped to achieve change via the electoral route, a somewhat forlorn idea given PRI hegemony, and became part of the "loyal opposition" within the Chamber of Deputies. This caused tensions within the UGOCM which in 1973 split between a pro-government faction and an independent faction.

Several peasant and ejidal leaders from the northwest states of Sonora, Sinaloa and Baja California formed the CCI in 1963, which affiliated with the National Liberation Movement (MNL) led by former president Lázaro Cárdenas and bringing together Cardenistas and Communists in a broad front. The MLN and the CCI came under attack by the right wing in the wake of the Cuban revolution. The government imprisoned leaders of the Communist faction, and the CCI split, with the pro-government faction collaborating in efforts to expel the Communist faction.

While both of these movements achieved national visibility due to their links with political parties and/or prominent political leaders, the majority of dissident rural movements were local or regional. The most important was a movement for agrarian reform and municipal democracy in Morelos led by Rubén Jaramillo. At the age of 15, Jaramillo had fought in the revolutionary army of Zapata, and he subsequently dedicated himself to continuing the agrarian struggle of the peasants in Morelos. In Morelos and other rural southern states, peasant villages and indigenous communities had a tradition of self-government. Many, however, had come under the control of *caudillos* (military leaders) or *caciques* (political bosses), and the struggle to retain, or regain, village autonomy was an important element in the agrarian struggle. Another major issue in Morelos was the corruption of sugar mill owners and their exploitation of both cane cutters and mill workers. Jaramillo's work on behalf of the cane workers brought him into conflict with local officials as well as the state and ultimately federal governments. He eventually took up arms and led the peasants in land invasions. In 1962, he, his pregnant wife and three sons were brutally murdered. Although it was generally known that military troops and the judicial police were responsible, the culprits were not brought to trial.

As these examples indicate, while some dissident leaders and groups were co-opted into the political system, receiving some concessions in the process, repression was a last resort in response to demands that the government could not contain or control. Police or military forces or in some cases hired thugs were involved in the harassment, imprisonment, torture and even assassination of leaders. Massacres of opposition activists, particularly in the countryside, were reported, if at all, as shootouts between rival peasant groups, or as police action against bandits. In effect, government repression was often "invisible": the imprisonment or assassination of dissident leaders, particularly in the rural areas, often received little publicity and were generally carried out by lower-level officials or hired goon squads, enabling the national government to maintain a posture of non-involvement.

The Student Movement of 1968

The student movement of the 1960s marked a turning point in Mexico's political history.[34] As was the case of other protest movements, the 1968 student movement had its origins in several states. During the 1960s students had mobilized in Puebla, Michoacán, Guerrero, Sonora, Tabasco, and Sinaloa. Although the issues varied, most were met with repression by authorities. The Mexico City rebellion began with a clash between students of a preparatory school and a vocational school following an informal football game, which was repressed by local police officers, resulting in several injuries. After riot police and shock troops attacked subsequent marches protesting police brutality, the student movement expanded to incorporate high school and university students throughout Mexico City and began to hold daily protests. Police violence escalated, resulting in various injuries and some deaths, as well as the arrest and imprisonment of several students, some of whom were tortured. Nevertheless, the movement continued to grow to include teachers, professors, and other non-students as well as students from universities and secondary schools in other parts of the country.

The movement in some aspects reflected student rebellions elsewhere during this period, including a generational uprising against authority, whether in the form of mediocre teachers, intransigent parents, or a reactionary government. Like many protest movements of the period, particularly in Latin America, students were inspired by the Cuban revolution, and particularly by Che Guevara, who had been assassinated the year before. Some students were well-versed in the works of Marx and Lenin, Herbert Marcuse and Franz Fanón; the membership included Marxists of various persuasions.

But it was primarily a Mexican movement. The students themselves saw it as embracing the protest movements of the past, particularly that of the railroad workers in the late 1950s, as well as the earlier student movements. Over time, objectives expanded from protest against police repression to include demands for release of political prisoners, condemnation of government failure to address the glaring poverty of many Mexicans, and opposition to plans to hold the 1968 Olympics in Mexico City, arguing that the money spent on elaborate preparations could be better used to alleviate poverty. It specifically targeted the governing party and the Mexican state, seen as concealing an ossified bureaucracy and repressive apparatus beneath a veneer of revolutionary rhetoric and democratic stability.

The harsh government reaction to the student marches and demonstrations during July and August in part reflected concern on the part of government officials that instability could result in cutbacks in U.S. investment or in U.S. intervention. The timing was also critical. Mexico would be the first developing country to hold the Olympics, which were scheduled to begin on October 12, and the government was afraid that the students would disrupt the Olympics or use the occasion to publicize abuses by the government.

For the students, the government reaction confirmed their accusations of government repression. In August the students called a national strike and formed a National Strike Council (CNH) with representation from 128 universities, technical schools and secondary schools, and a leadership that rotated among different members in an effort to prevent the government from identifying specific leaders and attempting to bribe or co-opt them. Each university and secondary school had its own committee, which in turn was responsible for the action brigades that carried out daily activities. These included printing petitions that were circulated on the streets, in markets, and on buses, making posters, painting slogans on walls, engaging in street theatre, and collecting funds to finance their activities. Medical students formed special brigades to take care of those injured in confrontations with the police or military forces; there were also special brigades for preparing food and other specific functions. Spontaneous street meetings of three or four students were sometimes joined by people on the street, offering their support.

Meetings were to be governed by the principle of direct democracy in which everyone had the opportunity to express his or her view, an idealistic position which sometimes led to long harangues as well as lengthy discussions and debates on Marxism, anti-imperialism and other issues. Many activists saw these discussions as an esoteric diversion from immediate tactical concerns. Given the differences among the students, the movement was not without its setbacks and divisions. Historical class divisions between the middle class and the working class had traditionally taken the form of rivalries between preparatory and vocational school students, and between students of the UNAM (National Autonomous University of Mexico) and of the IPN (National Polytechnic Institute). There were also differences between radical and more moderate groups, among different Marxist groups (Communists, Trotskyists, Maoists, and others), and between the "philosophers" and the pragmatists.

Despite these differences, the students were able to come together and achieve unity around basic goals and daily street actions, as well as massive marches and demonstrations. The movement issued six demands: (1) freedom for all political prisoners; (2) revocation of Article 145 of the penal code, which prohibited activities threatening the public order and Mexican sovereignty;[35] (3) disbandment of the corps of *granaderos* (riot police); (4) dismissal of the chief of police and his deputy; (5) payment of indemnization to the families of those injured or killed since the beginning of the conflict; and (6) determination of those government officials responsible for the bloodshed.[36] The demands were specifically focused on the repressive apparatus and actions of the state in an effort to obtain support from moderate as well as more radical sectors among the students and the society as a whole. Much of the street action was oriented to obtaining support from different sectors of the population, and students attempted, with mixed success, to gain the support of labor and peasant groups. In part because of control exercised by the CTM and the CNC, support from these sectors was limited, but individual peasants and workers as well as the unions of railroad and industrial workers and some independent labor and peasant organizations—and even some local CTM unions—supported the movement.

Mass demonstrations also attracted supporters among the population who marched along with the students and attended rallies in the Zócalo, the main plaza of Mexico City. Although the demonstrators were generally vocal and on occasion quite rowdy, with protestors shouting insults at the president as well as slogans, perhaps the most effective was a "silent demonstration" called by the strike committee to present the six demands of the movement to the president. As described by one CNH member:

> As soon as we left Chapultepec Park, just a few blocks further on, hundreds of people began to join our ranks. All along the Paseo de la Reforma, the side-walks, the median strips, the monuments, and even the trees were full of people, and every hundred yards our ranks were doubled. And the only sound from those tens of thousands and then hundreds of thousands of people were their footfalls. Footfalls on the pavement, the sound of thousands of feet walking on, step by step. The silence was more impressive than the huge crowd. It seemed as though we were trampling all the politicians' torrents of words underfoot, the flood of words that the facts belie, the heaps of lies; we were sweeping them all away with our feet . . . With our footsteps . . . we were avenging years and years of cowardly crimes, crimes that had been carefully covered up, crimes resembling those committed by gangsters . . . Since we had resolved not to shout or talk as we had during other demonstrations, we were able to hear—for the first time—the applause and shouts of approval from the dense crowds supporting

us along the line of march, and thousands of hands were raised in the symbol that soon covered the entire city and was even seen at public functions, on tele-visios, at official ceremonies: the *V of Venceremos* ["We shall win"].

—Luis González de Alba[37]

In an effort to diffuse the conflict, the government agreed to a dialogue, although at the same time it was running daily ads in the major newspapers denouncing the students. The student leadership insisted that the dialogue be public and transparent, given the government's practice of operating in secret and of attempting to co-opt, divide and neutralize opposition. On September 18, Army troops invaded UNAM, disregarding the university's autonomous status and arrested some 500 people, including university officials, resulting in a for-mal protest by the rector. Several days later, the army occupied the IPN, again arresting students. At this point, the movement had been considerably weak-ened; many of the leaders were in prison where they were subjected to brutal torture. The military forces remained on the two campuses until September 30.

The strike committee called for a demonstration on October 2 in the Plaza of Tlatelolco, which was to be followed by a march to the National Polytechnic Institute. On hearing that the police forces had blocked the route to the Institute, the organizers called off the march, but the demonstration went forward as planned. When the speeches began at about 5:30 PM, the plaza was packed with demonstrators, supporters, and bystanders: men and women of all ages (includ-ing some with children), street vendors, housewives and other spectators, while many people in the housing units watched from their windows. When police and military troops began moving into the plaza, the strike leaders, who were addressing the crowd from the fourth floor of one of the surrounding buildings, cautioned everyone to remain calm. In addition to the police and army forces, members of the Olympia Calvary Battalion (a force specifically trained for the Olympics), dressed as civilians but each wearing a white glove for purposes of identification, gathered at the entrances of the plaza and mingled with the crowd.

At approximately 6:30 PM, a helicopter, which had been circling overhead, fired two flares. This was the signal for members of the Olympia Battalion to surround the plaza, preventing any escape, while others ran up to the speakers' platform to arrest the strike leaders. Sharpshooters on the roofs of the surround-ing buildings began firing on the crowd. In the confusion that followed, the sol-diers and police also began firing at the demonstrators as well as at onlookers in the surrounding buildings. "The bullets were shattering the windows of the apartments and shards of glass were flying all over, and the terror-stricken fami-lies were trying to protect their youngest children."[38] Heavy weapons were used: in addition to rifles and bayonets there were bazookas, tanks and machine guns. One of the buildings caught fire, causing the evacuation of its terrified residents.

Unable to escape, students and their supporters and people forced out of the surrounding buildings ran in all directions as comrades and strangers fell at their sides, wounded or killed. Some, including young children, were trampled in the process; some jumped into the Aztec ruins, many landing on top of others. Some students were able to find refuge in the surrounding apartments; in other cases the terrified residents refused to open their doors. The shooting went on for several hours, finally ending at about 11:00 PM. Individual stories of survivors of the massacre, several of them interviewed while in prison, attest to its horror:

> There was a girl right next to me who had been hit square in the face by a dumdum bullet. It was ghastly! The entire left side of her face was gone . . . The shouts, the cries of pain, the weeping, the prayers and supplications, and the continuous deafening sound of gunfire made the Plaza de las Tres Culturas a scene straight out of Dante's Inferno.
>
> —Diana Salmerion de Contreras.[39]

> . . . when the machine gun started firing, two comrades, a boy and a girl, raised their hands way up in the air to surrender, and I don't know whether it was that the soldiers had been given drugs, or what, but they suddenly fired round after round at the two of them.
>
> —Daniel Esparza Lepe[40]

> A child no more than five or six years old who was running about crying fell to the ground. Several other children who had been with him fled in terror, but one six-year-old came back and started shaking him: "Juanito, Juanito, come on get up!" He began to pull at him as though that would revive him. "Juanito, what's wrong with you?" he asked him. He obviously had no idea what death was, and was never to find out that his little friend was dead, because his questions suddenly were heard no more, just a moan. The two tiny bodies were left lying there, one on top of the other.
>
> —Jesús Tovar García[41]

There are no final figures on how many people lost their lives that night. The government claimed that the number was 37; other estimates indicate that 200 to 400 were killed. Hundreds more were wounded. Many others, including members of the strike committee that had been addressing the crowd, were arrested and imprisoned. The government would argue that the shooting was instigated by the students, but reports by journalists and numerous eye-witnesses indicated no evidence of this, and that the police officers and soldiers who had been killed were, like many others, victims of the indiscriminate shooting into the crowds. Subsequent investigations reported that members of the president's guard who had taken positions in the apartment buildings surrounding the plaza had instigated the shooting.

Image 3-2 Students captured by police following a search of the Plaza de Tlatelolco, Mexico City, October 1968.

Throughout the night and the following days, desperate parents and other family members went from hospitals to morgues, from military quarters to courts, seeking their missing children and relatives. Many of the bodies they saw in morgues and hospitals were those of elderly women, middle-aged men, small children, pregnant women, as well as students. Some had been bayoneted; others had been grotesquely disfigured by dumdum bullets.

For those imprisoned before and during the massacre, the nightmare continued, as they were systematically beaten, tortured with electric prods, and told they would be executed if they did not sign documents attesting to their guilt or reveal the names or whereabouts of movement leaders and activists. Two years later many were still languishing in prison. Although some students continued to meet and stage protests, the movement was shattered. Many were demoralized by reports that some of the imprisoned students had fingered others under torture; mutual suspicions weakened the possibility of rebuilding a unified movement. The student movement was effectively crushed and the 1968 Olympics went ahead as scheduled.

Nevertheless, the movement, and its repression, represented a turning point. As one of the leaders of the movement stated, "There was one Mexico before the Student Movement, and a different one after 1968. T[l]atelolco is the dividing point between these two Mexicos."[42] The student movement and the

"Generation of 1968" would become the inspiration and impetus for many of the social movements that emerged in the 1980s and 1990s.

In the meantime, the movement had succeeded in publicizing the lack of democracy and the extreme poverty and inequality underlying Mexico's economic miracle, while the government repression had revealed the coercive authoritarianism underlying Mexico's political stability and eroded the legitimacy of Mexico's "perfect dictatorship." Mexicans did not cease to believe in the ideals of the revolution, but many ceased to believe in the Mexican state as the agent to realize its goals.

FROM VULNERABILITY TO CRISIS

Following 1968, the Mexican government confronted two major challenges: to restore the legitimacy of the system by incorporating groups "left out" of the Mexican miracle and to address the problems confronting the economy.

The 1970s was a period of significant changes in the international context. The liberation of several African countries from colonial rule, the industrial growth of certain developing countries, including Brazil and Mexico as well as the East Asian countries of Taiwan and South Korea, and the efforts of developing countries to assert their autonomy relative to the advanced industrial countries led to a new international emphasis on the "third world" countries of Africa, Asia and Latin America.[43] At the same time, these developments highlighted the increasing distinction *within* third world countries between the rapidly industrializing "middle level" countries and the poorer countries of these regions.

These changes were accompanied by the emergence of new perspectives on economic development and particularly the role of advanced capitalist countries in the economies of the less developed countries. While theories of modernization, prevalent in the 1960s, had assumed that the course of development of these countries would follow that of the advanced capitalist countries, that the benefits of growth would eventually "trickle down" to the most disadvantaged sectors of the economy, and that the impact of capitalist countries on the developing countries was generally positive, the new perspectives argued that growth was not occurring or that it was accompanied by acute dislocations, that it was not benefiting the poorer sectors of the population, and that the impact of the more advanced capitalist countries was often negative and even highly detrimental. Among those studying Latin America, the predominant theoretical approach was that of dependency, defined as a condition whereby the economy of a given country is largely determined by external forces.[44] One version of dependency theory, the "development of underdevelopment," argued that the advanced countries were actually "underdeveloping" the less developed countries, a process that in Latin America began with the European conquest and colonization, when the conquerors extracted the wealth of the colonies for the benefit of Spain and Portugal and imposed systems of monoculture, the production of a single product for export, in the new colonies, destroying viable systems oriented to self-sufficiency in food production. After these countries became independent, European countries and later the United States accumulated wealth through such mechanisms as investment with the repatriation of profits and loans with exorbitant interest rates, backed by political and military intervention. This process could end only by a socialist revolution, as occurred in the Soviet Union, China, and, of particular relevance for Latin America, in Cuba.

A more complex version of the dependency perspective, dependent development, asserted that the effect of dependency depended on conditions within the dependent country itself, particularly the nature of the class system and state-class relations. Where a domestic capitalist class had emerged, and received support and protection from an economically active state, foreign capital and technology could contribute to economic development. Such a model could lead to self-sustaining growth although the result would be uneven and inequitable.[45]

It is perhaps ironic that dependency theories became prominent at a time when some third world countries were asserting their economic power. This was particularly evident with OPEC (the Organization of Petroleum Exporting Countries), an oil cartel consisting of several Middle Eastern countries and Venezuela and Ecuador that was created in 1960. The ability of these countries to increase their control of their petroleum resources and thereby set prices and determine production quotas resulted in a dramatic increase in oil and gas prices in the 1970s, leading to an exponential growth in the resources of oil-exporting counties. The implications for developing third world countries were mixed. On the one hand, many of these "petro-dollars" found their way into European banks, expanding the reserves available for loans at a time when the newly industrializing countries offered attractive targets for loans. Countries like Mexico, Brazil, and Korea, among others, obtained increased access to foreign loans as a result. On the other hand, recession in the advanced industrial countries affected the economies of those third world countries that were dependent on them for investment and trade, as was the case of Mexico in relation to the United States, and steep oil prices negatively affected the trade balance of those countries dependent on oil imports.

Politically, the late 1960s were a period of growing political unrest in Latin America, including the increase of popular protests, the growth of leftist groups, and in some countries, the formation of guerrilla organizations inspired by the Cuban revolution. In 1970, elections in Chile brought a left-wing coalition, led by Socialist Salvador Allende, to power. Right-wing reaction to the mobilization and increased presence of the left resulted in the suppression of revolutionary groups and the destabilization and eventual overthrow of civilian governments in several South American countries, including the Allende government in Chile, by military coups. Those leading the military regimes were officers imbued with a mission to rid their countries of "Communist subversion," targeting not only guerrilla groups but also progressives and leftists, who were ruthlessly repressed. In contrast to previous military governments in Latin America, the new bureaucratic authoritarian regimes would remain in power for a much longer period; in addition to rooting out subversion their missions included economic goals. They were able to take advantage of the availability of loans from private U.S. and European banks to deepen industrial development and to upgrade military weapons and technology.[46]

The United States was deeply involved in these developments. U.S.-Latin American relations were largely defined by the Cold War, with frequent intervention and even the overthrow of governments considered too sympathetic to Communism. In the mid-1950s, the U.S. Central Intelligence Agency supported a coup against a democratically elected government in Guatemala, justifying this action on the basis of the presence of members of the Communist Party in the government, an act that led to increased levels of anti-Americanism in many parts of the region. The U.S. also supported Cuban exiles in an unsuccessful effort to overthrow the new revolutionary government in Cuba. In an effort to improve relations, and recognizing the importance of reform if more radical revolutionary change was to be avoided, the Kennedy administration promoted an Alliance for Progress in which the U.S. worked with Latin American governments to promote reform, resulting in a temporary thawing in relations.

At the same time, the United States sponsored counterinsurgency programs in several Latin American countries to train police forces to fight "internal subversion." Several officers trained at the U.S. School of the Americas (established in Panama to train Latin American military officers, subsequently moved to Fort Benning, Georgia, and more recently renamed the Western Hemisphere Institute for Security Cooperation) were heavily implicated in the repressive measures carried out by military regimes that came to power in the 1970s. The Nixon administration, in particular, targeted the democratically elected Allende government in Chile in a series of measures that combined economic destabilization, promotion of opposition groups, and direct support for a military coup.

In keeping with its nationalist emphasis and particularly its concern about foreign (notably U.S.) intervention in Latin America, the Mexican government opposed the Cold War position of the United States on several issues, condemning the overthrow of the Arbenz government in Guatemala as well as a subsequent marine invasion of the Dominican Republic to support a military coup. It also continued to recognize Cuba when other Latin American nations, prodded by the United States, withdrew recognition. The next two governments would continue to challenge U.S. Cold War policy in the region.

The Echeverría Government: The Limits to Reformism

Díaz Ordaz chose as his successor Luis Echeverría Alvarez, who as his Secretary of Government, shared responsibility for the tragedy of Tlatelolco. Echeverría's administration turned out to be one of the most enigmatic in Mexico's recent history; on the one hand promoting a broad range of social and economic reforms, and on the other continuing many of the most oppressive practices of the previous administration.[47] In an effort to restore the credibility of the government, Echeverría promoted a "democratic opening" to reach out to popular sectors. He freed political prisoners, including some of the labor leaders arrested in the 1950s and students imprisoned during the previous administration. The government also increased social spending on health, education and housing, and increased the number of Mexicans covered by social security, which by the end of his administration reached one-third of the population.

In contrast to previous administrations, the Echeverría government focused on small peasant holdings and ejidos of the rural sector, introducing measures to increase productivity on those producing for subsistence or domestic consumption and providing services such as credit, marketing and storage facilities designed to eliminate dependence on high-cost intermediaries. He also attempted, with limited success, to expand policies respecting CONASUPO (the government marketing board) to benefit peasants and farmers (e.g. through providing credit and assistance with marketing). Echeverría also declared an emergency wage increase for industrial workers and reformed the labor code to permit annual renegotiation of wages and responded positively—at least initially— to a resurgence of labor militancy, which included the establishment of independent unions and efforts to democratize existing unions.[48]

On the economic front, the government pursued a nationalist and statist agenda, establishing various policies to control and direct foreign investment, including a law in 1973 incorporating measures reinforcing "Mexicanization," the requirement that firms had to be at least 51 percent Mexican owned, in an effort to limit foreign, especially U.S., control, although foreign companies sometimes used Mexican *prestanombres* (name lenders) as fronts. He further sought to limit Mexican dependence on the United States by expanding markets for Mexico's exports, extending trade relations with Canada, Japan, China, the Soviet Union, several European countries, and Central and South America. Another mechanism for controlling foreign investment was the establishment of performance criteria, by which foreign companies were required to fulfill certain requisites that would benefit the national economy, such as obtaining a certain proportion of their supplies and inputs from domestic firms rather than imports, or exporting as much or more than they imported. As noted, performance criteria had been established for the automobile industry.

With respect to international relations, Echeverría pushed a "third world" policy, calling for a new international order that would give more favorable treatment to developing countries, through such policies as the stabilization of international prices for the commodities these countries exported. He also broke with U.S. policy in establishing relations with East European countries, and welcomed Chilean exiles following the military coup against the Allende government in Chile, which had been facilitated by the CIA, as well as exiles from other military dictatorships in the Southern Cone countries.

This period was also characterized by a vast increase in state economic intervention. Citing the stagnation of the private sector, the government increased its investment as a percentage of total investment from 35 to 55 percent, expanded the number of enterprises in the public sector—which tripled from 277 to 845 during his administration—and doubled the number of public employees from 500,000 to 1 million. These investments included both the expansion of public investment in heavy industries, such as steel, chemicals, and fertilizers, and the takeover of industries in such fields as textiles and sugar production that were facing bankruptcy, with the goal of maintaining employment levels. Approximately 17 percent of public investment went into expanding the oil industry in an effort to end Mexico's dependence on oil imports; by the end of Echeverría's *sexenio*, Mexico was again exporting oil.

The government attempted to pay for its increased social and economic investments by raising taxes and establishing a more progressive tax system. As noted, Mexico had one of the lowest tax rates in the world; the system was also highly regressive, with the workers and middle class bearing the brunt of the taxes. Officials within the Ministry of the Presidency proposed a tax reform that would enable the government to raise taxes on wealth, increase corporate taxes, and raise the income taxes of higher income groups. However, business interests, particularly the powerful Mexican Businessmen's Council, opposed it, as did their allies within the Central Bank and the Ministry of Finance. The result was a much more modest tax reform that did little to resolve the inequities in the existing system, an outcome that reflected the weight of the business sector and the continued importance of the informal alliance of officials in the Finance Ministry and Central Bank with the most powerful business conglomerates.[49]

As a result, the fiscal deficit (the amount of government expenditures minus that of government revenues) grew from an average of 2.5 percent of the total GDP in the period from the mid 1950s to 1972 to 8 percent annually in the three-year period from 1973 to 1976. The government became heavily dependent on borrowing, particularly from foreign banks, which were more than willing to lend to countries like Mexico with a promising growth record. Mexico's total foreign debt increased from $6 billion in 1970 to $25.9 billion in 1976, and interest payments on the debt grew from $720 million in 1970 to $2.3 billion in 1976.[50]

The policies of the Echeverría government had mixed results, but they failed to resolve Mexico's social inequities and economic difficulties. On the one hand, as a result of state spending the Mexican economy continued to grow, although unevenly, at an annual rate of 6 percent. Exports increased from $2.9 billion to $7.4 billion between 1970 and 1976. Increased social spending and wage raises resulted in a shift in income distribution that benefitted Mexico's middle sectors, including members of the working class, at the expense of the upper-level income groups, but failed to benefit the lowest population groups. Between 1969 and 1977, the proportion of income received by the top 20 percent declined from 64 to 55 percent of the total, and that of the lowest 20 percent from 4 to 3.3 percent, while that of the middle 60 percent increased from 32 to 42 percent.

On the other hand, because growth in consumer industries, dependent on private investment, was sluggish, Mexico increased its import of consumer goods, as well as its imports of machinery and other inputs for heavy industry in the public sector. Efforts to diversify export markets for consumer goods and reduce dependency on the United States were undermined by the poor quality of these goods relative to those produced in the advanced industrial countries. In addition, as mentioned earlier, Mexico had become increasingly dependent on food imports. As a result, imports grew faster than exports, leading to an increased balance of trade deficit.

In the meantime, state involvement in the economy, as well as the heavy leftist and anti-business rhetoric of the Echeverría government, had alienated business groups. In May 1975, they formed the CCE (Consejo Coordinador Empresarial—the Business Coordinating Council), an umbrella organization grouping the different business groups for the purpose of influencing government policy in the following (1976–1982) sexenio. Distrust of government intentions, as well as fear of devaluation, led to cutbacks in private investment as well as capital flight. Inflation also increased from 3.4 percent in 1969 to an average of 17 percent in 1973-75, fed in part by increased wages as well as increased government spending. In 1976, for the first time in 24 years, Mexico was forced to devalue the peso, which dropped to approximately half its previous value.

While business groups balked at Echeverría's economic reforms, bureaucratic inertia and local opposition stymied many of his social reforms. One example was an effort to reform CONASUPO in order to increase production, distribute income more equitably, and incorporate marginal groups into the economy. Despite the good intentions and motivations of the young technicians responsible for implementing the program, its effectiveness was limited by the resistance

of local interests, ingrained habits of paternalism which limited peasant participation, and political considerations in the last years of the sexenio, when officials
at all levels concentrated on securing a position in the next administration.[51]

In addition, while increased social spending had some effects on increasing
the availability of education, health services and housing and on reducing
income inequality, shifts in government policies alienated sectors of the left as
well. After initially supporting workers attempting to democratize their unions
or form independent unions, dependence on corporate labor leaders to control
labor demands in the context of growing inflation led the government to back
those attempting to block changes in the corporate labor sector.

Despite initial outreach to progressive groups, including students, the
Echeverría government grew increasingly repressive. In some cases, repression
was apparently instigated by paramilitary groups formed by right-wing elements,
possibly including some right-wing officials within the PRI opposed to Echeverría's policies. In an effort to rebuild the student movement, some of the newly
released student activists called a march, to take place on June 10, 1971. The
demonstration was interrupted when an armed paramilitary troop—*los halcones*
(the falcons)—infiltrated the march and attacked the students, killing some and
subsequently chasing those trying to escape, invading shops, churches, and even
hospitals to attack those seeking refuge as well as the wounded. Dozens were
killed or wounded, or arrested and imprisoned. Blame fell on the regent (the
mayor, an appointed position) of Mexico City, who was responsible for the paramilitary group, but while Echeverría had promised a thorough investigation of
the event, and the regent and the police chief were forced to resign, no charges
were ever brought.

Following the Tlatelolco massacre, some groups, including some of the students of the "Generation of 1968" had resorted to violence, forming urban guerrilla movements, which carried out a series of bank robberies and kidnappings.
The prominent Monterrey business leader, Eugenio Garza Sada, was killed in a
kidnapping attempt, further incensing the business sector. In the impoverished
southern state of Guerrero, a peasant guerrilla force, led by a rural schoolteacher
Lucio Cabañas, launched attacks on army bases in the state. Military and police
forces suppressed urban and rural guerrilla organizations, in some cases wiping
out entire villages accused of collaborating with the guerrillas. It also targeted
non-violent dissidents and opposition groups. Dissident labor and peasant leaders were persecuted and in some cases assassinated, and *porros*, provocateurs
often posing as students, attacked opposition movements in the university.
Although less extensive and less visible than those carried out by the military
regimes of South American, Mexico had its own "dirty war" that included the
torture, assassination, and "disappearance" of militants and those suspected of
supporting them.

Two events in the last months of the Echeverría administration further tarnished his reputation. Following growing media criticism of the administration and its policies, the administration maneuvered the dismissal of the editor of *Excelsior*, the leading national newspaper, in July 1976.[52] And in the last weeks of his administration, in response to a series of peasant land invasions in the northern state of Sonora, Echeverría turned over 250,000 acres of privately owned land to the peasants in a poorly planned move that incensed the landowners and business groups and was of limited benefit to the peasants, since landowners were able to recover much of the land through court proceedings. At the end of the Echeverría administration, the credibility of the regime was at its lowest point, and Mexico's economic system was confronting a major crisis.

Jose López Portillo: Oil to the Rescue?

Echeverría was succeeded by his Finance Minister Jose López Portillo, whose immediate priority was a rapprochement with Mexico's business sectors. In the last months of his administration, Echeverría had signed a stabilization agreement with the International Monetary Fund, which provided over $900 million in loans in return for which Mexico agreed to implement measures to bring its budget deficit under control. López Portillo reassured the business sector that he would maintain these policies.

In the meantime, new petroleum reserves had been discovered in the Gulf of Mexico in the 1960s, although the extent of these reserves was not known at the time. Mexico had of course been a major oil exporter through the 1930s, but following the petroleum expropriation in 1938 and throughout the period of Mexico's economic miracle, an increasing portion of Mexico's oil production had supplied Mexico's growing industries. By 1969, Mexico had stopped exporting crude oil, and it subsequently became a net importer of oil. The Echeverría government had initiated the development of Mexico's new oil resources, and by 1975 Mexico was again a net oil exporter. As the extent of Mexico's Gulf of Mexico resources became increasingly evident, the López Portillo government saw it as a new engine of growth and decided to devote extensive resources to its exploitation.

How to develop Mexico's oil resources was a subject of intense debate within Mexico.[53] Several Mexican intellectuals called for a gradual development of oil reserves, giving priority to maintaining a sufficient reserve for Mexico's own energy needs and for the production of other goods, such as plastics and fertilizer, that would provide inputs into Mexico's industry and agriculture. The leading proponent of this perspective was Heberto Castillo, a university professor and founder of a small political party, the Mexican Workers' Party. At the other extreme was the position of Jorge Díaz Serrano, the Director of PEMEX, who pushed for the aggressive development and export of Mexico's oil in an effort to resolve Mexico's balance of payments problems, a position that was also favored by business sectors. A third position was that of groups within the government, led by José Andrés de Oteyza, the secretary of National Resources, and Carlos Tello, who was briefly secretary of Budget and Planning. Like Castillo, they maintained that—as a non-renewable resource—oil reserves should be developed gradually, primarily for Mexican use, while also exploring other energy sources. Gradual development would also provide time for the extension of domestic capacity in exploitation, transportation and storage facilities. Resources from oil should also be used to deepen Mexico's industrial capacity, producing capital goods for the domestic market and for export.

Although López Portillo spoke of using oil wealth judiciously to expand Mexico's productive capacity, "emulating Japan rather than Saudi Arabia," in effect he followed the position of Díaz Serrano, taking advantage of the availability of foreign credit and high oil prices to promote the aggressive development of oil resources for export. Oil production increased from less than 1 million to 2.25 million barrels of oil a day by 1982, and oil exports grew from 94,000 to nearly 1.5 million barrels between 1976 and 1982.

Initially this policy appeared to be highly effective. Between 1978 and 1981, Mexico's GDP growth averaged 8 percent annually, and the value of Mexico's exports increased from $6.6 billion to $20 billion. In the same period, there was an annual increase in investment of 16.2 percent, including government investment in expanded infrastructure, such as roads, warehouses, and ports, to facilitate exports, and in complementary industries, especially petrochemicals. Private domestic investment also grew, much of it in real estate and construction as well as industry, and foreign investment increased fivefold. An estimated 4 million new jobs were created, reducing Mexico's chronic problems of unemployment and underemployment. The government also undertook several initiatives in agriculture to expand the production of basic food products and reduce Mexico's dependence on food imports, such as SAM (the Mexican Food System) which provided credit, seeds, fertilizers and other inputs, as well as assured markets, to peasant producers who pledged to meet government production goals in corn, beans, and other basic foods. Mexico's boom particularly benefited the new middle class, giving them access to an elite lifestyle exemplified by a dramatic increase in automobile ownership and frequent shopping sprees to the United States.

Oil wealth also increased Mexico's international status. The López Portillo government took an active role in supporting revolutionary movements in Central America, implicitly challenging the U.S. government, which, particularly during the administration of Ronald Reagan (1981–89), provided substantial military and economic support to the government of El Salvador in its effort to crush the revolutionary movement in that country. In 1981, Mexico and France issued the San José accord, which recognized the Salvadoran guerillas as a legitimate political force, and Mexico opened its territory to the members of the revolution's political front. Mexico also provided extensive economic and moral support to the Sandinistas in Nicaragua while the Reagan administration was supporting counter-revolutionary groups attempting to overthrow them.

Despite Mexico's spectacular growth in the late 1970s, however, Mexico's economy was becoming increasingly vulnerable.[54] First, oil exports were offset by increased imports. The rapid development of Mexico's petroleum generated a need for foreign technology to expand oil exploitation; imports also included machinery and other inputs for expanding industry. Consumer imports also grew, in part due to the growth of the domestic market and the inability of domestic industry to satisfy consumption needs. Buying sprees by upper and middle income Mexicans traveling to the United States added to the costs of imports. Mexico's trade deficit increased from $1.8 billion in 1979 to $5.4 billion in 1982 and to $14.4 billion in 1983.

A second factor in Mexico's external vulnerability was the fact that although Mexico had succeeded in diversifying its exports and increasing its industrial exports in the 1960s and early 1970s, Mexico now became increasingly dependent on the export of a single commodity. Oil exports increased from approximately 15 percent to 70 percent of total exports between 1976 and 1982, while the exports of manufactured goods stagnated in absolute terms and declined from 47 to 16 percent of the total. Thus Mexico's economic viability was closely tied to the international price and foreign market for oil.[55]

Third, dependence on foreign loans increased. Foreign banks were attracted by the discovery and development of Mexico's oil reserves. At the same time, Mexico needed foreign capital to develop its oil reserves and pay for industrial expansion. Mexico's foreign debt increased from approximately $28 billion in 1976 to $75 billion by 1981. (See Table 3-3) Most of this, $53 billion, was public sector debt. However, the foreign debt of the private sector, although lower, grew even more rapidly, from $1.8 billion to approximately $22 billion.[56] The cost of servicing foreign debt was a further drain on Mexico's current account balance.

Two additional factors aggravated Mexico's vulnerability. Inflation increased from an already high level of 30 percent in 1980 to 70 percent by 1982, cutting heavily into wage gains, and resulting in a significant decline in real wages. In addition, government efforts to maintain the exchange rate of the peso to the dollar meant that it was overvalued on the international market. This increased the cost of exports and decreased that of imports, with the effect of discouraging the former and encouraging the latter. In addition, fear of devaluation again led to capital flight into U.S. bank accounts and real estate markets.

The automobile industry demonstrates some of the problems confronting the Mexican economy. Foreign auto firms were required to obtain an increasing

Table 3-3. Factors in Economic Crisis: 1976–1981

YEAR	1976	1977	1978	1979	1980	1981
GDP (annual % change)	4.2	3.4	8.2	9.2	8.3	7.9
Fiscal Deficit as % of GDP	9.9	6.7	6.7	7.6	7.5	14.1
Total External Debt (billions of US dollars)	27.5	30.9	34.6	40.3	50.7	74.9
Total Public Debt (billions of US dollars)	20.8	22.9	26.3	29.8	33.8	50.3
Nominal U.S. Prime Rate	6.8	6.8	9.1	12.7	15.3	18.9
Share of Oil Exports in Total Exports (percent)	15.4	23.3	30.7	45.1	67.3	72.5
Current Account Balance (billions of US dollars)	-3.7	-1.6	-2.7	-4.9	-10.7	-16.1
Capital Flight (billions of US dollars)	3.0	0.9	0.1	0.02	-0.3	11.6

Source: Lustig, Nora Claudia. *Mexico: The Remaking of an Economy*, Second Edition. © 1998. Brookings Institution Press. Reprinted with permission.

proportion of their inputs from domestic suppliers and to increase exports of automobiles and auto parts to match and eventually exceed imports. However, with the rapid growth of the internal market as a consequence of the oil boom, automobile companies complained that Mexican suppliers were unable to keep up with the demand for inputs without increasing imports. Between 1977 and 1980, auto sales in the domestic market nearly doubled, from 286,725 units to 561,249; the import of automobile parts increased from $338 million to $937 million, while the exports of automobile parts stagnated at approximately $300 million. Automobile imports declined slightly but not sufficiently to make up for the increased imports of auto parts. The negative trade balance within the auto industry increased from $242 million to $822 million, a significant element in Mexico's overall balance of trade deficit.[57]

Two external factors transformed Mexico's economic vulnerability into a full-blown crisis. First, a substantial rise in U.S. interest rates—from 6.8 percent in 1977 to 18.9 percent in 1981—led to a drastic increase in the costs of loan repayment for Mexico and other countries that had borrowed heavily during this period. Second, a drop in the international price of oil in 1981 threatened the growth of earnings from Mexico's major export. Capital flight accelerated, reaching $11.6 billion in 1981.[58]

In August 1982, the government announced that Mexico would no longer be able to service its foreign debt. Given the heavy exposure of U.S. and European banks in Latin America, fear of a major crisis in international finance mobilized leading U.S. banks and central banks in the United States, Europe and Japan, which put together a series of loans to rescue Mexico (and subsequently other countries), as well as the financial system itself, from threatened collapse.

In the meantime, a study conducted by the government had revealed the dimensions of capital outflow, including $14 billion deposited in bank accounts in the United States and an additional $30 billion in U.S. real estate owned by Mexicans. Furious at what he termed a lack of patriotism on the part of financial groups, which he blamed for capital flight and accused of putting their interests above the welfare of the country, López Portillo announced the nationalization of the banks in his last State of the Union message on September 1, 1982. The bankers as well as the rest of the private sector were stunned by the announcement, particularly given the favorable treatment they had previously received from the López Portillo government.

But the move was broadly supported by popular sectors, including labor unions, peasant organizations, students, and some small- and medium-sized business groups. The banking establishment had the reputation of a powerful monopoly operating in the interests of a small number of wealthy families, concentrating loans, at low interest rates, among firms of their own respective groups and limiting the availability of credit to small and medium firms. The expropriation also represented a victory for nationalist groups within the state, who had been calling for bank nationalization and the establishment of exchange controls to control capital outflow and to facilitate the flow of financial resources to government priorities.

The apparent victory of the nationalist groups within the state and within the population would be short-lived, however. It was vigorously opposed by more orthodox economists within the government; the director of the Banco de Mexico resigned and the secretary of finance offered his resignation but López Portillo refused to accept it due to his importance in ongoing negotiations with the IMF, which demonstrated the weakness of Mexico's position as a result of the debt crisis. The IMF requested an end to exchange controls (introduced at the same time as bank nationalization) and a reduction of Mexico's budget deficit, from 17 percent in 1982 to 6 percent in 1983. The Mexican government argued for a reduction of the deficit to 14–15 percent. The final agreement was 8.5 percent in 1983, to be further reduced to 5.5 percent in 1984 and 3.5 percent in 1985. These reductions could only be achieved through drastic cutbacks in government spending, including the elimination of subsidies benefiting consumers and the private sector and the abolition of numerous government programs and services.

The repercussions from the economic crisis and austerity measures were devastating to the Mexican population. In 1982, an estimated one million workers lost their jobs as small and medium firms closed down or dismissed workers while the government eliminated over 100 agencies and programs.

Efforts of organized workers to obtain wage increases equal to the increase in the cost of living were frustrated. By the end of the year, radio and TV programs carried stories of poor urban and rural dwellers reduced to robbery to feed themselves and their families.

CONCLUSIONS

The political system that emerged from the violence and trauma of the Mexican revolution was a basically conservative regime, resistant to serious reform on behalf of the more disadvantaged population, but remarkable in the Latin American context for its political and economic stability and its legitimacy as an authoritarian regime that was also flexible and at least partly responsive to its constituents. This legitimacy rested in part on the genuine reforms of the immediate post-revolutionary period and the hopes engendered for the future by the continued use of revolutionary rhetoric, the frequent turnover of political office, and occasional examples of positive response to demands by constituent groups. It also benefitted from Mexico's economic growth, which brought significant sectors into the middle class.

The legitimacy of the Mexican state, its ability to control large sectors of the population through a sophisticated state-party apparatus that penetrated much of society, and the use of education and the media to advance the government's ideology and interpretation of events were major factors in its stability. At the same time, with few exceptions, the Mexican government was generally careful not to offend privileged economic groups, which exercised a powerful veto through their ability to withhold investment and to export capital, and which often enjoyed close ties with key government and political officials at various levels. These groups also benefitted from economic growth as well as tariff protection, tax breaks and subsidized inputs.

Following Mexico's conflicted relations with the United States in the 1920s and its affirmation of national sovereignty, particularly through the expropriation of U.S. and British oil companies, in the 1930s, Mexico collaborated with the United States during World War II, and relations in the post-war period were generally positive. Mexican policy makers conducted a dual policy, continuing to collaborate with the United States in domestic matters (e.g., efforts to remove Communist Party members from unions and other organizations) while frequently challenging its foreign policy—for example, in continuing to recognize Cuba following the revolution, and supporting the Central American revolutions during the 1980s. In the meantime, U.S. (and to a lesser extent European and Japanese) corporations, particularly in automotive and chemical industries, penetrated the Mexican market, in some cases establishing joint ventures with Mexican private groups. The United States continued to be Mexico's major trading partner as well as the major source of foreign capital.

Throughout this period various social and political actors sought to bring about reform: establishing independent parties, seeking union autonomy, or mobilizing guerrilla movements. For the most part, these groups were co-opted or repressed. The events of 1968, and the subsequent administrations of Echeverría and López Portillo, however, severely challenged the political and economic pillars of the system. The Tlatelolco massacre manifested the repressive nature of the regime, as did the subsequent repression during the 1970s. The Echeverría sexenio also demonstrated the difficulty of implementing significant reforms that threatened powerful interests, while that of López Portillo revealed the perils associated with economic dependence on foreign commodity markets, even for a strategic commodity such as oil. In both cases, foreign economic dependence grew, as the two administrations relied on foreign credit for their expansive projects, and the foreign debt skyrocketed.

In Mexico as in other Latin American countries, the debt crisis ushered in what became known as the lost decade, a period of stagnating or declining growth rates and painful adjustments as countries struggled to stabilize their economies. It also marked the end of the ISI model and its replacement by a radically different economic system. Political change would come more gradually, responding in part to the mobilization of those groups that had been marginalized or victimized by the political and economic system.

CHAPTER 4

Reorienting Mexico's Economy: The Process of Economic Liberalization

INTRODUCTION

Beginning in the mid-1980s, Mexico entered a period of rapid and profound economic transition. From an import substitution industrialization (ISI) model oriented primarily to production for the domestic market, Mexico shifted to an emphasis on production for export. From a highly regulated, mixed economy with a growing sector of state-owned firms, it moved to an open market economy dominated by private capital. From an emphasis on national control of productive resources, it became increasingly open to foreign investment. This transition involved not only a break with the previous model of economic development but also an implicit rejection of many of the principles of the Mexican revolution that had informed the ideology, if not always the practice, of the government party and the state. It involved a substantial restructuring of the state and of its relations with different groups in Mexican society and has had important implications for the welfare of Mexico's population.

This Chapter seeks to explain these changes and their consequences. The next section outlines the international and domestic context within which this transition occurred. It discusses why these changes took place, who supported them, and why. The following section examines the trajectory of change, focusing on economic stabilization and restructuring during the administrations of Miguel de la Madrid (1982–1988) and Carlos Salinas de Gortari (1988–1994), and assesses its effect. The subsequent section looks at events leading up to the peso crisis of 1994, its impact, and efforts to respond to it. The concluding section briefly summarizes some of the implications of these changes.

CHANGING CONTEXT/SHIFTING ALLIANCES

What led Mexican policy makers to embark on such a dramatic restructuring of the economy? What groups favored these changes, which ones opposed them, and why? To understand the causes of economic changes it is necessary to examine both the international context and factors specific to Mexico.

International Context

Changes in international economic conditions over the past three decades are often summarized in the concept of globalization, or economic globalization.[1] In many respects, globalization can be seen as a continuation, or a new stage, of a centuries-long process of the internationalization of capital, whereby capitalist firms, generally with the assistance of their respective states, moved into different regions and countries in an effort to maximize profits through control of natural resources, access to markets, or the availability of cheap labor. This process was non-linear, with periods of growth and expansion followed by contraction, or de-globalization, during recessions.

Over the past few decades, however, technological advances, particularly the accelerated development of transportation, communications and information technology, have greatly facilitated cross-border capital flows and international financial transactions. One result has been the outsourcing of different phases of production and their integration at an international, rather than simply a local or national, level. Individuals, banks, and other institutions with access to mobile capital—capital that is not tied into ownership of fixed assets such as real estate, factories, farms, etc.—can shift these resources to stocks, bonds, and other financial assets in other countries wherever they anticipate a higher return, with increasing ease and rapidity. And corporations can disperse various phases of production and marketing to different parts of the world on the basis of such factors as reduced labor costs, minimal regulation, or greater proximity to markets.[2]

To take advantage of these conditions, banks and other financial institutions as well as manufacturers interested in outsourcing production push for the elimination of any barriers or restrictions to capital flows or trade between countries. In the case of Latin America, while U.S. and other foreign corporations investing in Latin America had been able to take advantage of tariff protection during the ISI phase of production for the internal market, they became increasingly interested in being able to freely transport capital, products, supplies, equipment and other inputs across borders without tariffs and other restrictions, in keeping with the integration of an internationally based production strategy.

By the 1970s, and particularly the 1980s, international lending agencies such as the International Monetary Fund and the World Bank, as well as some

Western governments (most notably, the Thatcher government in England and the Reagan administration in the United States) were promoting an ideological shift toward economic liberalism and the reduction of the state role in economic intervention.[3] Economic liberalism, often referred to as neoliberalism,[4] calls for "the maximization of entrepreneurial freedom within an institutional framework characterized by private property rights, individual liberties, unencumbered markets, and free trade."[5] The role of the state is generally limited to establishing and conserving this framework and creating markets where they don't exist. The process of liberalization, therefore, involves the removal of any restrictions on the market, including barriers to trade or to capital flows as well as other forms of government intervention in the economy.

The orientation toward economic liberalism, which was later reinforced by the collapse of state-centered regimes in Eastern Europe and the Soviet Union, has been summarized in what became known as the Washington Consensus, linking U.S. government officials and economic agencies, international lending institutions, and think tanks. These agencies agreed on a series of conditions for loans to Latin American debtor countries, among them the elimination of government subsidies, the privatization of state-owned assets, deregulation, and trade liberalization.[6] The Latin American debt crisis gave considerable leverage to international lending agencies such as the IMF and the World Bank, which by the middle of the 1980s had shifted their primary focus from monetary stability and development lending, respectively, to making loans conditioned on fulfilling requirements for economic liberalization, often referred to as structural adjustment programs.[7]

Domestic Conditions

While changing international conditions, and the pressures of foreign governments and international institutions in the context of the debt crisis, were significant factors in Mexico's economic transition, internal conditions were also important. First was the economic crisis itself, which led to extended debate in Mexico and elsewhere regarding the future direction of the economy. Proponents of neoliberalism blamed the crisis experienced by Mexico and other Latin American countries on the ISI model, claiming that it was either problematic to begin with or no longer viable, and called for a shift toward an open model oriented to export with minimum state involvement. They pointed to the corruption and waste resulting from state intervention and particularly from state ownership, as well as the heavy and often arbitrary restrictions policy makers placed on various transactions including trade, investment, and financial activities which, they argued, undermined private sector initiative. A particular problem was rent-seeking, whereby private interests tended to seek advantage and maximize profits through concessions from the state (e.g., tax exemptions, subsidized inputs, tariff protection) rather than through production of goods and services in a competitive market.[8] Other analysts, while acknowledging some of the problems of excessive state intervention, believed that adjustments could be made to the existing model, which provided for expanding and upgrading production to expand exports; that some countries, such as Mexico and Brazil, had indeed begun to export manufactured products by the 1970s; and that these countries had established a firm industrial base under the ISI regime.[9]

Differences within the Mexican state were resolved with a shift in the balance of power within the government and the PRI, from a division of positions between the political and technical groups (*políticos* and *técnicos*) to the dominance of the técnicos, or what is sometimes referred to as a new techno-bureaucracy. As noted in Chapter 3, formerly the políticos had generally progressed through the electoral system and had controlled the presidency and certain ministries such as the Interior, while the técnicos were dominant in the Finance Ministry, the Banco de Mexico, and, after its creation in 1976, the Ministry of Budget and Planning.

This began to change with José López Portillo, who selected Miguel de la Madrid Hurtado—who had received an M.A. from Harvard University—as the PRI candidate for the presidency, reflecting a growing concern regarding economic issues and problems. Two earlier developments influenced these changes. First, while those holding economic positions within the government had consistently been influenced by Western economic trends, and some officials had been educated abroad, they had generally studied in England and in other countries of Europe where Keynesianism and notions of state-guided development were still in vogue and had sought to adapt foreign ideas to Mexican reality. Increasingly, however, young economists went to universities in the United States, where orthodox neoclassical economic theories were presumed to have universal applicability.[10] Second, the government of Echeverría (1970–76) significantly expanded the opportunity for young economists to study abroad through the creation of CONACYT, the National Council of Science and Technology, which funded hundreds of these scholars.

In addition to their training in classical economics, young Mexican economists often developed contacts with U.S. economists who held key positions in U.S. and international financial institutions. Upon their return to Mexico, these young technocrats were quickly recruited into economic positions with the government and with the administrations of Miguel de la Madrid (1982–88) and Carlos Salinas de Gortari (1988–94); they became dominant within the state. In the Salinas administration, Salinas himself had received an M.A. in Public Administration, and an M.A. and a Ph.D. in Economics at Harvard; Pedro Aspe, Secretary of Finance, had a Ph.D. from MIT; Emilio Lozoya, Secretary of Energy and Mines, received a degree in Public Administration at Harvard; Ernesto

Zedillo, secretary of Education (and later president), had a Ph.D. from Yale, as did Jaime Serra Puche, secretary of Commerce and chief NAFTA negotiator. Educated in the same universities and even under the same instructors as their U.S. counterparts, they shared a free market, internationalist approach to economics and developed contacts that would be important in their future transactions with foreign governments, multinational corporations, and international lending agencies.[11]

In what has been termed the "orthodox paradox," analysts of economic reform in Mexico and other countries have recognized that in order to implement reforms that would diminish the economic role of the state, the state, and particularly a cohesive executive that is able to insulate itself from pressures by political and societal groups opposed to liberalization, continues to have an important role. In the case of Mexico, the hegemony and corporate structure of the governing party, the concentration of government power in the presidency, and the role of the camarilla in ensuring the loyalty and cohesion of the governing team, were among the factors that enabled the technocratic faction to prevail against considerable opposition within the party, certain sectors of the state bureaucracy, and the population at large.[12]

But while the role of Mexico's techno-bureaucracy was critical, business groups also had an important indirect and direct influence on economic change. Business groups, particularly those with substantial economic resources and access to international markets, had the option to cut back production and export their capital when they felt threatened by government policies. As noted in Chapter 3, a significant factor in the Mexican economic crisis had been the export of capital by domestic and international investors.

Furthermore, bank nationalization had deepened business distrust of the Mexican state and further undermined the informal partnership between the state and business, already damaged as a result of the statist and nationalist initiatives of the Echeverría regime. Capital flight continued during the first years of the de la Madrid administration. Given the economic debacle and their political distrust of the government, investors were hardly anxious to invest in Mexico. By the same token, the Mexican government was desperate to attract foreign capital to the country and draw back domestic-flight capital, and needed to rebuild trust with the private sector—a concern which helps to explain why the government was not only willing to implement neoliberal reforms, but also in some instances to go beyond the requirements of international financial institutions. The government also took over much of the foreign debt of the private sector, which particularly benefited the large economic groups.[13]

The economic crisis strengthened the independent, market-oriented business groups centered in Monterrey relative to those businesses heavily dependent on government contracts and subsidies that had been considerably reduced as a result of the debt crisis and the cutback in government expenditures. In addition, manufacturing had become increasingly decentralized during the 1970s, as several firms in Mexico City began to shift production to other parts of the country to take advantage of lower wages. And economic growth had led to the emergence of new middle-level entrepreneurs in north and northwestern Mexico and other regional centers, which differed from traditional businesses in their free market orientation as well as their political activism. Several had been active in local business chambers and local and state politics and by the 1980s had obtained leadership positions in several national business organizations. As will be discussed further in Chapter 5, many of the more established economic groups as well as the new regional business interests became active in the PAN, at that time the principal opposition party.

Many of the new businesses already exported and/or had contracts with foreign, especially U.S., firms. Some of the more established economic groups benefited from their diverse holdings as well as their existing relations with foreign corporations and had also begun to export during the 1970s, often through joint ventures with foreign firms. Thus, while many within the private sector had benefited from protectionism, state subsidies, and other benefits of the ISI model, a substantial number of business leaders were prepared for—and in some cases actively pushing for—a more open economy, and certainly one in which the discretionary power of the state was reduced.[14]

Although suspicious of government action and often supporting the political opposition, business groups also pushed to take a more active role in the formulation of policy. For example, beginning in 1985 a small group of Mexican businessmen from Monterrey held regular meetings with President de la Madrid and submitted draft reform proposals to the Finance Ministry and other government agencies. Business relations with the government also improved as a result of the incorporation of representatives of the major economic groups in negotiations with the corporate sector of labor for wage-price controls in the late 1970s. Relations continued to improve under Salinas, who, in an unprecedented move, incorporated a major business leader, Claudio X. Gonzalez, president of Kimberly Clark de Mexico and head of the CCE (Business Coordinating Council) between 1985 and 1987, as an economic advisor. Throughout the 1980s business groups within the CCE and the CMHN (Mexican Council of Businessmen, an organization of Mexico's most powerful entrepreneurs) worked closely with the new techno-bureaucracy within the government and foreign creditors in reforms to open the economy and reduce the economic role of the state.[15]

Thus the new techno-bureaucracy was able to reconstruct and formalize an alliance with major economic groups and new export groups, many of whom would benefit from the neoliberal reforms of the 1980s and 1990s. At the same time, it succeeded in co-opting or neutralizing opposition to economic reforms. Ironically, a major instrument in this process was the corporatist party system, which was considerably weakened by the economic changes taking place. In effect, economic restructuring also involved a restructuring of state-society relations, from a balance between informal state-business relations and corporatist state-party relations with popular sectors, to a strengthening of ties between the state, major business groups, and foreign investors; while the corporatist sector, increasingly unable to deliver benefits, was largely limited to exercising control over its constituents.[16]

ECONOMIC STABILIZATION AND RESTRUCTURING: 1982–1994

The administration of Miguel de la Madrid marked the beginning of what would be a definitive transition from the state-guided ISI model to an open market, export-oriented model, although this was not immediately apparent.[17] What did become clear very quickly was that the new administration would represent a break with the nationalist and populist orientation of the last months of the López Portillo government. One immediate concern was to deal with the fallout from bank nationalization. Although de la Madrid did not try to undo the nationalization, which in fact had been reinforced by a constitutional amendment, the government provided substantial compensation to former bank owners and sold off one-third of the commercial bank shares. It also returned the firms that had been owned by the expropriated banks, and thus included in the expropriation, to the previous owners. In addition, the bankers were able to re-obtain possession of auxiliary financial services, including investment banks and brokerage firms, which subsequently led to the emergence of a private banking system parallel to that controlled by the state and the basis for the establishment or reconstitution of several economic groups.

Negotiations with the IMF and foreign banks to service Mexico's debt, initiated during the administration of José López Portillo, continued throughout the decade and were often acrimonious. Agreements with the International Monetary Fund (IMF) necessary to restructure debt payments (which would have totaled 62 percent of export earnings in 1982) were contingent upon measures to stabilize and restructure Mexico's economy. Following agreement with the IMF, foreign banks provided loans to enable Mexico to continue to service its debt, but they were not sufficient to relieve the international constraints Mexico confronted or to aid its economic recovery. The economy remained in a deep recession throughout most of the decade. GDP growth, which had reached 8.5 percent in 1981, stagnated throughout the rest of the 1980s and was negative in some years.

Opposition groups as well as some officials within the government called for Mexico to take a stronger stand against the demands of the IMF and foreign bankers, including a unilateral moratorium, or a moratorium in conjunction with other Latin American countries. But the governments of the major debtor countries were unable to come to agreement. Finally, renegotiations in 1989–1990 resulted in an agreement based on the Brady Plan (named for the U.S. Treasury Secretary), conditioned on Mexico's continued economic restructuring, which reduced the debt and enabled Mexico to re-enter international financial markets. This, in turn was critical in restoring investor confidence.

In keeping with the requirements of the international lending agencies as well as efforts to resolve the economic crisis and to restore favorable relations with the domestic private sector, the process of economic liberalization began under Miguel de la Madrid and accelerated in the subsequent administration of Carlos Salinas, who as Secretary of Budget and Planning had been the major architect of the reforms in the de la Madrid administration. The reforms for the most part followed the criteria outlined in the Washington Consensus and in some respects went beyond the demands of the IMF and the World Bank. The rapidity and extent of the reforms process can be explained by a combination of factors, including the further concentration of political control within the government by the president and a small number of officials in key ministries, the close collaboration of policy makers with owners and representatives of Mexico's major conglomerates and business groups, and the marginalization of groups and interests opposed to reforms. The latter included small and medium businesses in CANACINTRA oriented to the domestic market and those large businesses dependent on the state as well as labor and other popular sectors, a process that was facilitated by the control exercised by the state and the governing party.

Monetary Stabilization

Initial reforms by the de la Madrid government focused on efforts to control inflation, which was nearly 100 percent by 1982 and 150 percent by the middle of the decade, particularly by reducing budget deficits and stabilizing the peso. Deficit reduction was based largely on cutbacks in government spending (which now included the added burden of debt servicing). Public investment, notably in industry, rural development and energy, was reduced by as much as 87 percent between 1982 and 1991. Expenditures on health and education, while they increased in relative terms, declined in real terms—by 23.3 percent and 29.6 percent, respectively, between 1983 and 1988. Per capita social spending was down by 40.2 percent. The indexation of wages at a lower rate than inflation, which continued to be high throughout the decade, also resulted in a significant decline in real wages.[18]

Beginning in 1987 the government negotiated a series of pacts with representatives of business and labor that included wage and price controls, among other measures, and finally resulted in reducing inflation, which had reached 159 percent in 1987, to 8 percent in 1993. The fiscal deficit was reduced and in certain years there was a surplus in the primary budget (revenues minus expenditures, excluding interest payments). The devaluation of the peso helped to stabilize the exchange rate, although the peso again began to be overvalued in the early 1990s.

Trade Liberalization

Trade liberalization was a central feature of the neoliberal strategy.[19] According to those pushing economic reforms, trade liberalization would eliminate inefficiencies resulting from excessive protection and would expand markets for exports. Exporters would benefit from greater access to foreign technology and other inputs. Trade liberalization would also benefit consumers through the import of commodities at relatively lower prices and/or higher quality than heavily protected domestic goods. A turning point in Mexico's trade regime was the decision to join GATT, the General Agreement on Tariffs and Trade, in 1986. GATT had been established in 1948 for the purpose of gradually eliminating barriers to free trade among countries of the world; as of 1995, 100 countries were members. Previously, Mexico had rejected membership in GATT, which was strongly opposed by pro-protectionist groups within the PRI and the government as well as business groups dependent on the state. But by the mid-1980s, the pro-reform techno-bureaucracy was dominant within the state. Tariffs and other import controls were rapidly reduced. Until 1985, importers in Mexico had been obliged to obtain licenses for 90 percent of domestic production; the maximum tariff was 100 percent. By December 1989, import licenses were required for only 20 percent of domestic production; and the maximum tariff was 20 percent for all but a few imports—well below the GATT requirement of 50 percent. By the early 1990s the average tariff had been reduced to 4 percent.

The reforms were favored by foreign corporations, which preferred to obtain their supplies for production in Mexico from their home companies through intra-industry trade rather than rely on domestically produced inputs. As noted above, the large domestic conglomerates oriented to international markets generally supported them as well. Through joint investment with foreign firms, and access to funds from the parallel financial system, domestic firms that were part of these conglomerates had a competitive advantage over smaller, less well-connected firms, and some were already exporting. The reduction of tariffs and restrictive import licenses would facilitate the import of foreign technology and other inputs for their industries.

But trade liberalization was devastating for many of the small and medium firms producing for the domestic market, which lacked the resources and access to foreign capital and technology needed to become more efficient and competitive. Trade liberalization led to an increase in low-cost imports, and while consumers benefited, traditional firms in such areas as textiles, shoes, toys and furniture, unable to compete, were forced to close down or in some cases shift from manufacturing to import, in both cases resulting in substantial job loss. Various reports indicated that 2,400 furniture firms disappeared between 1985 and 1993; in 1992 alone an estimated 10 percent of shoe manufacturers shut down; employment in textile manufacturing dropped by 50 percent between 1989 and 1991, and 30 percent of Mexico's toy industries shut down in roughly the same period.[20]

According to some industrialists, the problem was not simply trade liberalization itself, but the way it was done. As described by the Bernardo Navarro, at that time the head of the Chamber of Electronic Industries, "There was no way to plan for the opening because we had no warning. Not only did the regime move without consulting the official representative organizations of industry and business, but these chambers and associations were not even given advance notice of what was to come . . . We would have been able to offer some suggestions on how to phase in an open economy without destroying a whole industry . . . If we take the twenty-five thousand jobs that were lost in the electronics industry plus all the jobs that have been lost in other manufacturing industries . . . this adds up to a very large number of people with nothing to eat."[21]

Privatization

A second major change has been Mexico's shift from a mixed economy with extensive state control of strategic and even non-strategic industries to a market economy based more exclusively on private enterprise in which state ownership has been substantially reduced.[22] Privatization was seen as a means to reduce the corruption, waste and inefficiency that was associated with state intervention and public enterprises; privatization would also reduce the drain on the government budget resulting from shoring up non-profitable firms and would attract investment funds from foreign investors as well as domestic groups. The process, more broadly called disinvestment, involved liquidation, particularly of poorly performing firms, mergers, and transfers (often to state or local governments, or in some cases employees), but the most important firms were sold to private groups.

Disinvestment began gradually under the de la Madrid administration, focusing primarily on small firms and less strategic industries, and accelerated during the Salinas administration. Ironically, the reduction of state ownership and control required substantial government intervention. To facilitate privatization, de la Madrid and Salinas initiated a number of measures to centralize control in the Finance Ministry, marginalizing those ministries with a vested interest in retaining parastatal firms. Between 1982 and 2000, the major mining and steel companies, the telecommunications system, banks, airlines, and television channels passed from the public to the private sector. The number of state enterprises was reduced from 1,555 to 202. Their share of the revenue of the top 50 firms in Mexico dropped from 72 to 21 percent of the total between 1984 and 1999, while that of private Mexican firms jumped from 18 percent to 56 percent and that of foreign firms increased from 11 percent to 23 percent.

Privatization entailed substantial restructuring of public firms to meet criteria of efficiency and rationality necessary to make them attractive to private owners—ironically achieving one of the alleged benefits of private ownership *before* they passed into private hands. Worker resistance to this process, which often involved laying-off workers and abrogating contracts, was effectively–sometimes brutally–suppressed. The government often provided additional incentives to attract foreign and domestic investors.

The most important public firms were sold in the form of large sections of shares to the highest bidder. Since a major goal of the government was to raise funds, the prices were set high, in some cases considerably higher than the book value of the firm. Given the costs involved, only the largest firms and dominant economic groups could participate, and often they were obliged to join with other groups, particularly foreign companies, and/or borrow heavily, in order to raise sufficient capital.[23] At the same time, the government provided various incentives to would-be buyers, including measures to limit competition. The rationale was that only large investors with considerable resources would be in a position to take responsibility for the firms and carry out needed and agreed upon investment. The effect, however, was often to transform public monopolies into private monopolies or oligopolies.

The largest single sale was that of Telmex, the giant communications firm, which was given a monopoly of long-distance telephone services until 1996. In return, Telmex was expected to carry out a series of measures to expand telephone service and to improve its quality. The government also streamlined the existing labor contract to increase management control of the work process, although in contrast to other privatizations this was achieved through negotiation with the Telephone Workers Union (STRM) in return for a promise to maintain current employment (although workers could be redeployed) and giving workers shares in the newly privatized firm.

Controlling interest in Telmex (51 percent) was sold in three parts, totaling $6.3 billion. The privatization plan also limited the number of voting shares and limited foreign ownership of these shares to 49 percent, thus ensuring Mexican control. The major sale (of 51 percent of voting shares, 20.4 percent of total stock) was to an investment group headed by Carlos Slim of Grupo Carso and including Southwestern Bell and France Cable and Radio. During the economic crisis and recession of the 1980s, Carlos Slim, along with other investors, had been able to buy up controlling interest in companies at a relatively cheap rate. Slim, a close associate of President Salinas, became the wealthiest man in Mexico (and today one of the three wealthiest men in the world), and Telmex quickly became the largest firm in the Mexican stock market. The value of its stocks soared from $1 billion to $30 billion between 1988 and 1992. Southwestern Bell's profits from Telmex in 1991 exceeded those from all of its U.S. operations.

The privatization of state-owned firms resulted in a one-time windfall of over $20 billion for the Mexican government, most of which was used to pay off the debt. At the same time, it led to monopolies in sectors such as telecommunications, and concentration of assets, notably in the banking sector. In just over a year, in 1991 and 1992, the government sold the 18 nationalized banks for a total of $12.4 billion. The buyers included some of the previous bank owners and especially economic groups that benefited from the creation of alternative financial channels in the 1980s. As of mid-1993, three bank-brokerage groups controlled 29 percent of GDP. The four largest banks controlled 70 percent of bank assets.[24] In short, privatization reinforced monopoly or oligopoly control in banking, telecommunications, and other areas, and resulted in an enormous cost to consumers, as buyers of privatized firms sought to recoup their investment by charging high prices or interest rates.[25]

Deregulation

Throughout this period, measures were enacted to decrease and/or rationalize state regulation of the economy. Price controls were eliminated in certain sectors and reduced in others. The Salinas government established an office for deregulation in the Ministry of Trade and Industrial Development to respond to business complaints regarding price controls and excessive bureaucratic red tape in obtaining import licenses and business permits. The extensive discretionary powers of the state as well as bureaucratic delays were reduced (although not eliminated).[26]

As a necessary condition for divestiture and privatization, a series of measures provided for the classification or re-classification of certain state-owned enterprises as non-strategic (and therefore available for privatization) as well as the redefinition of certain operations *within* strategic industries as non-strategic. A constitutional amendment was approved to permit re-privatization of the banks, and the petrochemical firms within PEMEX (which was off-limits to privatization given its historic and symbolic importance for Mexico's revolutionary ideology) were divided between basic and secondary petrochemicals, with the latter open to private investment.

The privatization of the banks was preceded by a series of reforms that among other measures reduced the reserve requirements from 90 to 30 percent of deposits. Taking advantage of their access to foreign financial markets, the banks contracted dollar loans, which were then used to provide loans in pesos at higher rates. The lack of government oversight was also an important factor in high-risk lending, with minimal checks on the credit-worthiness of borrowers.

Several other measures liberalized conditions for foreign investment, including opening up certain sectors to 100 percent foreign ownership; permitting foreign investment in Mexico's stock exchange, which grew rapidly in the late 1980s and early 1990s; and reducing or eliminating certain performance criteria, such as local content requirements, for foreign investors. In addition, following pressures from the United States, which was dissatisfied with Mexico's intellectual property rights provision, Mexico passed a copyright law in 1991 that gave copyright owners exclusive rights to reproduction and distribution for a period of 50 years.[27] Similar to privatization and trade liberalization, these measures were in keeping with the government's goal of placating the private sector (through simplifying bureaucratic procedures and reducing regulations in such sectors in banking) and attracting both domestic and foreign investment (by opening up strategic state-owned sectors to privatization, liberalizing requirements for foreign investment, and protecting intellectual property rights). They demonstrate the fundamental shift from the economic nationalism of the ISI period, oriented to protecting the domestic private sector and the national economy in general from external control (through such requirements as Mexicanization—majority Mexican ownership—and performance criteria) to the reduction of state economic control and intervention and the abdication of the state role in investment in strategic sectors.

The "Flexibilization" of Labor

The economic crisis, neoliberal reforms, and deliberate government policies significantly reduced the power of organized labor and had a devastating effect on workers in the formal sector.[28] In the context of the recession resulting from the economic crises of the 1980s, many firms were forced to close down or reduce their workforce. Trade liberalization led to bankruptcies among small and medium firms oriented to the domestic market that were unable to compete with cheaper imports. Privatization was often preceded or followed by layoffs of workers. With trade liberalization, over half of the small and medium manufacturing firms disappeared between 1988 and 1993, resulting in the elimination of 43,000 jobs, and thousands of jobs were lost in the state sector between 1983 and 1993, particularly in those firms slated for privatization. Because of inflation, real wages were reduced to between 40 and 60 percent of their pre-crisis value by 1988. Wage reduction was also part of a deliberate policy to attract investment on the basis of cheap labor.

Members of the private sector and the government saw the corporate union structure and the control exercised by unions over the workplace as obstacles to economic restructuring. Central to the restructuring process is the "flexibiliza-tion" of labor: the ability of companies to hire and fire workers as deemed necessary, to exclude certain workers from unionization by classifying their jobs as posts of *confianza* (trust) or ideally to do away with unions altogether, to employ (and dismiss) temporary workers as needed and to shift from full-time to part-time workers, and to promote workers on the basis of training or compe-tition rather than seniority.

Flexibilization in effect contradicted prerogatives won and exercised by unions in many enterprises and required changes in collective contracts. When workers tried to resist these changes, owners responded by such measures as declaring the firm bankrupt, dismissing workers, and reopening the firm on the basis of a new contract that eliminated clauses seen as detrimental to reform. For example, when workers at Ford Cuautitlán suspended work after management refused to grant an emergency wage increase authorized by the government and granted to workers at other Ford plants in Mexico, the managers fired the labor force, closed the plant, and rehired 2,500 of the original workers at terms favor-able to management, with the acquiescence of the CTM union. When workers continued to struggle to restore previous benefits and staged a work stoppage in January 1990, two hundred CTM strike-breakers attacked, resulting in the death of one worker and the wounding of nine others.[29]

The government also used its control over labor boards to refuse recogni-tion of dissident unions, to prevent strikes, and to side with employers in labor disputes. With some exceptions, corporate labor leaders, unable to deliver ben-efits to unionized workers as in the past and fearing militancy among the rank and file that might threaten their own position, collaborated in government efforts to control workers, in some cases brutally suppressing worker resistance, as the above case demonstrates. Corporatist union leaders also signed "protec-tion contracts" with management, forming "ghost unions" without the consent, or even the knowledge, of the firm's workers. Workers who attempted to orga-nize independent unions were fired and even blacklisted. The decentralization of production from Mexico City to other parts of the country, beginning in the 1970s; as well as the shift from permanent, full-time jobs to temporary and/or part-time positions; and frequent job turnover or rotation (particularly among the *maquiladoras* of northern Mexico, discussed later) in the 1980s and 1990s, also undermined labor organizing.

The Modernization of the Countryside

Measures to stabilize Mexico's finances and restructure the economy have had a major direct and indirect impact on the Mexican rural sector. Efforts to reduce the budget deficit under the de la Madrid administration included substantial cutbacks in programs of rural assistance, which were reduced from 11.7 percent to 6.4 percent of public spending between 1980 and 1987. The Mexican Food System program (SAM), an ambitious effort to make Mexico self-sufficient in basic food production, was eliminated. The budget of the Agriculture and Livestock ministry was cut by approximately 70 percent. During the 1980s and 1990s, rural credit programs, agricultural subsidies, and rural extension programs were eliminated or drastically cut.[30] In addition to these measures, reduction in trade protection for agricultural products also undercut domestic producers.

As in other sectors, the Salinas administration moved aggressively to modernize the agrarian sector, particularly the ejidal program. To some extent these reforms responded to long-term problems in the ejidal sector, among them corrupt ejidal authorities, illegal renting to private groups, boundary and ownership disputes, and the excessive intervention and corruption of government bureaucracies, which had been the target of frequent peasant mobilizations.[31] However, the Salinas reforms were primarily motivated by low levels of productivity in the rural area, which employed 22 percent of the labor force but contributed only 5 percent to the GDP.[32] The strategy entailed a re-conceptualization of food security from self-sufficiency in food production to concentration of resources on those products in which Mexico enjoyed a comparative advantage in exports, such as fruits, vegetables, coffee and sugar, while importing basic food products for domestic consumption. Central to this conception was the assumption, as expressed by the Under-Secretary of Agriculture, that poor farmers and peasants were a "dead weight on society" who should find work in better paid activities and leave agricultural production "to those who have what it takes to make it profitable and dynamic."[33]

The most dramatic initiative was the government's decision to end land distribution and permit the privatization of ejidal lands through a new Agrarian Law, enacted in 1992. Ejidal members could obtain individual certificates of title to their land, subject to approval by the ejidal assembly; the land could then be legally sold, rented or mortgaged. The expectation was that ejidatarios would sell their land or form associations with private investors (including foreign investors, who would be permitted ownership of up to 49 percent), resulting in a more rational use of the land.[34] Not only was this a devastating blow to landless or land-poor peasants who still had hopes of benefiting from land distribution, but an assault on one of the basic principles of the revolution.

The ejidal reform did not meet expectations. Many ejidatarios have been unwilling to alienate their land, even if its cultivation is not their major economic activity, since it offers a means of subsistence and thus a certain level of security in a situation in which other sources of income (such as labor on export-oriented farms in Mexico, or on U.S. farms) are low-wage and unstable. Other reasons may be historical factors, including long-term struggles for land, as well as shared cultural values and social ties.[35] By the same token, few investors were interested in ejidal land, which is often of poor quality and lacks the necessary infrastructure and other technological inputs to make it more productive.[36]

How have rural households coped with these changes? As indicated above, and contrary to expectations, many rural families did not abandon the land, even though its contribution to household income has been substantially reduced. For the most part, they have coped by further diversification of their sources of income and through an increase in the number of household members engaged in income-generating activities, notably women. In addition to farming, sources of income include wage labor, either in the rural sector or through migration to urban areas; self-employment in small-scale production (such as prepared food or crafts) which may be sold locally or in urban centers, small commercial establishments or providing services (such as sewing); and increasingly, through migration to the United States, with remittance income directed to basic consumption and/or invested in production (e.g., for starting a small business or purchasing livestock).[37]

In addition to individual solutions, members of some ejidos and communities have been able to draw on social networks and shared experiences in organizing and mobilizing to improve their conditions. In several ejidos, women's groups organized to collaborate with government programs in providing health, education, and nutritional meals for children. In the mid-1990s, local and regional peasant organizations collaborated to form ANEC, the National Association of Commercial Farming Companies, to market their produce. Another association, Comagro, formed by peasant organizations in the state of Jalisco, sells their corn to the food industry and provides distribution channels for Mitsibushi for fertilizer and other agricultural inputs for its membership.[38]

The endurance of peasant communities, in spite of government policies predicated on their demise, indicates their attachment to the land and their resiliency and creativity in coping with a deteriorating policy context. Through a combination of individual and collective initiatives, they have diversified their sources of income, organized to improve the conditions of their families and communities, and joined forces to facilitate access to market and agricultural inputs. The costs have been enormous, including the separation of families as a result of migration. Some households and communities have managed to improve their conditions, but others are barely surviving.[39]

The North American Free Trade Agreement

The culmination of the Salinas government's ambitious program of economic restructuring was the North American Free Trade Agreement (NAFTA) between Canada, Mexico and the United States, which went into effect in 1994.[40] Its purpose was to gradually eliminate tariffs and other barriers to trade between the three countries over a period of 15 years, in effect creating a single market. The advantage to U.S., Canadian and Mexican investors, and to a lesser extent other investors, was the ability to take advantage of relatively low wages to invest in Mexico, at the same time enjoying unrestricted access through trade to the lucrative U.S. market. Mexico would presumably benefit from the inflow of foreign investment, job creation, and increased export earnings. Because NAFTA incorporated rules of origin, non-NAFTA investors wishing to take advantage of unrestricted access to the North American market would have to produce a certain proportion of the inputs to their industries in the three member countries.[41] Given its low labor costs, Mexico could be expected to be the primary beneficiary.

NAFTA differed from previous regional free trade agreements as an agreement between two advanced industrial societies and a relatively poor, semi-industrial country. Although the European Community (EC), even prior to its incorporation of the Eastern European countries, included less industrialized countries, the difference between the United States and Canada, two of the wealthiest countries of the world, and Mexico was much greater. As of 1988, Mexico's GNP per capita was $1,760, while that of the United States was $20,000. Mexico was dependent on the United States for approximately 75 percent of its trade, while trade with Mexico represented only 4 to 7 percent of U.S. trade. In the past, Mexico had consistently rejected the possibility of a free trade agreement with the United States due to fear of U.S. domination. So why did the Salinas government take the initiative to begin negotiations in the 1990s?

One factor was undoubtedly the continued fallout from the economic crisis. Investment continued to be sluggish throughout the 1980s and government officials believed it was imperative to attract foreign capital.[42] Direct foreign investment was also essential for the technological advancement of Mexico's industries to enable them to compete internationally, given the context of globalization and Mexico's export orientation. Similar to his predecessors, however, Salinas had initially hoped to diversify Mexico's economic relations with other parts of the world rather than deepening dependence on the United States. During the 1970s and 1980s, European countries had indicated an increased interest in relations with Mexico and other Latin American countries. This had also been a period of substantial economic growth and international expansion on the part of Japan. However, with the changes in the Eastern European countries and the collapse of the Soviet Union in the late 1980s, the economic interests of the Western European countries shifted to East Europe. It also became evident that Japan was interested in Mexico chiefly as a conduit to the U.S. market.[43]

A second factor was the fear on the part of the Salinas administration that subsequent governments might attempt to undo its economic reforms. NAFTA would have the effect of institutionalizing the economic changes, making it difficult if not impossible for future governments to reverse the process of economic liberalization. This concern coincided with an aim of the U.S. negotiators to ensure that Mexico would maintain economic conditions favorable to U.S. trade and investment.

Since the United States and Canada had already established a free trade agreement, negotiations focused on issues involved in incorporating Mexico. The negotiations were characterized by two basic asymmetries. The first, mentioned above, was the sharp distinction in Mexico's level of development compared to the other two countries. Despite this disparity, NAFTA did not incorporate measures to compensate Mexico through a social policy or development funds.[44] This contrasts with the negotiations of the European Union, which incorporated a social policy component that provided funds for infrastructure and social development for the less advanced countries of Southern Europe (and later Eastern Europe), a difference that reflects the distinct histories and ideologies of the North American countries compared to those of Europe. Many of the EU countries have historically been characterized by a social democratic or welfare orientation in which the state has a prominent role in ensuring a basic level of welfare and addressing the economic disparities that result from the action of the market. In contrast, the North Americans negotiators, including the Mexicans, many of them trained in U. S. universities, were influenced by a strict pro-market ideology that was generally critical of government intervention in the operation of the free market.[45]

The second asymmetry, particularly affecting Mexico, was that between the more powerful sectors, which were fully represented in the negotiations, and other sectors—farmers, workers, small businesses—that were effectively excluded. The Mexican government encouraged business groups to form a coalition, the Coordinating Council of Foreign Trade Business Organizations (COECE), which worked closely with Mexican officials throughout the NAFTA negotiations by participating actively in designing and revising Mexico's negotiating positions.

Not only did business groups have privileged access to the negotiating process relative to other social groups, but only large business groups had the time, skills, and resources to participate actively. Despite representation of all the major business organizations in COECE, the large economic groups dominated the organization and the working groups. Negotiations respecting automobiles and the auto parts industry demonstrate the implications of this imbalance of power. While large firms producing vehicles each had their own representatives, small and medium auto-parts producers were dependent on associations such as CANACINTRA. Foreign vehicle manufacturers confronted the government, conditioning future investment on reforms such as a reduction of protection, but representatives of CANACINTRA complained that its proposals to help small firms adjust were routinely ignored. The final agreement called for an immediate drop in the requirement regarding the proportion of inputs from domestic suppliers, which would disappear altogether in 2004; according to one observer, this measure would condemn the small auto parts producers to oblivion.[46]

Despite the asymmetrical relationship among the three countries, analysts of the negotiation process have argued that the benefits to each country tended to reflect the priorities of the respecting negotiating teams, with the United States' position prevailing on issues of rules and principles, such as rules of origin, investment, and intellectual property rights, whereas Mexico was more likely to win on specific sectoral issues.[47] In several cases, negotiations resulted in compromises or trade-offs, and Mexico did gain certain concessions. For example, Mexican producers of oranges and orange juice would have tariff-free access to the U.S. market after a phase-out period of 15 years. In exchange, Mexico agreed to a 15-year phase-out of protection of corn and other agriculture products for the domestic market. The Mexican government subsequently accelerated the phase-out period, however, a move that proved devastating to small corn producers in southern Mexico.[48]

NAFTA was not only a trade agreement, but also an investment agreement, responding to the goal of corporations and financial institutions to reduce or eliminate any restrictions on investment in the member countries. The U.S. negotiators were largely successful in achieving favorable conditions for foreign investors. While Mexico was able to maintain its control over the energy sector, it was obliged to phase out its performance requirements for foreign investment (e.g., that foreign companies obtain a certain proportion of inputs from domestic suppliers and that their imports be linked to the value of their exports) after a period of 10 years. The Mexican government's ability to screen foreign acquisitions of domestic companies was also reduced to those cases in which foreign investors owned over 40 percent of the domestic company and the value of the purchase was over $150 million.

Negotiators reached an agreement in 1992, which then had to be ratified by the respective legislative bodies. Given PRI control of the legislature, there was relatively little debate in Mexico, where officials promoted NAFTA as a project that would create jobs and propel Mexico into the "first world" of advanced industrial countries. However, numerous groups in all three countries, among them independent unions and environmental organizations, concerned that their perspectives were not being taken into account, formed cross-sectoral coalitions in their respective countries and joined in cross-national coalitions with their counterpart organizations to establish priorities and demand their incorporation in the NAFTA agreement.

Although generally ignored by the negotiating teams, these groups were able to take advantage of the debate in the U.S. Congress, which had to ratify the agreement and where the outcome was far from certain. Mexican activists also recognized that U.S. pressures on Mexico were much more likely to be effective than their own, and thus saw lobbying members of the U.S. Congress as an effective strategy for presenting their perspectives. One result was the formulation of side agreements requiring foreign investors to respect labor and environmental laws in each country. Although the enforcement mechanisms, particularly for labor rights, have proved to be weak, the emergence of a "blue-green" coalition and its success in placing labor and environmental issues onto U.S. trade agreements represent an important achievement, and cross-national collaboration between the three countries has continued to be significant.[49]

NAFTA was a trade and investment agreement, not a jobs and development agreement. Nevertheless, it was promoted in Mexico as a measure that would increase employment and advance development goals. With some exceptions, the prevailing ideology of trusting market mechanisms to ensure growth and improve imbalances in income distribution precluded the implementation of state interventionist initiatives to provide assistance to sectors unprepared to confront the challenges and distortions resulting from an open market economy.

THE IMPACT OF ECONOMIC LIBERALIZATION

U.S. congressional approval of NAFTA (and its subsequent approval by the Mexican Chamber of Deputies) in late 1993 marked the culmination of the Salinas government's efforts to modernize Mexico on the basis of a new growth model that incorporated integration with the U.S. economy. As illustrated in Figure 4-1, in a little over a decade, the Mexican economy had been transformed. In addition, production, previously centralized in Mexico City and to a lesser extent Monterrey and Guadalajara, had become increasingly decentralized with new centers in the northern border region and cities of the central states, a process that had already begun to accelerate in the 1970s. Restrictions on foreign investment in terms of ownership and performance criteria had been reduced, and most were due to be eliminated. The previous nationalist ideology, emphasizing development through state promotion of domestic industry, had been replaced by neoliberalism, an ideology oriented to growth through a market economy integrated with the international market.

By the end of the Salinas administration in 1994, increased economic stability, the gradual elimination of restrictions on foreign investment, the privatization of state-owned enterprises, and particularly the prospects of the NAFTA agreement, had resulted in a massive increase in foreign investment as well as a return of domestic-flight capital. Most of this was portfolio investment (in government bonds and the growing stock market, following its opening to foreign investors in 1989), which increased from $3.4 billion in 1990 to approximately

$30 billion in 1993, providing a significant boost to Mexico's foreign exchange. Direct foreign investment, which had declined from $2.5 billion in 1980–1981 to $500 million in 1985, also grew rapidly, though less dramatically, to approximately $4.4 billion in 1993.[50]

Figure 4-1 Mexican Transitions: 1982–2000

Economic Model

ISI model, primarily oriented to domestic market, with high levels of protection.	Export oriented production, trade liberalization. NAFTA agreement to eliminate trade barriers between Mexico, U.S. and Canada.
Mixed economy with extensive state intervention, including public ownership of strategic and non-strategic industries.	Disincorporation, including privatization via sales, mergers, transfers and liquidation of industries; deregulation.
Centralization of production in Mexico City and (to lesser extent) other major cities (Monterrey, Guadalajara).	Decentralization of production with new centers in the north (particularly in the maquila industry) and mid-sized cities (Aguascalientes, San Luis Potosí).
Foreign investment encouraged in certain areas but restricted through performance criteria and in terms of ownership.	Increased opening to foreign investment, with removal of previous restrictions.

Socio-economic Structure

Agriculture sector characterized by division between commercial farms (especially north) and ejidos/small peasant production (center/south).	Agricultural sector characterized by growing pressures on ejido. Revision of Article 27 in 1991 eliminates support for ejidal sector. Increasing gap between commercial farms, many them producing for export, in northern states, and impoverished rural south.
Industrial/commercial sector with structure of large number of small firms with small share of investment and small number of large firms controlling majority of assets.	Industrial/commercial sector characterized by importance of independent middle level entrepreneurs, esp. in north, northwest. Many firms producing for domestic market unable to compete, close down.
Private sector dominated by foreign-owned firms and domestic economic groups combining major banks, manufacturing industries, real estate firms, insurance companies, etc. having disproportionate access to foreign capital and technology via joint ventures, foreign loans, technology transfers. Divided between those with close links to state (esp. in center) and more independent firms (esp. in north).	Economic groups temporarily weakened with bank nationalization but reconstituted (and new groups formed) in 1980s and 1990s, in part through constitution of alternative financial system. Further concentration with privatization, emergence of "new billionaires" Multinational corporations dominant in several sectors, notably the auto industry.
	Growth in drug trade; drug lords become important economic and political players.
Labor divided between organized sectors (in both corporate and independent unions) and non-unionized groups in small factories, shops, etc. State control via recognition of unions and of legality of strikes. Relatively high wages, benefits, and security via collective contracts for independent and corporate unions. Model: Petroleum workers union; independent auto workers union.	Reduction of state-guaranteed protection for workers. Decimation of independent unions, weakening of corporate unions. "Flexibilization" of labor, removal of union influence at work site. Also fragmentation due to decentralization "new unionism" based on labor-management cooperation and wages/benefits linked to productivity although recently wages have not kept up with productivity increases. Model: Telmex union.

(continued)

Figure 4-1 *continued*

Large informal sector of home workers, street vendors, domestics, etc. Rural-urban migration, especially to Mexico City, and emigration, especially from rural areas, to the U.S.

Growing informal sector, especially street vendors in major urban centers. Increased emigration involving not only farmers and peasants from traditional sending states but also urban groups, e.g., workers and middle class from Mexico city.

Political System

Dominant party system in which major party (PRI) controls all executive positions at national and state levels, as well as most lower levels. Based on corporate structure with labor, peasant, popular sectors. System of clientelism and widespread corruption.

Shift to dominant party system with increased space for opposition parties, including opposition control of legislature and state governorships, to pluralist system of competing parties. Persistence of clientelism and corruption, exacerbated by growth of drug cartels.

Government characterized by division between politicos (linked to party) and tecnicos.

Technocrats become dominant within the government.

Centralization of power in federal government (presidentialism).

Decentralization, with larger role for states and local governments and legislature; increased independence of judiciary.

Ideology of dominant party/state based on revolutionary nationalism, statism, social justice.

Ideological shift of PRI to "social liberalism," combining liberal economic reforms and anti-poverty programs. Policies continued under PAN governments.

Major opposition party, PAN, based on conservative ideology, with several smaller parties.

Three major parties: PRI, PAN, and PRD with several smaller parties.

Private sector formally excluded from official party with limited direct participation in electoral politics. Dominant economic groups have direct but informal links with the government.

Growing and open presence of private sector in both PRI and PAN; business candidates elected at state and local levels. Dominant economic groups have direct and indirect formal and informal links with government.

Independent labor, peasant, political organizations generally coopted or repressed.

Emergence of independent social movements and organizations, including those of workers, women, indigenous groups, environmental groups, human rights and civic action groups. New inter-sectoral and cross-border coalitions.

Direct foreign investment was particularly important in the two most dynamic sectors—in terms of both growth and exports—within manufacturing, the auto industry and the *maquiladora* industries. The maquiladora industries had initially been established along the border with the United States in the mid-1960s to manufacture consumer products such as garments and electronics; they imported most of their inputs, such as textiles or components, tariff-free, often from "twin" plants on the U.S. side of the border, and these were then processed or assembled in Mexico, with the final product exported to the United States. The number of firms in the maquiladora sector increased from 600 in 1983 to 1,954 in 1992 and 2,000 in 1995, and during the same period those employed rose from 198,500 to nearly 500,000. While the maquiladoras in the border cities grew rapidly, maquila production also began to be decentralized toward interior cities. This was particularly true of the apparel industries, where previously integrated firms producing for the internal market contracted with U.S. firms to assemble material designed and cut in the United States.[51]

The automobile industry underwent substantial restructuring in the 1980s, partly as a result of new performance criteria introduced in 1983, raising local content requirements to 60 percent, reducing the number of makes and models Mexico could produce, and mandating a favorable balance of trade, with exports to equal or surpass imports.[52] This resulted in new automotive investments in Mexico (in some cases through the export of U.S. firms). During the 1980s, automakers in Mexico began to export finished vehicles as well as engines and other parts, in some cases working with local suppliers to ensure quality.[53] In short, government-mandated performance criteria were instrumental in the growth of investment, technology transfers, and the expansion of production in Mexico. As noted above, however, NAFTA would eventually phase out performance criteria for the automobile industry by 2004, which was expected to seriously undermine the Mexican auto parts industry.

An increasing proportion of foreign investment went into services and commerce, including construction, restaurants, and retail and discount stores. There was a massive growth in franchises; restaurants such as Burger King, Domino's Pizza, and McDonalds, and convenience stores such as 7-Eleven, began to appear throughout Mexico City as well as other major cities. There was also an increase in joint ventures with Mexican firms; for example, between U.S. discount stores such as K-Mart, Price Club, and Wal-Mart with big Mexican retail chains, generally controlled by Mexico's most powerful economic groups.

With increased investment came increased trade. Mexico's exports rose from $18 billion in 1980 to $61 billion in 1994, and Mexico's trade structure again shifted, from dependence on oil for 75 percent of its total exports in the early 1980s to a significant increase in the export of manufactured goods, to 77 percent of total exports, by the mid-1990s. Much of the increase in exports was from the maquiladora and auto industries. Between 1988 and 1996, automobile exports grew at an annual rate of 27.3 percent, and auto sector exports increased from 11.3 to 29.6 percent of all manufactured exports.[54] Manufacturing exports also increased as a proportion of manufactured output, reaching 34 percent in 1994 (and would grow to over 60 percent by the late 1990s).[55]

Mexico's economic reforms were looked upon as highly successful by policy makers and investment companies in the United States and among international financial agencies. In the early 1990s, some were hailing a second economic miracle in Mexico. Macro-economic stabilization had been achieved, the budget deficit nearly eliminated, and inflation reduced from 159 percent in 1987 to 7 percent in 1994. After nearly a decade of stagnation and negative growth, the economy was beginning to expand, with foreign investment providing a major impetus.

Many Mexicans were also optimistic regarding promises of modernization and the prospects of NAFTA, which had been promoted in Mexico as a source of new jobs. The government had also instituted an anti-poverty program,

PRONASOL (National Solidarity Program), funded by part of the profits from bank privatizations and targeted at poor urban neighborhoods and rural communities, which was highly popular. The hopes and expectations of many Mexicans were reflected in the 1991 congressional elections, in which the PRI vote increased from 50.4 percent in 1988 to 61.4 percent, and the number of PRI deputies increased from 233 to 290.[56]

But the new economic model did not benefit everyone. A major result of the reforms of the 1980s and early 1990s was the growing polarization of society. Between 1984 and 1994 the income of the wealthiest 10 percent of the population increased while the relative income of the remaining 90 percent declined, and that of the lowest 20 percent declined absolutely as well as relatively. Poverty levels increased: those characterized by "moderate poverty" (an income of two dollars a day) increased from 28.5 to 31.8 percent and those in extreme poverty (one dollar a day or less) went from 13.9 percent to 15.5 percent of the total population. The impoverished were disproportionately those from the rural sector, those with little or no education, and those from the south, especially the states of Guerrero, Oaxaca and Chiapas.[57]

How could this increasing poverty in the context of apparent growth and prosperity be explained? At least part of the explanation has to do with the reduction in small and medium firms producing for the domestic market, the consequent decline in jobs in these sectors, and the dramatic drop in wages. Although new jobs were created in such sectors as the maquiladoras, jobs were lost in small and medium firms in traditional manufacturing, as a result of the bankruptcy of domestic firms due to the recession or their inability to compete with cheaper imports. Trade liberalization had exposed small- and medium-sized industries to international competition from cheaper exports without the necessary financial and technological resources to increase their competitiveness, and many were forced to close. The privatization of state-owned firms was preceded and/or followed by substantial downsizing, again resulting in job loss. In addition, small and medium firms that had been suppliers to state firms or had benefited from government contracts were often replaced through imports of supplies by now privatized firms.

There was little integration between the export sector and the rest of the economy. The maquiladoras import most of their inputs, and with the exception of the maquiladoras, the most dynamic sectors of manufacturing in terms of exports have had little impact on job creation. Between 1988 and 1996, the automotive sector increased its share of manufacturing exports from 11.3 to 29.6 percent of the total, but generated only 1.3 percent of the manufacturing jobs and 0.1 percent of total employment.[58]

Wages also dropped sharply during this period. Industrial wages declined by over 30 percent between 1982 and 1987. Although the wage and price controls introduced by the 1987 Economic Solidarity Pact had begun to reverse this trend, wages had not reached their 1980 levels by 1994. In addition, there was an increasing gap between the wages of skilled and unskilled workers.[59] One result of job loss and declining wages in the formal sector has been the growth of the urban informal sector, which according to one estimate was approximately 45 percent of total employment by the mid-1990s.[60]

The agricultural sector also experienced polarization and increased poverty, partly due to external factors such as a drop in the prices of commodity exports but also due to the withdrawal of state support to the rural sector in terms of credit, technical assistance, and other inputs. The failure of the government to promote alternative institutions to compensate this loss, the elimination of tariffs and price supports for most agricultural products, and the reform of Article 27 of the constitution, which ended land reform and permitted the privatization of the ejidos, also contributed to deteriorating conditions in the countryside. Agriculture has ceased to be a viable source of income for many Mexicans, resulting in extensive migration to other parts of Mexico (including seasonal migration to work on modern commercial farms in the north) and to the United States, in some cases involving the migration of whole families.[61]

At the other extreme has been the concentration of assets in a small number of large firms and economic groups. As of the early 1990s, CEMEX (*Cementos Mexicanos*), controlled 70 percent of national cement production, and VITRO, a Monterrey conglomerate, accounted for 90 percent of glass production. As noted above, the privatization of state-owned enterprises and banks was a further factor in asset concentration and the monopolization of certain sectors—for example, mining, where one company controlled 96 percent of Mexico's copper production.[62] One result was the astonishing growth of Mexican billionaires. According to a survey by *Forbes* magazine, in 1994 Mexico had 20 billionaires, more than any other country with the exception of the United States, Japan, and Germany. Seventeen of these had benefited from the privatization process, and three were from the Garza-Sada family of Monterrey.[63]

Modernization has also tended to aggravate regional inequalities. The wealthier areas, including Mexico City as well as several states in northern and central Mexico, have the infrastructure and human and capital resources to attract investment, domestic and foreign, which gives them a strong advantage over poorer agricultural states lacking these assets, particularly in southern Mexico. The decline in federal government resources has limited its ability to institute compensatory measures to redistribute resources to the more impoverished areas of the country.

Apart from income and wealth polarization, the Mexican economy was confronting certain macro-economic imbalances by 1993. While exports had grown dramatically, imports grew even more rapidly due to increased consumer spending, especially by upper-income groups, and to imports of machinery and other inputs used in production. The growing trade deficit was facilitated by the over-valuation of the peso, which meant lower prices for consumers and business firms but also discouraged exports. Consumer and industry spending was also encouraged by the expansion of credit by the newly privatized and poorly regulated banks.

Imports in the manufacturing sector grew faster than exports, with the result that the manufacturing sector had a significant trade deficit in the 1988–1996 period.[64] The major exporters—the maquiladoras and the auto industry—were also major importers, and a substantial proportion of U.S.-Mexican trade consisted of transfers within multinational corporations, such as the auto industries. Many of the new retail establishments in Mexico also imported much of their merchandise from the United States. In 1992, Mexico's total exports were $46 billion, but imports were $62 billion—a trade deficit of nearly $16 billion (see Table 4-1).

At the time, trade deficits were compensated by foreign investment. But, as noted above, most foreign investment was portfolio investment in stocks and bonds. This was a highly volatile form of investment since, in the absence of capital controls (e.g., stipulations that foreign portfolio investment, or a proportion of it, had to remain in the country for a particular period of time), it could be quickly withdrawn at a sign of increased risk or instability. In addition, the use of high interest rates to attract foreign capital to Mexico's bond market raised costs of borrowing for Mexican firms. Domestic investment levels were low, an

Table 4-1. Mexican Macroeconomic Indicators: 1989–1995

DATE	1989	1990	1991	1992	1993	1994	1995
GDP Growth (annual percent)	3.5	4.3	3.9	2.8	0.4	3.8	-6.2
Annual Inflation Rate	19.7	29.9	18.8	11.9	8.0	7.1	52.0
Exports (U.S. $ million)	35,171	40,711	42,687	46,196	51,885	60,879	79,543
Imports (U.S. $ million)	34,766	41,592	49,966	62,130	65,366	79,346	72,454
Balance of Trade	405	-881	-7,279	-15,934	-13,481	-18,467	7,089
Foreign Direct Investment	2,785	2,549	4,742	4,393	4,389	10,792	6,963
Portfolio Investment	354	3,369	12,741	18,041	28,919	8,185	-10,140
Total Reserves less Gold (U.S. $ million)	6,329	9,863	17,726	18,942	25,110	6,278	16,847
Real Exchange Rate (1980=100) Controlled Rate	112.8	105.4	92.4	82.5	77.5	79.5	115.2

Source: Drawn from Manuel Pastor and Carol Wise, "State Policy, Distribution, and Neoliberal Reform in Mexico," *Journal of Latin American Studies*, 29, 4 (1997): 333. Reprinted with permission of Cambridge University Press.

additional factor in unemployment and underemployment, and the growth rate, after reaching 4.5 percent in 1990, declined to 2.8 percent in 1992 and 0.6 percent in 1993.

At the same time, the weakening of banking regulations (e.g., lowering the requirement for bank reserves) also facilitated an over-extension of the financial system, with bank lending increasing 24 percent a year between 1991 and 1994 and an increase in non-performing loans.[65] In effect, the government had abdicated its regulatory functions, not only failing to exercise restraints but also encouraging loan expansion, especially for homes as well as consumer credit. By 1994, the overvaluation of the exchange rate, combined with high interest rates in the United States, was making investors increasingly nervous.[66] In 1994, a series of political shocks exposed the vulnerability of Mexico's economy and led to a new economic crisis.

FROM EUPHORIA TO DISILLUSION: THE PESO CRISIS

On January 1, 1994, the day that NAFTA went into effect, a guerrilla army of indigenous peasants in the state of Chiapas launched a dramatic offensive, attacking army posts in several parts of the state. Taking its name from the revolutionary leader Emiliano Zapata, the Zapatista Army of National Liberation (EZLN), or Zapatistas, were motivated by the reversal of the agrarian reform and the implications of NAFTA for the rural sector, as well as a long history of oppression under state authorities and local caciques. The government quickly repressed the rebellion, but the uprising, its motivations, and the government repression received massive coverage in the national and international press, generating an outcry from human rights organizations. Concerned about its international image, the government withdrew its forces and began negotiations with the Zapatistas.[67]

Less than three months after the Zapatista revolt, the PRI presidential candidate, Luis Donaldo Colosio, was assassinated at a rally in Tijuana. In the meantime, there was a spate of kidnappings, particularly targeting wealthy business leaders. Even after the July presidential election of Ernesto Zedillo, who had replaced Colosio as PRI candidate (see Chapter 5), there was another political assassination, this time of the Secretary General of the PRI and a brother-in-law of Salinas, in which members of the PRI and even the president's brother Raul were implicated (although Raul was eventually released for lack of evidence).

The political instability of 1994 (as well as the vulnerability of the peso) resulted in massive capital flight as both foreign and Mexican investors shifted their funds abroad. Between February and December, foreign exchange reserves plunged from $29.6 billion to $6.3 billion. In a desperate attempt to shore up the currency the new Zedillo government tried to float the peso. Its value dropped instantly by 55 percent.

The Clinton administration and the International Monetary Fund moved quickly to work out a rescue package for Mexico, with the assistance of other countries. Because of resistance in the U.S. Congress, with both Democrats and Republicans seeing the project as a bailout for wealthy investors and speculators, the administration bypassed congressional approval and drew on the Exchange Stabilization Account to make available $20 billion in credits to Mexico, which would be secured by the earnings of Mexico's oil exports. This was supplemented by loans from the International Monetary Fund and from other countries, bringing the total to nearly $50 billion.

Why was the United States willing to bail out Mexico in 1994, in contrast to its response during the debt crisis 12 years before? One factor was that the Mexican economy, despite its vulnerability, was in a stronger position than it had been in 1982 due to macro-economic reforms and stabilization policies. Also, from the perspective of Washington and the major lending agencies, Mexico was a "model reformer." Mexico's economic failure would send the wrong message to other governments attempting to carry out the economic reforms pushed by the United States and international financial institutions. It would also make NAFTA appear to be a mistake and undermine pending free trade agreements with other countries. Finally, there was fear of a contagion effect, that a crisis in Mexico could affect other markets in Latin America and throughout the world.

With the help of these loans, Mexico was able to repay its short-term debt in 1995. As imports declined due to the recession, and exports increased, helped by the devaluation of the peso, the balance of trade shifted from a negative $18.5 billion to a positive $7.1 billion in 1995. By 1997 Mexico's foreign exchange reserves had grown to $28 billion, and Mexico was able to pay off its loan to the United States by the end of the year.[68]

But for most Mexicans, the crisis and peso devaluation meant an immediate and stark deterioration of their conditions. Inflation increased from 7.1 percent to 52 percent between 1994 and 1995. An estimated one million jobs were lost in 1995. Those workers who retained their jobs saw their real wages, which after dropping dramatically in the 1980s had begun to increase in the early 1990s, again decline—over 13 percent in 1995 alone. As indicated above, the massive increase in interest rates meant that debtors, ranging from large firms to thousands of small firms and individual credit card holders, were unable to repay their debts. Coming after a period when, following the difficulties and sacrifices of the 1980s, Mexicans had begun to hope for a better future, the economic crisis led to a profound disillusionment and demoralization.

CONCLUSIONS

The liberalization of Mexico's economy was rapid and far-reaching. Both the pace and depth of this transition can be attributed to a combination of factors: the influence of international lending agencies in the context of the debt crisis; the rise of a politically connected and U.S.-trained techno-bureaucracy to the leadership of Mexico's government; the increased weight of the independent, export-oriented business sector; government efforts to regain the support of business elites alienated by previous government actions and particularly bank nationalization; and the government's ability to neutralize opposition to reforms on the part of popular groups and small and medium businesses as well as their supporters within the state.

But the specific liberalization strategy pursued by the Mexican government in the 1980s and early 1990s favored foreign corporations, large domestic businesses and conglomerates and export-oriented interests to the relative neglect of small and medium industries as well as small farmers and peasants producing for the domestic market. In effect, the process of economic restructuring involved a fundamental restructuring of state-society relations. On the one hand, state-business contacts were increased and formalized. Owners of Mexico's largest conglomerates and leaders of major business groups participated actively with government officials in various stages of the reform process of which they were, in many cases, the major beneficiaries. On the other hand, the traditional base of the state-party system, particularly workers, peasants and other popular groups, as well as significant sectors of the middle class, were generally excluded from the reform process and were often its victims. Among the consequences of this strategy have been the emergence or reinforcement of a dual structure in both industry and agriculture, in which export-oriented sectors have advanced while small and medium producers oriented to the domestic market have declined; an extreme polarization of wealth and income; the lack of articulation of Mexico's dynamic export sector to the rest of the economy; and increased external vulnerability due to close integration with the United States economy and dependence on foreign investment.

In the meantime, many of those groups excluded from economic policy debates became protagonists in Mexico's political transformation. The 1980s and particularly the 1990s saw the emergence of civic action groups, new labor alliances and confederations, indigenous movements, and middle-class groups alienated by the government's economic policies as well as the continued domination of the PRI. Directly or indirectly, these groups undermined PRI hegemony and supported the rise of opposition parties, resulting in the demise of the dominant party system and its replacement by a more pluralist political system. This transformation will be the focus of the following chapters.

CHAPTER 5

From "Perfect Dictatorship" to Imperfect Democracy

INTRODUCTION

In 1958, Dr. Salvador Nava, a highly respected physician, decided to run as an independent for municipal president of San Luis Potosí (the capital of the state of the same name) in an effort to undermine the corrupt political machine of Gonzalo Santos, a former PRI governor who continued to control state politics. Nava's overwhelming victory against the Santos candidate ushered in an era of "good government" in the city in which he eliminated the monthly municipal "kickback" to Santos, saving considerable funds; ensured transparency by publishing the budget showing income and expenditures; and expanded services such as drainage, electrical power, and street paving. He soon gained a national reputation and was even praised by the Mexican president. In 1961, however, when he decided to run for state governor, the national directorate of the PRI blocked his candidacy in spite of his popularity and support of the local PRI for his nomination. When Nava resigned from the PRI and ran as an independent his supporters were attacked, and on the day of the election military forces blocked the polling places, ensuring a PRI "victory." Protests by Nava and his followers were suppressed; Nava himself was arrested and tried for "sedition" although charges were dropped for lack of evidence. In 1962 Nava temporarily suspended his political activities, but *navismo* became an important model in the ongoing efforts toward electoral democracy and effective opposition government.[1]

The struggle for democracy in Mexico has taken various forms in the years following the Mexican revolution, among them labor movements struggling for internal democracy and union autonomy, the student movement of 1968, and efforts by opposition groups to challenge PRI hegemony in local and state elections. Beginning in the 1960s, several independent NGOs formed around such issues as economic development and human rights, and local grass-roots organizations emerged in several municipalities throughout the country. These included Christian Base Communities, sometimes formed at the instigation of a charismatic priest or bishop, such as Bishop Sergio Méndez Arceo of Morelos and Bishop Samuel Ruiz in Chiapas, although they generally lacked support from the conservative Church hierarchy. Political exiles escaping from military regimes in Argentina, Brazil, Chile and Uruguay during the 1960s and 1970s worked with Mexican groups and citizens in campaigns to protect political prisoners. These organizations expanded with the influx of Salvadoran and Guatemalan refugees in the 1980s.[2]

Independent voices in the media beginning in the 1970s offered expanded coverage and alternative interpretations of events and issues, a process that had begun with print media in the 1970s (see Chapter 3) and expanded to include radio and television as newly mobilized citizens demanded greater integrity in reporting, and market competition for listeners and viewers compelled media outlets to respond to their demands. The growth of independent media was accompanied by the growth of civil society and provided a space in which new social actors—associations, interest groups, opposition parties—could make their voices heard, raise issues such as human rights and the meaning of democracy, and challenge the institutions of the old order.[3]

In the context of the economic changes of the 1980s, new social movements emerged and political opposition expanded. Pro-democracy movements in the northern states of Baja California, Chihuahua, Durango, and Sinaloa, as well as Guanajuato and Yucatán, were instrumental in PAN victories in several municipal elections, and in the southern state of Oaxaca, a coalition of workers and peasants won the municipal elections of Juchitán in 1981 in an alliance with the Mexican Communist Party. In the 1988 presidential elections, left and centrist parties, protest movements, and social organizations rallied around an opposition candidate, ultimately leading to the formation of a second opposition party. Pressures for a more democratic and representative system grew, resulting in turn in a series of political and electoral reforms on the part of the PRI government.

Finally, on July 2, 2000, after 71 years of uninterrupted rule, the PRI was voted out of office. The presidential elections of 2000 were widely acclaimed as a critical point in Mexico's political transition from an authoritarian regime to a more democratic one. The victory of Vicente Fox of the National Action Party marked the official end of the hegemonic party system and Mexico's transition to a competitive system with three major parties and several smaller ones. Although Salvador Nava did not live to see this victory, the Potosí Civic Front and thousands of other civic groups and social organizations that had formed in Mexico in the preceding decades had an important role in this transition.

But just as the 2000 elections were not the beginning of Mexico's process of democratization, neither were they the end. In contrast to the euphoria surrounding the elections of 2000, the subsequent presidential elections of 2006 resulted in a contested outcome that raised questions regarding the meaning of Mexican democracy, including the reliability of the institutions that had been established to ensure democratic elections and the possibility that Mexico's new political system would be an elite democracy that excluded significant sectors of the population. While Mexico appears to have made a transition from an authoritarian, dominant-party system to a more pluralistic system of competing parties, elements of the previous system continue to exist that undermine the concept of competitive, fair elections and may even threaten the consolidation of democracy, particularly if the new system fails to effectively address the serious problems of poverty, inequality and crime that plague Mexico as well as other Latin American countries.

In short, Mexico's democracy is a work in process, forged through the interaction of social and political actors in a context in which global changes and the introduction of a neoliberal economic model have disrupted the traditional patterns of Mexican society. The previous Chapter traced the development and impact of economic changes. This Chapter examines the ways in which these developments have influenced Mexico's shift from an authoritarian to a more democratic system. In the next section we examine different conceptions of democracy, identify its basic characteristics, and examine the process of democratic transition. The following section is concerned with explaining this transition in Mexico and develops a model that attempts to identify the various factors that help to explain why this process has occurred at this particular time.

The rest of the Chapter is concerned with the trajectory, or process, of democratization during the period between 1988 and 2006, focusing on the presidential elections of 1988, 1994, 2000 and 2006 and encompassing the administrations of Carlos Salinas, Ernesto Zedillo, and Vicente Fox. A final section addresses the question of the extent to which Mexico can be considered a democratic country today and discusses some of the major challenges to the consolidation of democracy in Mexico.

CONCEPTUALIZATIONS OF DEMOCRACY AND DEMOCRATIC TRANSITION

Although most people assume they know what democracy is, it is in fact a highly contested concept, which various people have defined in different ways. Some definitions focus on electoral processes, and the procedures through which citizens choose their representatives. Some emphasize participation, in which citizens are directly involved in decisions affecting them. Some argue that real democracy cannot exist in conditions of economic inequality and argue for what is sometimes referred to as substantive democracy—involving a basic right to jobs, health care, education and housing—as an essential component of any concept of democracy.[4]

At its most basic level, democracy may be defined as government by the governed, involving some form of direct or indirect participation in government by the affected population. Central to most contemporary conceptions of democracy is the concept of citizenship, in which each citizen is equal before the law, with an equal right to participate in the political process. It thus contrasts with authoritarian governments in which the population has no input to government and rule is arbitrary. Democracy may be direct, with citizens participating directly in developing the rules governing society and in decision making, or indirect, with citizens choosing representatives who will be responsible for rule making and decision making. Direct democracy is usually associated with relatively small, homogeneous societies in which there are similarities in beliefs, interests and lifestyles. In the past, it was often assumed that democratic societies could not persist in the absence of these similarities; in some cases decisions are reached by consensus. The Greek city-state and the New England town meeting are models of direct democracy; it is also characteristic of some indigenous societies.

In large, heterogeneous societies with differences in class, religion, ethnicity, ideology, and interests, direct democracy and agreement by consensus are difficult, if not impossible. For democracy to exist, people must "agree to disagree." Citizens may not be able to participate directly in decision making, but they have the right to choose their decision makers. Participation is formalized through procedures, or rules, to elect their representatives, and while people may disagree strongly regarding specific issues there must be general agreement on the procedures and rules for resolving those issues. Conflict is institutionalized into non-violent contestation for offices and influence. Democracy has in fact been defined as "the institutionalization of uncertainty."[5]

The concept of participatory democracy goes beyond that of formal or procedural democracy to also incorporate two elements: the degree of *inclusiveness* in the democratic system, and the *scope* of participation. Both direct and procedural democracies often include certain members of the population and exclude others. In the Greek city-states, participation was limited to free men, excluding women as well as slaves. Many modern Western democracies initially included a small elite of white males, such as property owners. It was only over time, often through the struggles of excluded groups, that women, members of the working class, and minority groups have become part of the electorate in these countries.

The scope of participation in formal democracies may go beyond the selection of representatives to include membership in political parties, involvement in political campaigns, and running for office. Representative democracy may also coincide with forms of direct democracy through participation in grassroots or voluntary organizations, ranging from the local PTA to labor unions, environmental organizations, women's groups, or neighborhood associations—the institutions of civil society. Historically, participation in such organizations has been seen as important for the functioning of formal democracies, providing an opportunity for direct participation in decision making, inculcating democratic and participatory values, developing political skills, and in some cases providing channels or opportunities for the input of these groups in the formal democratic process. Ideally, civil society fortifies democratic regimes by facilitating communication among individuals and groups, in the process strengthening social networks and providing opportunities for the development of tolerance, mutual accommodation, and inter-personal trust, values seen as important for the functioning of democracy.

Thus, as the *inclusiveness* of political participation expands to incorporate previously excluded groups, the *scope* of participation may result in the incorporation of new issues in the political process such as labor rights, environmental protection, and gender equality.

Some analysts conceptualize democracy as including not only political equality, based on citizenship with each citizen equal before the law and with an equal right to participate in the political process, but also in terms of incorporating a goal of social and economic equality. They argue for what is sometimes referred to as substantive democracy, which includes the basic rights of all citizens to jobs, health care, education, and decent housing. In the absence of these rights, they argue, citizen equality is impossible, since deprivation weakens the options for effective political participation. In addition, massive inequality, involving an extreme concentration of wealth and power in the hands of a small elite, enables these groups to exercise undue influence on governments. From this perspective, substantive democracy is not only an end in itself but also a condition for the consolidation and stability of formal democracy. At the same time, in theory at least, formal democracy and participatory democracy, by enabling voters to choose representatives that will respond to their needs and by enabling disadvantaged groups to exert organized pressure on government officials, can increase substantive democracy.

While the concepts of formal and participatory democracy involve the direct or indirect participation of the citizenry in government, substantive democracy is a function of government performance. To the extent that it is an expectation by the citizenry and involves redistribution of a society's resources, e.g., through taxation, provision of basic services in such areas as education and health care (particularly to disadvantaged groups or areas), and job creation programs, it may be seen as an element of government accountability. At the same time, the high levels of poverty and inequality that characterize Mexico as well as other Latin American countries can threaten the long-term viability of democratic government, and the ability of governments to address these problems is an important condition for democratic consolidation.

The following discussion will focus on concepts of formal democracy and participatory democracy. A formal democracy is a political system in which the government is accountable to the governed (citizens) through competitive, fair, and regularly scheduled elections in which the entire adult population participates, in the context of the rule of law and guarantees for political freedom (e.g., freedom of speech, freedom of association).[6] *Competitive* elections imply the existence of alternatives: opposition parties and candidates that can be voted into office. Elections are *fair* if there is a level playing field, in which all candidates have an opportunity to present their ideas and perspectives, and citizens have opportunity to vote, with votes counting equally. Elections are *regularly scheduled* to provide opportunities to change government leaders, which help make governments accountable to the electorate. The *rule of law* and *guarantees of political freedoms* provide the conditions for citizens to participate equally and freely in the electoral process: candidates may express their opinions, and voters have the opportunity to hear the perspectives of all the candidates and to vote, without fear of reprisals.

An effective electoral democracy—in which all citizens are equal and government is accountable to the people—involves the development of institutions, including governmental institutions (executive, legislative, judiciary) and institutions that enable citizens to participate effectively in elections and hold governments accountable, including electoral institutions, political parties, a free and independent press, and civic organizations. Horizontal accountability refers to the autonomy of government institutions and the ability of each to act as a check on the other, while vertical accountability is exercised through institutions ensuring citizen input into government and the accountability of the government to its citizens.

There is an abundant literature on the process of regime change and specifically the transition from authoritarian to democratic regimes in Latin America and other parts of the world. In fact, democracy itself has been defined as a process of curbing the power of arbitrary, authoritarian rulers, replacing arbitrary rules with just ones, and giving the ruled a role in the process of rule-making.[7] Historical analyses of conditions leading to democracy in the United States and Europe have focused on the impact of capitalist modernization on different groups and classes and the formation of coalitions detrimental or favorable to democracy. Several analyses of Latin America have particularly emphasized the mobilization of the working class and organized labor against elite groups favoring the status quo. In general, the process of democratization, as well as increasing its inclusiveness and scope, involves an ongoing struggle between excluded groups seeking to broaden participation and those favoring the status quo who resist change or try to limit inclusiveness.

In South America, where military regimes had usurped civilian rule and overthrown democratic governments in several countries during the 1960s and 1970s, analyses of transitions from military to democratic regimes focused on the interaction of three processes: a gradual opening or liberalization by the regime; the mobilization of protest groups, which may undermine the legitimacy of the regime and push for increased liberalization; and elite bargaining between the regime and representatives of the opposition. The result was a democratic transition, but given the power of the military and fear by civilian politicians of regression to military rule, elite bargaining between opposition and regime leaders frequently involved the containment of democratic processes within specified parameters, excluding what military leaders identified as radical or disruptive elements, often of the left. Although Mexican authoritarianism was more flexible than those of South America, and the trajectory of change was unique, the interplay of regime liberalization, popular mobilization, and elite bargaining also characterized its political transition.

External forces may also influence regime change, and shifts in the international context have been particularly important in Latin America. The processes of democratization in Eastern Europe and the demise of the Soviet Union, as well as democratization (or re-democratization) in Southern Europe, had an influence in Latin America. More significant, the end of the Cold War eliminated anti-Communism as a major justification for U.S. support of authoritarian regimes in the region, although U.S. opposition to revolutionary and radical regimes and intervention in elections on behalf of conservative candidates have continued. The process of globalization has also been a factor in the increased alliances of groups promoting change with foreign and international NGOs, which can provide various forms of support.

There has also been extensive debate on the impact of globalization and neoliberalism on democracy. While some have argued that economic liberalization, by reducing the economic power of the state, facilitates political liberalization, others have argued that the process of economic reform has in fact resulted in greater polarization of society, reinforcing privileged groups at the expense of the majority of the population, which is detrimental to democratic participation. Still others suggest that there is no relation, or that it is highly complex, depending on different contexts and circumstances.

In the meantime, concerns regarding the stability of new democratic regimes in Latin America as well as the quality of the new democracies (including the continued presence of authoritarian tendencies and the limitations on participation) resulted in a shift in analyses of democracy and the process of democratization in Latin America, from an emphasis on conditions that facilitated a transition to democracy to the consolidation of democracy. Among the concerns raised in this literature are institution building and the strength of democratic institutions, such as the electoral system, political parties, and the courts; the extent of equality before the law of different regions and sectors; acceptance of the desirability and irreversibility of the democratic "rules of the game" by the population as a whole; and the accountability of the government to the governed.

In the case of Mexico, although democracy was a goal of many of the protagonists in the Mexican revolution in the early 20th century, what in fact resulted was a shift from a personalist dictatorship to a more institutionalized (and in some respects more inclusive) form of authoritarianism. Prior to the 1980s, Mexico's electoral system only fulfilled the condition of regularly scheduled elections. Although opposition parties existed, they were not really competitive; there were opportunities to vote but no level playing field, and fraud prevented votes from being counted equally. Presidentialism precluded horizontal accountability, and vertical accountability was undermined by the absence of effective opposition and by the top-down control exercised via the corporatist structure of the government party. Most important, the law was unevenly applied, and freedoms were limited by intimidation, clientelism, state domination of media, and fear of reprisals.

With respect to participation, the system could be considered inclusive in that the adult population, men and women, had the right to vote, and its scope extended beyond the electoral process in that people could and did participate in political parties and other types of organizations. But the lack of meaningful elections, and the fact that the PRI and/or the government dominated many of the major organizations, in effect limited meaningful electoral participation. Some liberalization occurred in the 1970s, in large part in response to the loss of legitimacy following government repression of the student movement. As noted in Chapter 3, the press became more autonomous as independent newspapers and journals emerged. Beginning in 1977 changes in electoral laws permitted greater participation by opposition parties in the legislature—a response to electoral abstention and the fact that in 1976 the PRI candidate had run virtually unopposed, a source of considerable embarrassment given the PRI claim of electoral democracy. The government also recognized previously outlawed parties, such as the Mexican Communist Party. Both changes led to increased participation by opposition parties. The growing salience of opposition groups, the emergence of a more critical media, and increased international exposure, were factors in the growth of greater awareness and a more informed political culture, particularly among the growing middle class. There was little indication, however, that these changes would be part of a more thorough transformation of the political system.

The following section presents a model of the process of political change, which will be the basis of the subsequent analysis of Mexico's political transition after 1980. A final section will examine the extent to which Mexico can be considered a democracy in terms of the formal characteristics of an electoral democracy, the extent of political participation, and the accountability of the government to the governed, and consider some of the obstacles and challenges confronting Mexico's democracy today.

A MODEL OF DEMOCRATIZATION IN MEXICO

Although Mexico's transition to a fully functioning democratic system is far from complete, there is little doubt that significant progress was made in the period between the early 1980s and the elections of 2000. The examination of this transition focuses on the interaction of different elements: (1) the economic crisis of the 1980s and the economic restructuring of the late 1980s and the 1990s, and the resulting dislocations affecting large sectors of the population; (2) the emergence and mobilization of civic organizations, protest movements and opposition parties; (3) an increase in Mexico's international exposure and the growing significance of international influences, and (4) government initiatives in response to these processes that have resulted in changes in government institutions, shifts in electoral rules and procedures, and the increased salience of the opposition. These processes and their impact on political changes, are summarized in Figure 5-1.

Figure 5-1 Mexico: Model of Political Transition

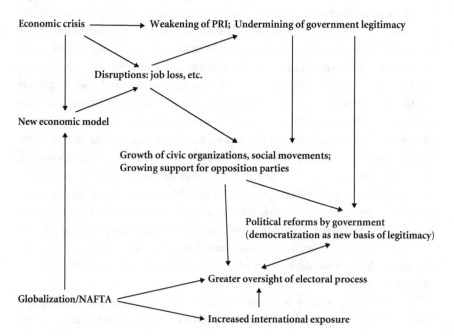

As shown in Chapter 4, the economic crisis and new economic model resulted in dislocations and increased insecurity for various sectors of the middle and lower classes as a result of the disappearance of jobs, the decline in wages, and the elimination of job security. While economic restructuring led to increased opportunities for some, it sharpened the income gap between the wealthy and the poor. It also weakened the economic basis for the clientelism that underpinned the corporatist system of the PRI, reducing the resources available to the state and party to deliver benefits, bribe opponents, or carry out reforms and thus undermined the legitimacy of the government.

Increased dissatisfaction among the population affected by the economic crisis, economic reforms, and the withdrawal of the state from its redistributive functions were important factors in the growth of opposition parties, civic organizations, and social movements (discussed in Chapter 6). Although labor was considerably weakened by the economic crisis and reforms of the 1980s, the crisis and austerity measures resulted in new movements and coalitions, including peasant movements, teachers organizations, and community and neighborhood organizations. After two massive earthquakes in 1985, groups left homeless or jobless as a result and frustrated by the inadequacy of the government response, became especially militant.

At the same time, business groups, antagonized by the government's nationalization of the banks in 1982, became increasingly active politically, pushing for democracy and for reduction of state control over the economy. The major opposition party at that time, the PAN, attracted some of these groups, giving the party a new dynamism and transforming it into a major opposition party. In addition, a dissident group broke off from the PRI and became the nucleus of a new left-center party, the PRD (Democratic Revolutionary Party) which attracted many of the new social movements and organizations as well as others opposed to the economic trajectory of the PRI government. The PRI now found itself confronting two major opposition parties at a time when its legitimacy had been seriously eroded.

Finally, the international context of increased economic integration as a result of globalization, and, in the case of Mexico, the negotiations over NAFTA, as well as the political implications of the end of the Cold War, and the process of democratization in other Latin American countries, also influenced events in Mexico. During the NAFTA negotiations, opposition political leaders and human rights groups pressured for the inclusion of a democratic requirement for countries participating in the free trade agreement, as was the case with the European Union. While they were unsuccessful, the NAFTA debate in the U.S. Congress raised concerns about the absence of democracy in Mexico to which the Mexican government was somewhat more responsive. Mexico's increased international visibility was also a factor in support provided by foreign and international organizations to efforts by domestic human rights groups, civic organizations, and others to bring about a more democratic system.

In the context of an authoritarian system that had experienced a major erosion in its legitimacy and basis of support, the emergence or resurgence of social organizations, the formation and consolidation of opposition parties, and Mexico's increased exposure to foreign and international opinion, exerted considerable pressure on Mexico's government, which responded with recognition of opposition victories and electoral reforms that have gradually leveled the electoral playing field.

THE 1988 ELECTIONS AND THE ADMINISTRATION OF CARLOS SALINAS DE GORTARI (1988–1994)

Although it was far from evident at the time, the elections of 1988 represent a critical turning point in Mexico's transition to democracy.[8] Growing dissatisfaction with the PRI regime had been a factor in the growth of political opposition. As noted in Chapter 4, business groups became increasingly active politically following bank nationalization, and while the PRI succeeded in co-opting some of them, others were attracted to PAN—notably young, well-educated small and middle level entrepreneurs who had not been active politically but had been leaders in local business organizations.[9] Disaffected members of the middle class, many of who had benefitted from the boom of the late 1970s and early 1980s and blamed state economic intervention for the crisis that had ended their privileged situation, were also drawn to the PAN. The party was particularly strong in the states of Guanajuato and other west central states, Yucatán, and the northern states of Baja California, Sonora, Durango, Coahuila, Chihuahua, Sinaloa, and Nuevo León.

The influx of small and medium level entrepreneurs brought new energy to the party, expanding its efficiency and competitiveness. At the same time, they challenged its identification. Prior to the 1980s, the party had been a relatively small, ideologically oriented opposition party. Participation in elections served an educational purpose: calling for democracy and respect for the rule of law, an end to corruption, and limits on the power of the state. The party also stood for conservative Catholic values, opposed such government policies as land distribution, and upheld the rights to private property. While the young entrepreneurs who entered the party in the 1980s and 1990s generally shared these values, they were more focused on winning elections, resulting in a more pragmatic orientation. For example, many of them were willing to accept public funds for electoral campaigns, a practice that was counter to the wishes of those wanting to protect ideological purity.

In the 1980s, the party won a number of municipal elections in those states where it had been politically active. In Chihuahua, for example, the PAN won seven major municipalities, which incorporated 75 percent of the state population, in 1983. But opposition success aroused the concern of the national PRI machine, which ensured the defeat of PAN in the 1986 gubernatorial and municipal elections through massive fraud. Although the PAN launched a spirited campaign to protest the fraud, the defeat led to a decline in the political activity of the new entrepreneurial leaders, antagonizing some longtime rank and file PAN militants who felt that the newcomers were simply using the party for their own electoral ends and lacked a real commitment to the party's core values and its day-to-day functioning. These concerns led the traditional *Panistas* to impose stringent criteria for membership in the party and marked the beginning of tensions between the ideological purists and pragmatists, which has continued to characterize the party.

While the PAN was attracting disaffected young business leaders in several Mexican states, a group of leftist politicians within the PRI itself, many of them friends and associates of Cuauhtémoc Cárdenas, son of Lázaro Cárdenas and governor of Michoacán (1980–1986), were growing increasingly dissatisfied with the direction of government policies. A particular concern was the government's adhesion to the IMF guidelines on the debt issues and the costs the harsh austerity measures imposed on the Mexican people. In 1987 they formed the democratic current within the party (partly modeled on the critical current that emerged at that time in the Spanish Socialist party) and issued a series of documents calling for debt reduction and a return to the basic values of social justice of the Mexican revolution. Recognizing that a change in policy would not be possible if de la Madrid was allowed to choose his successor, they also called for internal democracy and pushed for a nominating convention within the PRI to select the next presidential candidate.[10]

President de la Madrid refused to go along with this proposal, and the dissidents were expelled from party. The democratic current became the nucleus of an electoral coalition, the FDN (National Democratic Front) which also incorporated some existing parties, including the Communist party and other parties of the left, as well as newly mobilized social movements and groups. Cárdenas became its presidential candidate for the 1988 elections.

The Cárdenas candidacy was very popular. The campaign appealed to the ideals of Mexico's revolutionary heritage—nationalism and social justice, in effect, taking over the traditional ideals of the PRI, as well as promoting democracy and an end to PRI hegemony. Fond memories of his father, Lázaro Cárdenas, and of the reforms carried out during his administration, particularly in the rural sector, also strengthened the appeal of Cuauhtémoc Cárdenas. In the meantime, de la Madrid not only did not democratize the nomination process, but selected Carols Salinas de Gortari, who as secretary of Budget and Planning had been responsible for the modernization and austerity program under de la

Madrid, as the PRI presidential candidate. Despite the experience and expertise of the PRI in getting out crowds, Cárdenas was the obvious favorite during campaign. Nevertheless, when the votes were counted, Salinas was declared the victor in the elections by a bare majority (50.1 percent). Mexicans were highly suspicious of this outcome, particularly as the computer system tallying the votes allegedly broke down in the middle of the vote count. Many in fact believed that Cárdenas actually obtained the most votes, in spite of the usual fraudulent practices by the PRI machine, especially in the countryside, where PRI officials and caciques were accustomed to controlling the vote through intimidation or various favors. Groups within FDN refused to accept the outcome of the election, and formed the Democratic Revolutionary Party, the PRD, headed by Cárdenas.

The period between the presidential elections of 1988 and those of 1994 was a critical one in Mexico's transition toward free and fair elections. In addition to the formation of what would become an important new opposition party, the Cárdenas candidacy in the 1988 presidential campaign raised the possibility of change through the electoral process. The obvious fraud of the 1988 elections and the questionable victory of Salinas led to a focus on electoral transparency and the mobilization of Mexican citizens to monitor local and state elections.[11] The pro-democracy groups and networks that had emerged in the previous decades were mobilized, and by 1994, approximately 400 civic action groups existed in 20 of Mexico's 31 states. In April of that year, the Civic Alliance was formed, linking these groups in a loose confederation, which would play an important role in the presidential elections of 1994 as well as subsequent elections.

In the meantime, the new Salinas government confronted several challenges. The PRI now faced two major opposition parties. The opposition also had gained positions within the legislature, although it continued to be PRI dominated. The economic difficulties resulting from the crisis and the austerity measures instituted by the de la Madrid administration had resulted in widespread popular alienation, evident in the growth of opposition forces and support for opposition parties. The groups that formed the traditional base of PRI support, including labor, the peasantry, and small businesses, had been weakened due to the inability of the PRI to deliver benefits as in the past. The legitimacy of the PRI government was further eroded as a result of the flagrant manipulation of the 1988 electoral outcome.

While continuing and expanding the economic restructuring of the de la Madrid administration, discussed in Chapter 4, the Salinas government sought to counter the erosion of support. One form this took was to respond to opposition accusations of fraud in local and gubernatorial elections allegedly won by the PRI. In some cases, particularly where the contested electoral outcomes generated embarrassing national and international publicity, there were negotiations between the opposition party and the PRI, resulting in a third person taking office, and/or new elections. In the 1991 gubernatorial elections in San Luis Potosi, Dr. Salvador Nava, who had re-emerged politically in the 1980s and had been elected a second time as mayor of the city of San Luis Potosí, ran as an independent in a somewhat uneasy coalition that included the PAN, the PRD, and a local right-wing party, as well as the Potosí Civic Front, which Nava and his supporters had formed in the 1980s. Despite their differences, the parties shared with the Potosi front the goal of ending the one-party system, and could unite around Nava's platform calling for democratic elections, freedom of the press, independent electoral institutions, and an end to corruption. The campaign succeeded in attracting national media attention as well as support from national political and intellectual leaders and human rights organizations. The electoral process itself was monitored by electoral observers from human rights organizations in San Luis and Mexico City who reported numerous instances of PRI manipulation and fraud both prior to and during the election, among them the removal of thousands of voters from the electoral role, intimidation of voters, and stuffing of ballot boxes.

When the PRI candidate, Fausto Zapata, was declared winner, Nava and his followers accused the Salinas government of failing to ensure democratic elections as promised and staged a series of mobilizations, including the formation of a human chain by women supporters around the government palace to prevent Zapata from taking office, and a dramatic 265-mile "Dignity March" to Mexico City which was joined by prominent national leaders. As the march, led by the now elderly and ailing Nava, gathered hundreds of thousands of adherents, the Salinas government agreed to negotiate; he called for the resignation of Zapata and the appointment of a new interim governor, a member of PRI who arranged for new elections in 1993.[12]

In other cases, the victory of the opposition candidate was recognized by the government, as occurred in the gubernatorial elections of Baja California (1989) and Chihuahua (1992) where the PAN candidates were declared winners. Recognition of these as well as PAN municipal victories was part of an agreement between PAN and PRI leaders whereby the government would respect electoral outcomes benefiting the PAN in return for PAN support for recognition of the Salinas victory in the 1988 elections as well as other legislative initiatives, and reflected the affinity between the PAN and the technocratic branch of the PRI with respect to the government's economic liberalization policies. The government was less willing to recognize the validity of electoral victories by the PRD, which had challenged the PRI's claim to be the party of the revolution, was adamantly opposed to economic liberalization, and was thus considered a more serious threat.

Some analysts have suggested that Salinas' goal was a virtual two-party system, with the PRI and the PAN contesting elections while the PRD was effectively neutralized. The PRD was indeed considerably weakened during this period, in part due to its own internal conflicts and divisions, but also due to PRI machinations, such as use of the media to associate the PRD with incompetence, violence and disorder, and in some cases more violent tactics: PRD leaders claim that 68 of its activists and officials in the state of Michoacán were assassinated in the period between 1988 and March 1994.

Both Miguel de la Madrid and Salinas carried out reforms of the electoral system, which responded to pressures from opposition groups and parties but at the same time ensured continued PRI hegemony, particularly as votes for opposition parties in the Chamber of Deputies increased following the 1977 reforms, eroding the PRI majority.[13] The de la Madrid government expanded the number of proportional representative seats in the Chamber of Deputies, which were distributed to opposition parties, from 100 to 200, thus increasing opposition presence, but subsequently gave the PRI access to these seats (previously solely for the opposition) in order to ensure an absolute majority in the Chamber. The Salinas reforms of 1990 and 1993 were similar in manipulating the number of majority party seats to ensure an absolute PRI majority. The 1990 reforms established a Federal Electoral Institute (replacing the former Federal Electoral Commission) to oversee elections, but it was under the control of the Ministry of the Interior and the president appointed its members. The 1993 reform did respond to opposition requests for representation in the Senate, increasing the number of senators per state from three to four with two senators from the majority party, a third allocated to the party with the second highest number of votes, and the fourth allocated according to the overall national vote.[14] (See Figure 5-2.)

The Salinas government also attempted to restructure the PRI and establish a new basis for PRI support. In an effort to undermine the control exercised by leaders of the corporatist sectors of the party, Salinas instituted internal reforms enabling individuals to join the party without being a member of a sectoral organization, and established representation on a geographic as well as a sectoral basis. In 1991, the CNOP (the National Confederation of Popular Organizations) was expanded to incorporate territorial as well as organizational members, and renamed FNOP (the National Front for Organizations and Citizens) two years later. But Salinas, like his predecessors, was ambivalent toward the corporatist sectors of the PRI; while they were regarded as corrupt, and were generally opposed to the economic changes that the technocrats were seeking to implement, he needed them to ensure political support and electoral victories.

To establish a new basis for PRI support, Salinas sought to appeal to groups that benefitted from the economic reforms, including business groups benefiting from

Figure 5-2 Electoral Reforms: 1977–2000

1997 (Lopez Portillo). Expanded number of Chamber of Deputies seats to 400 with 100 distributed to minority parties according to their share of the vote. Facilitated registration of new parties (by providing for conditional registration prior to elections, to be confirmed if and when vote for party attained sufficient threshold) and gave legal standing to several parties that had been outlawed, including Mexican Communist party. Public funds would be distributed to parties according to their share in the previous elections.

1986 (de la Madrid). Increased number of seats in Chamber of Deputies distributed by proportional representation from 100 to 200, permitting increase in opposition.

1987 (de la Madrid). Established Tribunal for Electoral Disputes to adjudicate electoral disputes. Gave the PRI access to seats distributed by proportional representation by granting the relative majority party a sufficient number to make it an absolute majority ("governability clause"). Also made party registration more difficult. Created Federal District representative assembly.

1900 (Salinas). Introduced "sliding scale" in Chamber of Deputies to enable largest party to obtain 2 additional seats for every percentage point above 35 percent of total vote, further ensuring its absolute majority. Creation of Federal Electoral Institute formally independent of government but still under control of Ministry of Interior with majority PRI representation. Reintroduced conditional registration.

1993 (Salinas). Reallocated distribution of 200 proportional representation seats in Chamber according to each party's share of total vote. Introduced minority representation in the Senate, increasing number of senate seats per state from 3 to 4, with two going to the party with majority vote, the third to the party with the second largest number of votes, and the fourth allocated according to the overall national vote.

1994 (Salinas). Federal Electoral Commission remained under control of the Interior Ministry, but other members were non-partisan citizen representatives elected by major parties. Permitted international electoral observers.

1996 (Zedillo). Replaced the Minister of the Interior as head of IFE with an independent non-partisan citizen, making it completely independent. Replaced the Tribunal for Electoral Disputes with the Electoral Tribunal of the Judicial Branch, which ensured its independence of the executive. Established that majority party representation in Chamber could not exceed its vote by more than 8 percent, and established that no party can have more than two-thirds of the total. Federal District Electoral Law reformed, enabling citizens of Federal District to elect their own government. Private sources of campaign funding limited to ten percent of the total; remaining funds would come from government and be distributed by the IFE. Parties given greater access to free media coverage on radio and television.

the privatization of state assets, new export interests, and new urban groups. He envisioned a shift in the basis of PRI legitimacy: from representation and implementation of the populist goals of the revolution to an emphasis on Mexico's modernization and integration with the world economy and becoming a "first world" nation.

In keeping with his rejection of the corporatist model, he advocated a new type of labor relations based on cooperation between management and workers, epitomized by negotiations between the telephone workers union and Telmex at the time of its privatization, in which unionized workers retained their jobs and obtained a small share of the stock of the company in return for management control over hiring and wages tied to productivity increases. The leader of the union, Francisco Hernández Juárez, was hailed as a model of the "new" labor leadership, and the government supported his formation of a new federation, FESEBES (Federation of Goods' and Services' Unions), in spite of CTM opposition. The government also instituted social programs to respond to the needs and enlist the support of the more disadvantaged sectors of the population. Salinas advocated an ideology of "social liberalism" that would combine economic liberalization with social concern for the poorest sectors, at the same time promoting the ideal of a leaner but more effective state through targeted aid rather than blanket subsidies as in the past. The most important program was the National Solidarity Program, or PRONASOL, which provided funding for a range of services in rural and urban municipalities including schools, health clinics, electricity, and potable water. PRONASOL involved collaboration between the federal government and local organizations designed to bypass local PRI representatives, although PRI officials often took credit for and benefited from PRONASOL programs. PRONASOL also had a partisan component: much of its funding went to areas such as Michoacán, where the PRD had a strong following, in an apparent effort to undercut its support.[15]

As indicated in Chapter 4, the events of the early 1990s appeared to justify the policies and optimism of Salinas and the technocrats. Mexico had succeeded in reducing its budget deficit, and inflation was down from 160 percent in 1987 to 19 percent in 1991. Attracted to Mexico's growing stock market, foreign investment poured into the country, reaching $20 billion in 1991 alone. NAFTA, which was scheduled to go into effect on January 1, 1994, had been presented as an agreement that would provide business opportunities and jobs, "a rising tide that would lift all boats" and in the process lift Mexico into the ranks of a first world country. Promises of future prosperity, as well as the popularity of programs such as PRONASOL, had re-established the legitimacy of the government among broad sectors of the population. Previously seen as a weak and ineffectual candidate, Salinas had proved to be a popular and effective president, both in Mexico and among international financial circles, where he was being discussed as a candidate to head the new World Trade Organization. Events of 1994 would provide a rude awakening.

1994 AND THE ADMINISTRATION OF ERNESTO ZEDILLO (1994–2000)

The year began with the Zapatista uprising in Chiapas on January 1, the date that NAFTA went into effect. The uprising focused national and international attention on the fact that the new economic program was leaving significant sectors of the population behind, worse off than before. It also threatened to undermine the political and economic stability necessary for business confidence and foreign investment that Salinas had sought to cultivate. The immediate reaction of the government was to send in the military to repress the uprising. But in contrast to the repression of previous guerrilla movements, the abuses of the military in Chiapas were widely publicized, in part the result of the large number of international journalists in Mexico to cover the initiation of

NAFTA as well as the increased independence of the Mexican press. The result was widespread protests by both Mexican and international human rights groups against repressive government tactics.[16] The government called off the military assault and initiated negotiations with the Zapatistas, which continued for several months.

Less than three months later, however, Mexico faced another crisis: on March 23, the PRI candidate for the 1994 presidential elections, Donaldo Luis Colosio, was assassinated at a rally in Tijuana. The gunman was arrested and convicted but many were suspicious that he was not acting on his own. Although subsequent investigations failed to find evidence of a conspiracy, it was widely believed that members of the drug cartels or even groups within the PRI disgruntled at political reforms were behind the assassination—the first of an official at this level since the assassination of president-elect Alvaro Obregon in 1928.

In addition to the Zapatista uprising and the assassination of Colosio, the climate of political instability was aggravated by a series of kidnappings of high-level business leaders. Political instability was a factor in the growing flight of capital, although economic factors were responsible as well, among them an overvalued peso and fear of devaluation.

It was in this uncertain climate that the Salinas government enacted another set of electoral reforms, responding to pressures by the PRD, which had rejected the earlier reforms as superficial and insisted it would not accept the election results without further changes. The most significant development was the change in the composition of the Federal Electoral Institute; it would continue to be headed by the Ministry of the Interior but the other officials would be non-partisan citizens nominated by the major opposition parties. It also permitted international observers for the first time. (See Figure 5-2)

In addition, as noted above, the Salinas sexenio had been a period of increased civic activism. In April 1994, several human rights and pro-democracy organizations that had formed after the 1988 elections established the Civic Alliance, which was joined by other NGOS, labor unions, and social movements. The members of these groups were from different political and ideological perspectives and included professors, students, citizen groups, social activists, and members of Christian base communities. During the 1994 presidential campaign, the Civic Alliance carried out campaigns to inform citizens of their political rights and mobilized some 20,000 observers to monitor the elections throughout Mexico. The presence of electoral observers was undoubtedly a factor in the relative transparency of the 1994 elections compared with those of the past, although there were widespread electoral violations, notably in the rural area.[17]

Following the assassination of Colosio, Salinas picked Ernesto Zedillo, another technocrat and secretary of Education in the Salinas administration, to be the PRI candidate. The two other major candidates were Cárdenas of the PRD, and Diego Fernández de Cevallos of the PAN. Elections were now more competitive in that opposition candidates and parties were recognized and able to participate effectively in the electoral campaign. Thus, although some opposition groups and electoral observers found instances of fraud, the victory of the PRI candidate was not as controversial as it had been in 1988. Most observers agreed that the elections were the most honest in Mexico in a long time and that the Zedillo victory was legitimate.

Under these conditions, how can the Zedillo victory be explained? First, although Zedillo was not a charismatic candidate, the two major opposition candidates did not appear sufficiently strong or prepared to govern in an unstable situation. Given the critical situation in the country, many may have felt that despite its problems, the PRI was the only party with sufficient experience to deal with the economic and political problems Mexico was confronting. Second, although fraud was reduced, the electoral arena was not a level playing field. PRI's control of government gave it several advantages. Although the media was more autonomous than before, the PRI had greater access to media coverage, particularly through the two major television networks, Televisa, which was closely aligned with the PRI, and Azteca, which, though privatized, also followed the government line. And although weakened, PRI's clientelist networks still existed, particularly in rural areas, and the practice of using threats, intimidation, bribes and promises to secure votes continued to be widespread in some areas.

Finally, while the Salinas government wished to maintain at least a façade of democracy and transparency while the NAFTA deal was pending and to end PRI dependence on government financing, the PRI could count on substantial support by business groups that had benefitted from privatization and other measures by the Salinas administration. A particularly scandalous example is an intimate dinner party given in February 1993 and attended by top party and government officials, including Salinas himself, as well as many of the new billionaires. The ostensible purpose was to discuss a five-point program for the next PRI administration, but the climatic event was a discussion of contributions by business groups to the pending campaign, culminating with a pledge of $25 million by each participant for a total of $750 million—five times what the Democratic party in the United States had spent on the 1992 elections.[18] Thus, while the actual vote on election day was relatively transparent, events preceding the vote virtually ensured the continued hegemony of the PRI.

Zedillo took office in a climate of continued political and economic instability. In September there was another high-level assassination, this time the secretary general of the PRI, José Francisco Ruíz Massieu. Ruíz Massieu was the former brother-in-law of Salinas, and high-level PRI politicians were implicated,

one of whom subsequently disappeared and was believed to have been murdered. Kidnappings of top businessmen for ransom continued; there were frequent demonstrations, and rumors of peasant revolts in different areas of the
country. Capital flight continued, with both Mexican and foreign investors with-
drawing funds from Mexico. Finally, in December, when Mexico's foreign
reserves were dangerously low, Zedillo attempted to float the peso. Instead, it
plunged on the international market, revealing the precariousness of the economic recovery. Mexico was again confronted with an economic crisis, with
inflation over 40 percent and prospects of more unemployment and underemployment. As noted in Chapter 4, the costs of the peso crisis were enormously
high in terms of jobs lost—an estimated one million in 1995—and declining
wages.

Zedillo's first years in the presidency were spent coping with the crisis. He
secured a loan of $48 billion from the United States, the International Monetary
Fund, and other countries and international lending agencies, and he initiated a
massive austerity program, which helped to restore Mexico's macro-economic balance. He succeeded in repaying the debt to the United States three years early, in
part by raising interest rates to encourage the sale of government bonds. Interest
rates went up from 20 percent to 120 percent in the first few months of 1995, leading to a wave of bankruptcies by businesses and individuals unable to repay their
debts, and banks threatened to repossess farms, businesses, and other possessions.

This in turn led to a major crisis in the banking system. In the absence of
sufficient regulatory controls, the excessive borrowing of the 1990 to 1994 period
had already resulted in an increase in the ratio of non-performing loans
(loans that could not be repaid). With the peso crisis and the massive increase
in interest rates, non-performing loans increased to 30 percent of the total by
1997, and many banks were also facing bankruptcy. The Zedillo government
enacted a rescue package for the banks, in effect taking over their debt at the cost
of an estimated $100 billion—more than eight times what the government
received from re-privatizing the banks, and vastly increasing the government's
debt-service burden.[19]

The Zedillo administration continued to target strategic government sectors for privatization, including Mexico's port facilities, which, as in the past,
were restructured prior to sale to make them attractive to private investors. The
government has also opened certain operations of PEMEX and CFE (the Federal
Electric Commission) to private investment, although PEMEX is off-limits for
full privatization and labor and other social groups have strongly resisted the
privatization of Mexico's electric power system. Mexico's social security system
was partly privatized, however, with workers obliged to choose among private
banks, designated as Retirement Fund Administrators (Afores), to administer
their pension funds.

Zedillo also liberalized foreign investment in the financial sector, permitting foreign banks, previously restricted to 15 percent of ownership, to acquire up to 100 percent of private banks.[20] The result was a spurt of foreign investment in Mexican banks and an increase in foreign bank-ownership, either through joint investments with private Mexican owners or complete ownership. While in 1994 only one bank (of a total of 20) was foreign owned, by 2000 the number was 20 out of 34. Between 1999 and 2004, foreign bank control of bank assets rose from approximately 20 percent to over 80 percent of the total.

While international bankers and investors were pleased with these initiatives, many middle-class consumers and small businesses that confronted financial ruin were added to the ranks of those affected by the peso crisis. One result was a resurgence in anti-government demonstrations including middle-class groups that had never demonstrated or participated in politics before. One example (discussed in the next Chapter) is *El Barzón*, initially consisting of farmers threatened with foreclosure, which expanded to include families threatened with eviction, middle-class credit card debtors and small business groups. There was also a resurgence in labor mobilization, and a new independent labor confederation was formed that challenged the dominance of the CT. A second guerrilla group, the EPR (Revolutionary Popular Army) emerged in southern Mexico in 1996 and carried out attacks against military posts and convoys. Peasants and ejidatarios staged land invasions, and in some cases peasants attacked trains and warehouses for grain and other food supplies.

Crime levels also increased. In the border city of Juarez, dozens, and eventually hundreds, of young women—many of them maquiladora workers—disappeared and were later found murdered and often sexually abused. Local law enforcement agencies were not only ineffective in resolving these crimes but frequently implicated in them. Crime victims also included members of the upper and middle classes kidnapped for ransom.

Much of the crime was related to drug trafficking. Following the U.S. closure of the Caribbean corridor as a major conduit for drug trafficking from Colombia to the United States, the Colombian cartels had shifted their transportation routes to Mexico, which became the major channel for the transfer of cocaine as well as a significant producer of marijuana and heroin. This was accompanied by an increase in corruption, as drug dealers bought off or intimidated local officials, as well as in violence, as drug dealers targeted leaders and members of rival drug cartels, journalists who exposed drug dealers, and judges and prosecutors who attempted to bring them to justice. High-level government officials were also involved in corruption. When the Zedillo administration sought to shift responsibility for drug control from the corrupt federal police to the military, General José de Jesús Gutiérrez Robello, appointed to head the

National Institute to Combat Drugs, was subsequently discovered to have connections with Mexico's major drug cartel.

In addition, human rights organizations estimated that there were some 300 political assassinations in the period 1994–1997, including journalists, government officials, members of political parties, and leaders of social organizations, as well as guerrillas, soldiers and policemen. In some cases, PRI militants and/or government officials were involved in the slayings. In 1995, policemen massacred 17 peasants in the state of Guerrero, an event that was captured on video. In December 1997, paramilitary forces linked to the PRI surrounded a church in Acteal, Chiapas where families had gone for protection and killed 45 men, women and children.

There were efforts during the Zedillo administration to reform the judicial system but these affected mainly the upper levels.[21] Reforms initiated in 1994–95 reduced the membership of the Supreme Court from 25 to 11, had judges nominated by the president and approved by two-thirds of the Senate, and reduced the term of members from a lifetime to 15 years. The Supreme Court was also able to rule on constitutional matters, veto legislation through judicial review, and resolve conflicts between branches and levels of government. However, high levels of corruption and incompetence in law enforcement agencies at the state and local levels continue to undermine the rule of law, with contradictory results: on the one hand, failure to effectively prosecute criminal behavior, as evident in the Juárez case, on the other, arbitrary arrests and practices such as the use of torture to obtain confessions.

The emergence of the EZLN (Zapatistas) and the EPR and the increase in crime and drug trafficking led to an expansion in the internal security role of the Mexican military. During the Zedillo administration, the ranks of the armed forces expanded to nearly 240,000 by 2000. Another major change beginning in the Zedillo administration was the growth in collaboration with the U.S. military, which had formerly been regarded with suspicion. This was evident in a marked increase in the number of military personnel receiving training in the United States, including the School of the Americas, the Inter-American Air Force Academy, the Inter-American Defense College and the CIA, which provided intelligence and counter-narcotics training to several officers. The United States also encouraged greater involvement of the Mexican military in the drug war as it was considered relatively immune to corruption compared to the police force.[22] This collaboration has increased in subsequent administrations, particularly with the Mérida Initiative, an extensive program of U.S. aid to Mexico and Central America to combat drug trafficking (see Chapter 8). The augmented role of the military in combating drug trafficking as well as crime has increased its visibility, giving rise to internal debates regarding the role of the military in civilian activities.

In response to the growth in protest movements as well as the increasing economic polarization and poverty in the 1990s, the Zedillo administration sought to compensate for government neglect of the domestic business sector and to expand efforts at poverty alleviation. It initiated programs to assist small and medium producers, often entailing collaboration between the federal government, state governments, and business groups. One of the more effective of these is CRECE, a network of Regional Centers for Business Competitiveness, established in each of Mexico's states and funded by the Mexican government and regional business chambers.[23] It also instituted PROGRESA (National Education, Health and Nutrition Program), which provided direct assistance to poor rural households for health care, education, and child nutrition. Subsequently during the PAN administrations, the program was renamed OPORTUNIDADES and expanded to include the urban as well as the rural poor.

In the meantime, the Civic Alliance continued to organize election monitoring of local and state elections by local citizens and to push for electoral reforms. It also promoted citizen monitoring of the media and carried out investigations of vote buying and forced voting. As a result of pressures from both the PAN and the PRD, the Zedillo government passed what it called the definitive electoral reform, which established that the chairperson of the Federal Electoral Institute would be a non-partisan citizen, making the Institute fully autonomous, placed the Electoral Tribunal under the judicial branch of government, thus freeing it from executive control, and eliminated the ability of any party to obtain control of the Chamber of Deputies if it did not have a majority vote. It also increased public financing and media coverage for the opposition parties. Finally, it permitted the election of the mayor of the Federal District, which had previously been governed by a regent appointed by the president. (See Figure 5-2.)

These reforms, as well as the appointment of a member of the Civic Alliance to head the Federal Voter Registry, helped to build confidence in the electoral process. In addition, as noted previously, the media had become increasingly independent of the government. Zedillo also continued the Salinas policy of recognizing opposition victories, and PAN candidates became governors in several states, the most important of which was that of a businessman, Vicente Fox, the representative of Coca Cola in Mexico, who was elected governor of Guanajuato.

One result has been the increase in alteration in office at the state and municipal levels, as well as divided governments, with different parties controlling the federal, state and local governments. The Zedillo government also expanded efforts to decentralize government resources, a process that began in the 1980s through transferring revenue, notably for education, health care and infrastructure, to states and municipalities. By the end of the 1990s, approximately half of government expenditures were under the jurisdiction of sub-national governments. The erosion of federal centralization means that state governors have become more powerful political actors. At the same time, the federal government has retained and even increased its control over taxation, which enables it to focus resources on poorer states and has led to increasing conflict between poor states favoring redistribution and wealthy states resenting the use of their taxes for this purpose.[24]

Just how much the political scene had changed became evident in the legislative and municipal elections of 1997, which turned out to be another major turning point in Mexico's political transition. PRI control of the legislature was eliminated, with four opposition parties—the PAN, the PRD, and two smaller parties, the Labor Party and the Green Party (PVEM)—collectively holding the majority of seats in the Chamber of Deputies.[25] The PAN was the major beneficiary of what was, in part, a "punishment" vote against the PRI, but the PRD also improved its position in the legislature, and PRD candidate Cuauhtémoc Cárdenas won the first mayoral electoral contest in Mexico City. The PRD has continued to control this position in subsequent elections, and Mexico City mayors, first Cuauhtémoc Cárdenas and subsequently Andrés Manuel López Obrador, became the PRD candidates for the presidency in the 2000 and 2006 elections, respectively (See Table 5-1).

By 2000, electoral reforms and election outcomes had had the effect of eroding the concentration of power in the federal government and particularly the executive. Opposition victories at the local and state levels as well as decentralization measures, including an increase in government revenues destined to state and local governments reduced the dominance of the federal government. At the same time, opposition victories in the legislature, which previously could

Table 5-1. Composition of Chamber of Deputies: 1997–2009

Political Parties	1997	2000	2003	2006	2009
Institutional Revolutionary Party (PRI)	239	208	224	106	237
National Action Party (PAN)	121	205	151	206	143
Democratic Revolutionary Party (PRD)	125	54	97	125	69
Ecological Green Party of Mexico (PVEM)	8	17	17	17	21
Labor Party (PT)	7	8	6	11	13
Party of Convergence for Democracy (PCD)		8	5	18	8
New Alliance Party				9	9
Social Democratic and Peasant Alternative				5	
Independent/Other				3	
TOTAL	500	500	500	500	500

Sources: Klesner, Joseph L. "Institutionalizing Mexico's New Democracy," in *Changing Structure of Mexico: Political Social and Economic Prospects*, Second Edition. Edited by Laura Randall. Armonk, New York: M.E. Sharpe, 2006; Mexico: Cámara de Diputados, "Composición por tipo de elección y Grupo Parlamentario" (http://www.diputados.gob.mx).

be counted on to automatically approve executive initiatives, limited the power of the presidency. The relative independence of the Supreme Court in recent years has been demonstrated by rulings against both the Zedillo and Fox administrations. Mexico had made significant progress toward what has been termed "horizontal accountability," and for the first time Mexicans began to view an opposition victory in the presidential elections as a real possibility.

The hope for a defeat of the PRI in the presidential elections of 2000 generated considerable excitement among the opposition groups. Some efforts were made to field a coalition candidate of the two major opposition parties, but they were unable to reach agreement and ultimately the PAN and the PRD ran their own candidates. Cuauhtémoc Cárdenas was the candidate of an alliance of the PRD and smaller parties, and the governor of Guanajuato, Vicente Fox, became the candidate of an alliance led by the PAN, although he also formed his own electoral group, the Amigos de Fox. One of the business leaders who had become involved in PAN electoral politics in the 1980s, Fox had been supervisor of Coca Cola in Mexico and later for all of Latin America, and he had served as a federal deputy as well as governor of Guanajuato. For the first time in its history, the PRI candidate was selected through a primary, with Francisco Labastida, a technocrat supported by Zedillo, edging out Roberto Madrazo of the party's traditional wing.

Despite the failure to field a single candidate, some PRD voters (as well as some from the PRI) switched their allegiance to Fox, a charismatic candidate who was the clear favorite. Fox won a sweeping victory, obtaining 42.5 percent of the vote compared to 36.1 percent for Labastida and 16.6 percent for Cárdenas. Much of the vote for Fox was undoubtedly a vote against PRI and a vote for change. Nevertheless, the defeat of the PRI, which turned the Mexican government over to the opposition for the first time in 71 years, was a significant step in Mexico's transition toward a more pluralistic system, and the Fox victory was widely acclaimed as evidence that Mexico was now a formal democracy.

MEXICO'S POLITICAL TRAJECTORY: A SUMMARY

As elsewhere in Latin America, the transition from an authoritarian to a more democratic regime in Mexico included elements of popular mobilization, regime liberalization, and elite bargaining, which interacted within the context of Mexico's economic crisis, the introduction of a new economic model, and the particular character of Mexico's political system. The economic crisis weakened the corporatist PRI model, reducing the resources it could draw on to meet the demands of constituents and buy off dissident groups. At the same time the crisis resulted in economic hardship for substantial sectors of the population, which was in many cases aggravated by the disruptions introduced in the new economic model, which further reduced government legitimacy and was a factor (though not the only one) in the growth of social movements, civic organizations, and opposition parties, including the FDN and its successor, the PRD, which won the support of many of the disaffected groups. The erosion of government legitimacy was also a result of populist PRI politics in the 1970s, culminating in the nationalization of the banks in 1982, which alienated business sectors and increased their political activism, evident in the emergence of the Panista entrepreneurs who were important in the growth of the PAN and its electoral victories in several cities of the north and center.

The process of globalization was also a factor in Mexico's transition to a new economic model and had the effect of increasing Mexico's international exposure, particularly with the NAFTA negotiations in the early 1990s, which raised the issue of democracy in Mexico.

These processes directly and indirectly prompted the government to make changes in the electoral laws during the 1980s. The increase in opposition victories in legislative elections during this period threatened the hegemony of the PRI in the Chamber of Deputies; thus several reforms of the 1980s and early 1990s could be seen as regressive, intended to ensure the PRI's continued control of the legislature. At the same time, the PRI's loss of legitimacy following the 1982 economic crisis and the bank nationalization was a factor in the increased recognition of opposition victories, particularly of the PAN, in municipal elections, although this was suspended when the extent of support for the PAN became clear. The obvious fraud and problematic victory of Salinas in the 1988 elections further undermined the legitimacy of the PRI government and alerted the administration to the new threat it confronted on the left. Because the PAN generally supported the government's economic policies, it was seen as the lesser of two evils, with the result that the government began to recognize PAN victories at the state level while attempting by various mechanisms to neutralize the threat of the PRD. Thus began what can be seen as a series of formal or informal pacts between the PRI and the PAN opposition, in which the PAN supported government initiatives in return for recognition of its electoral victories as well as further reforms. Although the government sought to ensure continued PRI domination, as evident in the reforms of the early 1990s, Salinas recognized that the days of a one-party system were numbered, and presumably saw a virtual two-party system in which the PAN and the PRI would contest power as the most desirable alternative.

However, the impetus for the major electoral reform of the Salinas administration came from the left—indirectly, in the Zapatista uprising and the highly unstable economic and political conditions that ensued, which enabled the PRD as well as the PAN to pressure for meaningful reforms as a condition for accepting the results of the pending presidential elections. The 1994 electoral reforms increased the independence of the Federal Electoral Institute and permitted international election observers for the first time. Combined with the growth of civic action groups and the formation of the Civic Alliance following the 1988 elections, the 1994 reform ensured greater oversight over the 1994 elections, which were generally seen as the most transparent up to that time.

The devastating effects of the peso crisis (1994–95) resulted in increased mobilization of various groups. In a climate of political and economic uncertainty, the PAN and the PRD both pressed for further changes, and Zedillo passed the 1996 reforms which made the Federal Electoral Institute fully autonomous and incorporated other changes to ensure the transparency of the electoral process and level the playing field for opposition parties. The 1997 elections increased the presence of both the PAN and the PRD in Congress, eliminating the PRI majority, and strengthened their position in state and local governments. The process of political transition culminated in the 2000 presidential elections and the defeat of PRI after 71 years in power.

THE FOX ADMINISTRATION (2000–2006)

Those hoping for major changes as a result of the Fox victory, however, were disappointed. President Fox confronted a more complex system than the previous presidents in a PRI-dominated system. Reduction in executive control, decentralization of the government and the presence of viable opposition parties meant a more pluralist system but one that is also more contentious. Relations between different levels of government may be complicated if each is controlled by a different party.[26] In terms of executive-legislative relations, initiatives that were automatically approved by the legislature in the past were now subject to debate, and delays and obstruction as a result of inter- and even intra-party differences and conflicts. Fox could not necessarily depend on PAN support; as one of the new "entrepreneurial" Panistas, whose political action group, Amigos de Fox, had to some extent bypassed the PAN during the electoral campaign, Fox was not entirely trusted by traditional Panistas. Economic reforms proposed by Fox, including expansion of the value added tax to include food and medicine, the privatization of the electric power industry, and labor reforms, were opposed by the PRI and the PRD. Proposed legislation to recognize indigenous rights— the result of prolonged negotiation between the EZLN and the government— was diluted by both PRI and PAN representatives in Congress, which placed limitations on the local autonomy of indigenous groups, resulting in its rejection by the EZLN.

In contrast to Salinas, a weak candidate who proved to be a strong president, Fox was a strong candidate but was generally seen as an ineffective president. While the loss of presidential authority and intra- and inter-party conflicts within

Congress were undoubtedly factors, Fox failed to work effectively with the legislature, and presidential domination was replaced by stalemate. In the absence of a strong executive power, other actors have filled the vacuum: state governors who took advantage of the increase in state revenues to create new centers of power; Mexico's economic elite, including 10 billionaires whose combined fortunes rose over 200 percent during the Fox sexenio; and drug lords who have been able to take advantage of the growing market for drugs in both the United States and Mexico as well as the easy supply of weaponry from the United States.[27]

Fox also suffered from a slowdown in the economy. After recovering in the late 1990s, Mexico's growth rates were sluggish in the first years of the 2000s, averaging less than 1 percent a year. They improved to 4 percent in 2004 but fell to a disappointing 3 percent in 2005. One problem was the lack of credit available to firms, especially small businesses, even after the denationalization of the banking sector; between 1994 and 2004 bank loans fell from 33 percent of GDP to 15 percent.[28]

The governments of Fox and his successor, Felipe Calderón, can be credited with the expansion of the anti-poverty programs introduced in the previous administrations, particularly OPORTUNIDADES (formerly PROGRESA), which now includes five million families and incorporates approximately a fourth of the Mexican population.[29] According to virtually all studies and evaluations, the program has been successful at several levels. Poverty has been reduced; rates of extreme poverty, which had increased from 21.2 percent of the population in 1994 to 37.4 percent in 1996, following the peso crisis, had dropped to 13.8 percent by 2006. Infant mortality has declined by 11 percent, and malnutrition, anemia, and both childhood and adult diseases have been reduced, as has the consumption of alcohol and tobacco by youth. Secondary school attendance has increased, notably in the countryside.

A significant, although unmeasured, result has been the implications for the empowerment of women. Because women were more likely to spend extra income on their families, the funds were dispersed to women rather than men, which, given patriarchal norms, particularly in the countryside, could result in jealousy on the part of spouses and even domestic violence. The program sought to compensate by setting up self-esteem workshops for women in addition to programs on such issues as health and nutrition. These programs, as well as growing manifestations of the benefits of the program over time, could reduce patriarchy in the affected areas.

The program is highly cost-effective, with 97 percent of the funds going to beneficiaries, and has been a model for similar programs in other parts of the world—even New York City. At the same time it confronts a variety of problems in Mexico, among them the poor quality of education and overcrowded classrooms, particularly in rural areas; it also raises questions regarding the availability of jobs to employ the youth who benefit from more education and healthcare.

Apart from anti-poverty programs, the decline in poverty has been attributed to factors such as the demographic dividend (the decline in fertility rates, population growth, and dependency ratio and the increase in the percentage of the economically active population), increased levels of emigration (from approximately 250,000 annually in the 1980s to 400,000 in the early 2000s), and the growth in remittances (which increased four times between the early 1990s to the 2000s and go primarily to poorer sectors of the population).[30] Migrant remittances have become a mainstay of the Mexican economy, and the Fox administration made efforts to improve the conditions of Mexicans who migrate to the United States, cooperating with the U.S. government to obtain work permits and/or amnesty for Mexicans working there. Fox also suggested the establishment of a $20 billion fund that would help bridge the development gap between Mexico and the other two NAFTA countries, based on the European integration experience (a proposal that became known as NAFTA-Plus). But these efforts were stymied by increased U.S. security concerns resulting from the attacks of September 11, 2001 and by opposition within the U.S. Congress.

The Fox government also made various efforts to expand human rights, in keeping with a campaign promise to make human rights a priority. Among the groups that have benefitted are sexual minorities, despite Fox's conservative orientation. Although sexual minorities had begun organizing in the 1970s and had made considerable advances in terms of the acceptance of homosexuals in Mexico, homophobia continued to be a problem and resulted in extreme violence, including an estimated 1,200 killed between 1994 and 2006 due to their sexual identity. After Fox became president he appointed a committee to suggest measures to attack discrimination; the committee proposed legislation to provide protection against discrimination against various groups, including those with unconventional sexual preferences, which was approved by the president and passed by congress in 2003.[31]

Corruption continued to be widespread, now aggravated by the ease of financial gain through the expanding drug trade, which also became increasingly violent in the last years of the Fox sexenio (see Chapter 8). Extreme problems of crime and insecurity, and the continuing economic hardships of significant sectors of the population, resulted in widespread disillusion with the Fox administration and by extension with the PAN. As the campaign for the presidential and legislative elections of 2006 began, large sectors of the population were looking at the charismatic mayor of Mexico City, Andrés Manuel López Obrador, the prospective PRD candidate for president.

THE CONTENTIOUS ELECTION OF 2006

If the victory of PAN candidate Vicente Fox in the 2000 election convinced many Mexicans and international observers that Mexico had successfully made the transition to a democratic country, the elections of 2006 demonstrated how far that process had to go.[32] The three major candidates were Felipe Calderón of PAN, who had been energy secretary under the Fox government and was supported by a coalition that included the Green party as well as the PAN; Roberto Madrazo, a former governor and president of the PRI; and Andrés Manuel López Obrador, former PRD president and major of Mexico City, who ran with several smaller parties in a coalition, FAP (Broad Progressive Front). As PRD president, López Obrador had been credited with reorganizing the party and attracting new voters. When he became mayor of Mexico City he carried out a range of popular reforms, among them the distribution of free medicine to the poor and the inauguration of high schools in impoverished areas, as well as ambitious public works projects, including the restoration of the historical area of downtown Mexico and the construction of a second level peripheral highway.

Because of his popularity as mayor (with 80 percent support by residents) López Obrador was seen as a key threat to the other two major parties, which attempted to derail his candidacy even prior to the electoral campaign. In 2003, PAN and PRI legislators had excluded the PRD from the selection of delegates to the Federal Electoral Institute, which had previously been selected by the three major parties.[33] President Fox and the two parties attempted to have López Obrador impeached as mayor for a minor violation, which could have led to his imprisonment and would have disqualified him as a presidential candidate. Massive street demonstrations in Mexico City protesting this maneuver as well as international pressure convinced PAN and PRI leaders of the inadvisability of pursuing this track, and the charge was dismissed on a technicality.

Madrazo's reputation for fraud and corruption and his unpopularity with important segments of his own party—resulting in an unsuccessful attempt to launch a rival PRI candidacy and the decision of the powerful head of the SNTE (National Union of Education Workers), Elba Esther Gordillo, to leave the PRI and form her own party—weakened his candidacy. By the time the campaign began in January 2006 it had become in effect a two-way race between Calderón and López Obrador. Throughout most of the campaign, polls showed López Obrador with an advantage of several percentage points over Calderón, although this lead was significantly weakened in the final weeks before the election. The PAN and Mexican business groups launched a series of negative ads linking López Obrador to contentious Venezuelan president Hugo Chávez and labeling López Obrador a demagogue and danger to the country. These ads, as well as intervention by President Fox on behalf of Calderón, were illegal according to

Image 5-1 A street vendor in Mexico City sells masks resembling presidential candidates Manuel López Obrador, Felipe Calderón, and Roberto Madrazo prior to the 2006 elections.

Mexican electoral laws, but effective, as successive polls showed a gradual drop in support for López Obrador relative to Calderón. López Obrador also made mistakes, including refusing to participate in one of two major televised debates and responding too slowly to the negative campaigning against him.[34]

In addition, not all on the left were united in favor of López Obrador. Sub-Commandante Marcos of the EZLN issued a statement in which he denounced all of the parties, including the PRD, and advised EZLN sympathizers not to vote. The EZLN instead launched "the other campaign" to coincide with the presidential campaign, in which Zapatistas traveled throughout the country, meeting with various social and grassroots organizations in an effort to unite them in the search for alternative forms of governance. Marcos' opposition to the PRD could be partly explained by the fact that the PRD had supported the watered-down version of the indigenous bill that was passed unanimously by Congress in 2001. Since that vote, the Zapatistas had virtually disappeared from the national headlines, and Marcos had antagonized many of his former supporters, including progressive intellectuals, journalists and politicians with his acerbic and sometimes vitriolic comments. Given the waning of support for the Zapatistas, the antagonism of Marcos probably had very little influence on the election outcome, but it was resented by López Obrador supporters.

The initial vote count gave Calderón a slim majority of 244,000 votes—less than 1 percent of the total of 41 million. López Obrador challenged these results in the courts and in the streets, demanding a recount of the vote and charging that a series of irregularities committed by PAN, President Fox, and business groups had undermined the validity of the electoral process. The Electoral Tribunal agreed to a recount of 9 percent of the votes from those districts in which there were specific claims of voting irregularities but refused to order a complete recount. Based on the partial recount the tribunal ruled that errors and irregularities reflected honest mistakes rather than deliberate fraud and did not affect the outcome. Most international observers as well as national monitors believed that the actual electoral process had been free and fair. Although the tribunal denounced the negative campaigning against López Obrador, and ruled that private sector advertising had been illegal and that Fox's involvement undermined the integrity of the electoral process, it did not support López Obrador's claim that these activities invalidated the electoral process, and on September 5 ruled that Felipe Calderón had won the elections.

While pursuing legal channels, López Obrador brought his supporters into the streets in massive demonstrations. On August 1, while the electoral dispute was still undecided, hundreds of thousands of his supporters occupied the Zócalo and the major downtown streets, Avenida Juárez and Paseo de la Reforma, of Mexico City creating a tent "city," which they occupied until mid-September. This protest was remarkable in terms of its size, discipline, and the level of commitment and organization of its participants. Supporters of López Obrador came from all parts of the country to participate in the demonstrations and join the encampments, which included makeshift kitchens where food was provided for free, portable toilets, medical tents staffed by doctors, classes for children, and numerous forms of recreation and entertainment including games of various kinds and evening films and live music. The protestors, who included farmers and workers, housewives, grandmothers, politicians, and even entire families, endured inclement weather, including heavy rains and occasional hail storms, and for the most part maintained strict order following López Obrador's instructions to conduct a peaceful civil resistance and to avoid any form of violence.[35] When asked why they were there, participants gave a variety of responses, among them justice, equality, and preserving democracy.[36]

Although initially projected to remain until the Electoral Tribunal responded to the demand for a total recount, the "tent city" was finally dismantled on September 15. Mexico City residents and businesses complained about the disruptions caused by the occupation of its major thoroughfare, and by this time, López Obrador's support had begun to erode even among members of the PRD, who were turned off by his intransigence and escalating rhetoric, including the denunciation of the electoral institutions. Nevertheless, López Obrador continued to draw massive crowds to demonstrations, including a "convention" in which he was acclaimed as the "legitimate" president, and another massive demonstration on November 20 in which he took the "oath of office" and named his own cabinet. Although the controversy faded after Felipe Calderón was sworn into office on December 1, approximately one-third of the Mexican population continued to be convinced that the election was fraudulent.

The 2006 election demonstrated a strong geographic polarization between northern and center states, which were won by Calderón, and the southern states and Mexico City, in which López Obrador had the largest number of votes. (Madrazo did not carry a single state.) Although this division reflects to some extent the economic polarization of the country, the socio-economic breakdown indicated a somewhat different pattern, in which Calderón drew voters primarily among the wealthy and more highly educated and Madrazo among the poor and least educated, while López Obrador drew votes more or less equally from all socio-economic sectors, although slightly less from the highest income group.[37]

The elections, which included legislative as well as presidential elections, also suggested a further weakening of the PRI, which not only came in third place in the presidential election but became the smallest of the three major parties in the legislature, displaced from second place by the PRD, which as a result of the election became the largest opposition party. PRI continued to have major strength among state governors, however, and was further strengthened as a result of the 2009 midterm elections, which increased its number in the Chamber of Deputies, where the PRI alliance with the Green party (PVEM) constituted a majority (see Table 5-1), and the number of PRI governors.

The 2006 election also led to a serious split within the PRD, between a faction led by López Obrador, *Izquierda Democrática* (Democratic Left), which contended that the election was stolen and refused to cooperate with the Calderón government, and the *Nueva Izquierda* (New Left), a more moderate faction led by former PRD senator Jesús Ortega and aligned with former presidential candidate Cuauhtémoc Cárdenas, which is more open to cooperation with the PAN and the PRI.

The Calderón administration confronted a number of challenges during its first years in office, several of which have had implications for the nature of democracy in Mexico. One of the most pressing issues was (and is) the drug trade, which had escalated into a drug war among the different cartels and between the cartels and the government, with some 2000 people killed as a result of drug-related violence in 2006. Within weeks of taking office, Calderón dispatched military forces to nine states where drug production and/or trafficking were major problems, a move that was initially popular but has raised major concerns among human rights organizations, which have identified numerous violations committed by the military against civilian populations, and among pro-democracy groups, who are concerned about the militarization of the drug war and its implications for the corruption of the military and for civilian-military relations. The United States has pledged substantial aid to assist the Mexican forces in the drug war, which some critics contend may exacerbate these problems. In the meantime, the violence has escalated, with approximately 15,000 killed during the first three years of Calderón's administration.[38]

Calderón proved to be more adept in working with the legislature than Fox had been. In his first year in office, all the parties voted in favor of a moderate fiscal reform, which, among other conditions, increased taxes on corporate income. At the instigation of the PRD, the legislature also passed an electoral reform that would enable all of the three major parties to participate in electing representatives to the Federal Electoral Institute and eliminates campaign financing for radio and television ads, with TV stations required to provide free time for political campaigns. These measures would appear to rectify some of the issues that emerged during the 2006 campaign, although smaller parties complain that they were excluded.

Other measures were more controversial. A proposal to permit foreign investment in PEMEX, the state-owned oil company, initially met with resistance from both the PRI and the PRD. The Calderón government proposed the measure as a means to deal with the problem of insufficient funds for investment in upgrading PEMEX infrastructure and equipment as well as the need for foreign capital and technology to develop offshore oil resources. Petroleum is Mexico's major export earner, but Mexico had been unable to take advantage of the escalating price of oil earlier in the decade due to a decline in production. Both the PRI and the PRD expressed concern over foreign control of a major resource and symbol of Mexico's sovereignty; other groups were concerned that a Mexican owner could turn PEMEX into a private monopoly, as was the case with the privatization of Telmex. Critics also pointed out that the company's shortage of investment funds stemmed from the government's appropriation of a substantial proportion of PEMEX earnings as taxes and proposed that they be retained by PEMEX for reinvestment, a proposal that was incorporated in the final bill.[39] The measure, which would permit private companies, including foreign companies, to work with PEMEX to develop oil fields in the Gulf of Mexico, but does not permit foreign or joint ownership, was finally passed, with PAN, PRI, and the moderate faction of PRD voting in favor, while the López Obrador faction opposed.

The Calderón government moved more forcefully in the sphere of electric energy. Two state-owned companies have controlled its production and distribution: the Electric Light and Power Company (LFC), which services the Federal District and surrounding areas, and the Federal Electricity Commission

(CFE), responsible for the rest of the country. While the workers of the latter belong to a corporatist union, those of Electric Light and Power are members of the militant Mexican Electrical Workers Union (SME), which has resisted government efforts to upgrade the plant through foreign investment due to fears it would result in privatization and/or a foreign takeover of the plant. On October 11, 2009, charging that the company was inefficient, the Calderón government took advantage of an internal conflict within the SME and sent federal police to take over the company, liquidating it and firing its 44,000 workers.

Business leaders, many of whom agree with the Calderón government that the inefficiency of the company has been a major obstacle to economic growth, applauded the move. The SME and its supporters agree that the company has been inefficient but blame the problems on management, and even many who blame the union for its recalcitrant opposition to reform of the industry objected to the manner of the takeover. The union held several demonstrations protesting the takeover; it launched legal appeals in Mexico and has received support from international unions and labor organizations. However, the operations of the company have been taken over by the Federal Electricity Commission, and the majority of workers have accepted the government's invitation to apply for employment there or for compensation. It thus appears that the SME, one of the oldest and most independent unions in the country, has been effectively neutralized if not totally destroyed.

The Calderón government moved against other unions, including the Mine and Metalworkers Union. PAN governments have also attacked dissident social movements, notably in the case of APPO (Popular Assembly of the People of Oaxaca), a movement that originated around a teachers' strike in 2006 and expanded to incorporate numerous other groups when the PRI governor attacked the teachers (see Chapter 6). The Fox government eventually sent in the federal police to quell the movement and several of its leaders were arrested during both the Fox and Calderón governments.

DEMOCRATIZATION IN MEXICO: ACHIEVEMENTS AND OBSTACLES

A child of twelve in 1976 . . . knew that political representation was controlled by a single party, that the president, the governors, the immense majority of municipal presidents, as well as all of the senators and most of the deputies belonged to a single political organization, the PRI. A child of twelve today, in the Federal District, knows that his city is governed by the PRD, that the PRI governs the state of Mexico, and that the President of the Republic belongs to the PAN

—Woldenberg, 2007

Over the past 20 years, Mexico has made significant progress in the transition toward a more democratic system. Among the factors in this change were social dislocations resulting from the economic crises of the 1980s and the subsequent economic restructuring during the 1980s and 1990s. The general result was a de-legitimization of the PRI government, resulting in the mobilization of business groups in northern Mexico and in some central-west states which became active in the PAN and the emergence of an opposition party of the center left, composed of a dissident faction of the PRI and some small center-left parties and supported by new social groups and protest movements. The growing strength of the opposition was an impetus to increased activism by local action groups and national NGOs, which undertook various initiatives to ensure electoral transparency. The international context, including the democratic transition occurring elsewhere in Latin America and increased international scrutiny of Mexico's politics in the context of NAFTA negotiations were also influences in Mexico's transition process. In response to these pressures, successive governments carried out a series of electoral reforms which gradually established the conditions for democratic elections.

As a result, Mexico has made a successful transition from a dominant party system to a competitive system in which different parties contend for office at all levels of government. The emergence and expansion of opposition parties, sharply contested elections, opposition victories at the local and state levels, and finally the election of a non-PRI candidate as president, demonstrate that the hegemonic party system has ended in favor of a pluralist system of competing parties.

In addition, the playing field is considerably more level than before. For the most part, the political freedoms necessary to enable candidates to campaign and voters to vote without fear of reprisal exist, although voters may be subject to intimidation by local authorities in some localities. The monitoring of elections by civic organizations in Mexico and international observers reduces the possibilities for fraud, and problems of partisan control of the electoral institute and campaign financing that surfaced during the 2006 election appear to have been mitigated. The Federal Electoral Institute and the Federal Electoral Tribunal, which adjudicates electoral disputes, continue to be among the most respected institutions in Mexico. Partly as a consequence of citizen mobilization, there has been an increase in the independence of the media, and the government monopoly of financial resources has been reduced as a result of reforms allocating public funds to the major political parties.

Furthermore, largely as a result of political pluralism and institutional guarantees of (relatively) free and fair elections, presidential control has been reduced. The Congress no longer automatically approves legislation proposed by the executive. Members of the Supreme Court are nominated by the president but must be approved by two-thirds of the Senate, and recent court decisions have demonstrated the relative independence of the judiciary, at least at the higher levels. State governors and municipal officers are no longer appointed or approved by the president but subject to the electoral process, and have access to an increased share of federal resources.

In short, Mexico has made and continues to make progress toward fulfilling the minimal conditions for formal democracy. The Mexican system has also become more participatory. Large numbers of citizens have become directly involved in the political process through civic action committees and other institutions. In addition, certain social groups, notably women, are participating at a higher level than in the past. The number of women in the Chamber of Deputies has increased, representing 17 percent of the total following the 1997 congressional elections and 23.2 percent in 2006. Women have also held top cabinet-level positions and have headed both the PRD and the PRI in the recent past. The growth of civic organizations and social movements has expanded opportunities for participation in non-governmental organizations as well as providing opportunities for gaining political skills; today an estimated 15 percent of the urban population participates in voluntary organizations other than religious or recreational associations (see Chapter 6).

At the same time, democracy in Mexico is very much a work in process, and important obstacles remain to its consolidation. What are some of the challenges to democracy in Mexico today?

First, as in other democratizing countries, elements of authoritarianism continue to coincide with new democratic institutions and practices. Given the peculiar nature of Mexico's hegemonic system, which oversaw a long period of economic growth and combined repression with at least some efforts at redistribution and social reform, one of these elements is the continuation of clientelist practices and what some analysts define as habits of dependency and political passivity on the part of the population accustomed to relying on the dominant party and the state, although these tendencies have been mitigated by the growth of a range of social movements and civic organizations.

Second, despite the increased participation in civic activities, there is evidence that Mexico's system is becoming an elite democracy in which a substantial proportion of the population feels it is excluded, both politically and economically. The intervention of economic elites in the electoral process to block candidates of the left, as well as the agreements and tradeoffs between the PRI and PAN to the exclusion of the PRD, point to an exclusive system. The results of the 2006 election left a substantial proportion of the population feeling disenfranchised, and the use of coercion against dissidents, as indicated in the treatment of the activists of APPO and the neutralization of the SME, undermine other forms of participation by disadvantaged or excluded groups.

A third and related issue is the weakness of the rule of law. High-levels of crime and the resulting sense of insecurity are seen as a major problem by many Mexicans. The corruption and ineffectiveness of local law enforcement agencies and officials, many of whom are complicit in crimes and their cover-up, have undermined the effectiveness of judiciary reforms at the higher level. Mexico's position as a conduit for drugs going to the United States has aggravated the problem of corruption at all levels of government. At the same time, government efforts to deal with this through the militarization of the drug war raises questions regarding human rights abuses and civilian-military relations. As will be further developed in Chapter 8, the United States is deeply implicated in these problems as a major market for drugs, a supplier of weaponry that has raised the level of violence in recent years, and supporter of militarization of the drug war.

Finally, one of the conditions for the legitimacy of a political system is its effectiveness in resolving the major problems of society. Neoliberal reforms that reduce the role of the state have in many instances weakened a major instrument for the redistribution of resources and the implementation of policies that can confront the causes of poverty and ensure the basic right to health services, education, and other necessities to all sectors of the population. Although targeted programs such as OPORTUNIDADES can be effective in reducing the poverty of the poorest sectors of the population, they are less effective in attacking its causes, and the economic initiatives pursued by successive governments have failed to expand employment opportunities sufficiently to compensate for job losses that occurred.

Mexico's political transition has been a dynamic process involving the changing relationship between changing economic conditions; the mobilization of social organizations, civic institutions, and political parties; and reforms strengthening electoral institutions and facilitating electoral transparency. While this particular conjuncture can obviously not be replicated, it indicates the significant role that various socioeconomic and political actors can have in ensuring the continuation and/or deepening of the process of democratic transition and consolidation.

CHAPTER 6

Mobilization and Resistance: Grassroots Organizing, Social Movements and Cycles of Protest

eginning in the 1980s, new challenges resulting from changing economic and social conditions combined with long-term grievances led to the mobilization of different sectors of Mexico's population who organized protests, formed social movements, established new organizations and forged networks and alliances linking different sectors and localities. This social mobilization in turn had an effect—sometimes direct, often indirect—on Mexico's transition toward a more pluralist and democratic political system.

While the form and trajectory of social movements and organizations in the late 20th century was influenced by specific events and policies, many had roots in Mexico's earlier history. As noted in Chapter 3, in the post-war period various groups resisted state and party control, protested fraudulent elections, formed democratic movements within PRI-controlled unions, called upon the government to adhere to the promises of the revolution for land reform and social justice, and, in some cases, took up arms in protest against government repression. Although these groups were generally neutralized, co-opted or repressed, they provided an inspiration and served as a catalyst to subsequent mobilization.

This Chapter examines continuity and change in Mexico's social movements: the ways in which prior experiences interacted with the challenges and options resulting from changing international and domestic conditions to influence the direction, goals and strategies of Mexican social actors in the late 20th and early 21st centuries. It begins with a brief discussion of social movements and raises questions regarding the origins, trajectories, goals, tactics, and achievements of Mexico's social movements during this period. It then examines several of the most important cases of social mobilization in Mexico beginning in the mid-1980s through the following decades. A final section draws on these cases to address the questions raised below.

PERSPECTIVES ON SOCIAL MOBILIZATION AND PROTEST MOVEMENTS

Social movements may be defined as voluntary movements formed by particular groups around a specific or limited number of goals who organize and mobilize support to meet those goals. As such, they differ both from one-time, spontaneous movements (such as revolts or riots) and from more permanent formal organizations or institutions (such as political parties, labor unions, and advocacy groups): they are more enduring than spontaneous movements, but less formal than institutions. The goals of social movements range from demands on public officials, e.g., for urban services, land titles, housing, etc.; to protests against certain laws or policies; or even to demands for a change in the government or regime itself, as in the case of pro-democracy movements. They are by definition *mobilizational,* generally involving a high degree of participation. Their tactics may include legal initiatives, petitions, and letter-writing campaigns, and negotiations with political leaders or government officials; or more dramatic and sometimes disruptive activities, including marches, demonstrations, guerrilla theater, and in some cases forms of civil disobedience, such as land occupations, or takeovers of government offices. Protest movements may be considered a particular type of social movement, which engage in disruptive tactics as a means of publicizing grievances and/or demands and increasing pressure on government officials and other targeted individuals or groups.[1]

In contrast to social movements, civic organizations are more formal, relatively permanent institutions. Civic organizations, including cooperatives, unions, peasant associations, environmental organizations, and other institutions that are independent of the state, are the components of a functioning civil society, which is important in the consolidation of democracy. In practice, it is often difficult to distinguish between the two: they have in common that they are participatory, voluntary and, ideally at least, autonomous. They link together groups and individuals having common demands, needs, or claims. Social movements, although by definition temporary, may and do transform themselves into more permanent organizations or become institutionalized. At the same time, established institutions may mobilize around particular issues, such as a proposed law perceived as unjust. And social movements, including protest movements, continue to have a role in established democracies, including the incorporation of new groups, such as women and minority groups, into the political process. Finally, both social movements and civic organizations are potential vehicles for the expansion of a participatory democracy that goes beyond the formal institutions of electoral democracy.

Several factors account for the increased attention to social movements in Latin America in the last decades of the 20th century. First, as indicated in previous chapters, the process of globalization has resulted in substantial changes in the international and national context. On the one hand, as noted in Chapter 4, economic globalization was a factor in the emergence of neoliberal economic regimes, which have disrupted the lives of substantial sectors of the populations of Mexico and other countries, providing a motivation for organizing around economic issues. On the other hand, the process of globalization, and the corresponding spread of information and facilitation of communications, provided new opportunities for movements and groups in Latin America and elsewhere to form alliances with similar movements in other countries or regions and to obtain moral support and economic resources from international movements and organizations with shared goals.

Second, and related to this, this period has seen the emergence of new groups and organizations around new identities and new issues. Women's movements and environmental movements have become increasingly important in several countries, including Mexico, since the 1970s. Indigenous movements are taking an increasingly important role in redefining the culture and politics of their respective countries. The ability of these movements to network with foreign and international environmental movements, women's groups and indigenous organizations has, in many respects, enhanced their access to resources and support.[2]

Third, much of the literature on social movements originated with the emergence of protest movements in the 1970s and 1980s during the military dictatorships in South America and the period of transition toward more open regimes. During the dictatorships, traditional forms of organization, based on class interests, such as trade unions and peasant associations, and representative institutions, such as political parties and legislatures, were often repressed. Some of the groups that might have joined labor unions or peasant associations in the past now organized on the basis of neighborhood or community. The Church—one of the few institutions that was not suppressed by military regimes—also had an important role. Changes in the Catholic Church as a result of the Second Vatican Council and the Medellin Bishops conference in the 1960s gave a new impetus to progressive groups within the Church, and Christian Base Communities were formed to involve the laity more directly in applying the precepts of religion to their daily life, in some cases leading to questioning existing socioeconomic and political systems.[3] In some cases, social movements challenged the legitimacy of authoritarian regimes, and some movements expanded their focus to include democracy.

Although Mexican authoritarianism was generally less repressive than the military dictatorships of South America, Mexico's traditional class-based union and peasant organizations were weakened by the neoliberal reforms of the 1980s which also diminished the ability of the state to respond effectively to the needs and demands of disadvantaged groups. Many of these organizations regrouped, and new organizations and movements formed to address new issues, such as NAFTA (North American Free Trade Agreement). The process of political liberalization and democratization, as in former South American dictatorships, provided increasing space for social and popular movements, which in turn often pushed for greater liberalization and democratization.

There has been considerable discussion and debate regarding the extent to which social movements in Mexico, and in Latin America in general, are new. An earlier emphasis on the "newness" of Latin American social movements has given way to a more nuanced recognition that they have important similarities to earlier movements in terms of composition, strategies and goals; at the same time they may also incorporate new issues (such as environmental and gender issues), new strategies (such as the use of the Internet), and new structures (such as Christian Base Communities). Another issue is the extent to which these movements, which have often had an important impact on democratic transitions in their respective countries, are themselves democratic. Although efforts have been made to open up participation and institute democratic processes, frequently decision making is controlled by a small group of leaders. Movement members may be more concerned with the effectiveness of leaders in providing for their needs than with democratic participation, and there may in fact be a trade-off between democratic participation, on the one hand, and coherence and effectiveness on the other—particularly if a movement is broad and heterogeneous.[4]

Social movements are generally temporary: either they disappear, or they turn into something else. To the extent they require a high level of participation and mobilization; they are difficult to sustain over long periods of time. And to the extent that they are organized around one or a small number of specific goals, they may dissipate once this goal is met, or eventually decide that they are not likely to achieve it. The process of democratization has mixed implications for social movements: on the one hand, it opens spaces for social participation, contested elections, the transition to democratic regimes, and the emergence of independent political parties, on the other hand political parties provide institutional channels that may replace social movements as vehicles for making demands on the system and siphon off leaders who opt to become part of the formal political process.

However, there is often an element of continuity in that major movement adherents may continue to be active, drawing on skills and experiences from previous mobilization. In some cases, the achievement of an initial goal may lead to mobilization or organization around further goals, e.g., a settler community that initially mobilizes around obtaining land titles to legalize its holdings may then organize to obtain urban services, such as street paving or electric power.

In the process, they may become more permanent organizations and institutions. Another process is "scaling up": when several local movements form links, eventually establishing regional or national networks, involving increasing formalization and institutionalization.[5]

Under certain conditions, a broad array of different movements organized around particular grievances may come together in large-scale protest movements, or cycles of protest, around a broader issue. This was the case in some of the pro-democracy movements in Latin America and other parts of the world. Some analysts have credited social movements with an important role in the transition to democracy in several of these countries. At the same time, some observers suggested that they would disappear once a democratic regime is in place. Demands previously channeled through social movements would now be channeled through newly formed, or re-emergent, institutions, including electoral systems, political parties, and legislative bodies. Some have argued that social movements, especially protest movements, are no longer necessary and even dysfunctional in a democratic context. Others, however, have suggested that while cycles of protest are temporary, social movements may shift strategies or take on new issues as the context changes.[6] In addition, the weakness of many of the new democracies and the unmet needs of substantial sectors of the population continue to be motivations for social mobilization.

A further issue is the ability of social movements to maintain their autonomy vis-à-vis the state and other political entities and the types of tactics and strategies they enlist in order to meet their goals. Given the clientelist traditions and co-optation skills of Mexico's traditional state-party system,—which have to some extent been carried over into the current relatively pluralist context— social movements in Mexico are particularly concerned with maintaining their autonomy. At the same time, social movements and civic organizations often make demands on the state, requiring negotiations with public officials, who in turn may require certain favors in return for acceding to demands, such as support for a particular political party or government initiative. Movements must often walk a fine line between eschewing all contact with official groups, thus risking ineffectiveness and a resulting loss of membership, or working with government and political officials to resolve problems at the risk of becoming incorporated into their political agenda with the corresponding loss of organizational independence.

Tactics vary according to a range of factors, among them the possibilities for working effectively within the existing system and taking advantage of legal channels, as opposed to the options in a system that is closed or unresponsive, which may call for more confrontational tactics. In both cases, but particularly the latter, an important element is to raise consciousness through marches, demonstrations, acts of civil disobedience, and other means of achieving visibility, and to elicit publicity through media coverage as a means of enlisting public sympathy and support. Some analysts of social movements see raising consciousness as one of the most important long-term effects of social movements. This may include not only a greater public awareness of the issue but also a changed perspective on the part of the participants themselves, who may gain a new sense of empowerment and efficacy.

The following discussion will focus on movements that emerged in Mexico between 1985 and 2006 and will address several issues. First, what were the origins of these movements? Do they have precedents in previous movements and organizations? What role have external groups or organizations (such as church or religious groups, student activists, trade unions) had in their formation?

Second, how have constraints and opportunities resulting from changing domestic and international contexts shaped the form and trajectory of these movements? How are they similar to or different from organizations and movements in the past?

Third, how have they engaged with the state and/or other targeted entities? Is it possible to obtain concessions and/or collaborate with the government and at the same time maintain autonomy?

Fourth, what kinds of strategies and tactics do they use? To what extent does this involve collaboration with other sectors of the population, or cross-border collaboration?

Finally, what have been the achievements of these movements? To what extent have their initial goals been met? What kind of impact have they had in terms of the issues they address? What other implications have they had?

URBAN PROTEST MOVEMENTS AND THE *ASAMBLEA DE BARRIOS* (NEIGHBORHOOD ASSEMBLY)

In September 1985 two massive earthquakes struck Mexico City. Hundreds of buildings collapsed, burying thousands of people and revealing the shoddy construction that characterized many of the structures in the capital city. An estimated 10,000 people were killed. Hundreds of thousands were left homeless. The immediate response of the government was to minimize the damage and refuse offers of international aid. In the days and weeks that followed, city residents rallied to rescue survivors trapped in the rubble, provide care for the injured, and demand assistance for those left homeless.

The sharp contrast between the inadequacy of the government response and the effectiveness of ordinary citizens gave rise to a new sense of empowerment and was an important catalyst in the upsurge of independent urban protest movements in the 1980s. The origins of many of these movements, however, went back at least to the early 1970s. Rural-urban migration over the previous decades had resulted in overcrowding and the severe deterioration of inner cities as well as the proliferation of large and often precarious squatter settlements in the urban peripheries. Prior to the 1970s, however, demands for land and services had been channeled by the organizations of the PRI, notably the CNOP, the major organization of the popular sector of the party, in return for support for the party and government.[7]

In the early 1970s, the democratic opening under Echeverría, combined with the organizing efforts of the students of the generation of 1968, resulted in new opportunities for the organization of independent urban movements. In 1969 students formed the *Política Popular* (Popular Politics) movement, and student brigades went to poor urban as well as rural areas to engage in grassroots organizing, meeting with residents to determine their needs, which included reductions in rates charged for water, demands for land and support for land invasions, and opposition to tax increases. Organizing around specific urban demands, as well as support for labor and peasant struggles, resulted in the emergence of grassroots movements which in turn formed coalitions consisting of student activists, squatter settlements, tenant groups, ejidos and labor groups. This occurred in several states, notably the northern states of Chihuahua, Nuevo Leon and Durango as well as the southern state of Oaxaca.[8]

Although the Echeverría government was initially responsive to these movements, business pressures led to a shift in policy and efforts to repress these movements in the mid-1970s, which continued under the subsequent administration of José López Portillo. It was in this context that approximately 60 organizations from 14 states as well as Mexico City formed a national coalition, CONAMUP (*Coordinadora Nacional del Movimiento Urbano Popular*, or Coordinating Council of the Urban Popular Movement) in 1981 to protect and support urban movements throughout the country.[9]

In the case of Mexico City, CONAMUP linked popular movements that had emerged in the 1970s as the demands of poor and middle-class city residents and small businesses for urban services confronted the priorities of the national government and the mayor (at that time appointed by the federal government) for infrastructure and prestige projects, such as the Mexico City Metro. These projects not only consumed budgetary resources, ultimately leading to enormous fiscal deficits, but in many cases also disrupted or destroyed urban neighborhoods. Cutbacks in federal government subsidies to Mexico City as a result of the debt crisis and austerity program of the early 1980s resulted in further sharp reductions in Mexico City's transportation, public health, and other urban services at a time when employment was declining and costs were rising, resulting in an acceleration of urban protests.[10]

When the earthquakes struck in September 1985, Mexico City residents were able to draw on social networks and experiences derived from prior mobilization and protests. Those who had lost their homes in the worst affected neighborhoods organized rapidly into neighborhood associations and mobilized 15,000 people for a protest march in early October. On October 24, several of these associations and pre-existing urban movements came together in the CUD (*Coordinadora Unica de Damnificados,* or United Coordinating Committee of Earthquake Victims). Its members included not only those left homeless by the earthquake but also renters of the inner city areas, where owners of damaged rent-controlled housing attempted to raise rates and evict residents. Government officials also sought to relocate earthquake victims and other inner city renters to peripheral areas in order to make way for the redevelopment and gentrification of the central city.[11]

Following a CUD march on October 26 calling for a debt moratorium with funds saved to be spent on reconstruction, the government formed the Program of Popular Housing Construction. Over the next two years, 44,000 new units were constructed; in many cases former renters became owners, and the practice of raising rents and evicting tenants was halted. But the CUD was unable to protect tenants in areas slated for gentrification, and reconstruction was often subject to bureaucratic delays; in some cases the disbursement of benefits to earthquake victims was based on membership in the PRI.[12]

An agreement between the government and the member organizations of the CUD in May 1986 led to a split in the movement. Some felt that with this agreement, in which the government pledged to construct housing for 250,000 people, their goals had been met, and they should concentrate their efforts on monitoring the process of reconstruction. Others wanted to go beyond the CUD and demand fair housing for everyone, as called for in the Mexican Constitution. They were particularly concerned with the needs of renters, which were not being met.

Four CUD organizations associated with the Mexican left formed the *Asamblea de Barrios* (Neighborhood Assembly). Established on the principle of housing for all who need it, the Asamblea called for an end to state-supported landlord evictions, the expropriation of unused state or private land for the construction of low-cost housing, the reform of the civic code to include rent control and new rules regarding eviction, and adherence to laws prohibiting political favoritism, as well as a reduction in the payment of the foreign debt.

The Asamblea provided legal counsel for families threatened with eviction and established workshops to inform people of their rights. It also defended renters threatened with eviction. When thugs, recruited to carry out evictions, surrounded a house in a poor neighborhood, the family sounded an agreed-upon alarm and hundreds of neighbors would appear to defend the house with sticks and stones.

Members of the Asamblea included middle-class residents and professionals, although most of the rank and file consisted of poor urban residents. The heterogeneity of the membership, including the presence of professionals—who could provide legal, financial and technical assistance to the Asamblea and its members and negotiate on a relatively equal basis with government officials—was undoubtedly a factor in the organization's effectiveness. The leadership attempted to avoid the rigidity and authoritarian tendencies associated with many left organizations through a decentralized structure; much of the work of the organization was carried out through commissions, and each housing project had its own organization. But while participation was encouraged, most decisions were made by four leaders at the top or, to a lesser extent, by mid-level leadership. Women, who constituted the majority of the rank and file, were important among the mid-level leaders but not at the top. Women did have their own commission to deal with women's issues, which also became involved in a range of other projects, among them the preparation of a pamphlet on AIDS and the organization of all phases of the Asamblea's electoral participation.[13]

The Asamblea leadership wanted to establish an alternative culture and formed a commission concerned with the social and political education of the membership. A particularly innovative strategy was the creation of a super-hero, *Superbarrio*, complete with red and yellow costume, boots, mask and cape, but with a collective identity personifying the popular struggle of the urban poor. In keeping with a sport that is very popular in Mexico, *Superbarrio* was a wrestler and participated in wrestling matches against *Catalino Creel*, a soap opera character representing a slumlord. *Superbarrio* was also an articulate spokesperson for the rights of renters and the urban poor, participating in negotiations with government officials and traveling throughout Mexico and to other countries to rally public opinion.[14]

By the mid-1980s, the political challenges to the PRI government were growing. In the 1988 elections, the urban popular movements, including the Asamblea, were a major source of support for the candidacy of Cuauhtémoc Cárdenas. While in the PRI, Cárdenas, as part of a democratic group within the CNOP, had established ties with grassroots, urban groups and pushed the PRI and the government to be more responsive to the needs of the population harmed by the debt crisis and austerity measures. The platform of the FDN incorporated demands by the Asamblea for a renters' law and for full democratic rights for people of the Federal District. Members of the Asamblea monitored the elections at polling places throughout the city, limiting the possibility of electoral fraud. In contrast to the official national returns, Cárdenas won a resounding victory in Mexico City, obtaining 49 percent of the vote to 29 percent for Salinas.[15]

Following the official defeat of Cárdenas in the elections, the Asamblea supported the refusal of the Cardenistas to recognize the outcome, and was involved in the formation of the PRD. This alliance with Cárdenas and the PRD was costly for the organization, however, which suffered from the hostility of the Salinas administration and its efforts to marginalize Cárdenas and organizations and groups that had supported him.[16] Control of housing funds shifted back to the government, and a substantial proportion of government funding was funneled through PRONASOL, the National Solidarity Program. In contrast to other urban organizations, including those of CONAMUP, the Asamblea initially refused to accept funds from PRONASOL (although later PRONASOL funds did go to some Asamblea projects). Another result of the association with the PRD was that many of the leaders of the Asamblea became active in the party leadership and shifted their focus from the movement to politics.[17]

The defeat of the FDN in 1988 marked a turning point for urban protest movements. In Mexico City, the needs of the population for urban services were marginalized as Salinas and his appointed mayor, Manuel Camacho, focused on the national goals of redevelopment and gentrification, including the displacement of poor urban residents in the interests of high income housing and tourism, resulting in the further disarticulation of urban popular networks.[18]

The CUD and its successor, the Asamblea, had emerged in response to a crisis, and succeeded in mobilizing people and resources for those who had been made homeless by the earthquake and in defending tenants threatened with eviction. They demonstrated the efficacy of ordinary citizens in a context in which the government seemed to have abdicated its responsibility. As successive governments cut back resources to support the basic needs of the population, citizens would be increasingly called upon to fulfill the obligations formerly performed by the government. In the meantime, as noted in Chapter 5, the 1988 elections were a catalyst in the organization of the Civic Alliance, which was to play a significant role in efforts to ensure the openness of the electoral process in local and national campaigns.

CHIAPAS AND THE ZAPATISTAS

On January 1, 1994, a guerrilla army of masked indigenous peasants emerged from the tropical forests of Chiapas into national and international headlines.[19] Declaring war on the Mexican armed forces, they seized cities in central and eastern Chiapas, occupied city halls, and kidnapped a notorious former governor. In flyers and broadcasts they proclaimed a revolution against a system that had for 500 years denied them basic rights, called for the removal of the "illegitimate" president of Mexico Carlos Salinas and appealed to the Mexican people to support their struggle "for work, land, housing, food, health care, education, independence, liberty, democracy, justice, and peace" through the formation of a "free and democratic government."[20]

The Mexican government responded by sending 12,000 troops into the region, backed by air strikes, forcing the insurgents to retreat to their forest strongholds. But media coverage of the uprising, and reports by human rights organizations in Chiapas of army abuses against guerrillas and civilians, led to a surge of support for the Zapatistas and widespread condemnation of government repression by national and international human rights organizations. The government changed its tactics, firing the interior minister (another former Chiapas governor), declared a unilateral cease-fire, and called on the Zapatistas to lay down their arms. The Zapatistas released the kidnapped governor and, despite their distrust of the Salinas government, began peace talks with government representatives.[21] At the same time, through their articulate spokesperson, *Subcomandante* Marcos, the Zapatistas made extensive use of the media, particularly the Internet, to spread information about their cause throughout Mexico and to international circles.

The immediate origin of the Zapatista movement was in the early 1980s, when a small group of leftist activists from northern Mexico came to eastern Chiapas to work with indigenous peasants in the Lacandón Forest. But its roots can be traced back at least several decades, if not centuries. Chiapas, a poor rural state in southern Mexico, has a large indigenous population comprised chiefly of different Mayan groups, but is dominated by a small number of non-indigenous landowners and ranchers. Throughout much of the colonial and post-colonial period indigenous groups in the area have been exploited, initially by Spanish colonists and subsequently by a succession of coffee and sugar plantation owners, logging firms, and ranchers, through land takeovers, forced labor recruitment, and debt peonage.

The Mexican revolution had mixed implications for the indigenous populations. On the one hand, government policies toward indigenous groups were based on an integrationist model that assumed that these groups were backward and promoted their integration into the dominant *mestizo* culture, in some instances forbidding the use of indigenous languages and dress.[22] On the other hand, the agrarian reform, particularly during the 1930s, brought some improvements in the conditions of indigenous communities, including the abolition of debt peonage and the expropriation of some of the private land holdings and their distribution to peasants and indigenous communities. This reform resulted in substantial support for the government party on the part of beneficiaries as well as many who hoped to eventually obtain land under the reform.

Much of this support was squandered over the succeeding decades, however, as a result of inconsistent government policies, long delays in providing land titles, takeovers of peasant land and indigenous communities for government programs, and favoritism to PRI supporters in conflicts over land claims, as well as the corruption and repressive policies of local and state officials. As the population grew, and land-poor peasants competed for scarce land, new conflicts developed, often deliberately exacerbated by government officials and landowners. Beginning in the 1950s indigenous peasants from different parts of Chiapas, and later migrants from other states, settled in the Lacandón forest in the southeastern part of the state, where intensive farming quickly exhausted the land. Government colonization programs, which in some cases settled new colonizers on land already claimed, further alienated many of the indigenous and non-indigenous peasants of the region. Another effect of pressures on the land was the increasing diversification of peasant and indigenous families into activities other than cultivation, including wage labor on rural estates, commercial activities, and handicrafts for the tourist trade.

Religious differences further complicated this picture. Protestant missionaries and churches working among indigenous populations began to attract converts on the basis of their more open, inclusive and egalitarian practices in contrast to the aloof and hierarchical culture of the Catholic Church, and to traditional practices in some of the indigenous communities. These conversions sometimes led to conflicts with indigenous communities, due to the emphasis of some of the Protestant churches on abstention from alcohol and refusal to pay religious taxes or participate in indigenous religious festivals.[23]

In the early 1970s, two important developments influenced the indigenous movement in Chiapas. First, as noted above, student activists from the generation of 1968 began to work in poor urban neighborhoods and rural neighborhoods throughout Mexico. Second, the growing influence of Liberation Theology and what became known as the preferential option for the poor within the Latin American Church in the 1960s and 1970s led to increased grassroots organizing by progressive groups within the Church. In Chiapas, student activists and catechists (lay preachers) influenced by Liberation Theology often worked together to form independent organizations that carried out various programs, among them the formation of credit co-ops and marketing organizations, and mobilized to resist government plans for the relocation of their communities. Bishop Samuel Ruiz, the bishop of the eastern part of Chiapas centered in San Cristóbal de las Casas, took a leading role in promoting indigenous organizing, and in 1974, under his leadership, the Catholic Church organized an indigenous congress including groups from different parts of the state. The demands presented at the congress included the restitution of communal lands, support for indigenous markets, guaranteed prices for crops, support for cooperatives, indigenous teachers who could communicate in their languages, and better health care that included respect for traditional medicine.[24]

In the meantime the integrationist orientation of the national government had begun to change in the 1970s due to the influence of a new group of "critical anthropologists" within the government who promoted a more *indigenista* perspective, as well as the influence of the emerging indigenous movements. The government was also interested in developing new mechanisms to enlist the support of indigenous populations in a context in which government institutions had been discredited. In 1975, the government organized a national indigenous congress that brought together indigenous groups from all over the country.

The two congresses were important in raising awareness of shared problems and facilitating networking and communications among different groups—in effect, drawing indigenous peasants into the national arena.[25] By the early 1980s indigenous peasants in eastern Chiapas were participating in a variety of organizations that had formed coalitions with national organizations and other sectors such as teachers, workers and students, and utilized a dual strategy of negotiations with government officials and mobilization, including marches, hunger strikes, and occupations of municipal buildings.[26]

With the economic crisis beginning in the early 1980s, the government reduced or eliminated rural support programs throughout the country, further eroding the conditions of peasants dependent on price supports and subsidized credit. In the meantime, the mobilization of peasant organizations led to repression by government forces, which was aggravated by the selection of General Castellanos Domínguez as state governor in 1982 and the increasing militarization of the border area with Guatemala, ostensibly to guard against incursions by Guatemalan military searching for guerrilla combatants from the revolutionary movements of that country.

Conditions continued to deteriorate with the presidency of Salinas beginning in 1988. On the one hand, the government's agrarian modernization policy projected the elimination of the "inefficient" small peasant sector, epitomized in the reform of Article 27, ending the land distribution program (and thus any remaining hope for land among the landless and land poor). On the other, co-optation efforts of the government through such programs as PRONASOL undermined independent organizations, aggravating differences within them regarding cooperation with the government and leading to splits in several organizations. The establishment of the PRD following the 1988 elections brought a new element of political conflict—not only between supporters of the PRI and the PRD, but also between those who supported these parties and those who rejected formal politics altogether. Thus on the eve of the Zapatista revolt, Chiapas was not only afflicted by poverty and a series of brutal and corrupt governments but also characterized by ethnic and religious differences, sharp economic distinctions, political conflicts, and a profound disillusionment with the possibility of finding redress of the existing situation within the law, particularly with the new agrarian law.

The Zapatista movement emerged through a dynamic process of interaction between outside organizers and indigenous and peasant groups in eastern Chiapas in the context of the complex class, ethnic, religious and political conflicts and alliances that had evolved over the previous decades. Throughout the 1980s the Zapatista movement expanded its base among indigenous communities in several municipalities, attracting members of peasant organizations, young men who saw their prospects derailed by government policies, as well as women for whom the Zapatistas provided unprecedented opportunities to learn to read and write and liberation from traditional gender roles. After repeated experiences of broken promises, political manipulation, and increasing violence and repression at the hands of the military and local government officials, many indigenous peasants within the movement were ready to take up arms. By 1992 the decision was made to begin the armed struggle, and following a year of preparation the Zapatistas launched their attack on January 1, 1994, timed to coincide with the beginning of NAFTA.[27]

Following the government counter-attack and the initiation of negotiations, the Zapatista movement continued to develop in a dynamic interaction with the dramatic events and changes of the succeeding years. The negotiations between the Zapatistas and government representatives, led by Manuel Camacho, the former governor of Mexico City, reached a tentative agreement in February 1994, but the accord was subsequently rejected by the Zapatista base. Over the next several months the Zapatistas concentrated on reinforcing and expanding their base in Chiapas and outreach to the national and international community. In Chiapas, the Zapatistas and other indigenous organizations created de facto autonomous municipalities and regions, characterized by various forms of self-government.

The focus of the Zapatistas on indigenous autonomy raised numerous issues in the debates that followed. Autonomy is not a monolithic concept and there were differences regarding the form autonomy should take. The Zapatistas claimed to be open to a "pluralism of autonomies," "a world in which all worlds would fit," and they themselves experimented with different models of self-government in the communities under their control.[28] However, the issue of autonomy challenged the traditional emphasis of Mexico's post-revolutionary governments on the assimilation of indigenous communities into the mestizo population and resulted in debates regarding national sovereignty versus territorial autonomy and individual rights versus collective rights. Some feminists were also concerned that indigenous autonomy could reinforce traditional gender roles to the detriment of women. In indigenous communities the lives of women are often severely circumscribed, beliefs in male superiority are deeply engrained, and there is continued resistance to seeing men and women as equal.

Within the EZLN itself, women took an active role in promoting gender issues. Women constituted 30 percent of the Zapatista forces and were an important element in its leadership. In the days after the revolt they issued the

Revolutionary Law for Women, which called for personal autonomy, including the right to choose whom to marry and the number of children they should have; a prohibition against violence toward women; as well as demands for education and health care, equal salaries, and access to positions of leadership. In practice, adherence to these principles was mixed within the Zapatista communities, although generally more broadly respected than in many non-Zapatista communities.[29]

The Zapatistas also continued to reach out to national and international civil society organizations by issuing a series of declarations, taking positions on various issues, and explaining their goals and promoting dialogue, which were widely publicized—notably on the Internet. They also organized marches, demonstrations, and referenda, and held a series of meetings, solidifying their support among national and international solidarity, human rights and other social and civic organizations. For many of these groups, Subcomandante Marcos became an icon.

The Zapatista challenge to the prevailing and ostensibly highly successful program of neoliberal reform was undoubtedly a factor in the enthusiastic support the movement received from different sectors of the population—the extent of which apparently surprised the Zapatistas themselves.[30] Immediately following the Zapatista revolt there had been further municipal revolts in several parts of Chiapas and PRI officials were replaced in approximately half of the municipalities of the state. Over the following year guerrilla movements emerged in other Mexican states. This popular enthusiasm—and the strong and immediate response of national and international human rights and civic organizations to government efforts to repress the movement—appear to have been important in the Zapatistas' increasing emphasis on democracy, including its recognition of the significance of civil society in the transition to democracy and its redefinition of democracy to include not only free and fair elections but also, and especially, the sovereignty of the people as proclaimed in the constitution.

The Zapatista revolt added a new dimension to the tensions within Chiapas itself, between those supportive of the Zapatistas and those opposed, including independent peasant organizations as well as those linked to the PRI. In February 1995, under pressure from international investors to "get rid of the Zapatista problem," the Zedillo government began a new offensive against the Zapatistas, including the "unmasking" of Subcomandante Marcos as a university professor. More seriously, the government sent 30,000 government troops into Chiapas who surrounded the Zapatista-controlled areas and the new autonomous indigenous regions. Although ostensibly intended to provide security, the military did little to control violence in the area and added new tensions and problems, invading communal land to build military camps and leading to the growth of prostitution as well as drug cultivation and consumption.[31]

In an effort to diffuse the tensions, Congress passed a law calling for new negotiations, which began in October 1995. By this time, indigenous rights had become a central issue for the Zapatistas, reflecting the growing importance of the indigenous movement in Mexico and increasing contact between the Zapatistas and other indigenous groups throughout Mexico. Many of these groups sent representatives to advise the Zapatistas during the negotiations with the government. Negotiators reached an agreement in February 1996, the San Andrés accords, which provided for constitutional changes that would recognize the collective rights of indigenous peoples, including the right to autonomy, in specified territorial boundaries. On the basis of the accords, a multiparty congressional Commission on Concordance and Pacification (COCAPA) drew up a constitutional reform recognizing the indigenous people as social and historical subjects, enabling indigenous communities to choose their own community and municipal authorities, utilize their own normative systems of justice and administration, and exercise control over land and resources within their jurisdictions.[32] Although initially accepted by the EZLN and the federal government, the Zedillo administration subsequently rejected the proposed reforms.

In the following months conditions in Chiapas deteriorated with attacks by paramilitary groups linked to local officials and landowners opposed to the Zapatistas. The worst attack took place in December 1997, following a series of skirmishes, paramilitary attacks and warnings by human rights groups of increasing violence in the area. On December 27, an armed group believed to be linked to state PRI officials surrounded a church in the small village of Acteal where members of a non-governmental human rights group fleeing from violence had gathered, and massacred 45 men, women and children. This act, and apparent PRI complicity in it, was an added factor in popular rejection of the PRI and in opposition victories in the Chiapas gubernatorial elections as well as the presidential elections in 2000.

Following the 2000 elections, President Vicente Fox sent legislation to Congress based on the constitutional reform called for in the COCAPA document, which would recognize autonomy in indigenous municipalities and provide for the possibility of regional autonomy. In 2001, the Zapatistas staged a triumphal march to Mexico City to address the legislature, where the reform was being debated. However, the law was weakened by Congress, omitting the possibility of regional autonomy and leaving implementation to state governors, and the version that passed unanimously in the Chamber of Deputies was rejected by the Zapatistas and other indigenous groups. The law does permit municipal autonomy, and the Zapatistas have maintained their autonomous communities in Chiapas, forming five relatively independent self-governing units, which have responsibility over education and health care and have the right to choose their own leaders.

After Subcomandante Marcos' rejection of the existing political system, including all three of the major parties following their support for the indigenous legislation and particularly his strong attacks against PRD candidate López Obrador during the 2006 election campaign, Marcos lost the support of progressive intellectuals and politicians in Mexico as well as many Mexican citizens. Some cite the authoritarian tendencies of the EZLN and the cult of personality that had developed around Marcos. International solidarity and financial support also declined. The EZLN leadership forbade members of Zapatista communities to receive funds from government programs such as OPORTUNIDADES, with the result that the Zapatista communities are generally much more impoverished than their non-Zapatista counterparts. The resulting hardship led some families to leave in order to accept government aid. At the same time, some observers have noted that the Zapatista communities have made important social advances compared to other communities, evident in a decline in alcoholism and domestic abuse as well as in infant mortality; the construction of new schools and clinics; and the access of girls to education.[33]

The autonomy of the Zapatistas has come at a high cost, not only due to their rejection of government aid, but most importantly they have been under relentless surveillance and, in some cases, direct attacks by government and paramilitary forces, which have some 56 military bases around Zapatista territory. The situation has been described as an "armed peace" in which the Zapatistas, paramilitary forces, and other armed groups control different parts of the region, while the government has attempted to co-opt or split the communities and to claim parts of the Zapatista controlled territory for redistribution to other communities or for projects in such areas as bio-prospecting and ecotourism.[34]

Although the issues raised by the EZLN have not been resolved, the achievements of the Zapatistas are significant. First, as noted above, they focused national and international attention on the failure of neoliberalism to respond to the basic needs of a broad sector of the population. Opposition to neoliberalism attracted immediate and widespread support among the Mexican population and continued to be a factor in international support and solidarity for the Zapatistas. It was also an important catalyst for other protest movements that emerged in the mid-1990s, such as the Barzón movement.

Second, they had an important impact on the process of democratic transition. Although democracy may not have been a major issue at the beginning, it became increasingly important as a goal of the movement, which has emphasized the importance of civil society. The Zapatista revolt was at least indirectly responsible for the electoral reforms preceding the 1994 elections,[35] although they have subsequently become disillusioned with electoral democracy, promoting participatory democracy in its place.

Third, changes in traditional gender relations were also an important component of the movement. It was in the Zapatista movement that many women learned to read and write; they not only participated in the armed struggle but held leadership positions and have consistently struggled for women's rights both within the movement itself and in the larger society.[36]

Fourth, while the indigenous movement in Mexico did not begin with the Zapatistas, they have reinforced the struggles for indigenous rights and autonomy. Through much of Mexico's post-revolutionary history, indigenous groups were defined as peasants for purposes of benefiting from state reforms, reflecting the Mexican government's emphasis on promoting the assimilation of indigenous groups into the dominant mestizo population. The abdication of the role of the state in the agrarian sector, combined with the rise of the indigenous movement throughout the Americas beginning in the 1970s, led to redefinitions of identity to encompass an increasing focus on indigenous rights and political autonomy.

Finally, the trajectory of the Zapatista movement and the strategies it has evolved demonstrate the ways in which globalization has redefined the options for social movements. Modern communications technology, especially skillful use of the Internet, has facilitated widespread publicity about the movement and its goals and the formation of national and international support and solidarity networks. These as well as national and international human rights and civic organizations have played an important role in the defense of the Zapatistas and in limiting the ability of the government to act with impunity to repress rural mobilization.

DEBTORS IN REVOLT: THE BARZÓN MOVEMENT

Over the spring and summer of 1993, while the Zapatistas were preparing their revolt, farmers in the states of Chihuahua, Jalisco, Sonora, Tabasco, and Zacatecas were engaged in another type of protest. Their actions ranged from parking tractors in the major plazas of the capital cities to occupying a bridge linking the cities of Juarez, Chihuahua and El Paso, Texas. Thus began one of the most unusual social movements of the 1990s, the Barzón debtors' movement, or El Barzón.[37] Within two years it had expanded to urban areas as well as rural communities throughout the country and incorporated small and medium businesses, merchants, homeowners, and credit card holders, as well as farmers.

The Barzón movement was a direct response to the fallout from government economic policies of the 1980s and early 1990s. It began in the rural sector, where trade liberalization and a consequent decline in agricultural prices, as well as sharp reductions in government support to agriculture, resulted in an increase in costs for credit and other agricultural inputs and reduced prices for output.

Rural protests in the 1980s over falling prices often took the form of occupation of government buildings, such as the food-marketing agency CONASUPO. With the sharp increase in interest rates in the early 1990s, many farmers dependent on loans to finance production were unable to repay their debts, and banks began to repossess property that had been mortgaged.[38] This rate increase affected not only farmers but also urban enterprises, homeowners, and even credit card holders who, encouraged to borrow in the general euphoria accompanying the growth in foreign investment and the prospective NAFTA agreement in the early 1990s, suddenly found themselves with debts they could not repay and threatened with losing their houses and other possessions. The 1994–1995 peso crisis resulted in a further increase in interest rates as well as a 40 percent reduction in buying power, again leading to rising costs, falling sales and increasing indebtedness for many small businesses and industries (including exporters dependent on the import of inputs).

Many of the founding members of El Barzón were rural organizations and political activists, including local leaders of the PRD and even some PRI politicians and government officials. But the Barzón movement was unusual because it recruited middle-class debtors who had little previous experience in protest movements. In the rural sector, it included medium and relatively large farmers and ranchers producing for domestic markets. For both rural and urban debtors, the impact of the real or threatened evictions and foreclosures was devastating, in some cases resulting in suicides.

El Barzón was less a national movement than a number of state and regional movements united around the goals of protecting members threatened with dispossession of their property, providing legal services and technical advice to the membership, and demanding a response to the problem of rural and urban debtors who suddenly found themselves unable to repay their debts. *Barzonistas* established guards to protect the homes, farms, or other property of members threatened with foreclosure and "liberated" goods they contended were unjustly confiscated. El Barzón also provided legal assistance to members as well as technical and professional advice on how to restructure their businesses to avoid indebtedness or how to shift to more valuable crops. At a broader level, the Barzonistas demanded a restructuring or pardoning of debts and basic economic changes, such as modification of banking practices, the reinstitution of subsidies, and the renegotiation of NAFTA.[39]

El Barzón engaged in a broad range of dramatic and imaginative forms of direct action and street theatre to confront bankers and/or government officials. Many of its activities were designed to demonstrate the links between government policies and the difficulties many sectors of the population were experiencing, as well as the intransigence of government officials and bankers who generally refused to negotiate with the Barzonistas. Farmers trucked farm produce into the cities and dumped it in front of banks. They paraded farm animals to the government palace in Mexico City. In a clear reference to the actions of the bankers and police they staged demonstrations in which some members, dressed as doctors, chased "patients" with syringes to "draw blood" in lieu of cash. They staged backward marches to demonstrate the "backwardness" of unresponsive government bureaucrats, wore chains or handcuffs as "slaves" or "prisoners" of the banks, and held mock funeral processions. They occupied banks and public buildings and blocked highways and bridges. Large groups would make out checks for one peso and line up at the banks to cash them, bringing business to a virtual halt.[40] These tactics were highly effective in drawing media attention and attracting new members, who eventually numbered between an estimated 500,000 and 2 million.

As its tactics suggest, El Barzón made effective use of symbolic politics. The name itself refers to a part of a yoke used on oxen and is based on a song, which compares the Barzón to the situation of a debt peon, who is never able to fully repay his debt and remains in bondage to the landlord. As noted above, farmers would occupy the central plaza of towns and cities with their tractors, and a green tractor became the symbol of the movement.[41]

In addition to substantial and generally sympathetic media coverage, El Barzón obtained support from several movements and institutions, including the Zapatistas, the Civic Alliance, university students, the Catholic Church, and various local groups. The Barzón movement in Zacatecas—a state where substantial migration to the United States was occurring—gained the sympathy of migrants when it led protests against California's Proposition 187, a 1994 ballot initiative which would have prohibited services, including education and health care, to undocumented immigrants.

El Barzón's relationship to political parties was somewhat ambiguous. The movement avoided alliances with existing parties, but many of the leaders were active in the PRI or the PRD. This was in fact a major source of division between the Zacatecas branch, which was led by individuals who had been and continued to be active in the PRD, and that of Jalisco, whose members were tied to the PRI. There was also substantial disagreement over other issues, such as whether the organization should lobby politicians or should negotiate with the government. Efforts to negotiate with the national government, which was in the process of restructuring the banks on highly favorable terms, in fact had limited success, one reason for the confrontational tactics of the movement. To the extent that the government responded, it facilitated debt restructuring on an individual basis, often favoring debtors not aligned to the movement. But the movement did receive support from within the legislature, including some members of the PRI as well as opposition representatives, and from state-level officials. In the context of the massive upsurge of mobilization following the peso crisis and 1995 revelations of corruption by the government and bankers, banks were eventually forced to restructure loans and desist from repossessions of houses and other property.[42]

The movement began to lose momentum by the end of the 1990s. In part, this was a result of success: some members who were able to restructure their debts withdrew from active participation in the movement and returned to their businesses or farms. With the process of democratization, several leaders of the Barzón movement in Zacatecas ran for national office as PRD candidates. In addition, with the opposition victories in the 1997 elections, many leaders and activists looked increasingly to the democratic process as a means to address the economic issues that had brought so many to the streets in the mid-1990s. One result was a division between the leaders, who opted to work within political institutions, and the rank and file, which continued to favor direct action protest. The movement itself was extremely heterogeneous, linking groups with strong differences who had even been antagonists in the past, such as peasants who had been involved in land disputes and the large landowners who opposed them, and small farmers and grain merchants who had haggled over grain prices.[43]

Although El Barzón failed to mount an effective long-term challenge to the dominant economic paradigm, it was successful in responding to the immediate needs of its membership and, at least to some extent, in achieving the restructuring of individual debts in the wake of the peso crisis. The decentralization of the movement also provided opportunities for democratic participation at the local level and facilitated the empowerment of those members who became active in the movement, particularly women, some of whom became national leaders of the movement.[44] El Barzón was remarkably effective in energizing significant groups of the population and mobilizing middle-class sectors that had participated in protest movements rarely, if at all, in the past. Through its spirited defense of its membership and dramatic street actions it captured the attention and imagination of a public profoundly disillusioned with the economic policies of the government and the corruption of its leaders.

THE RISKS OF BEING AN ECOLOGIST: COMMUNITY FORESTRY AND HUMAN RIGHTS IN GUERRERO

In 1999, Rodrigo Montiel and Teodoro Cabrera, two outspoken environmentalists and members of OCESP (Peasant and Environmental Organization of the Sierra de Petelán) in the southern state of Guerrero, were arrested and tortured into confessing to charges of drug dealing and armed rebellion. Their real "crime" had been opposition to clandestine logging and rapid deforestation in the surrounding area. In 2000, their lawyer and human rights activist Digna Ochoa was found dead and presumably murdered in her Mexico City office. In a similar though unrelated action, two members of the Tarahumara indigenous community in the northern state of Chihuahua who had been active in a campaign to halt logging were arrested in 2003 and charged with drug and weapons violations.

These cases generated considerable national and international outrage. Responding to international and national pressures, President Vicente Fox ordered the release of Montiel and Cabrera in 2001. The two Chihuahuan activists were released a year after their arrest when a federal investigation determined that the charges against them were fabricated. The Sierra Club gave its annual Goldman award to Montiel and Cabrera for grassroots environmental efforts, delivering the award to Montiel in 2001 while he was still in prison. Nevertheless, the climate of violence in the region had a chilling effect on environmental activism. Montiel and Cabrera left the state following their release, and many members of OCESP dropped out of the organization.

One of the few who remained active was Felipe Arreaga, a self-taught peasant with little formal education who had a passion for ecology and dreamed of a peaceful path to revolutionary change based on respect for the land and natural resources.[45] He had been among dozens of farmers whose successful campaign against illegal logging groups—including blockades of logging trucks—had angered landowners on cleared forestland and their allies among local caciques. Arreaga was arrested in November 2004 and accused of involvement in the murder of the son of a cacique who benefitted from ties with logging groups. Amnesty International adopted Arreaga as a prisoner of conscience, and he was finally acquitted (based on lack of evidence) and released in September 2005.

The arrests and even torture of grassroots environmentalists on trumped-up charges demonstrate the risks of environmental activism in Mexico, particularly in Guerrero, one of the poorest states of the country. Prior to the 2005 elections, the PRI had controlled the state government for 76 years—longer than its control of the federal government. Dominated by a small number of agro-livestock interests and local caciques, Guerrero seems an unlikely venue for grassroots environmental activism. But the state also has a long tradition of resistance to exploitation of its forestry resources, which can be traced back to uprisings in the early 20th century against foreign companies controlling the marketing of agricultural and forestry products in Guerrero's Costa Grande, which culminated in support for Emiliano Zapata's forces during the Mexican revolution.

Mexico's post-revolutionary history has been characterized by shifts between the empowerment of the peasantry and an emphasis on community forestry on the one hand, and a lack of trust in the peasants, evident in a certain element of state paternalism as well as an emphasis on commercial forestry, on the other. In the immediate post-revolutionary period forested areas passed to a small number of national owners, but the agrarian reform carried out by the Cárdenas government during the 1930s awarded a substantial portion of Mexico's forestry reserves to ejidos. After the Cárdenas administration, however, government support for these communities ranged from sporadic to non-existent, reflecting inconsistent forestry policies that fluctuated between concessions to private and public enterprises for commercial logging, protection of the environment, and policies to encourage community maintenance of forest and biodiversity resources. By the 1960s private companies again controlled most of the forested area, often in collusion with local officials and/or ejidal leaders.[46]

Contradictions in government policy were particularly evident during the administration of Luis Echeverría (1970–1976), whose interventions included the National Land Clearing Program, an aggressive program to shift forested area to agriculture and livestock, but also incorporated the initiation of programs based on grassroots development of forest resources by indigenous communities and ejidos. The latter initiatives were in response to pressures by peasant communities, which organized against timber interests and were promoted by a group of reformers (among them Cuauhtémoc Cárdenas) in the forest agency of the Agriculture ministry during the 1970s and early 1980s. The efforts of this group culminated in the Forestry Law of 1986, which combined economic, environmental, and social goals by enabling peasant and indigenous communities to participate in decisions for the production and management of forest resources, and even to control timber production, on the basis of an environmentally sustainable model. Today, approximately 80 percent of Mexico's remaining forestry reserves are held and operated by peasant ejidos and indigenous communities, a highly unusual situation in the Latin American context.[47]

The experiences of the peasant environmentalists of OCESP indicate several of the issues at stake in the development of Mexico's forestry resources.[48] The first is the competing goals of economic development, environmental protection, and the promotion of community goals and welfare. A second and related issue involves contrasting development models: a top-down approach which privileges national companies and transnational corporations, and a grassroots-oriented approach that fosters organized community involvement in investment decisions and their implementation. In Mexico's forestry development, the conflict between these models has taken the form of the plantation model versus the community-forestry model. Mexico's market driven economy, as well as international agreements such as NAFTA and WTO, privilege corporations. In this context, support for a community-based model, which often requires substantial state input in such areas as credit, training, technical assistance, and other services, tends to be discouraged. The abdication of the government role in such areas as regulation and oversight has been an additional problem in securing a balanced approach that will benefit forest communities.

Mexico's increasing integration into the world economy has resulted in new complications and controversies with respect to the protection of natural resources. Specifically, principles of private property rights and the patenting of life forces prioritized by the WTO and NAFTA come into conflict with principles of national sovereignty over genetic resources, the rights of indigenous and peasant communities that have developed and maintained biological resources, and the principle that knowledge and control of life forms belongs in the public domain. In the case of Mexico, Mexican government officials anxious to secure foreign investment facilitate foreign initiatives to obtain intellectual property rights over natural resources, genetic sequences and biological materials. Negotiations and agreements between foreign companies, Mexican government officials, and universities are often surrounded by secrecy, in some cases without the knowledge of the affected communities, which receive little or no compensation in return.

The control of much of Mexico's forestry resources by peasant and indigenous communities does give them leverage they would not otherwise enjoy. At the same time, the experience of OCESP demonstrates the severe challenges environmental activists face when they confront powerful groups at the local level. Despite progress in liberalization and democratization, the old political system of domination by local caciques remains deeply entrenched in impoverished states such as Guerrero. Their experiences also demonstrate the importance of allies among national and international NGOs, whose support has been noteworthy in campaigns for the release of imprisoned activists and in the linking of human rights and environmental issues. In short, to the extent that environmental activism challenges powerful groups, whether entrenched local interests or national and international groups that hope to benefit from the new market reforms, it is linked to the need for protections against human rights abuses by authorities.

Many communities in the area continue to resist the issuing of permits to logging interests, and reforestation campaigns are gradually repairing some of the earlier damage done by loggers. Among the latter is the work of the Women's Environmental Organization of the Sierra de Petetlan (OMESP), founded in 2002 and led by Celsa Valdovinos, the wife of Felipe Arreaga, which has planted 176,000 cedar saplings around 13 villages in the Coyuquilla River Valley. It has also promoted the creation of family vegetable gardens and education campaigns on hygiene, the environment, and reforestation, particularly targeting youth.

In September 2009, four years after his release from prison, Felipe Arreaga was killed in an automobile accident. In the meantime, in spite of a new PRD governor elected in 2005, political corruption and repression have continued in Guerrero. In addition, the Costa Grande as well as other areas of Guerrero have been affected by the drug violence that has become particularly virulent in parts of Mexico over the past five years. Nevertheless, Arreaga's widow, Celsa Valdovinos, has pledged to continue the work that she and her husband shared, planting trees, training youth, and promoting the ecological awareness of the rural communities of Guerrero.[49]

LABOR MOBILIZATION AND THE NEW TRADE UNIONISM

As indicated in Chapter 4, workers were among the major victims of the economic crises and neoliberal reforms of the 1980s and 1990s.[50] Recession and inflation, the liberalization of trade, cutbacks in public spending, and the privatization of state firms, led to job loss, cutbacks in wages and benefits, the elimination of job security, and the increased informalization of labor. One result was the weakening of the corporatist labor sector, a traditional pillar of the PRI regime, which was no longer able to provide the same level of benefits to its membership and increasingly sided with the government and business groups in confrontations with workers.[51] At the same time, the repression of independent unions and of rank and file mobilization meant that independent labor leaders and organizations were unable to take advantage of the decline in the corporatist sector of labor to recruit members or resist the anti-labor practices and policies of the government and business.

Two factors precipitated a change in this situation. First, the debate around NAFTA gave a new impetus to cross-border organizing among workers as well as other sectors. Second, the peso crisis of 1994–1995 resulted in the mobilization of workers as well as other sectors and generated cross-sector alliances.

Cross-border labor organizing has a long history. During the late 19th and early 20th centuries, U.S. mineworkers, railroad workers and agricultural workers (many of them Mexican immigrants who had been contracted to work in the United States, often by companies with properties in both countries) collaborated with their counterparts in Mexico. In some cases, Mexican workers in the United States carried back organizing skills and strategies learned in the United States to their country of origin. In other cases, workers in Mexico assisted workers in the United States, especially Mexican immigrants.

As noted in Chapter 3, in the post-war period the policies of the CTM leadership were generally congruent with the Cold War anti-Communism policies of the United States, purging Communist party leaders and members from the confederation. Cross-border solidarity among labor unions was limited in the post-war years due to nationalist ideologies, conflicting interests among workers in the same industry, and distinct union structures.[52] But there were instances of cross-border labor collaboration during this period, including cooperation on labor issues between the FAT (Authentic Labor Front), a small independent Mexican federation formed in 1960, and the United Electrical Workers of the

United States, which helped finance FAT efforts to organize plants in Mexico.[53] Other transnational organizations have been working to organize *maquila* workers and to improve health and safety conditions in the border region, among them the Coalition for Justice in the *Maquiladoras*, formed in 1989, which now includes 150 labor, human rights, environmental, religious and community groups in Mexico, the United States and Canada.[54]

Organizing among workers around the NAFTA negotiations was complicated by differences in the interests between workers in the United States, and to a lesser extent Canada, who feared that NAFTA would mean a massive loss of jobs to Mexico—the "great sucking sound" warned of by former presidential candidate Ross Perot—and Mexican workers, who feared that organizing to resist NAFTA could undermine their own job prospects. This assumption was repeatedly emphasized by the Mexican government, business groups, and corporatist labor leaders who claimed that Mexican workers were being manipulated by U.S. labor leaders. As in other efforts at cross-border collaboration, activists from the three countries also differed in terms of strategies and tactics, and both Canadian and Mexican leaders complained about the arrogance of some U.S. activists who failed to take their positions into account and often knew little of conditions in Canada and Mexico.

Labor activists, however, could agree on the need to protect labor rights and respect the labor laws in each of the three countries. Although they were unsuccessful in having such a provision included in the NAFTA agreement, it was incorporated in a side agreement that provided for the establishment of the National Administration Office (NAO) to rule on complaints brought by workers against companies accused of disregarding labor rights.[55]

In practice the side agreement proved to be a weak instrument in protecting labor rights due to the lack of enforcement mechanisms. While violations of certain principles (such as child labor laws and health conditions) may lead to investigation, arbitration and fines, violations of other principles—the right to organize, bargain collectively, and strike—result simply in consultations among the labor ministries of the relevant countries.[56] For example, the NAO ruled in favor of workers in a Sony plant in Mexico who filed a complaint against the company for blocking the formation of an independent union, but there was no enforcement of the ruling, and workers were turned down when they sought a new election. Efforts of workers to form independent unions in the maquiladoras are systematically met by intimidation on the part of owners and corporatist unions—ranging from refusal to permit a secret ballot on votes for union representation, to the firing of leaders and activists involved in organizing efforts, and to attacks on activists by thugs paid by the corporatist unions.[57]

With some exceptions, cross-border labor cooperation as a result of NAFTA has had limited success in ameliorating conditions of the majority of Mexican maquila workers, but it has been important in publicizing abuses and in developing and expanding relations among labor organizations in the three member countries. Unions in the three countries have collaborated frequently in campaigns against labor law violations. The AFL-CIO has worked with confederations and unions in Mexico on joint publications; in denouncing labor law violations; and by exchanging university researchers, lawyers, and labor leaders.[58]

Collaboration among labor organizations and between these and other sectors in different countries, and international labor solidarity, also go beyond the three member countries of NAFTA. In 2005, the Mexican Miners and Metalworkers' Union staged a protest in conjunction with metalworkers federations in the United States and Peru to oppose labor violations by Grupo Mexico, a Mexican mining consortium. Students at U.S. universities and colleges have been active in consumer boycotts of products made in sweatshops in Mexico and elsewhere.[59]

The second major factor in labor mobilization in the mid-1990s was the devastating effect of the peso crisis, including the loss of approximately one million jobs in 1995. One of the results was the formation of an independent labor confederation, the National Union of Workers (UNT), which became a major rival to the corporatist labor sector. The UNT had its origins in the Union of Telephone Workers, STRM, which in 1976 had elected Francisco Hernández Juárez, the leader of a pro-democracy group within the union, as secretary general. With the restructuring of Telmex in 1989 prior to privatization, the union took a different route from that of independent unions that had tried to resist restructuring and privatization. During the negotiations at the time of restructuring, Hernández Juárez obtained an agreement with management to retain jobs, or to provide generous benefits to those dismissed as a result of restructuring, in return for which he agreed to the reclassification of workers and to tie wages to productivity.[60]

In 1990, Hernández Juárez formed FESEBES (the Federation of Unions of Goods and Services Enterprises), a new federation that included workers in airlines, electric power, and film and television, autoworkers, and streetcar operators as well as telephone workers, to challenge CTM dominance within the Labor Congress (CT). The Union of Telephone Workers and FESEBES were hailed by then President Salinas as examples of a "new type of unionism" that would be based on cooperation between labor and management to raise production and productivity in return for increased wages and benefits. With the approach of the 1994 election, however, Salinas shifted his favor to the CTM, which could be depended on to deliver votes.[61]

With the renewed decline in standards of living resulting from the peso crisis, several unions led by Hernández Juárez broke with the Labor Congress and the CTM, and in 1997 formed the UNT. The independent union movement was a major protagonist in the surge of protests of the mid-1990s. As of 2001 the

UNT included 1.5 million workers, among them social security workers and university workers, as well as the FAT, and was the second largest federation in Mexico following the CTM, which claimed about 5 million workers.[62] Thus, while the CTM continues to represent the largest number of organized workers, the labor sector is now pluralist, with a second major confederation, the UNT, and several smaller labor organizations.

With the victory of the opposition PAN candidate in the 2000 presidential elections, the UNT had hoped to establish a working relationship with the new Fox government. But Fox preferred to work with the more established Labor Congress and CTM, resulting in continuity in corporatist state-labor relations even after the defeat of the PRI. Individual union efforts to improve wages in line with productivity increases have been undermined by business and government emphasis on keeping wages low, often with the complicity of corporatist labor leaders. Independent labor organizations, and in some cases those linked with the Labor Congress, have for the most part taken a defensive position, opposing the privatization of PEMEX and the electric power system as well as proposed labor legislation, which (among other provisions) would make it more difficult for workers to get rid of an existing union, to vote for a new union, to bargain collectively, or to strike.

At the same time, democratization and the increase in political pluralism has opened new opportunities for labor unions and confederations to seek political allies among government officials and legislative leaders at different levels of government and with political leaders from different parties for particular campaigns and initiatives. Congressional allies have blocked reforms seen as detrimental to labor. In some cases, corporatist union leaders at the local level or in specific plants have been responsive to rank and file mobilization. And on occasion labor boards have defended the rights of workers, as when the labor board of León, Guanajuato ordered a secret ballot election for adult-education workers to decide on representation by an independent union.[63]

Cross-border collaboration has continued. Campaigns on behalf of workers in Mexico have received support from U.S. and Canadian community organizations, churches and religious groups, and student activists. In short, neoliberalism has worsened the conditions of workers and weakened organized labor; at the same time, global changes and democratization have provided new options for workers in terms of cross-border organizing and solidarity, an increase in union autonomy, and forged new political and social alliances.

GRASSROOTS PROTEST IN OAXACA: LOCAL 22 AND THE POPULAR ASSEMBLY OF THE PEOPLE OF OAXACA (APPO)

On May 22, 2006, members of Local 22, the teachers' union of the state of Oaxaca, called a strike and occupied the major plaza of the state capital (Oaxaca

City). They demanded a wage increase, a new contract, and improved conditions in the schools, particularly in the impoverished rural areas. The *plantón*
(encampment), following efforts to negotiate with the government of Oaxaca,
had been a common practice in conjunction with state contract negotiations
since 1989. In the following weeks the teachers set up a radio transmitter, *Radio
Plantón*, staged marches, and sent a commission to Mexico City in what would
be the first of several efforts to dialogue with the federal government to find
solutions to the conflict.[64]

Prior to 2006, the combination of negotiations and the plantón had ended
with an annual contract. However, on the night of June 14, the government of
Ulises Ruíz Ortíz (sometimes referred to as URO), launched a violent attack on
the teachers, including bombing them with tear gas canisters thrown from a
helicopter, and injured several. This transformed a routine event into a major
confrontation which affected the state through the rest of the year.

Along with Chiapas and Guerrero, Oaxaca is one of the poorest states in
Mexico. It is also a largely indigenous state, with 14 distinct ethnic and cultural
groups. In addition, it has a history of political activism. In the 1970s and 1980s,
a number of organizations and movements emerged dedicated to the protection
of indigenous rights, gender equality and improved conditions for women, and
grassroots community development. An independent political movement, the
Coalition of Workers, Peasants and Students of the Isthmus (COCEI) succeeded
in gaining control of the municipality of Juchitán in the 1980s. In 1995, in the
wake of indigenous activism and the 1994 Zapatista uprising in Chiapas, the
state of Oaxaca passed the Law of the Indigenous Peoples and Communities of
Oaxaca, officially establishing that indigenous municipalities could elect their
authorities according to the customs and uses of the respective indigenous
groups. Today most of Oaxaca's municipalities have their own form of indigenous government.

Teachers have had an important role in the activism in Oaxaca as well as
other areas. Historically, teachers have had a unique influence in Mexico—both
for the status quo and for social change. Teachers, along with other local rural
leaders, were often a significant voice in articulating the grievances and organizing the resistance of peasant communities in the Mexican revolution.[65] As
noted in Chapter 2, during the 1920s and 1930s, rural teachers promoted agrarian reform, reinforcing and in some cases going beyond the agendas of the
post-revolutionary governments. In the case of Oaxaca, a rural and largely
indigenous state, this resulted in an enduring alliance between teachers and the
communities.

After the establishment of the PRM (later the PRI) on the basis of a corporatist structure in 1938, the SNTE (National Union of Education Workers)
became the largest organization in the CNOP (the National Confederation of

Popular Organizations), which grouped the organizations of the popular sector. Throughout the period of PRI dominance, teachers, for the most part, transmitted the values of the regime and led mobilizations and demonstrations on behalf of the party. The teaching profession was also widely seen as a means of mobility for members of the working class and peasantry into the middle class, another factor in its conservative influence. At the same time, many teachers in rural or poor urban areas were sympathetic to the grievances of these sectors and their demands for change. In Oaxaca, the teachers developed close relations with other sectors, including indigenous groups, as well as parents, and over the years they mobilized frequently for improvements in labor conditions, education, and infrastructure.

The political opening beginning under the Echeverría government in the early 1970s, followed by the electoral reforms of 1977 and the oil boom at the end of the decade, provided opportunities for mobilization and organization, which in several unions took the form of demands for higher wages, union democracy and labor autonomy in relation to the PRI labor structure. During this period, dissident movements of teachers emerged in several states, including Oaxaca, in opposition to the leadership of the National Teachers' Union, widely regarded as both corrupt and ineffective in representing the rights of teachers. The wages of teachers stagnated during the oil boom of the 1970s and 1980s, even though wages had increased in other sectors. Subsequently, the real wages of teachers dropped by over 60 percent during the economic crises between 1982 and 1989.

Similar to other protest movements, the dissident teachers were influenced by activists from the student movements of the 1960s and 1970s. In 1979 they formed the CNTE (National Coordinating Committee of Education Workers), a progressive coalition within the national union. Although united in their opposition to corrupt leadership and promotion of union autonomy, different state movements had varying organizational structures and tactics. The Oaxaca movement focused on grassroots organization with a democratic decision-making process that took into account different tendencies, reflecting the heterogeneity of the movement and keeping with the political line favored by some student activists.

The Oaxaca movement also differed from those that favored complete independence and opposed all contact with government. The movement maintained organizational autonomy, but it negotiated with the government to advance its constituents' interests and often combined negotiation (with state and federal officials and the national union leadership) with marches, demonstrations and disruptive tactics, including the plantón.

The state government's attack on the plantón in June 2006 had the unanticipated effect of rallying sympathy and support for the teachers among large sectors of the population, including some parents who had initially resented the interruption in their children's education and residents who had been annoyed at the inconveniences caused by the plantón. Following the destruction of the transmission equipment of *Radio Plantón*, students at the Benito Juárez Autonomous University of Oaxaca invited the protestors to broadcast from the university radio station. The attack also mobilized support from popular organizations throughout the state. Many individuals and groups had their own grievances against the authoritarian and corrupt practices of PRI Governor Ruíz Ortíz and of the PRI itself, which had controlled the government of the state for decades. Indigenous groups accused the government of ignoring the needs of the impoverished majority and concentrating resources on mega-projects oriented to tourism, industry and commerce, arguing that they threatened the economic resources or the cultural heritage of the indigenous people. The Ruíz Ortíz administration was also accused of a pattern of increasing repression; human rights organizations documented 30 political murders and the imprisonment of dozens of indigenous activists in the year following his inauguration.

After the attack on the plantón, several organizations, ranging from artists' groups to unions and indigenous organizations, formed the Popular Assembly of the People of Oaxaca (APPO), which eventually encompassed between 200 to 300 groups. APPO joined the teachers in retaking control of the plaza and public buildings, forcing the Ruíz Ortíz government to move to the outskirts of the city, and established a tent city of thousands, which controlled major parts of the city throughout the following months. Although the local police forces withdrew after the first attack, intermittent attacks by individual plainclothesmen and paramilitary forces on the plantón resulted in several injuries and deaths. The protestors set up barricades at strategic points throughout the city for self-defense, which remained in place until the end of October.

The demands of the movement expanded to incorporate the removal of Ruíz Ortíz from office; government support for education, healthcare, and other needs for the state of Oaxaca; and an extension of democracy. The nature of democracy was a subject of extensive dialogue and debate among the protestors; e.g., to what extent should they focus on strengthening the institutions of formal democracy versus developing various forms of participatory democracy based on indigenous practices? In order to govern the plantón and maintain order in the city they drew on indigenous traditions to establish an alternative form of democracy based on consensual decision making.

During this period, APPO held numerous marches and demonstrations, in which up to a million people participated from throughout the state. On August 1, following a women's march of "pots and pans," several of the women went to Channel 9, the government-owned radio and television station which, like most others in the city, had been disseminating negative reports regarding the movement, to ask for time to explain the APPO position. When they were refused, they took over the station, using it to disseminate the ideas and initiatives of APPO and opening it to members of the public to express their own ideas and grievances. After police invaded the station, the women and other members of APPO temporarily took over all radio and television stations of the city. Subsequently, most stations were returned to their owners but APPO retained control of one station, which continued to broadcast throughout the state until the end of October.

The APPO-controlled media served to coordinate activities, warn of government attacks, and issue calls to action. It was also a forum for dialogue and debate on issues important to the state of Oaxaca and the character and future of the movement itself. In addition to the radio and television broadcasts, people from various walks of life participated in assemblies, informal gatherings on the streets and at the barricades, workshops and other venues to discuss issues of importance to the movement, the city of Oaxaca, and the state.

APPO also held cultural events, including an alternative *Guelaguetza*, a celebration of the distinct indigenous cultures of Oaxaca, following the cancelation of the official annual event, which the protestors argued had been taken over by the tourist industry. Artists played an important role in movement, forming a collective, ASARO (Assembly of Revolutionary Artists of Oaxaca), and chronicling events in various forms of graphic art that were displayed throughout the city. Oaxacan artist Francisco Toledo, one of the leading contemporary artists in Mexico, established a group of mediators to negotiate with the government and APPO and, following the arrest of some of the protestors, raised funds to contribute to their defense.

Image 6-1 *Marcha de APPO* (Popular Assembly of the People of Oaxaca). The banner reflects the APPO demand for the resignation of Ulises Ruiz Ortiz, the governor of Oaxaca.

In late August and September, APPO representatives met with officials of the Fox government and members of the legislature, but while the government was responsive to the request for a salary increase and other labor-related issues, it refused to deal with the request for the dismissal of Ruíz Ortíz, recognizing that PAN would need PRI legislative support to govern effectively during the next six years. Subsequently the legislature, including some members of PRI, passed a resolution urging Ruíz Ortíz to resign, but the resolution was nonbinding. The Fox government also urged Ruíz Ortíz to resign but the governor refused to comply.

In the meantime, the conflict and the occupation of the central part of the city of Oaxaca had taken a toll on tourism, a major source of income for the city and the state. The population was increasingly polarized between those supporting the strike and those opposed, including residents, parents of school children, and small businesspeople angry at the loss of tourist income. Teachers were under pressure to return to the classrooms as the school year began. In October, a majority of the teachers decided to accept the contract offered by the government and return to their classes, but pointed out that they continued to support APPO and the removal of Ruíz Ortíz. Nevertheless, although accepted by the APPO leadership, the decision resulted in divisions between teachers who settled with the government and some members of APPO as well as those teachers that refused to return to classes, who maintained that they should hold out until the governor resigned.

Throughout the conflict, President Fox, who was concerned about the repercussions a violent confrontation between federal troops and protestors in Oaxaca might have in the context of the national electoral campaign and its contentious aftermath, seemed reluctant to intervene despite repeated requests by the Ruíz Ortíz government and president-elect Calderón, who finally stated that he wanted the issue resolved by the time he came to office on December 1. On October 27, an attack by state forces on the protestors resulted in the death of four Oaxacans, including a teacher and three other citizens, and a U.S. journalist.

This was apparently a catalyst for action by the federal government. Two days later the Federal Preventive Police (PFP) and riot police entered the city to dislodge the protestors, using helicopters, water cannons, and tear gas and retook control of the city. Nevertheless, in the following days APPO continued to hold demonstrations and marches demanding the release of prisoners and an end to government occupation of the city. Although APPO representatives called for peaceful demonstrations, there were attacks on the federal police, and protestors were blamed for setting fires that destroyed public buildings, which some protestors in turn blamed on the infiltration of the movement by government provocateurs or "rogue elements." Repression of popular protest continued under Calderón, who became president on December 1. On December 4, several representatives of APPO, including APPO leader Flavio Sosa, were arrested when they came to Mexico City to negotiate a solution to the conflict. During the period between the entry of federal troops into the city of Oaxaca and their withdrawal in mid-December, several people were killed and hundreds were arrested. Many of them, including Sosa, were sent to high security prisons in other parts of the country, where they remained for several months and in some cases for over two years.

Studies and reports by various human rights organizations documented at least 23 people killed in the period between June and December, including teachers, journalists, APPO members and bystanders, as well as numerous disappearances. While many of the charges against the protestors were later dismissed, including charges of "sedition," "criminal association," and "property damage" against Sosa, some continued to be charged with various crimes, and death threats against some protestors and their families forced them to go into hiding. Human rights organizations reported that several of those imprisoned recounted experiences of severe mistreatment, including beatings, sexual abuse, and torture.

The plantón ended without APPO achieving its major objective of removing the government of Ruíz Ortíz, let alone obtaining substantial changes in the economic and social conditions in Oaxaca. Although the movement was subsequently weakened by internal conflicts, it did succeed, during this brief period in 2006, in creating a space in which ordinary citizens could be heard and experiments in popular democracy could flourish. At the same time, the failure of the federal government to deal effectively with abuses by the Ruíz Ortíz administration, and the repression of the movement by both state and national forces, indicate the failure of Mexico's democracy to provide legal protections for many of its citizens.

WOMEN IN SOCIAL MOVEMENTS

In these and other movements of the past 25 years, women emerged as key actors, but they were not the first social movements in which women were active. During the Mexican Revolution, women participated not only as cooks and nurses but also as soldiers and even commanders. In the 1920s and 1930s, as teachers, they were in the forefront of efforts to provide education and promote agrarian reform in rural areas. In more recent years they have been the backbone of protest movements. But women had to struggle constantly and on numerous fronts to obtain recognition of their civil and legal rights and to end discrimination in the political, economic and social spheres. Their efforts have been complicated by entrenched patriarchal concepts and practices, rooted in indigenous and colonial Spanish traditions, that have relegated women to the private spheres of home and church, subordinated them to the authority of fathers and husbands, and fostered a stereotypical view of women as either docile, self-abnegating wives and mothers, or whores and prostitutes.[66]

Following the revolution women won several social and civil rights, such as the right to own property and labor rights. Over the next several decades, women, chiefly from the middle and upper middle class, campaigned for the right to vote, finally achieving it in 1952. Small but dedicated groups of middle-class activists continued to work to eliminate discrimination against women. While poor and working-class women were often at the forefront of movements oriented to social change, they were rarely involved in campaigns oriented to women's issues. Some believed that feminist agendas were a means of undermining the unity necessary for promoting social goals.

The 1970s and 1980s were characterized by an upsurge in women's social activism. First, the grassroots organizing efforts of the student generation of 1968 in urban neighborhoods led to increased women's involvement in urban-based movements. Second, the Women's Conference held in Mexico in 1975 was an important catalyst for women organizing around feminist issues. Third, the impact of the economic crisis of the 1980s pushed a number of poor and working-class women to organize to compensate for cutbacks in household incomes and government services.

Women often constituted the majority of members in urban movements in the 1970s and 1980s and could be quite audacious in demanding their rights, often taking the lead in direct action tactics. One example was a campaign to extend the water system to the poor areas of the city of Monterrey, home of the powerful Monterrey industrial groups, in early 1983. Residents organized a program, *Agua para Todas* (Water for Everyone), to petition the state and national government for the extension of water service. Women staged sit-ins at government offices and temporarily kidnapped water authority personnel. As with other groups, they combined negotiation with the government with direct action tactics. On one occasion, they bathed their children in the city fountains as a way of dramatizing their lack of access to water. The incident received broad national and international media coverage, to the considerable embarrassment of government officials and the city's industrial elite. The protests were eventually successful; President de la Madrid extended the water system to all homes that lacked water, serving some 300,000 residents.

The earlier 1975 Women's Conference resulted in tensions between Mexican feminists and those from the United States and other first world countries, due to concerns that the latter were pushing their own values and agendas, which were incompatible with those of third world women. At the same time, the conference was a catalyst for an increase in feminist activities in Mexico as well as alliances between Mexican feminists and international women's organizations. During the 1970s and 1980s, several feminist journals were founded and women's studies programs were established at universities throughout the country, including the UNAM and the Colegio de Mexico in Mexico City. Middle-class women also began to form cross-class connections, linking their demands for gender equity with the demands of popular groups and pushed efforts to end violence against women and to support rape victims.

The economic crisis beginning in the early 1980s impacted women in several ways. The elimination of price supports and rise in the prices of basic consumer goods meant that women, who were generally responsible for managing household budgets, were forced to cut back on family expenditures and/or find new sources of income. Cutbacks in government services, particularly affecting poor urban and rural women, were an additional source of strain. In many cases, men who lost jobs or suffered wage reductions migrated to other parts of Mexico or to the United States, leaving their spouses to head their households. A growing number of women entered the labor force, with the proportion of women increasing from 19 percent to 34 percent of the total labor force between 1979 and 1995. Although working and earning an income for the first time could be liberating for women previously confined to the private sphere, it also increased the responsibilities of women, who continued to have the major, if not sole, responsibility for household work and child care, resulting in the "double day" for many working women.

The practical concerns of women, stemming from their role as caretakers of children and family, were a further impetus to grassroots organizing as women engaged in various strategies to deal with these conditions. In some cases, women in particular neighborhoods organized collective kitchens or child care to share household responsibilities. Women also participated extensively in other social movements, such as CONAMUP, the Coordinating Committee of Urban Popular Movements established in 1981. Two years later, women formed the Women's Regional Council as an autonomous group within CONAMUP, in part to share survival strategies in order to improve living conditions and to provide services, such as breakfasts for children and care for the elderly.

Organization around practical goals often led to organizing around strategic, feminist goals.[67] On the one hand, women's participation in social movements was frequently the source of tensions within the household as male partners resented the time women spent outside the home, in some cases leading to domestic violence. On the other hand, women found that although they often constituted the majority—and the most active members—of social movements, they were generally excluded from the leadership. Thus a major goal of the Women's Council was to democratize CONAMUP and place more women in leadership positions. The Council also provided workshops for women on issues related to health and domestic violence.

Mobilization around the 1985 earthquakes in Mexico City was an important impetus for the social movements of the 1980s and for combining feminist and social agendas: linking commitment to the basic survival of families with efforts to end women's subordination to men and calling for "democracy in the home and in the government." Women increasingly organized on the basis of both social reforms and gender issues, reconciling feminism and class in what became known as grassroots feminism. Several NGOs concerned with women's issues also formed at this time, in Mexico City and in other areas, and worked with popular groups throughout the country.

Women have also been particularly active in human rights organizations. In 1977, Rosario Ibarra de Piedra, whose son had "disappeared" in the government repression of the1970s, formed the *Comité Eureka de Desaparecidos*. Women also were a majority within the civic action groups that formed throughout the country to monitor elections following the fraudulent elections of 1988.

The emergence of the EZLN in 1994 was another important moment in the women's movement as well as pivotal in the social movements of the 1990s. As noted previously, the Law of Revolutionary Women, issued on the day of the 1994 Zapatista uprising, called for women's right to personal integrity, including control over marriage, the number of children to have, and freedom from violence, as well as the elimination of gender discrimination in the home and society. The incorporation of indigenous women into the feminist agenda in effect indicates the compatibility of women's rights and indigenous rights, although not always realized in practice. Women continue to have an important role in Zapatista leadership as well as in confrontations with military forces surrounding the Zapatista areas. Women were active in the dissident teachers' movement in Oaxaca and elsewhere and in the APPO protests in the city of Oaxaca, where the takeover of the government radio and television station by women activists was a major turning point in the 2006 plantón.

Similar to other social movements that emerged in the wake of the student mobilization in the 1960s, women's groups sought to maintain their autonomy in relation to the government. At the same time, they did not hesitate to negotiate with the government for certain services and support, sometimes combining negotiations with more militant and confrontational tactics. The Women's Council of CONAMUP resorted to occupying offices of the relevant government bureaucracies in campaigns to improve living conditions, e.g., by obtaining control over the sale and distribution of cooking oil and subsidized milk in urban neighborhoods. In contrast to some movements, it also collaborated with the Salinas government in PRONASOL, the National Solidarity Program, in which women played a particularly important role as members and leaders of local solidarity committees.

Women have made some gains within the labor movement, political parties and government, although men continue to be dominant, even in unions in which women are the majority. In 1995, Alejandra Barrales became the first woman head of the flight attendants' union (*Asociación Sindical de Sobrecargos de Aviación*, ASSA) and in 1998 she successfully led its first strike for improved wages and benefits. In 1999, following a campaign linking women in labor unions, NGOs, and the three major political parties, Congress passed a reform to the Labor Law ending discrimination against women in the workforce.

Politically, women have held positions in municipal governments and the national legislature; the most significant growth took place during the legislative elections of 1997, in which 17 percent of the deputies and nearly 15 percent of the senators were women. The number and proportion have fluctuated since then, but in the 2006 elections women were 23 percent of the federal deputies. Several women have been state governors, and some have been cabinet members. The PRD and the PRI are both headed by women, and all three major parties have established quotas, requiring that 30 percent of all candidates for office should be women. Gender issues have now become institutionalized into the national debate and discourse.

But resistance to greater gender equality and even the basic rights of women continues to exist. Most disturbing has been the high level of violence and crimes against women. The most blatant example was has been the murder of women in the border city of Juárez. Beginning in the early 1990s, young women, many of them workers in the border maquila industries, began to disappear. Later their bodies would be found, often with signs of rape, torture and mutilation. Between 1993 and 2005, over 400 women were killed; hundreds of others disappeared. Local law enforcement officers were slow to respond, suggesting that the women were isolated victims of personal crimes, or worse, that they were prostitutes and in effect "asking for trouble." Local investigations were haphazard, characterized by inadequate record-keeping and little follow-up. Over the years, approximately 160 individuals have been convicted and imprisoned, but the crimes have continued. Many are convinced that the local police are involved in a cover-up of the crimes or even complicit in the crimes themselves. The murders and the failure of officials to respond adequately have given rise to the term "femicide," defined in a legislative report as combining misogynist acts against women with the "institutional violence" of government authorities that block justice against the perpetrators.

The failure of local police to adequately investigate the crimes led the mothers of the victims to take on the responsibilities of investigation. Two organizations, Justice for Our Daughters and Our Daughters Coming Home, documented approximately 430 women murdered between 1993 and 2005 as well as 600 unsolved disappearances; they also pressed state and government to intervene.

Only in 2003 did the federal government become involved, convening the Commission to Prevent and Eradicate Violence against the women in Juárez, which demonstrated that femicide was a widespread phenomenon not only in Juárez but throughout Mexico. But the commission did not receive sufficient federal support to function effectively; when the initial head of the commission resigned the government failed to replace her.

In August 2007 a coalition of women's and human rights groups formed the Citizen Observatory of Femicide to identify femicides on a national level and to make policy proposals. The national legislature conducted its own investigation, as have various foreign and international organizations, including the European Parliament. Several of these pointed out the failures of law enforcement, the creation of a climate of impunity, and the need for education on human rights and gender equality.

The investigations led to new legislation including the General Law of Access of Women to a Life Free of Violence and legislation in the state of Chihuahua increasing penalties against sexual harassment and stating that rape within marriage constitutes a crime. But the inadequate response of government at all levels to femicide in Juárez and elsewhere raises obvious questions as to how effectively these laws will be enforced. More broadly, it demonstrates the formidable obstacles that women have confronted and continue to confront in their struggles for women's rights.

DISCUSSION

What insights can be drawn regarding social movements and civic organizations in Mexico on the basis of the cases outlined above? What do they tell us about the origins, trajectories, goals and strategies of these movements? How similar are they to previous movements? To what extent, and how, have they maintained their autonomy in relation to the state, political parties, and other political actors? What have been their achievements?

With respect to their origins, these cases indicate that the emergence of social movements on the national scene is often preceded by years and even decades of organizing and that much of it occurs at the local level and around local issues.[68] The mobilization of citizens—in response to the Mexico City earthquake, the Zapatista revolt in Chiapas, the teachers' plantón and the formation of APPO in Oaxaca, the ecologists in Guerrero—occurred around particular local issues or events, although in some cases they had national and international implications. The Barzón movement was less of a national movement than a coalition of local movements.

At the same time, even movements that begin spontaneously, such as the rapid mobilization of individuals and communities in the immediate aftermath of the 1985 earthquake in Mexico City, have origins in long-term organizing: leaders and activists from urban protest movements that emerged in several states as well as in Mexico City in the 1970s had an important role in the formation of the CUD and later the Asamblea de Barrios. Similarly, in the case of El Barzón, in which middle-class farmers, small businesspersons, and homeowners participated for the first time, several of the leaders had been activists in local or state politics in states such as Jalisco and Zacatecas. The emergence of the Zapatistas was preceded and influenced by a long history of indigenous organizing in Chiapas, while Section 22 of the teachers' union, and many of the other social groups that became part of APPO, had a history of activism in Oaxaca. And, as seen in Chapter 5, the formation of the Civic Alliance was preceded by the organization and mobilization of civic action groups in San Luis Potosí and other parts of Mexico.

Political openings also provided opportunities for organizing. In Mexico, the "democratic opening" under Echeverría in the early 1970s, although short-lived, was a factor in the successful organizing of urban movements in several parts of the country and in the responsiveness of some reformist government officials to demands for urban services in Mexico City and elsewhere.[69] It also provided a catalyst for the initiation of grassroots programs to develop forest resources by indigenous groups, as evident in the case of Guerrero. The emergence of the Cárdenas candidacy in 1988 and subsequent formation of the PRD, and the victories of opposition parties in municipal and state elections in the 1980s and 1990s (which raised expectations regarding the possibility of a substantial change in the political system) provided an impetus for the organization of local grassroots election monitoring campaigns and the formation of the Civic Alliance in 1994.

Globalization and neoliberalism were also important. Negotiations around NAFTA reinforced the development of cross-border collaboration as well as the formation of cross-sector networks in Mexico. The Agrarian Law of 1992 was a deciding factor in the Zapatista uprising. The peso crisis of 1984–1985 was a catalyst in expanding the numbers and level of mobilization of the Barzón movement, as well as the mobilization of labor and the emergence or consolidation of independent labor organizations.

How do the social movements that emerged in the last decades of the 20th and the early 21st centuries compare with earlier movements? There are both continuities and differences—in terms of actors, goals and strategies—with the earlier experiences of the post-war period. First, while labor organization at the workplace was less central than in the past, workers, including labor activists, were involved in organizing in their neighborhoods and communities. Second, women were active, in some cases constituting the majority, in both early and more recent movements, but were more likely to have, and demand, a leadership role, and to organize around issues of gender, as was the case in the EZLN.

Third, indigenous groups have mobilized in the past, but often it was as peasants around land issues, reflecting the class focus in the constitution and among pro-agrarian groups within the government. As government officials became less responsive to agrarian needs, particularly under the Salinas government, and with the increasing visibility of indigenous movements in Latin America and elsewhere, these groups stressed issues of identity and autonomy. Similar shifts occurred among indigenous movements in the Andean countries, demonstrating the ability of social groups to select among multiple identities in response to contextual changes, including changes in relations with the state and the influence of other social actors. Fourth, some middle-class groups that had never participated in protest action became more mobilized—such as small and medium farmers, small urban business groups, and middle-class homeowners and consumers threatened with loss of property in the Barzón movement. In sum, new social actors emerged, while long-term social actors shifted their locus of mobilization, embraced new issues, and took on new roles and identities.

In addition, many of the social movements of the 1980s and 1990s were more heterogeneous than in the past. The Asamblea de Barrios included middle-class residents although the majority of the rank and file were the urban poor. The civic action groups included professors and students, citizen groups and social activists, members of Christian Base Communities and NGOs, as well as different political and ideological perspectives. The constituency of El Barzón was both urban and rural and included small and medium farmers, owners of small firms, and credit card holders. This heterogeneity was a source of strength, since it broadened the base of the movement, and also enabled it to draw on the skills and experiences of different constituencies. However, it could also undermine the cohesion of the organization, particularly in the long term, given the diverse character, experiences, and interests of the membership.

The issues of organizational autonomy and relations with the state were resolved differently in different cases. The frequency with which independent organizations in Mexico had been co-opted by the state or taken over by PRI elements led to a determination on the part of students and other activists to maintain organizational autonomy and a rejection of any collaboration with the government or party that entailed tradeoffs in terms of support. At the same time, the goals of many of these organizations—housing for earthquake victims, relief from debt, and self-government of indigenous communities—involved interaction with the government, and several movements were directly involved in negotiations with the government. The CUD and subsequently the Asamblea de Barrios met with government officials around housing for earthquake victims and poor tenants. El Barzón negotiated for the restructuring or pardoning of the debts of its members. Even the Zapatistas met with government representatives to negotiate various issues, notably community self-government and regional autonomy, although they broke off all relations with the government following the passage of the indigenous legislation of 2001.

Government decentralization and the emergence of viable opposition parties presented new opportunities and challenges. The issue of political collaboration became more controversial with the Cárdenas candidacy and the formation of the PRD, which raised the question for activists in several organizations of possible collaboration with what appeared to be a viable left or center-left opposition. On the one hand, some social organizations such as El Barzón were able to obtain support from Congress or state officials even when negotiations with the federal executive were unsuccessful. The Asamblea de Barrios collaborated with the Cárdenas campaign in 1988 and subsequently the PRD, a move that proved costly when the Salinas government marginalized supporters of Cárdenas. Some of the leading activists in El Barzón were already activists in the PRD or the PRI, which led to some divisions in the leadership. The decision of some leaders to work within the new political institutions also alienated members of the rank and file who preferred direct action tactics. At the other extreme, the Zapatistas rejected all relations with political parties, particularly after the unanimous vote for the 2001 indigenous law. This too has had consequences in cutting off EZLN communities from government assistance.

The transition to democracy has not eliminated the need for social mobilization to confront continued economic exploitation, social injustice and political repression. The nature of democracy itself has become an issue, as movements seek to redefine it to incorporate greater participation and to expand the presence and role of civil society. The "other campaign" of the Zapatistas and the intense debates and discussions of APPO may be seen as experiments in alternative forms of democracy.

With respect to tactics, social movements drew on a familiar repertoire, including marches and demonstrations, land invasions, strikes, street theater, and civil disobedience, combined with legal cases, negotiation and other forms of interaction with government officials at different levels. They also took advantage of new technologies, such as the Internet, which became a major instrument in publicizing the proclamations and documents of the Zapatistas. In addition, movements benefitted from the international solidarity found in human rights, environmental, labor and other organizations—evident in the Amnesty International defense of Mexican environmental activists, as well as the international and national protests against government repression of the Zapatista movement. When NAFTA was being debated in the U.S. Congress, representatives from Mexican organizations lobbied members of Congress for the inclusion of labor rights.[70] The congressional debate also provided a window of opportunity for groups working on behalf of maquiladora workers to publicize abuses in the maquiladoras.[71]

Intra-sector and cross-sector alliances were also increasingly important as different organizations joined forces or collaborated around particular events or issues. Human rights organizations, labor unions and other social movements joined forces to form the Civic Alliance. The RMALC (Mexican Action Network on Free Trade), linking environmental organizations, labor unions and confederations, women's groups, and human rights organizations, among others, was formed to have an input into NAFTA. Following the peso crisis, the UNT, El Barzón, and other organizations joined forces in opposing the government's economic model. Alliances also crossed borders, as was evident in the Coalition for Justice in the Maquiladoras.

What have these movements achieved? Most social movements organized at least initially around concrete objectives, such as the provision of urban services, housing for earthquake victims, protection of renters and debtors, protection of forest resources, and labor contracts. In the context of economic and political changes beginning in the 1980s, however, movements and groups have taken on more ambitious goals having to do with national issues. The Asamblea de Barrios called for a debt moratorium or a reduction in the payment of foreign debt. In the aftermath of the peso crisis, the UNT and other labor organizations as well as El Barzón called for the repudiation of the neoliberal agenda and a renegotiation of the NAFTA agreement. The EZLN called for a constitutional amendment recognizing Mexico's indigenous communities and granting them political autonomy.

For the most part, they failed to achieve these more far-reaching goals. There was no repudiation of the debt or re-negotiation of NAFTA, and there has been limited impact on the neoliberal agenda, although popular movements and their allies in Congress have succeeded in blocking certain initiatives, such as the expansion of the value added tax to include food and medicine. Following the mobilization of the Zapatistas and other indigenous groups, the indigenous law of 2001 was passed, but in a truncated version that was rejected by these groups.

However, to focus on dramatic changes is misleading. Mexico's social movements have been effective on several levels. First, they did succeed in meeting some of their immediate goals. The CUD and the Asamblea were successful in obtaining housing for earthquake victims and to some extent in protecting renters in Mexico City, although not those in areas slated for gentrification. The Civic Alliance and its member organizations have been important in the substantial improvement in electoral transparency and in promoting Mexico's transition from a dominant party to a pluralist system. El Barzón protected debtors threatened with repossession of their property and enabled some members to restructure their debts. The EZLN established a zone of indigenous autonomy in Chiapas although it has suffered continued harassment from the government and PRI-related organizations, and there has been an increase in de facto self-government by indigenous groups in Chiapas and elsewhere. The formation of RMALC and the mobilization of labor, environmental and other organizations in Mexico, the United States, and Canada, around NAFTA, led to the inclusion of labor and environmental issues in the NAFTA side-agreements, although their implementation has proved to be difficult.

At the same time, social movements and civic organizations had an important role—often indirectly—in Mexico's transition from an authoritarian to a more democratic regime. In Mexico, as elsewhere in Latin America, the mobilization and organization of different social groups called into question the legitimacy of the existing regime and exerted pressures on the government to which it had to respond. Democracy was a demand of many movements and the specific goal of civic action groups and the Civic Alliance. The mobilization around the candidacy of Cuauhtémoc Cárdenas in the 1988 presidential election, protests against fraudulent PRI victories in local and state elections, the emergence of the Zapatista army on January 1, 1994, and the social unrest following the peso crisis of 1994–1995 were followed by electoral reforms, eventually leading to a more level playing field and increasing recognition of opposition victories (see Chapter 5).

Finally, the impact of social movements may be long term. First, while social movements are ephemeral, social activists endure and become involved in other movements or organizations, often drawing on prior experiences. In many cases, participants gain skills and a new sense of empowerment that can be carried into other areas. The achievements of a given movement, however incremental, may constitute the basis for subsequent organizing. Second, although specific events or policies (the earthquakes of 1985, the 1992 agrarian law, NAFTA, the peso crisis) were catalysts in the emergence of social movements in the 1980s and 1990s and help explain the specific forms they took, these movements had antecedents in prior experiences and earlier movements and in many cases were the result of long-term organizing efforts. While social movements may disappear or become institutionalized, and cycles of protest dissipate as conditions change, they are part of an ongoing historical process that forms the basis for the emergence of new movements and cycles of protest in the future.

CHAPTER 7

Mexicans on the Move: Migration, Settlement and Transnational Activism

INTRODUCTION: MIGRATION STORIES

Juan Carlos Payan and his brothers followed in the footsteps of his uncle and other members of the small community of Zapotillo who have migrated from this impoverished region of the western state of Sinaloa to work in the coal mines of Utah. This migration trajectory had its origins several decades ago when, in the words of Payan's uncle, "really tall, really blonde men" came from Utah to recruit workers. Today the population of Zapotillo consists largely of women, children and the elderly. Most men of the community have migrated to Utah where they earn over $20 an hour, the amount they earn in a week in the corn and tomato fields in Sinaloa. But Payan's trajectory—and that of two other Mexican migrants—ended tragically in August 2007, when they were among the six miners buried in the collapse of the Crandall Canyon Mine. In spite of this, it is likely that migration of men from Zapotillo to the mines in Utah will continue. As stated by a former classmate of one of the miners: "here there is no work. We don't have options."[1]

Lucino Canseco came to the city of Santa Ana in Southern California in 1990, at the age of 22, with the aim of making and saving money and then returning to Mexico. He took a job in a restaurant, bussing tables. Fifteen years later he was still in Santa Ana—and still bussing tables. In the meantime, he has married, has a son, now nine, and lives with his family in a two-bedroom apartment in a neighborhood east of downtown Santa Ana. The family rents out one of the bedrooms to new immigrants, and with his wages—approximately $15,000 a year, the rental income, and what his wife earns through part-time babysitting they are able to make ends meet. Lucino could earn more by working double shifts, but that would leave little time with his family. Life is better in the United States than it would be in Mexico, but he has hopes that his son will be able to go to college and have opportunities that he lacked[2].

Like several other men from his village, Erasmo Alonzo Sánchez migrated from Santa Maria Ayoquenzo, a Zapotec community in the state of Oaxaca, when it was no longer possible to make a living there growing corn. He went to the lettuce fields near Salinas, California where he worked ten-hour days for eight years, developing chronic back pain, but earning enough money to send $500 home to his family every two or three months. While some of his remittances went to buy food and other necessities, his wife Catalina Sánchez recognized the potential market for nopal cactus among Mexicans in the United States, and began investing some of her husband's earnings in a nopal garden. She was joined by other women whose husbands were in California, who formed a co-op to grow and market cactus. With migrant earnings and assistance from the Mexican government they built a plant to process nopal for export, which opened in May, 2007, and are seeking markets for distribution in Los Angeles, San Diego, and Salinas. In 2004, Erasmo Alonso returned home and now works with his wife. The hope of the families in Ayoquen-zo is that the nopal project will reverse the process of migration, enabling family members to return from the United States and providing sufficient opportunities for the younger generation to earn a living in Oaxaca rather than migrate.[3]

Every migrant has his or her own story; each migrant family has its own history. Together, they are part of a broad movement that in the case of Mexico encompasses millions of families and a long historical trajectory that predates the Spanish conquest and extends into the foreseeable future. This trajectory is deeply intertwined with the histories of Mexico and the United States: relations between the two countries have propelled and facilitated migration which in turn has had a profound effect on each and on the relations between them.

This Chapter begins with an introduction to concepts and issues in the study of migration. It then goes into the history of Mexican migration, focusing on the changing conditions in both Mexico and the United States that have influenced migration between the two countries, and a brief overview of Mexicans and Mexican Americans in the United States. The following section examines relations between Mexican immigrants and their home countries and communities. Two case studies illustrate different patterns of migration, those of Zacatecas, a traditional migration state, and Oaxaca, an indigenous state of relatively recent U.S. migration. A concluding section examines Mexican migration to the United States as both cause and consequence of the growing economic, social and cultural integration of the two countries.

CONCEPTS AND ISSUES

Migration refers to a relatively large scale movement of people within or across borders. It encompasses both internal migration (i.e., within a given country) and international migration (from one country to another). In the case of international migration, the country of emigration may be referred to as the home country, sending country or country of origin, while the country of immigration may be referred to as the host country, receiving country, or point of destination. Migration to another country may be official (i.e., with documents that legalize immigration status) or unofficial (without documents). Undocumented or unauthorized immigrants have crossed the border without documents or in many cases have simply overstayed their visas which permitted them to remain in the host country for a specified period of time.

Patterns of migration vary. *Cyclical* migration, which is often seasonal, involves repeated migration (internal and/or international) to and from a particular location. This is frequent in rural areas of Latin America, in which a small farmer or peasant may migrate to another part of the country or to another country to harvest crops during part of the year, then return to work on his or her own farm. *Temporary* migration refers to short-term migration, generally ranging from six months to two years. Temporary migrants, or *sojourners,* often migrate to earn money for a particular purpose (e.g., to buy land, or build a house), and are sometimes referred to as *target earners.*

Permanent migration refers to migration for the purpose of settling in a new location; in contrast to sojourners, permanent migrants are settlers. As the case of Lucino Canseco indicates, sometimes temporary migrants (sojourners) and cyclical migrants become permanent as a result of changing circumstances. In the case of international migration, the shift from a sojourner to a settler may be due to a change in type of job (from temporary to permanent), the decision to marry or to bring family from the home country, and/or to change one's legal status—from undocumented to documented or to permanent resident—in the host country. It often accompanies increased integration into the host society, indicated by such factors as fluency in the host country language and familiarity with its customs. The shift from temporary to permanent may be a conscious decision; often, however, it is the product of circumstances that accumulate over the years.

Finally, refugees are migrants who are fleeing from violence, war, persecution, or in some cases natural disasters. Migration is generally involuntary, and refugees may or may not control the possibility of return. The UN definition of a refugee, which was adopted in the U.S. Refugee Act in 1980, is anyone who leaves his or her country and is unable to return due to a well-founded fear of persecution due to religion, race, ethnicity, or membership in a particular group.

Why do people migrate?[4] Explanations for migration tend to focus on individual (or in some cases household) decisions, on the one hand, and broader contextual conditions in the home country (sometimes referred to as "push" factors), the receiving society ("pull" factors), or the relationship between the two, on the other hand. Individual (or household) decisions consider the costs and benefits of migrating vs. the costs and benefits of remaining. However, these decisions are related to context—such as the absence of opportunity in their communities of origin (a reason to leave, or "push" factor) and the actual or perceived opportunities at the point of destination (a place to go to, or "pull" factor).

Contextual explanations also look at relations between the point of departure and the point of destination, which explains why migrants go to one region or country as opposed to another. Migration from developing countries to more advanced countries, for example, often reflect historic patterns of colonization, settlement, foreign investment, and other types of intervention, or in some cases direct recruitment. Thus Algerians have traditionally migrated to France, Indians and Pakistani to England, Turks to Germany, and Mexicans and Dominicans to the United States.

Once a pattern of migration is established, migration may continue or increase due to the creation of *migrant networks*—social ties linking countries and communities of origin to communities of migrants in the receiving country, which facilitate migration for later migrants. Contacts (such as relatives or friends) in the host country may help in financing the trip of the migrant, finding a job in the host country, locating a place to live, or other assistance. Over time, migrant communities may form in the host country of individuals and families from the same country or even the same community, which facilitate subsequent migration, even when the initial reasons for migration no longer hold.

International migration has increased dramatically in recent years, reflecting the rapid growth in economic integration, communications, and cultural influence that has accompanied globalization.[5] Increased migration has involved not only a larger number migrating, but also the diversity of regions of origin, and the extension of destination points. Successive economic crises and neoliberal reforms often result in severe dislocations, including job loss and reduction of wages, in certain areas of sending countries. At the same time, developments in communications technology and the spread of media access, including TV, video, film, and the Internet, to all areas of the world, have led to increased information about conditions in destination countries, such as the United States, European countries, and Japan. The globalization of production, including the outsourcing of jobs to various parts of the world, which familiarizes job recipients with companies based in advanced countries, and in some cases direct recruitment of skilled and unskilled labor from developing countries, are further factors in migration.

International migration raises numerous issues regarding migrant relations with countries of origin and countries of destination. For international migrants planning to return to their home countries—including seasonal migrants, temporary migrants such as target earners and, in some cases, refugees—social and cultural assimilation into the host society may be minimal. Permanent migrants, or settlers, however, are expected to become incorporated into the host society, and there is a considerable literature on this issue. Earlier U.S. immigration literature was often based on the assumption that assimilation involved an erosion of ties with the home society and the previous culture and adopting the social norms and values of the host country.

Subsequently, the concept of assimilation has been rejected (or modified) in favor of concepts of adaptation or incorporation, which do not necessarily imply rejection of home country values, customs, or contacts.[6] Successful incorporation into the host society is seen as the result of two factors: the socio-economic characteristics of migrants, such as the level of education, language ability, and job skills; and what is referred to as the *context of reception*, i.e., conditions facilitating or impeding incorporation in the host society. This includes:

1. The structure of the labor market, i.e., what types of jobs are available? While the socioeconomic characteristics of immigrants will influence the type of work they can do, they may be constrained by the conditions of the labor market, e.g., whether they have access to unionized jobs that provide some security and generally better wages and working conditions.

2. Government policies toward immigrants and refugees (sometimes referred to as the gate-keeping function), which include official designations of documented (legal) or undocumented and therefore subject to deportation (illegal), as well as the extent to which these policies are enforced. Undocumented immigrants often lack the options of legal immigrants in terms of access to jobs and services; they can also be more easily exploited since they are less likely to complain to authorities for fear of deportation.

3. Mainstream attitudes, ranging from acceptance to discrimination and hostility. Although attitudes vary, immigrants have often been subject to discrimination and scapegoating, particularly in periods of recession or depression.

4. The existence and nature of an ethnic community in the host society to which new migrants can relate. An immigrant or ethnic community may facilitate immigration and incorporation as a source of information about conditions and opportunities in the host society; it may also ease adjustment through a culturally familiar environment. However, it may also delay incorporation into mainstream society by limiting interaction with other groups in society and restricting opportunities outside those available to the ethnic group.

Incorporation is often partial. Migrants may be incorporated into the mainstream society economically but retain social and cultural norms from the home country. This is particularly true of first generation immigrants who migrate as adults, many of whom continue to be nostalgic for the home country even after remaining in the host country for many years. Their children, however— including those born in the host country (the second generation) as well as those who came at an earlier age (sometimes referred to as the 1.5 generation)— generally adapt more quickly as a result of socialization in host country schools and peer group pressures. But for immigrants living in depressed inner city areas, these pressures may result in downward assimilation into a marginalized underclass rather than into mainstream society. The concept of segmented assimilation has been used to define the various possible outcomes of second-generation incorporation.

The emergence and development of a migrant community may reinforce identification with the home country or, over time, result in the development of a specific ethnic identity through interaction with other cultural or ethnic groups. This may be reinforced if newcomers and their descendants experience discrimination or hostility from the host society, leading to forms of cultural resistance in which immigrants assert their national and/or ethnic identity as a source of pride.

Globalization has also fostered a new way of looking at the issue of immigrant incorporation into host societies. The traditional concept of a "melting pot" has been replaced by that of cultural pluralism, in which immigrants and their children retain elements of their former culture and social practices while at the same time adapting to the culture of the host society. Biculturalism— including fluency in two languages and understanding of two cultures—can be an asset in an increasingly integrated world.[7]

Globalization also facilitates what is sometimes referred to as transnationalism, defined as the establishment and expansion of links by immigrants and immigrant communities in the host country with their families and communities in the country of origin.[8] Some definitions refer to the establishment of "social fields" that consist of networks connecting both migrants and non-migrants living in both sending and receiving countries. Individual immigrants maintain connections with families and communities in their home countries through letters and phone calls, videos, periodic visits home, (e.g., for national and religious holidays) and remittances—earnings sent by immigrants to family members back home. This is of course particularly the case when the spouse, children, and in some cases parents remain in the home country—a situation that is sometimes referred to in terms of binational families.

Over time, particularly with the growth of migrant communities in the host country, these social networks become increasingly dense. In some cases immigrants from a particular community establish informal or formal associations that facilitate these connections, such as home town associations, that raise funds for particular civic projects in their home countries. Migrants who visit or return permanently to their home communities may also bring cultural and social influences from the host country (sometimes referred to as social remittances), in some cases reinforcing other external influences (e.g., through the media).[9] Some migrants become involved in the politics of the home country or of their particular home community on their return or while maintaining their base in the host country.

For the most part, these types of migrant-related cross-country connections are not new, as we will see.[10] What is different today is again the impact of globalization, both directly and indirectly. As communications and information technology facilitates widespread knowledge about advanced countries, it also facilitates communications across borders. The growth of migration has also meant a growth in remittances, particularly since the difficult economic conditions in the home country that have often fueled migration in the first place also mean that family members are more dependent than ever on migrant earnings. The amount of remittances has grown exponentially in recent years, to the point that they not only assist families but also provide a major source of foreign exchange for many home countries, in some cases surpassing revenues from major exports.

Home country states have historically taken an interest in their emigrant populations. In many cases, this has taken the form of efforts to block emigration, prevent assimilation in the host country, and/or facilitate migrant return. In some cases, they have attempted to protect emigrants from discrimination in the host countries. In other cases, emigration has been seen as an escape valve for surplus labor and may even be encouraged; although at the same time the home country governments seek to retain the loyalty of their emigrants.[11] In recent years, partly as a consequence of economic dependence on migrant resources, home country governments (and in some cases business interests) have taken an increased interest in their nationals abroad and the role they can play as sources of income, markets for home country exports, and possible sources of investment.

It goes without saying that migration is a transformative experience for the migrants themselves. In going from one country to another, migrants often cross not only geographical borders but also class, cultural and ethnic boundaries.[12] How migrants, as well as their home and host countries and communities, are transformed through international migration is an important part of the migrant story.

Based on these perspectives, the following discussion of Mexican migration will address the following questions. First, how can Mexican migration to the United States be explained? More specifically, how do the motivations of individual migrants intersect with contextual factors to explain changing migration patterns and trajectories? With respect to contextual factors, how has migration been influenced by U.S.-Mexican relations? How have such factors as U.S. immigration legislation, economic conditions, and mainstream attitudes affected the reception and incorporation of Mexicans in the United States? How has globalization influenced patterns of migration and settlement? What has been the economic, social and cultural impact of Mexican migration in the United States? In Mexico? How has migration affected those who migrate and their descendants?

MEXICAN MIGRATION IN HISTORICAL PERSPECTIVE

"The border crossed us."

Not all Mexicans in the United States crossed the border. As noted in Chapter 2, prior to the mid-19th century, Mexican territory extended north into what is now the Southwest United States, including California, Arizona, New Mexico, Texas, and much of Utah, Nevada, and Colorado. Even prior to the Spanish conquest, indigenous groups such as the Yaqui and Mayo lived on both sides of what is now the U.S.-Mexican border. As the Spaniards traveled north from central Mexico, Franciscan missionaries established missions throughout much of the Southwest, and Spanish colonists and their descendants established ranches in different parts of the region. Much of the area was controlled by nomadic indigenous groups, however, who resisted Spanish (and later Mexican and U.S.) encroachment, and the Spanish settlements in the region were generally isolated from each other as well as being separated from the center of Mexico.[13]

With Mexico's independence in 1821, what are now the southwest states of the United States became part of Mexico, and many Mexicans and Mexican Americans[14] today continue to see this area as their historic homeland. Following the independence of Texas and its subsequent incorporation into the United States and the defeat of Mexico in the Mexican American war, the current boundaries between the United States and Mexico were established, separating Mexicans living in the United States from those in Mexico. As some Mexicans and Mexican Americans put it: "We didn't cross the border. The border crossed us."[15] The Mexican ancestry population continued to be a majority in certain areas of the region until late in the 19th century. Although Mexicans living in the United States at the time the southwest region was annexed officially received U.S. citizenship, they were treated as second-class citizens and often subjected to harsh discrimination.[16]

Migration during the Porfiriato and the Revolutionary Period

In the late 19th and early 20th centuries, Mexican-U.S. migration grew rapidly as a result of several processes: the swift development of the southwestern U.S.

states, with mining and agriculture in particular requiring low-wage labor; the expansion of investment, including foreign investment, in agriculture, mining, and other activities in Mexico; and the disruptions resulting from the expropriation of Mexico's rural communal settlements and peasant holdings as the expansion of agricultural estates and expropriation of rural communal settlements and peasant holdings led to masses of landless, impoverished rural workers.

Linking these processes was the expansion of railroads in both the United States and Mexico that facilitated the demographic and economic growth of the U.S. southwest, connected production sites and markets in Mexico with U.S. cities and railroad centers, and fostered the development of a mobile labor force. These mobile workers moved from rural states in western and central Mexico to northern Mexico and on to the United States—occupying a variety of temporary and seasonal jobs in agriculture, railroads, manufacturing and mining in both countries. U.S. and Mexican labor contractors cooperated in recruiting Mexican workers to work on the railroads, particularly after the 1882 Chinese Exclusion Act and other restrictive U.S. measures in the late 19th and early 20th centuries virtually eliminated the flow of migrant labor from China, Japan and other Asian countries. Mexican workers had a major role in constructing the railroads in the U.S. Southwest as well as their maintenance and repair. Mexicans also found jobs in local industries in major railroad centers such as Los Angeles and El Paso as well as Chicago and other industrial centers of the Midwest.

Mexican migration to the United States expanded during the revolution, as Mexicans escaping violence in their home country continued to find work in expanding U.S. industries and agriculture, and continued to grow in the 1920s, particularly from central western states affected by the Cristero conflict. Large-scale irrigation projects opened up previously arid land for agriculture in the U.S. Southwest, and the expansion of cotton, sugar beets, fruit and vegetable production, facilitated by Mexican labor, helped to transform this region into a major agricultural center. By this time, Mexican immigrants had begun to form enclaves in several cities, including Los Angeles, San Antonio, and Chicago. In Los Angeles, Mexicans began to move out of the central-plaza area of earlier settlements to an area east of the Los Angeles river. It was during this period that several communities in East Los Angeles that are now predominantly Mexican or Mexican American were settled.[17] These and similar communities in other cities provided a combination of shared language and culture, as well as a barrier against the prejudice that Mexicans continued to experience in United States.

With the depression of the 1930s, the U.S. government expelled over 400,000 Mexican migrants. At the same time, in Mexico, the agrarian reform during the Cárdenas administration ended the debt peonage system and redistributed land to an estimated 810,000 peasants, reducing the landlessness of the Mexican population.

The Cárdenas government also encouraged Mexicans in the United States to return to Mexico, which at this point was considered to be under-populated, a concern which continued during the following decades.

Migration between the 1940s and the 1970s

As noted in Chapter 3, support of the agrarian reform beneficiaries in Mexico, particularly small farmers and ejidos, declined in the 1940s, as governments concentrated on industrial expansion to the relative neglect of agriculture. One result was large-scale rural-urban migration. Although the number of agricultural workers grew, due to a population increase, the proportion of rural workers was reduced from 65 to 30 percent of the total labor force in Mexico between 1940 and 1980. Migrants to cities, especially Mexico City and other large cities, worked in manufacturing or services, including expanding government services. These migrants included women who obtained jobs as domestic servants. But despite the growth associated with the "Mexican miracle," particularly in manufacturing, it was insufficient to absorb the growing labor force, including Mexicans coming from the countryside. This resulted in the growth of the informal economy and of squatter settlements in the environs of major cities, and was a factor in continued migration to the United States.

At the same time, the Second World War offered new opportunities for Mexican immigrants as well as Mexicans living in the United States. The scarcity of labor resulting from the enlistment of U.S. workers in the military during World War II led to creation of the bracero program, an agreement between the United States and Mexico which brought Mexicans into the United States to work temporarily in agriculture. Concerns about the mistreatment of Mexicans in the United States led to periodic efforts of the Mexican government to renegotiate bracero contracts and at the same time prevent undocumented emigration, which undercut contractual agreements. As the U.S. economy continued to expand in the post-war period the bracero program was extended, ultimately lasting from 1942 until 1965. During that period, 4.5 million Mexicans came to the United States under the auspices of the program, nearly half from four western states in Mexico: Michoacán, Jalisco, Guanajuato, and Zacatecas. Many were small farmers or ejidatarios, who used their earnings from the bracero program to provide inputs needed for farming on their return to Mexico.

Initially, this migration was cyclical; migrants would harvest for part of the year and then return to their home communities for the rest of the year. Some also came as temporary migrants, often target earners who worked in the United States until they had earned enough for specific projects, such as buying more land or adding on to a house. In spite of the efforts of the Mexican government to prevent it, undocumented emigration also continued and was in fact encouraged

Image 7-1 Mexican migrant workers, employed through the Bracero Program, harvest chili peppers in California, 1964.

by the United States. By the 1970s, Mexican population growth had led to new problems of insufficient jobs for the growing labor force, resulting in greater acceptance of undocumented emigration as well as the introduction of population control policies on the part of the Mexican government.[18]

A number of Mexican Americans joined the U.S. Armed Forces and served during World War II; several received the Congressional Medal of Honor and many died in the conflict. Following the war, veterans were eligible for higher education through the G.I. bill, and Mexican Americans began to enter professional and managerial positions and to take a more active role in U.S. politics.

Many Mexican immigrants began to settle permanently in the United States. The growth of manufacturing and heavy industry in the United States provided opportunities for Mexicans and Mexican Americans as well as African Americans in unionized, relatively well-paying industrial jobs. Migrant networks expanded between place of origin in Mexico and points of destination in the United States; migrants who had already traveled to the United States brought sons, nephews, or other relatives with them on subsequent trips, while immigrants in the United States found jobs for others from their communities. The development of migrant communities in the United States meant that migrants had a place to go for legal help, a Spanish-speaking community, and job contacts.

At the same time, Mexican immigrants continued to experience discrimination in the United States. As the expulsion of 400,000 Mexicans in the 1930s indicates, they were generally viewed as a "disposable labor force." Again in the early 1950s, "Operation Wetback" led to the expulsion of one million Mexicans as well as some naturalized Mexican Americans. Some Mexicans deported in the 1950s settled in border cities, such as Tijuana and Mexicali, which became part of the migration route for Mexicans coming from western Mexican states to the United States.

As of 1960 the Mexican ancestry population in the United States was estimated at 3.5 million. Approximately 80 percent of this population lived in the Southwest—the border states of Texas, New Mexico, Arizona and California, and Colorado, and roughly 80 percent was urban. The vast majority—85 percent, had been born in the United States and were therefore U.S. citizens by birth.

Beginning in the 1960s, as migrant networks increased, patterns of Mexican migration to the United States began to change. First, there was a shift in U.S. employment opportunities from temporary or seasonal agricultural employment to permanent jobs in urban areas, in industry or service jobs (gardeners, janitors, dishwashers and for women child care, domestic service, and health care workers). Second, while Mexican immigrants were initially considered sojourners, increasing numbers were now permanent, indicated by the number of marriages and children born in the United States as well as increased home ownership. Finally, the composition was shifting from predominantly young male workers to also include women and families, although males continued to dominate Mexican migration due to labor recruitment. The migration of women was associated with settlement: women migrated alone or with their families to join their spouse, or families migrated together. At the same time, a growing number of women migrated alone, establishing their own networks.[19]

One effect of the growth of migrant networks and the increase in permanent settlement was the decline in the working-age population and productive activities in Mexico in areas of traditional migration. Some villages were inhabited chiefly by women, children and the elderly, except for annual or biannual visits by migrants who returned to celebrate the holidays with families and friends in their home communities. Life for women left behind could be difficult. In some cases, the male breadwinners in the United States sent part of their earnings, if at all, for a brief period of time; some established a new family in the United States. Even if remittances were sent regularly, the women left behind in traditional rural villages, where patrilocal conditions prevailed, lived with their in-laws and were often subjected to severe restrictions with respect to their personal behavior and in some cases became virtual slaves to their in-laws.[20]

In the United States, migrant families encountered cultural challenges that single male migrants did not confront. This was particularly significant in gender relations and inter-generational interaction. In the United States, women working outside of the home, in many cases for the first time, earned their own income, resulting in increased independence, which could be problematic for husbands accustomed to asserting patriarchal norms. Children, influenced by U.S. schools and peer groups, became aware of the greater freedom of their U.S. counterparts and chafed under the stricter behavioral patterns that their parents attempted to impose. At the same time, Mexican traditions of strong family bonds, often extending over three generations, served as a bulwark for many Mexican families against the hostility and discrimination many experienced in the United States.

Political Activism among Mexican Americans in the United States

The 1960s and 1970s saw an increase in the political activism of the Mexican ethnic population in the United States, reflecting the growth in the proportion of Mexican Americans in the middle class and the influence of the civil rights movement, as well as conditions of exploitation, discrimination and exclusion that many Mexican immigrants and Mexican Americans experienced in the United States.[21] During the 1960s, they created new organizations oriented to the Mexican American population, such as the Southwest Voter Registration and Education Project (SVREP) and the Mexican American Leadership, Development and Education Fund (MALDEF). Mexican Americans became increasingly active in politics and were elected to city and state offices in areas with substantial Latino populations.

Beginning in the 1960s, Mexican and Mexican American farm workers led by César Chávez joined Filipino organizers and workers in the United Farm Workers movement (UFW) to promote unionization and improved wages and working conditions among farm workers in California. The UFW succeeded in capturing the imagination of important sectors of the U.S. population and obtaining widespread support for a grape boycott designed to pressure California growers to sign a contract with the farm workers. The campaign was eventually successful and was followed by strikes and boycotts confronting growers in California, Texas and the Midwest. The campaigns of the UFW also attracted young Mexican American as well as non-Latino activists and provided organizing skills that they were able to take into new leadership positions. Chávez himself became an icon and role model for Mexican Americans.

The Chicano movement also emerged at this time. In 1968, Mexican American high school students in East Los Angeles, frustrated at the failure of schools to prepare them for college or to recognize the historical role and contributions of Mexicans and Mexican Americans, staged a series of walkouts, demanding college preparatory courses, bilingual education, Mexican American teachers, and classes in Mexican American history. The movement spread throughout the Southwest, and in 1969 student activists met in Denver, Colorado at the First National Chicano Youth Liberation conference where they formally adopted the concept of *Chicano* to replace that of Mexican American and to distinguish themselves from both white Americans and Mexicans. Subsequently, the Plan of Santa Barbara called for Chicano studies programs in colleges and universities and for the unification of student groups in the Movimiento Estudiantil Chicano de Aztlán, or MEChA.[22]

The movements of the 1960s and 1970s succeeded in raising awareness of the Mexican ancestry population in the United States through the creation of Chicano studies programs, the publication of numerous histories and contemporary analyses of Mexican Americans/Chicanos, the establishment of bilingual programs, and the gradual increase in the number of Mexican Americans teaching at the college level. There has also been a growth of Mexican American businesses, a proliferation of Mexican American, and more generally Latino, organizations; and an increase in the Latino media. Nevertheless, the Mexican ancestry population in the United States continues to be predominantly of the poor working class, in part due to the continuation of new immigration, and their struggle against discrimination and institutionalized racism is a continuing one.

Economic Crisis, Neoliberalism and Contemporary Migration

Patterns of immigration again shifted in the 1980s. As noted in Chapter 4, the Mexican economic crisis of the 1980s led to a sharp drop in wages, a decline in formal employment, and an increase in informal employment and in the number of family members employed. It also led to an increase in migration and in dependence on remittances from family members in the United States as household survival strategies. These changes were also reflected in new migration patterns: migration from traditional sending states in western Mexico continued to grow, but there was also increased migration from urban areas, notably Mexico City, and other parts of the country, where emigration had been limited in the past. And in addition to rural workers, there was an increase in migration by other socio-economic groups, including some middle-class professionals (such as teachers and architects) and indigenous groups from Oaxaca and other states.[23] These patterns were reinforced with the economic restructuring beginning in the late 1980s, which brought a further deterioration in conditions for many Mexicans.

In the meantime, the U.S. economy was also undergoing significant change as a result of the globalization process. Beginning in 1970s, middle-level jobs in manufacturing industries (production of automobiles, auto parts, tires, chemicals, etc.)

declined as factories closed down and in some cases moved abroad. This resulted in a shift in the labor market as manufacturing jobs that had been an important avenue for income mobility for Mexicans and Mexican Americans as well as African Americans and other sectors of the population began to disappear. At same time, there was an increase in high-end occupations in such fields as communications and information industries, as well as trade, transport, real estate, finance and other services, and a massive growth in low-skilled, low-wage jobs in manufacturing, construction, and services. New immigrants from Mexico, as well as the growing number of immigrants from Central America and other countries, were able to find work as hotel and restaurant workers, -janitors, gardeners, domestics, and construction workers and in low-wage manufacturing industries such as the garment industry.

As a result of the new surge in immigration from Mexico and other Latin American countries, an increasing portion of the Latino population was foreign born. Between 1970 and 2000, the number of foreign-born Mexicans in the United States grew from 760,000 to 8.8 million, at which time Mexicans represented 28 percent of all immigrants and 59 percent of all Latinos in the United States. As of 2006, the number of foreign-born Mexicans in the United States was estimated at 12 million.

The massive influx of Mexican and other immigrants into the United States led to changes in settlement patterns. In the Los Angeles area, which continued to be a major destination of Mexican immigrants, there was a dramatic growth in areas of traditional Mexican settlement, such as East Los Angeles; at the same time the influx of immigrants meant that some of these areas became increasingly "Mexicanized," shifting from predominantly fourth and fifth generation Mexican American to predominantly first and second generation Mexican. Many Mexicans who came to the Los Angeles area in 1970s and 1980s also settled closer to the central city, near jobs in hotels and restaurants, construction, and other fields.

While the majority of ethnic Mexicans are in the southwestern states (with half in California and Texas), increasing numbers have gone to the American South and Midwest to find jobs in agriculture, food processing, meat and poultry packing, and textile manufacturing. In some cases they are directly recruited by agents who travel to Los Angeles from meatpacking plants in Omaha, Nebraska or poultry processing plants in South Carolina, among others. Mexican and other immigrants have also found jobs in other parts of the country; today there are Mexican immigrants in every state of the union, including Alaska and Hawaii. There are also new centers of Mexicans and Mexican Americans in cities such as New York, where the Mexican-origin population increased from approximately 40,000 in 1980 to approximately 250,000–300,000 in 2000.

The U.S.-Mexican border, long an area of U.S.-Mexican interaction, also grew rapidly. U.S. investment in the maquiladora border industry beginning in the 1960s and its rapid growth starting in the 1980s drew a large number of Mexicans to the border region and intensified cross-border contacts, including the expansion of twin cities linking population on both sides. By the 1990s the 2000-mile border was home to over 12 million people, approximately half on either side, and the population of twin cities, such as Tijuana and San Diego, Ciudad Juárez and El Paso, and Matamoras and Brownsville, grew rapidly. Over time, a distinct bilingual, binational culture developed, with frequent contacts between inhabitants on both sides, many of whom cross the border on a daily basis for work, shopping, or social visits.

The Mexican Presence in the United States Today

Although Mexican immigrants continue to find work and settle in various parts of the United States, the context of reception, or opportunity structure, in the United States has changed in ways that make their economic and social incorporation in U.S. society difficult. First, in contrast to the traditional manufacturing jobs of earlier immigrants, the service jobs that migrants find today provide little security and few opportunities for mobility. Second, particularly in the large cities, immigrants are often forced to settle in ghetto areas characterized by crowded housing, poor schools and inadequate services and in some cases a prevalence of gangs and drug activity, which not only affect the quality of life but may draw younger generations into a disaffected, marginal underclass. Third, there has been an increased hostility toward immigrants and particularly undocumented immigrants, fed by misconceptions—or deliberate distortions—e.g., that immigrants are taking the jobs of U.S.-born workers, that they don't pay taxes, or that they come to the United States to take advantage of welfare and other services.[24] Between 2005 and 2007, the number of anti-immigrant groups in the United States increased 600 percent, from 40 to 250.[25]

Negative perceptions and stereotypes resulted in pressures for new legislation to control immigration, and with the recession of the early 1990s, there were several new anti-immigrant initiatives. In California, voters approved Proposition 187 in 1994, which would have eliminated access to numerous services (including schools and health services) for undocumented immigrants. Although it was eventually overturned as unconstitutional, it marked a shift to increasingly restrictive measures on a national level beginning in the 1990s, including legislation restricting access of legal and unauthorized immigrants to certain benefits, and policies such as Operation Gatekeeper to fortify the border through the addition of border patrol agents and surveillance technology. The September 11, 2001 attacks on the World Trade Center and the Pentagon led to increased concerns about security and efforts toward border control, frequently conflating undocumented immigrants with terrorists and drug smugglers.[26] In 2006 the U.S. Senate passed legislation to build a 700-mile wall along the border.

Measures to control the border, at least until recently, have had little effect in controlling undocumented immigration. The inability of the Mexican economy to provide sufficient employment for its population meant that Mexicans (as well as immigrants from other countries, particularly Central America) continued to attempt the trip to the United States, although numbers have fallen off recently due largely to the U.S. recession. But increased surveillance has made the trip more dangerous and costly: immigrants are forced to use more difficult and dangerous terrain, particularly through long stretches of desert, and smugglers are charging increased prices. One result is an increased number of deaths as immigrants become lost in the desert, in some cases abandoned by smugglers, and succumb to heat and dehydration. Between 1995 and 2008, it is estimated that over 5,000 migrants died in efforts to cross the desert.

Partly as a result of anti-immigrant activity, Mexican American and other Latino groups are becoming increasingly organized around immigration and other issues. In the spring of 2006, an estimated 3.6 to 5 million people—many of them Mexican immigrants, including undocumented immigrants—participated in dozens of marches throughout the United States in response to the immigration debate in Congress. In some cities, such as Los Angeles and Chicago, these were the largest demonstrations in their respective histories.[27] Latinos are also becoming increasingly active politically, although the number of registered voters is still considerably lower than the proportion of eligible voters among the Mexican American population. In the meantime, Mexican Americans and other Latinos are a growing presence in city, state, and national governments. In California, the mayor of the city of Los Angeles and several members of the city council are Latino, as are recent leaders of the State Senate and Assembly. Latinos also hold positions in other state and city governments as well as in the U.S. government.

Living across Borders: Mexicans as Transnational Actors

Even after they have lived in the United States for several decades, some first generation Mexican migrants continue to be involved with their communities of origin and many think of returning to Mexico eventually. Contacts with their families and communities are facilitated by the fact that Mexico shares a long border with the United States, which has traditionally permitted visits back and forth, as well as letters, telephone calls, and other forms of communication.

As stated previously, the relations that migrants construct and maintain with their communities and countries of origin are sometimes referred to as transnationalism. The concept of transnationalism challenges notions like assimilation that assume that migrants break all ties with their countries of origin when they become incorporated in the receiving country. It also challenges concepts of migrants as essentially passive: through the relations they establish, they often have a significant impact on their countries and communities of origin. Some lead binational lives, traveling back and forth on a regular basis for business or social reasons, or engaging in politics on both sides of the border.

Cross-border activism by Mexican immigrants in the United States goes back at least to the mid-19th century, when clubs were formed in the U.S. Southwest to support exiled president Benito Juárez. In the late 19th and early 20th centuries Mexicans worked on both sides of the border, shifting among different types of jobs as opportunities presented themselves. Workers in the United States and Mexico often cooperated in organizing workers in areas like mining and agriculture. Mexicans in the United States were also active in initiatives to support the Mexican Revolution. Mexican exiles from the Porfirian government—among them the Flores Magón brothers, whose newspaper *La Regeneración* was published in the United States and smuggled into Mexico—found temporary homes in Texas, California, and other states.

With the resurgence of Mexican migration to the United States beginning in the 1940s, migrants frequently divided their time between the United States and Mexico. Those contracted through the bracero program for temporary work in the United States often returned with sufficient earnings to buy land or invest in agricultural inputs. Earnings that were small by U.S. standards could go much farther in Mexico. And while Mexican migrants worked at menial jobs and often experienced discrimination in the United States, they were able to enjoy a higher status and become part of the middle class in Mexico as small farmers or entrepreneurs, i.e., crossing class boundaries as well as national borders.[28] Many saw the United States as a place to work and earn money, while Mexico was a place to relax and enjoy life.[29] After Mexican immigrants began to settle in the United States, they would often return home for family visits during the holidays, and construct new houses in their home country for an eventual return. In the meantime, both contracted workers and undocumented immigrants continued to cross the border for temporary work, a process that was facilitated through the creation of migrant networks linking migrant communities—sometimes referred to as "daughter communities"—in the United States with their home communities in Mexico.

Although contacts of Mexicans in the United States with their compatriots in Mexico have a long history, these contacts have intensified in recent decades as a result of globalization. As noted above, globalization has led to increased migration, resulting in the growth of binational families and a dramatic increase in remittances, migrant earnings sent to their families and communities in their home countries. These links are further facilitated by the development of communications technology, adding new means of communication to existing ones and in some cases leading to what has been termed a "sense of simultaneity"—simultaneous participation in the communities of origin and destination.[30] A 2004 survey indicates that 20 percent of Mexican immigrants travel to their country at least once a year and that 44 percent call relatives at home at least once a week[31] Some first generation migrant families have homes in both countries or plan to build a second home in Mexico.

Remittances sent by Mexican migrants have increased from $700 million in 1980 to $2.5 billion in 1995 and to $23 billion in 2006, at which point they were the largest source of Mexican foreign exchange other than exports, greater than foreign investment and second only to petroleum exports in foreign trade. Remittances are sent primarily to families and for the most part are used for basic consumption—food, clothing, health, housing and school fees. In some cases, remittances represent all or a substantial portion of the migrant family's income.[32] Since remittances generally go to relatively poor families (although not the most destitute), they have an impact on income redistribution and on the alleviation of poverty.[33] At the same time, they may increase inequality within a given community between families that receive remittances and those that do not and provide an additional incentive to migration.

Although most remittances are used for consumption, some remittances and savings migrants bring with them on their return, are invested in production, through the purchase of land or agricultural implements, for example, or in some cases, the establishment of commercial ventures and even small factories or workshops. And expenditures on consumption can stimulate production in the home community: building a new house requires cement, lumber, and other inputs. Expenditures for health and education, particularly if families could not otherwise afford health services or school fees, can also be considered investments in human resources.

In addition to remittances, there is a substantial exchange of goods. Migrants returning to Mexico bring TV sets, CD players, and other appliances and household goods; migrants returning from Mexico to the United States frequently bring back "nostalgia" products—especially particular kinds of food that remind them of home. In the village of Laguna Grande in the southern part of the Zacatecas, for example, nearly every family has a dairy cow, and cheese production, often using recipes handed down through generations, is a major household activity. The cheese is given as gifts or sold locally and in other parts of Mexico, and is also a favorite of Laguna migrants longing for a taste of home.[34] In the case of the *nopal* cooperative begun by Catalina Sánchez and the other women of Ayoquenzo using remittances sent by their migrant husbands, the expectation is that migrants in the United States will constitute an important market for the *nopales* they produce.

Mexican migration to the United States, return visits and more permanent returns to home communities, have reinforced other cultural exchanges. One of the most evident examples is the creation of social spaces—immigrant or ethnic communities, cultural centers, etc.—in U.S. cities where the experience of Mexico and/or the home community is to some extent reproduced. One can hear Spanish spoken as it is spoken in the home community, enjoy authentic Mexican food, listen to Norteño music and mariachi bands, compete in soccer tournaments, participate in religious practices such as the Posada, commemorate the Day of the Dead, and buy products made in Mexico, in some cases at branches of Mexican stores. Mexican restaurants have become increasingly widespread throughout the United States, and fusions of Mexican and U.S. art, music, and recreation have become transnational.

In addition to material goods, Mexicans returning to their home country reinforce elements of U.S. culture spread through U.S. media, such as hip hop and rap, as well as fashion, particularly among the younger generation. These influences may be negative: youth active in gangs in U.S. inner cities who return or are sent back to their home communities have been instrumental in spreading U.S.-based gangs throughout many parts of Mexico, particularly among poor youth. In other cases, returning migrants who have internalized perspectives on more equitable gender relations may have some influence on others in their home communities, although there are also cases in which they revert to more traditional patriarchal norms once they return. The process of negotiating gender and inter-generational relations between traditional norms and the expectations derived from the immigrant experience is a particularly complex one for returning women and youth.

Another impact of migration is an intensification of cross-border organizing. One form this has taken is the growth of hometown associations, or clubs, as they are called among Mexicans, which group migrants from a particular sending community living in the United States.[35] These associations collect funds and send what are sometimes referred to as "collective remittances" for projects in their home communities. Mexican associations have their origin in voluntary mutual-aid groups that go back at least to the 1920s and that initially focused on collecting funds to help families of the deceased or to return the deceased for burial in Mexico, a practice that continues.[36] Some also sent money to their home communities for such projects as church repairs, subsequently expanding to other community projects. Over time, some clubs shifted to projects focused on the incorporation of Mexicans in the United States, but others continued their hometown focus, and new hometown associations were formed. When migrants from a given sending community live in several different locations in the United States, they may have clubs in several different cities.

Funds are raised through parties or dances, which often include raffles and the selection of a queen from the migrant community. Projects include church repairs, recreation centers, school books, construction of schools and clinics, road paving, potable water systems, and electricity in the home community. The initiative for a given project may come from the club or from the home community.

Some clubs have counterpart organizations in their home community; in others they may work with the local priest or village authorities. For example, when the mayor of the municipality of Talpa de Allende in the state of Jalisco needed funds to complete the construction of a hospital, he contacted the hometown club in Reseda, California, which came through with sufficient funds to finish the building project. The Talpa de Allende Club has also contributed funds for a school bus, earthquake repairs, and a home for the elderly in their home town.[37]

Like other migrant organizations, the hometown associations also have a social function, providing opportunities for immigrants from a particular community to get together for parties, dances, and other fundraising events. The clubs and other organizations also sponsor events to reinforce identity with their place of origin, such as the annual celebration of the community saint's day. Indigenous groups are particularly concerned with maintaining their culture and languages and their ties with their home communities, and in some cases sponsor language classes and cultural programs for youth to ensure that they don't forget their roots.

As noted, migration and migrant earnings may enable individuals or families to achieve higher economic status and social prestige in the home community. They may also be a source of political power. Returning migrants who have amassed substantial savings in the United States may invest in particular projects in their home communities with the ultimate aim of running for office. One example is Timoteo Manjarrez, who migrated from a village in Guerrero to Chicago in 1980. Starting as a dishwasher, he eventually opened three Mexican restaurants. On returning in the late 1990s he invested in several projects, including a restaurant and a hotel, and in 2004 he was elected mayor of his hometown, where he continued to promote development, including street paving and a new recreation center.[38]

Leadership in hometown associations may also be a step toward political influence at home. Members of hometown associations have been very active in lobbying on behalf of Mexicans in the United States, including efforts to achieve dual nationality, the right to vote in the U.S. for candidates in Mexican elections, and the right to run for local and state office, arguing that because of their remittances, leadership in hometown associations, and initiatives on behalf of the community, they have a stake in the municipality. Several Mexican states, including Michoacán and Zacatecas, permit emigrants to run for local office. Although some municipalities reject the idea on the grounds that one can't really run the community or municipality if one doesn't live there, in some areas, emigrant candidates have been elected and many "commute" between jobs in the United States and political obligations in Mexico.

Hometown clubs/associations generally focus on issues and programs in Mexico, but some are becoming increasingly involved in the United States, for example, encouraging Mexicans and Mexican Americans who are U.S. citizens to register to vote and raising scholarship funds for students in the United States. Contrary to popular assumptions, studies have shown that there is no contradiction between concern for conditions in one's ancestral country and active involvement in the country to which they have migrated, and that immigrants interested in conditions in Mexico may be more likely to be interested in U.S. politics. The hometown associations may in fact constitute a training ground for activism in the United States as well as political involvement in the home community. Fabian Morales, from a small town in the state of Guerrero, founded one of the first hometown associations in Chicago in 1970 and subsequently helped establish a confederation grouping Mexican clubs throughout the Midwest. He was also a co-founder of the Mexicans for Political Progress, a political action committee which raised funds for political campaigns in Illinois.[39]

The growth of remittances has also been a factor in the increased interest and involvement of governments of sending communities in migrant communities abroad. One of the major catalysts to increased Mexican government involvement with the migrant community in the United States was the Mexican presidential campaign of 1988. As an opposition candidate, Cuauhtémoc Cárdenas brought his campaign to the United States, where he had substantial support among the Mexican immigrant communities, including many recent migrants who had been negatively affected by the recent economic crisis in Mexico.[40] Although they were unable to vote without returning to Mexico, migrants in the United States were believed to have significant influence on their families at home.

Cárdenas officially lost the elections, which were heavily tainted by fraud, but his strong support in the United States led to a new recognition on the part of the PRI and the incoming Salinas government of the potential significance of Mexicans in the United States for Mexican politics. The government initiated programs "to redefine and reincorporate Mexicans living abroad as members of the nation" including an amendment to the Mexican constitution ensuring that Mexicans living abroad could maintain their national identity. The Mexican government also saw the Mexican community abroad—particularly those who had become U.S. citizens—as a potentially significant source of influence in the United States in promoting and lobbying for projects of interest to the Mexican government, such as the pending North American Free Trade Agreement.

The Mexican government also established PCME—Program for Mexican Communities Abroad—which among other projects undertook several initiatives to promote the hometown associations. Working through Mexican consulates throughout the United States, PCME encouraged the establishment of additional clubs and established a two-for-one program in which both the federal and state governments would match funds sent by the associations. Subsequently some municipalities also began to contribute, transforming this into a three-for-one program, which meant that for every dollar sent by the hometown association, three additional dollars were contributed by the three levels of government. The impetus from the Mexican government resulted in an exponential growth in the clubs as well as an increase in their degree of institutionalization, with several forming federations grouping clubs from a particular state.

This was a turning point in the orientation of Mexicans and the Mexican government, involving a reinterpretation of Mexican migrants in the United States, who previously had been disparagingly referred to as *pochos* (Mexicans who had abandoned their homelands and culture). With the recognition of their economic importance because of the growing role of remittances and their potential political importance—both in Mexican politics and in lobbying efforts in the United States—Mexican migrants became much more respected at home, and successive administrations, as well as state and local governments, began to regard them as a political and economic resource. The 1995–2000 National Development Plan of the Zedillo administration stated explicitly that "The Mexican nation extends beyond the territory contained within its borders." A 1997 constitutional change permitted dual nationality for Mexicans who became U.S. citizens.[41] Governors from migrant-sending states began to travel frequently to Los Angeles and other major U.S. cities where daughter communities are located, as did many municipal mayors, who may have as many "constituents" in the United States as in their home community.

Increased institutionalization and the development of links with the Mexican government at different levels enabled hometown associations to increase the scope of their activities. In 2004, donations from Mexican hometown associations with matching government funds financed over 1,250 projects. At the same time, it has complicated the process of decision making, and in some cases resulted in tensions and conflicts. These may arise over differences in priorities between the clubs in the United States and authorities in the respective municipalities or states,[42] actual or perceived lack of cooperation from government authorities, or competition between the clubs and officials in home communities who see the clubs as undermining their authority. These tensions may be reinforced by personal and/or political rivalries, particularly as the shift from the hegemonic party system has meant that different parties may control different levels of government.

Recently some clubs and federations have begun to concentrate on funding productive programs that provide employment for Mexicans in their home communities and thus reduce the incentive to migrate. A local priest in Atacheo, Michoacán initiated a program to train youth in entrepreneurship through projects in such areas as the production of fruits and flowers and raising turkeys, which is financed by local sources as well as emigrants with government support through the three-for-one program. In other instances, projects are funded by

Mexican migrant entrepreneurs, or, as in the case of the nopal cooperative in Santa Maria de Ayoquenzo, by individual migrant remittances.

Not all of these projects have been successful. Among the problems encountered were a lack of cooperation between the hometown associations and government authorities in Mexico; the absence of technically proficient local personnel who can oversee the projects; and the failure to conduct feasibility and marketing studies to determine whether local conditions and resources, including sufficient labor, exist for a particular project and whether there is a market for the what is produced. In those communities that have become virtual "ghost towns" due to out-migration, it may already be too late to generate projects that can stem migration by providing jobs for would-be migrants at home.

Nevertheless, many see migrant remittances and especially the contributions of businesspersons and hometown associations as having a potentially important role in providing opportunities for Mexicans in their home communities. Learning from experience, some of the more successful projects sought out technical assistance through government or private sources or NGOs. The nopal growing co-op formed by Catalina Sánchez and other migrant wives in Santa Maria de Ayoquenzo in Oaxaca benefited from both the remittances sent by their husbands in the United States and government assistance in building a plant to process nopal to be marketed among Mexicans in the United States.

MIGRATION FROM A TRADITIONAL SENDING AREA: THE CASE OF ZACATECAS

Zacatecas is one of a small number of Mexican states that are identified as traditional states of emigration to the United States. A relatively large, arid, and sparsely populated state in north-central Mexico, at the time of the Spanish conquest it was inhabited by the semi-nomadic Chichimec tribes, including the Zacatecos, from which the state took its name. During the colonial period it became a major center of silver mining, drawing on indigenous workers who labored in the mines, often under harrowing conditions. The wealth accrued by the mine owners is still evident in the handsome rose-stone buildings and the baroque cathedral in the city of Zacatecas.

A fall in silver prices in the late 19th century resulted in the ruin of some mine owners, while others modernized their mines with the help of U.S. and British investment. Modernization replaced workers with machines, and unemployed mine workers migrated to other parts of Mexico, particularly to the northern states where they found mining jobs, and in some instances to the United States, where they worked on the railroads and formed settlements in California and elsewhere.[43] The disruptions and violence resulting from the revolution and counter-revolution and the subsequent Cristero rebellion led to further emigration from the state, resulting in a sharp decline in the population between 1890 and 1930.

Pressures for agrarian reform in the aftermath of the revolution led the Zacatecas state governor to promulgate some of the first agrarian laws in Mexico. Agrarian reform expanded during the Cárdenas government, resulting in the establishment of new rural population centers scattered throughout the state. The world depression of the 1930s also cut off employment opportunities in the United States and many Mexican migrants were deported back to Mexico. Mexico's shift from an outwardly oriented to an inwardly oriented development strategy led to an emphasis on agricultural production for the internal market, and the states of Durango and Zacatecas became the leading producers of corn and beans. Beginning in the 1930s, emigration declined and the state population grew.

Not everyone benefited from the agrarian reform, however, and with the introduction of the bracero program in the United States, and the post-war expansion of the U.S. economy, emigration from Zacatecas to the United States again increased. At this stage, migration was primarily male, generally the heads of households, and migrant earnings supplemented farming as a source of family subsistence, consolidating the economic model of small peasant production that predominated in the state. Although migration was cyclical, tied to seasonal agricultural work in the United States and subsistence agricultural production in Mexico, increasing numbers of migrants began to find more permanent jobs and sometimes brought their families and settled in the United States. The establishment of daughter communities in the United States and the growth of migrant networks facilitated the migration of other family members, friends, and neighbors. Permanent migration is now more typical than cyclical or temporary migration.

As noted earlier, the crisis of the 1980s and the neoliberal reforms of the 1990s resulted in a substantial increase in Mexico-U.S. migration. In Zacatecas, further consolidation of the mining industry resulted in the elimination of small-scale mining and increased concentration of ownership, with three mining companies controlling 90 percent of production, again leading to a decline in mining jobs. Employment in agriculture and livestock production, the other major economic activities, dropped by 50 percent, and efforts to expand manufacturing and the tourist industry have had a minimal effect on employment. Over half of the Zactatecan population lives outside of Zacatecas—in the United States or other parts of Mexico. In Zacatecas itself, a substantial part of the population consists of families, or in some cases elderly parents, dependent on earnings from abroad. It is estimated that Zacatecans in the United States send a total of $1 million a day in remittances to their families at home.

Zacatecans in the United States have become highly organized.[44] As early as the 1920s they were involved in civic clubs, and because of the deportations in the 1930s these became benefit committees to help migrants deported back to Mexico. The origins of the present hometown associations have been traced back to the 1950s and 1960s, when Zacatecans in Southern California began to collect funds to help compatriots who were ill or to transfer the bodies of the deceased to their home villages. Subsequently, they began to provide funds for investment in projects in their home communities.

In 1986, the Federation of Clubs of Zacatecans in Southern California linked the Zacatecan clubs in the region; Zacatecan clubs in Chicago, as well as other cities, also formed federations. Also in 1986, a matching fund was initiated with the governor of Zacatecas, which doubled the contributions of the respective clubs to projects in their home communities. As noted above, the increased involvement of the Mexican government and the establishment of the PCME in the 1990s gave an added boost to the formation of clubs in Los Angeles and elsewhere, and in 1992 the matching funds program became a two-for-one program, with the participation of the federal as well as the state government. In 1997, the Confederation of Clubs of Zacatecas linking Zacatecan federations throughout the United States was officially established.

Although hometown associations representing municipalities from other states have formed federations and some have instituted two-for-one or three-for-one programs, the Zacatecan clubs are the most institutionalized and their relations with the state government the most developed. By 2003, the three-for-one program had invested $20 million in 308 projects throughout the state, including the expansion of potable water and sewerage systems; the construction of roads and highways; street paving and electric energy systems; school construction and repair, as well as computers and other equipment for schools; and parks, plazas, and sports fields. The Zacatecan clubs from specific communities or municipalities have also cooperated with their counterparts in other parts of the United States on particular projects. For example, clubs of several communities in the municipality Francisco R. Murguia located in Dallas and Austin, Texas joined forces to raise funds for a highway that would link isolated communities of the municipality.

The hometown associations reinforce transnationalism—the links between migrant communities in the United States and their home country and communities—in several ways. The Southern California Federation publishes a newsletter with information about the clubs and their respective communities as well as more general information of interest to migrants. Work meetings are held annually in Los Angeles, attended by the governor and often several municipal mayors from Zacatecas as well as the leaders of the different clubs, to review existing projects and to plan future ones. This usually coincides with the celebration of the *Día del Zacatecano* in November, when a prominent Zacate-can is chosen as the Zacatecan of the Year.

Zacatecan clubs were very active in efforts to enable immigrants to vote in the United States in Mexican elections. As with other hometown associations, Zacatecan clubs provide leaders with opportunities for political participation and some have run as candidates for mayor in their respective home communities. Andrés Bermúdez, a Zacatecan who migrated from the town of Jerez to the United States as an undocumented immigrant in the early 1970s, worked initially as a farm laborer, and eventually amassed a fortune growing tomatoes, earning him the name "Tomato King." He was also active in the Northern California Federation of Zacatecan clubs and became its director. He decided to run for mayor of Jerez in 2001. All five candidates for the office came to California, and the first debate of the campaign took place in Los Angeles. Bermúdez, who ran as a PRD candidate with a promise to create jobs and promote development in Jerez, won the election but was unable to take office because he had lived in Jerez for less than a year. He ran again in 2004, after the year's residency requirement had been dropped and again won, becoming the first non-PRI mayor of the municipality[45]

Zacatecan clubs and federations have had their own share of tensions and conflicts. Political conflicts combined with tensions over controlling funds were factors in the Zacatecan gubernatorial election of 1998. Although the Southern California Federation had developed close relations with the respective PRI governors of Zacatecas prior to this time, some members of the federation were dissatisfied with what they saw as excessive control being exercised by the PRI governor. When the PRI rejected a popular Zacatecan, Rafael Monreal as its gubernatorial candidate, Monreal ran as a candidate for the PRD, campaigning heavily among Zacatecans in the United States, and won the election. Monreal continued to work closely with the federation, creating a cabinet-level position for this purpose, and promoted several initiatives to increase its autonomy.

Zacatecan clubs (as well as others) have concentrated increasingly on funding productive programs that will provide employment for Zacatecans and reduce the migration from the state. A group of businesspersons from the Southern California Federation formed the Group of Zacatecan Entrepreneurs to develop projects in the state, which include the production of fruit and vegetables, agave plants, cattle, tequila, and charro-style shirts. In the village of Lagunera Grande, projects include a mattress factory as well as a cheese export business. Some projects have run into problems, however, including the limits of local market demand for some goods, which reflects the lack of studies assessing the market.

Today many small villages in Zacatecas have paved streets, drinking water, new municipal buildings and parks, largely as a result of the collective remittances of migrants and the three-for-one program. But, like the village of Zapotillo in Sinaloa, from which Juan Carlos Payan made his fateful journey that ended in a mine in Utah, some villages are virtual ghost towns, with many of their inhabitants living in the United States or elsewhere. In some cases, schools have closed due to lack of students or have been able to remain open only by bussing in students from other communities. The modern homes built by migrant earnings stand empty, awaiting the occasional visit or eventual return of their owners.

INDIGENOUS MIGRATION: MIXTECS AND ZAPOTECS FROM OAXACA

The southern state of Oaxaca is home to 16 different indigenous groups organized in hundreds of communities, over 400 of which are governed by their own customary law. Land is held in common and generally only members of the community in good standing have access to it. Government is conducted through a council of elders or a general assembly. All adult males under 60 are required to participate in the *tequio*, a form of communal labor for the construction and maintenance of public works. In some communities, membership also requires participation in the cargo system, whereby public office is rotated among community members.

Like Zacatecans, Oaxacans have a long history of migration, dating from the early 1900s, although prior to the late 20th century it was primarily to urban areas of Oaxaca or to other parts of Mexico.[46] Different indigenous groups have distinct migration patterns. The Mixtecs are for the most part concentrated in a poor area in western Oaxaca characterized by extensive deforestation and soil erosion. Since the mid-20th century they have migrated annually to northwestern Mexico, particularly Baja California, often recruited by labor contractors for seasonal work on commercial fruit and vegetable estates. Some took part in the bracero program in the 1940s and 1950s, but it was in the 1970s and especially the 1980s that the Mixtecs have migrated in large numbers to the United States. In the United States they initially worked primarily in the agricultural regions of California, Oregon, Washington, Florida, North Carolina, New Jersey and New York. Over time, some began to work in other fields, such as in canneries and in the service sector. Mixtecs have established daughter communities in several locations in Mexico, particularly Baja California, and in the United States, particularly in the western states.

In contrast, the Zapotecs, located in the Central Valley and coastal area of Oaxaca, initially migrated to urban areas, principally Oaxaca City and Mexico City, although some also participated in the bracero program in the United States. Like the Mixtecs, they began to migrate to the United States in larger numbers in the 1970s, a migration that was reinforced by the crisis of the 1980s, but instead of going to rural areas they migrated to urban areas, primarily Los Angeles, where they found jobs in the service industries, working as dishwashers, janitors, and busboys in local restaurants. Many have worked their way up, saved their money, and after 10 or 20 years some opened their own restaurants, taking advantage of the unique cuisine of Oaxaca and hiring recent immigrants from Oaxaca as staff. As of 2004 there were an estimated 28 Oaxacan restaurants in Los Angeles—18 owned by migrants from a particular Oaxacan community, Tlacolula.[47]

Similar to other indigenous groups, Zapotecs and Mixtecs often suffer from discrimination by their Mexican compatriots as well as the bias and hostility experienced by immigrants in the United States. As field workers in Northwest Mexico as well as in the western United States, living in isolated areas and often lacking both Spanish and English language ability, the Mixtecs have been particularly exploited and suffer from harsh conditions, including low income, unstable jobs, and poor housing and living environments. Partly as a result of this, reinforcement of their indigenous Mixtec identity has been a significant focus of their organizing efforts.

At the same time, migration has resulted in broadening the definition of identity. Prior to migration, identification was primarily based on allegiance to the local community. Intra- and inter-ethnic rivalries among indigenous groups in Mexico were a factor in preventing a broader identity. Migration has resulted in a process of "scaling up," i.e., from identity strictly with one's particular community to a broader Mixtec identity along with efforts to preserve the Mixtec language and culture. Mixtecs have also formed coalitions with Zapotecs and other indigenous groups from Oaxaca in what became the Oaxacan Indigenous Binational Front (FIOB). Indigenous groups from Oaxaca also worked with other indigenous groups to oppose the 1992 celebration of the 500th anniversary of the European conquest of the Americas. In 2005, the FIOB changed its name (while retaining its initials) to the Indigenous Front of Binational Organizations, in effect incorporating indigenous groups from other Mexican states on both sides of the border.

Numerous other organizations have been formed representing Oaxacans from specific areas or focused on specific issues. Like other Mexican migrants, some Oaxacans had organizing experience in Mexico before coming to the United States, e.g., in the CIOAC (Independent Central of Agricultural Workers and Peasants), and have participated in labor organizing in the United States. In Oregon, for example, they have leadership positions in the Northwest Treeplanters and Farmworkers Union, which by 2000 succeeded in signing contracts with growers that recognize unions and provide for seniority rights, grievance procedures, and overtime payment.

Because of their communal traditions, Oaxacans and other indigenous migrants feel a special obligation to support their communities of origin, and their hometown associations link different migration destinations in both Mexico and the United States with their home communities. At the same time, migration places considerable strains on home communities due to the large number of migrants. As in other parts of Mexico, many municipal communities in Oaxaca are heavily dependent on migrant resources. Indigenous immigrants continue to be responsible for cargo (participation in public office) and *tequio* (participation in communal labor) obligations in their home communities, which means that they must return to their home communities for a period of one or two years or risk losing status and even membership in the community. In some instances they can postpone their tequio services, provide substitutes (for example, family members) or pay others to take on these responsibilities. Performing community-designated leadership roles, however, often means that the migrant must return, leaving jobs in the United States or elsewhere at considerable economic sacrifice. Migrants can also participate in the electoral process in their respective municipalities and often have an important impact on election outcomes.

In 2001 the Oaxacan Federation of Indigenous Communities and Organizations of California (FOCOICA) was formed, with the aim of incorporating all Oaxacan migrant organizations in the state—and eventually the United States—including hometown associations, sports clubs, and education and cultural associations. Similar to other state federations, the Oaxacan federation has signed a three-for-one agreement with representatives of the Mexican government at all three levels. Both the FIOB and the federation also have programs dedicated to working with migrants in the United States, including health programs, civic training, education programs, and efforts to preserve different indigenous roots, such as the annual Guelaguetza celebrating the different indigenous cultures of Oaxaca.

MIGRATION AND PERSONAL TRANSFORMATION

The experience of migration from one country to another is a transformative experience for the individual migrant; in Stephen's words, it includes crossing class, cultural and ethnic as well as geographic boundaries.[48] Mexicans who migrate to the United States, as well as their families at home, are affected in multiple and complex ways. Migration may result in new roles and identities: a farm worker in Mexico may become a factory or service worker in the United States and return to Mexico with sufficient funds to become a property owner or open a small business, thus improving his status and class position. Or, as in the case of several migrants from Oaxaca, one may begin working in a restaurant as a busboy and end up owning one or more restaurants in the United States. As indicated earlier in the case of indigenous groups from Oaxaca, ethnic identity may also shift, from an identification with one's particular community to a broader ethnic identity.

For family members who remain in Mexico, remittances may enable them to enjoy a higher standard of living and to obtain resources they would not otherwise have access to. At the same time, the prolonged absence of family members—leaving wives without husbands and children without parents, often for many years—can be a painful and sometimes traumatic experience.[49] Some studies suggest that women left behind enjoy increased autonomy and authority, challenging the patriarchal norms that continue to characterize Mexican society. In those rural villages where patrilocal norms prevail, however, young married couples move to the home of the husband's parents, and the wife is subject to the authority of her mother-in-law, an authority which may be abused if the husband is absent. There are apparently numerous instances in which this relationship involves severe exploitation and mistreatment, where young wives are forbidden to leave the house or are subjected to extensive surveillance by family members and neighbors in the interest of protecting the honor of the husband and his family.[50]

Under these circumstances, migration for women, particularly rural women may be a liberating experience. Although in some instances their spouses may impose the same patriarchal norms that are customary in traditional villages, in other cases—particularly when women are working outside of the home and earning their own income for the first time—they may gain a certain amount of financial independence as well as freedom from the social constraints they would experience at home. Mexican and other Latina women in the United States are often active in organizations outside the home, especially those involving families and children, such as health, education, and the local environment. The separation between the public and private spheres, in which men have privileged access to the former while women are confined to the latter, is gradually being eroded.

The transformation of women migrants is often affected by the circumstances of migration and conditions at the point of destination. In the case of Oaxaca, migration has resulted in gradual changes in social and cultural norms and practices with respect to women. Generally, patriarchal norms have prevailed in both home communities and in migrant communities, where women are often obliged to ask their fathers or husbands for permission to leave the home for work and other public sphere activities. In practice, however, there is considerable variation; in some Oaxacan communities, women can fully participate, voting in assemblies and holding office; in others they cannot vote and their participation is minimal. Women do have certain roles and responsibilities within the public sphere, particularly in religious and cultural activities, and women whose husbands have migrated may take their place in performing tequio obligations. This increases their public presence but also means additional work; in fact it is frequently the case that women are obligated to take on additional tasks and responsibilities without the authority or recognition that these responsibilities should entail.

Women who migrate may have limited decision-making power even when they work outside the home and are active in organizations. Women are very active in Zacatecan hometown associations, for example, but rarely hold leadership positions. In the case of Mixtec migration to Baja California, which is often family-based migration, women work in the fields in addition to their domestic responsibilities (rarely shared by male members of the family) and participate in different organizations and in mobilizations (e.g., for urban land or services), but organizations also tend to be male-dominated. Mixtec women may be more active in Tijuana and other cities, where they often become street vendors, resulting in contacts with government officials and the acquisition of linguistic skills, and in street vendor associations women are the major leaders and actors.[51]

Indigenous organizations in Mexico and the United States have sought to promote the participation of women, although generally through encouraging husbands to grant them permission to be active rather than questioning the system of male dominance. At the same time, women's participation in these organizations, including informational workshops and training sessions, have given many of them the self-confidence to assert their independence and question traditional practices. Indigenous women have formed their own organizations in migrant communities in Mexico and the United States (as well as Oaxaca) which focus on issues of family support, domestic violence, alcoholism, and sexual harassment and other forms of discrimination. In effect, these organizations erase the line between the private sphere, to which their lives have been traditionally relegated, and public spaces in which issues are debated and decisions made. Women in field work and street vending who have family-support responsibilities due to the absence of their husbands have formed savings clubs to help meet expenses. Through these and other practices women are confronting the patriarchal norms that have traditionally governed gender relations in many indigenous communities.

Migration also affects inter-generational relations. Children who come to the United States at a relatively early age are quickly socialized through school and peer group interaction—particularly with respect to social freedom and relatively liberal childrearing practices—that may conflict with those of their migrant parents, accustomed to exercising greater social control and expecting strict obedience from their children. Parental authority may also be undermined by the fact that children often learn English first and speak it more fluently than their parents, and they may act as brokers and intermediaries between their parents and teachers and other public officials. Some migrant children who come to the United States at an early age grow up without speaking their native language, which may pose particular difficulties if they are sent back home. Because first generation parents often work long hours at relatively low-wage jobs, some immigrant and second generation children have little parental supervision. In addition many immigrant families are forced to live in low-income inner city neighborhoods. Youth may experience downward socialization, evident in such behaviors as school drop-outs, teenage pregnancies, drug use and gang activity. At the same time, studies have shown that, for the most part, children of Mexican migrants experience upward mobility relative to their parents in terms of education, income, and other socio-economic conditions.

Children who are left behind when both parents migrate confront particular difficulties. Generally they are left with relatives, and while this may result in the development of particularly close bonds between the child and his or her grandmother or aunt, in other cases it may result in severe problems of discipline, particularly if the emotional pain of separation from one's parents is accompanied by resentment. Poor children in this situation are particularly susceptible to recruitment into gangs by returning gang members.

In summary, the experience of migration has a significant impact on individuals, families, and their relations both in Mexico and in the United States, but the nature of this impact varies significantly according to such factors as the context in both the sending and receiving communities, as well as the characteristics of the individual migrant and migrant families.

REVIEW AND DISCUSSION: MEXICAN MIGRATION AND U.S.-MEXICAN RELATIONS

Mexican migration to the United States has both reflected and influenced economic and social conditions in the two countries and the relationship between the two. Spanish and Mexican migration to the northern part of what was initially the Spanish empire and subsequently Mexico, although limited, established a presence in what would become the Southwest United States, still evident in California missions, Spanish architectural influences, and place names like San Francisco, Los Angeles, El Paso and San Antonio.

Subsequently, conditions and events in Mexico and United States have affected migration. Labor recruitment frequently established initial migration trajectories. The expansion of U.S. economic interests into Mexico during the Porfiriato in the late 19th and early 20th centuries was accompanied by the recruitment of Mexicans to work in U.S. agriculture, mines, and railroads on both sides of the border; then the revolution and the Cristero rebellion drove many Mexicans across the border. After a hiatus during the depression of the

1930s, when thousands of Mexican migrants returned to Mexico, U.S. labor shortages during World War II led to a renewed interest in contracting Mexicans to work in the United States on a temporary basis. The bracero program, initiated in 1942, was periodically renewed until 1964, by which time increasing numbers of undocumented workers were also coming to the United States, drawn by the booming U.S. economy and the availability of jobs.

While labor recruitment and the availability of jobs drew Mexicans to the United States, events and conditions in Mexico helped to explain why many were willing to leave. One effect of the Porfirian modernization beginning in the late 19th century was the takeover of peasant land by Mexican landowners and in some cases U.S. companies, resulting in a large landless population that migrated to other parts of Mexico and to the United States for work—a process that continued into the 1920s due to the disruptions resulting from the Mexican Revolution and the Cristero rebellion. The migration process was reversed in the 1930s with the U.S. depression and deportation of Mexicans, while the land distribution program and other reforms of the Cárdenas administration provided opportunities for Mexican peasants in the Mexican countryside. During and following World War II, the government neglect of peasant agriculture, combined with population pressures in the countryside, led to an exodus of rural workers and peasants to increasingly overcrowded cities, and many took advantage of the bracero program to migrate for work in the United States.

With the economic crisis of the 1980s and the subsequent restructuring of the Mexican economy, migration again increased, with migrants from traditional sending areas being joined by migrants from areas and sectors where migration to the United States had been limited. One element of the impact of globalization and economic restructuring in the United States had been an increase in low-wage service jobs, which were filled by new immigrants from Mexico and other countries.

Aside from structural conditions in the United States and Mexico, migration to the United States was facilitated through the creation of new structures - migrant networks linking Mexicans in the United States with their families and communities in Mexico. As Mexican migrants began to settle, creating "daughter communities" in the United States, established migrants recruited relatives and friends to work in agricultural, industrial and service jobs, often in the same place of employment. These networks had become increasingly complex over time and now constitute an important element in U.S.-Mexican relations.

The experience of Mexican migrants and their descendants in the United States have been mixed. Reflecting their rural background, the majority of first generation Mexican migrants generally have lower levels of education than the U.S. average, and have typically worked in relatively low-wage agricultural and service jobs, reflecting the availability of these types of jobs in the U.S. labor market. The situation of first generation immigrants is complicated by the fact that a large number are undocumented, limiting their educational opportunities and employment options. Their children generally achieve higher levels of education and during the mid to late 20th century some were able to move into more secure manufacturing jobs and higher level technical and professional positions.

The impact of U.S. immigration policy on Mexican migration reflects a perspective in which Mexican migrants have been historically regarded as a cheap, disposable labor force, reflected in both labor recruitment (e.g., during the geographic and economic expansion of the United States at the turn of the twentieth century and the *bracero* program during World War II) and deportations (as during the depression of the 1930s and in Operation Wetback in the 1950s). In general, recent efforts to curtail migration, particularly undocumented migration, such as Operation Gatekeeper, have been less successful at keeping migrants out of the United States than limiting opportunities for them once they are in the country. One ironic result has been that immigrants tend to remain in the United States rather than returning home due to the anticipated difficulty of re-entering. Fears generated by the September 11, 2001 attacks on the World Trade Center and the Pentagon, as well as increased hostility toward immigrants, have led to more draconian measures, including substantial increases in the number of border patrol agents and equipment as well as a 700-mile fence along key border areas, and round-ups and detentions of immigrants at their homes and workplaces (see Chapter 8).

Mexican migration to the United States has transformed both countries. Traditionally, Mexican immigrants have been drawn from poorer sectors of the population, and the conditions of their migration as well as their reception in the United States have tended to limit or delay their integration into the mainstream of U.S. society. Many Mexicans were, at least initially, seasonal or temporary migrants for whom migration was a way to earn money and improve their standard of living in Mexico. Even after Mexicans began to settle in the United States many continued to look to Mexico as a place to which they would eventually return, undoubtedly due in part to the discrimination they experienced in the United States as well as the proximity of their home country, which facilitated contact and a constant renewal of ties with their families and communities.

At the same time, Mexicans and their Mexican American descendants have transformed the United States, spatially, culturally, economically and politically, a process that has become increasingly evident with the increase in settlement and the growing number of migrants beginning in the 1970s and 1980s. Early Mexican settlements expanded into barrios and eventually major sectors of cities, particularly in the Southwest as well as parts of the Midwest. Mexicans and other Latin American immigrants have become an important sector of the labor force and dominate in certain service occupations in areas such as Southern California, Texas and parts of the Midwest, and are becoming increasingly evident in non-traditional migrant regions, such as the Northeast and South. Mexican immigrants have also been a major element in the focus of the labor movement on organizing immigrants, particularly in service occupations, beginning in the late 1980s.

Mexican restaurants, *taquerías* and markets can be found in many cities throughout the United States, and tortillas, tacos, burritos, and quesadillas have become an important part of the diet of many Americans not of Mexican descent. Wall murals, norteño music, soccer games, Mexican American theater groups have been integrated into U.S. culture, and Spanish language radio and TV stations are among the fastest-growing media outlets in the United States. The political impact of Mexicans and their descendants is evident in issues such as bilingual education, movements such as the Chicano mobilization and MEChA, organizations such as MALDEF and the United Farm Workers, and the presence of Mexican Americans in elected offices at all levels of government.

Mexican migration to the United States has also had a major impact in Mexico itself, due to the ties that Mexican migrants create and sustain with families and home communities in their country of origin. The most immediate effect is in the small rural sending communities, where migrant remittances have improved the levels of consumption of their families, at the same time resulting in increasing inequality between these and those families without relatives in the United States. Migration influences are also evident in the modern houses, new clinics, paved roads, and other civic projects financed by individual donations and collective remittances. The impact of migration is also visible in the fact that some of these towns have become virtual "ghost towns" with little evidence of social or economic activity, while many of the working age population is in the United States.

Migrants have also established formal organizational links through hometown associations, state federations, and other binational groups such as the FIOB, which interact with counterpart organizations, community leaders, and government officials in their home states and communities. In addition to civic projects, some of these organizations, as well as individual entrepreneurs, have invested in productive activities in their home communities. Migrants have an important influence on home country politics, and some participate directly, particularly at the local level, using the status and reputations they obtain through economic success in the United States, leadership in hometown associations, and individual and collective donations to the community.

Beginning in the 1980s, Mexican migration has also had an increasing impact on Mexico at the national level. Migrant remittances have not only reduced poverty in migrant sending areas, thus constituting the largest—and perhaps most effective—form of foreign aid to the country, they also provide a major and (at least until recently) growing contribution to Mexico's foreign exchange. Similar to other migrant sending countries, Mexico's national economy has become increasingly dependent on migrant remittances. One result has been increased government attention to the migrant community in the United States, evident in new government programs to assist migrants, the promotion of hometown associations by Mexican consulates in the United States, and the frequent travels of municipal officials and state governors from migrant sending areas to visit their "constituents" in the United States.

Finally, migration has been a transformative experience for migrants themselves. One of the most important areas of this change has been in family relations. For many, migration has meant family separation, and the existence of binational families, often for long periods of time. In the United States, families often include both undocumented immigrants and U.S. citizens, and the deportation of undocumented family members is another way in which families are separated.

Family migration and settlement in the United States has also led to changes in gender and inter-generational relations in ways that challenge traditional patriarchal norms. In some cases, women have been empowered through working outside the home and earning their own income. Many women also enjoy greater freedom in the United States compared with their lives in rural Mexico. Children exposed to the greater freedom experienced by their U.S. peers challenge the strict requirements their parents attempt to impose in keeping with traditional upbringing.

Collective organizing has also been a source of empowerment. Members of hometown associations gain increasing influence in their communities. Indigenous organizations challenge traditional ethnic discrimination, demand a reinterpretation of indigenous-nonindigenous relations and strengthen the indigenous presence and identity in the United States and Mexico. Women's groups challenge patriarchal traditions and confront the dichotomy between the private sphere to which they are normally relegated and the public sphere from which they have traditionally been excluded.

Collectively, as in the case of other immigrant groups, the experiences of Mexican migrants in the United States have been partly shaped by their encounters with a population having a distinct cultural identity and language. This has led to the formation of Spanish-speaking barrios in some of the major centers of Mexican immigration. The discrimination that many experience in the United States, which has racial and ethnic overtones, has reinforced their own Mexican and/or Mexican American identity. Migration has also affected the identity of indigenous groups, whose self-perceptions have shifted between identity with their particular community or municipality to a broader ethnic identity and in some cases pan-ethnic or indigenous identity.

In summary, Mexican migration to the United States is a major element in the dynamic relationship between the two countries, one which both reflects and reinforces that relationship, and has decisively shaped its character and trajectory. It is also a process that presents significant challenges to policy makers in both countries, an issue that will be taken up in Chapter 8.

CHAPTER 8

U.S.-Mexico Relations: Current Issues

Poor Mexico! So far from God, so close to the United States![1]

A century after
General Taylor and General Scott,
Come General Electric and General Motors
As they are now known.
Through every border and every port
And even by air
Comes the invasion.
We all know very well
The traitors of the past,
But do we know who are those of today?[2]

Since the Mexican American War, when the United States established its southern land border in the middle of Mexico, the two countries have had a complex, often contentious, and highly unequal relationship. Prior to the 1930s, it was characterized by frequent political and threatened military intervention, often to protect U.S. economic interests. Since the 1940s the relationship has been less abrasive, but Mexico continued to dwell in the shadow of its stronger neighbor, fearing intervention based on its own experience as well as continued U.S. political and even military intervention in much of Latin America throughout the 20th century.

During much of this period, U.S.-Mexico relations were structured by the U.S. status as a world power and its efforts to secure its economic and security goals in Latin America. Within this context, Mexico has been at the forefront of Latin American efforts to contain U.S. intervention in the region. At the same time, Mexico continued to be economically dependent on the United States as Mexico's major export market and as its most important source of foreign investment.

In recent years, the rapidly changing global context has resulted in new uncertainties affecting the U.S. global position and its relations with Latin

America. Among other changes, these include the growth of emerging economies and the weakening of the U.S. economic position relative to the rest of the
world, evident in its massive trade deficit and indebtedness; the launching of the
U.S. "war on terror"; and more recently the U.S. recession and its implications
for other countries, particularly those that, like Mexico, are closely tied to the
United States. One element in this change has been the growing autonomy of the
Latin American states relative to the United States. This autonomy is evident in
the selection of José Miguel Insulsa, a Chilean Socialist, as Secretary General of
the OAS (Organization of American States) against the preferred candidate of the
United States; the election of several left and center-left governments in South
and Central America; the growth of Brazil as a regional power; and the growing
economic presence of other countries, notably China, in the region.[3] South
American governments have also formed institutions excluding the United
States, implicitly challenging the hegemony of U.S.-dominated institutions in
the region, among them TeleSur (a South American television network), the
Bank of the South, and UNASUR.[4]

These changes have had an impact on Mexico and U.S.-Mexico relations.
What is ironic, however, is that Mexico, which had taken the lead in efforts to
contain U.S. hegemony in the past, has had a limited role in current challenges
to U.S. dominance in the region. This is due in part to its close economic ties
with the United States and, since the mid-1980s, greater policy convergence
between the governments of the two countries. Thus Mexico has become
increasingly linked economically with North America, while it maintains cultural ties with the rest of Latin America.[5]

At the beginning of the 21st century, the two countries are more highly integrated than ever. The United States continues to be Mexico's major trading partner; meanwhile Mexico is the primary or second most important export market
of 22 U.S. states, including California, Texas, Arizona, Nebraska, and Iowa. U.S.
capital finances some of the largest corporations and banks in Mexico, and Mexican workers labor on farms and in factories throughout the United States—
their remittances providing a significant contribution to the Mexican economy.
Wal-Mart, McDonald's and K-Mart have outlets throughout Mexico; Mexican
and Mexican American restaurants are ubiquitous in certain parts of the United
States, including at least 18 Oaxacan restaurants established by indigenous
immigrants in Los Angeles alone. Television and computer components are
shipped from U.S. companies to Mexican factories across the border, where they
are assembled and exported back to the United States as TV sets and computers.
Migrant organizations such as hometown associations in the United States have
established a close working relationship with their hometowns in Mexico, while
indigenous groups have established binational organizations concerned with the
welfare of indigenous group in both countries.

Relations between the two countries are particularly evident in the U.S.-Mexico border region, which extends from the Pacific Ocean to the Gulf of Mexico. Mexican families—and some U.S. families—live on both sides of the border. Citizens of both countries cross the border on a regular basis, in some cases daily, to visit family and friends or for work or shopping on the other side; it has been estimated that there are roughly a million such crossings every day. Twin cities of the U.S. and Mexican border states line the region, among them San Diego, California, and Tijuana, Baja California; Nogales, Arizona, and Nogales, Sonora; El Paso, Texas, and Ciudad Juarez, Chihuahua. These cities have established collaborative relations on such issues as public health and the environment. At the national level, a number of joint U.S.-Mexican commissions have been formed to deal with border issues such as the North American Development Bank, the Border Environment Cooperation Commission, and the Border Health Commission, although inadequate funding has sometimes limited their effectiveness. Social organizations span the border, among them the Coalition for Justice in the Maquiladoras as well as numerous others concerned about labor and environmental and health conditions on both sides of the border.

However, there are still unresolved issues and areas of friction, among them NAFTA and more generally U.S.-Mexican economic relations, the drug trade, and the migration of Mexicans to the United States. One of the manifestations of the continuing asymmetric relations between the two countries is that the United States has generally had a leading role in defining the nature of these issues and their proposed solutions. In the following three sections these issues will be examined with an emphasis on their implications for Mexico, the respective roles of Mexico and the United States in efforts to define and resolve them, and the effectiveness of Mexican and U.S. policies in addressing these issues.[6]

NAFTA AND THE MEXICAN ECONOMY

The North American Free Trade Agreement was the linchpin of the economic restructuring that established the neoliberal model in Mexico—a model that had been promoted by U.S. economic interests and international lending agencies as well as U.S.-trained policy makers in Mexico.[7] As noted in Chapter 4, business groups were the major participants in the negotiations that linked Mexico with the United States and Canada aside from government officials. It is therefore not surprising that among the major beneficiaries of NAFTA have been relatively small groups in both the United States and Mexico (as well as Canada): U.S. corporations, such as General Motors and Ford that are able to take advantage of cheap labor; financial investors who benefit from the removal of restrictions on investment in Mexico; U.S. corporate farmers who receive government subsidies; rural exporters in northern Mexico who have benefitted from long-term government investment in infrastructure, particularly irrigation; and Mexican businesses that have the financial resources and international connections to compete effectively in the international market.

The market-oriented approach precluded measures to compensate for Mexico's lower level of development and government intervention on behalf of more disadvantaged sectors. At the same time, there has been extensive government intervention in the operation of the market to the benefit of more powerful groups in both the United States and Mexico. As noted above, U.S. corporate farmers benefit from government subsidies to agriculture, which enable them to export corn at prices below the costs of production, while farmers in northern Mexico benefit from earlier investments by the Mexican government in infrastructure as well as a disproportionate share of supports and subsidies in the NAFTA era. In the meantime, institutions such as the North American Development Bank, initially intended to promote development by providing loans and grants for infrastructure and other investments in Mexico, has received a fraction of the resources it needs to function effectively.[8]

As indicated in Chapters 4 and 5, the new model has had mixed results. Since Mexico began its liberalization policy that culminated with NAFTA, the Mexican economy has become more open: trade increased from 7.6 to approximately 30 percent of Mexico's GDP between 1980 and 2008. Exports are more diversified: in 1980 oil accounted for over 60 percent of all exports, compared to 7.3 percent in 2000, at which time 90 percent of Mexico's merchandise exports were in manufactured products.[9] High-tech exports as a proportion of total exports increased from 8 to 22 percent in the 1990s.[10] Furthermore, although Mexico's overall trade balance is negative, reflecting an increase in imports from the rest of the world, it has enjoyed a favorable trade balance with the United States for much of this period.

Foreign direct investment (FDI) peaked at $27 billion in 2001 (reflecting the opening of investment in the financial sector to foreign banks), after which it has fluctuated between $14 billion and $23 billion. Most of this investment is in manufacturing, particularly machinery and equipment (including automobiles) and increasingly in services, notably trade, finance (reflecting foreign investment in major Mexican banks) and business services. There has recently been a shift in the character of foreign investment in Mexico; new investment, which predominated prior to 1998, has declined, while mergers and acquisitions, and reinvested earnings, have increased. Foreign investment in Mexico is highly concentrated geographically in the center of Mexico, particularly in Mexico City, and in the northern states. Over half is in the Federal District although the share is declining relative to the states of Mexico, Jalisco, Nuevo Leon, Chihuahua, and Baja California. It is also concentrated in the largest Mexican firms: between

1999 and 2005, over 50 percent of new investment and 60 percent of reinvestment have gone into the 500 top firms in Mexico, and 70 percent and 80 percent, respectively in the 1,000 major firms.[11]

The Mexican economy continues to be heavily dependent on the United States both as a market for its exports and as a source of investment. Of a total of $293 billion in exports in 2008, $234 billion, or roughly 80 percent, went to the United States.[12] While Mexico's trade had been dependent on exports to the United States prior to NAFTA, what has changed is the greater openness of the Mexican trade regime, which means that the Mexican economy is much more dependent on trade revenue and, by extension, the U.S. market, than before.

The United States is also Mexico's major source of foreign direct investment in manufacturing and services (excluding finance). Of the 15 largest foreign affiliates in manufacturing (based on sales in 2000), 12 were U.S. based, particularly in motor vehicles and electronic equipment. U.S. companies, led by Wal-Mart, also control nine of Mexico's 15 major foreign affiliates in trade and services. Only in finance, where European banks, particularly Spanish, are dominant, does U.S. capital have a smaller presence, with six of the 14 foreign-controlled banks and only one of the top four.

Mexico's trade with the United States is closely related to U.S. investment in manufacturing. A large proportion continues to be intra-industry and even intra-firm trade. The top U.S. exports to Mexico consist of electronic equipment, motor vehicle parts, and chemicals; the major Mexican exports to the United States are petroleum, cars, and electronic equipment.[13] As noted in Chapter 4, Mexico's major export industries are the maquiladora industries, which import components and parts from U.S. suppliers and in many cases export the final product to the U.S. market, sometimes to the same firms, and the automotive industry, with a large back-and-forth trade of vehicles and vehicle parts. In addition, Mexico is a major exporter of oil to the United States (although it has dropped recently and is now in fifth place, following Canada, Saudi Arabia, Venezuela and Nigeria) and visitors from the United States are an important source of Mexico's earnings from tourism. Finally, as detailed in Chapter 7, remittances from Mexican migrants in the United States constitute another major source of Mexican foreign exchange.

One of the implications of Mexico's economic dependence is that its exports as well as other sources of foreign income, and consequently its overall growth, tend to fluctuate with the economic health of the United States: both exports and growth increased significantly during the second half of the 1990s, reflecting the boom in the United States; stagnated or contracted in 2001–2002 during the U.S. recession; and rebounded along with the U.S. recovery in subsequent years. This dependence is exemplified in the U.S. (and world) recession beginning in 2008, resulting in an estimated contraction of 7.1 percent in Mexico's GDP in 2009. Hundreds of thousands of jobs had already been lost in 2008, particularly in the maquila sector, and it is expected that more will be lost in 2009. Migrant remittances were 2 percent less in 2008 than in the previous year and dropped by 18 percent within the period between April 2008 and April 2009, as U.S. jobs in such areas as construction, which employ a large number of migrants, dried up. Tourism has also been reduced—in part a result of the drug trade and the apparently brief but devastating impact of the H1N1 (Swine flu) epidemic. Oil exports—an important source of government revenues as well as foreign exchange—have also declined.

Finally, the initial economic advantages Mexico enjoyed as a source of cheap labor with privileged access to the U.S. market have declined as a result of U.S. trade agreements with other countries and the access of countries such as China to the WTO. Companies may now invest in countries in which labor is even cheaper than in Mexico and still enjoy access to the U.S. market. They may also compete effectively with Mexican producers in the domestic market. The rapid growth in Chinese trade is only partly due to cheaper labor, however; in comparison to Mexico it has also invested heavily in economic development, including education and infrastructure, and it now sells more electronic products and equipment to the United States than Mexico. At the same time, the value of Chinese exports to Mexico, which were less than $100 million in 1994, grew rapidly in the 1990s and particularly after 2000, reaching $7.4 billion in 2008, third only to the United States and the European Union. China is also undertaking computer, infrastructure and automotive investments in Mexico, including joint investments with Mexican companies, oriented to the U.S. market.

Although NAFTA was not explicitly oriented to development or the creation of jobs, it was widely promoted as an agreement that would promote jobs in Mexico and, by extension, reduce Mexico's migration to the United States. Sixteen years after NAFTA went into effect, it is evident that neither has occurred.[14] Migration from Mexico to the United States has increased steadily during this period (prior to the recession beginning in 2008), and while jobs were certainly created, notably in the maquiladora sector, jobs have also been lost in small and medium industries unable to compete with less expensive imports or with foreign affiliates in Mexico. The number of workers in the major FDI industries is actually less than in 1994, and while FDI wages are relatively high, wages in general have failed to keep up with productivity, which increased 178 percent between 1994 and 2001.

The impact of NAFTA on Mexico's small farmers has been particularly devastating. While fruit and vegetable exports to the United States from large and medium farms on irrigated land in northern Mexico have increased, imports of subsidized products from the United States, notably grains, have undermined small producers in southern Mexico and resulted in an overall deficit in Mexico's agricultural trade with the United States. The effect on Mexico's rural sector was not unanticipated by NAFTA's negotiators; the assumption on the part of policy makers seemed to be that the small farm and peasant sector was anachronistic and would disappear with modernization. The relatively long phase-out period (up to 15 years) for the removal of Mexican tariffs on inputs of basic foods such as corn and beans was meant to provide time for small farmers and peasants to shift to other employment.

But while the number of agricultural workers has declined sharply, the availability of alternative jobs in Mexico has been weak at best, and the government has not only failed to prepare farmers for this change but removed price supports and subsidies for staple goods and withdrawn much of the funding for rural assistance programs for small farmers that had existed prior to NAFTA.[15] The government also dismantled CONASUPO, which had purchased staple products at guaranteed prices for farmers, during the 1990s. Public credit to agriculture was greatly reduced; while the government provided 55 percent of agricultural credit in the 1980s, in the 1990s 73 percent of the agricultural credit was private, going chiefly to commercial farmers.

The government has established new programs to subsidize farmers, but Mexican agricultural subsidies are a fraction of those in the United States. In addition, with some exceptions, such as Financiera Rural, which provides microcredits to small farmers, many government subsidies are oriented to commercial production for export. For example, ASERCA (Support Services for Agricultural Marketing), created in 1991 to provide marketing support and information and to promote exports, has been oriented primarily to northern Mexico, which in 2002 received 89 percent of the ASERCA budget.[16] Ironically, in many cases Mexican subsidies go to U.S. companies in Mexico, such as Cargill, a major recipient of subsidies in the state of Sinaloa. Procampo, a special government fund to provide subsidies to poor farmers, has provided much of its aid to large commercial farmers, many of them linked to drug cartels and to government officials.[17] Small farmers and peasant producers have been able to survive due largely to the expansion of unpaid family labor and remittances from family members in the United States.

It should be pointed out that not all of the gains or the losses experienced by Mexico and Mexicans over the past 15 years can be attributed to NAFTA. In terms of gains, while NAFTA contributed to the increase in Mexico's exports and foreign investment, Mexico's growth has been less dynamic than that of other Latin American countries. And NAFTA cannot always be blamed for the economic disruptions affecting workers, peasants, and small businesses in Mexico since globalization and economic liberalization have resulted in similar disruptions elsewhere.

At the same time, NAFTA has aggravated Mexico's dependence on U.S. trade and investment. As indicated previously, foreign investment in Mexico has increased geographic and social polarization within Mexico, with the bulk of foreign investment in the Federal District and a few central and northern states, and the concentration of investment in the largest firms of a few key sectors. Employment in FDI manufacturing sectors has declined, while wages in these sectors, although higher than those for manufacturing in general, have failed to keep up with productivity increases.

Quite apart from its costs and benefits, NAFTA has become a powerful symbol for those who have suffered from the effects of globalization and economic liberalization throughout the three member countries. As noted in Chapter 6, their exclusion from the negotiation process was the impetus for cross-border mobilization and organization. Today, various groups in each country have been pushing for a renegotiation of NAFTA that would respond to these problems. In Mexico, opposition has been led by small farmers and peasants whose viability has been undermined by the competition of subsidized imports of basic foods from the United States as well as the withdrawal of rural support programs and the 1991–92 agrarian law. Peasants and indigenous communities, as well as environmental groups, are also concerned about the import of genetically modified agricultural grains from the United States, fearing contamination of native grains and a loss of biodiversity.

In 2007, a number of peasant, indigenous, and small farmer organizations launched the campaign "*Sin maíz no hay país*" (Without Corn there is no Country) and have mobilized for food self-sufficiency, public policies oriented to self-determination and sustainable agriculture, prohibitions against the use of food crops for production of bio-fuels, and renegotiation of NAFTA and the WTO to guarantee food sovereignty. With respect to GMO (genetically modified organisms), they have called for a moratorium on the planting of genetically modified corn, the creation of a special Protection Regime of Corn—which will guarantee genetic diversity of corn—and required labeling on all GMO products. More basically, they have called for recognition and respect for peasant agriculture and the importance of the peasantry in maintaining biodiversity and environmental protection.

In the United States the loss of factory jobs has been an element in the push for NAFTA renegotiation. In February 2009, the AFL-CIO in the United States and the Canadian Labour Congress presented a joint letter to President Obama and Canadian Prime Minister Stephen Harper outlining problems with the existing NAFTA agreement, among them the weak enforcement mechanisms of the labor and environmental side agreements and the excessive protection provided to investors, often at the expense of domestic laws. In both Mexico and the United States, demands for renegotiation have been taken up by legislators;

during the 2008 presidential campaign in the United States both Barack Obama and Hilary Clinton called for the renegotiation of NAFTA, as did López Obrador, the losing candidate in the Mexican presidential campaign of 2006. However, President Calderón has opposed renegotiation and it appears that none of the three leaders plans to give priority to this issue.

In the meantime, the Mexican government has taken steps to limit dependence on the United States, as have individual firms. As of 2009, the Mexican government had signed free trade agreements with 44 countries. Mexican exports to the EU more than doubled following a free trade agreement signed in 2000; it has also expanded trade with Latin America. However, this expansion was based on relatively low levels of trade in both cases, and Mexico continues to have a substantial trade deficit with both regions as well as China. Some of the maquiladoras, which depend on the United States for 80 percent of their exports, have been trying to diversify markets into other countries of Latin America. There have also been government efforts to assist less competitive firms and growers, as well as anti-poverty programs, which have had some effect in ameliorating the conditions of the poorest sectors of the population (see Chapter 5).

Some analysts are calling for a long-term national development strategy involving trade and investment policies that would focus on the production and export of higher value products, the creation of jobs, technology transfers, and the establishment of linkages between foreign investment and other sectors of the Mexican economy. Although President Calderón has announced some measures to respond to the crisis, such as creating new jobs through investment in infrastructure, critics contend that the Mexican government seems to be focusing on maintaining macroeconomic stability to draw foreign investment rather than initiating development policies that would respond more effectively to Mexico's needs in the areas of technological development, competitiveness, and employment.

THE DRUG TRADE

I cannot welcome you here . . . We are living the consequences of a war we did not ask for."
(Luz Maria Davila, addressing President Calderón on a visit to Ciudad Juárez, quoted in Wilkinson, "A tipping point for Mexico?")

Apologize, then resign!
(Protestors addressing President Calderón in Ciudad Juárez, quoted in Wilkinson, "Calderón visits Juárez.")

On January 31, 2010, a group of gunmen attacked a party of teenagers in Ciudad Juárez, most of them high school and college students, killing at least 15 and wounding several others. There is no evidence that any of the victims were

Image 8-1 *No Pais sin Maiz* (no country without corn). Denotes the significance of the cultivation of corn, a basic food staple of Mexico, which has been undermined by imports of subsidized U.S. grains.

linked to the drug trade. It was a shocking act of violence even for a country that witnessed 3,700 deaths in Juárez in a two-year period and 15,000 deaths in Mexico as a whole in the three years after Calderón took office and launched a military war on the drug cartels.[18] When Calderón visited Ciudad Juárez in the wake of the tragedy, he was greeted by an angry crowd, including civil leaders, educators, clergy, businesspersons, and relatives of the young victims, among them Luz Maria Davila, a maquiladora worker and mother of two of the youth who were killed.

There are few issues in which Mexico and the United States are more thoroughly intertwined than the drug trade.[19] Mexico is the major foreign supplier of drugs to the United States; the United States is the major market for drugs produced in or trafficked through Mexico and, by extension, the source of the funds fueling the drug trade.[20] Ninety percent of the cocaine that comes to the United States comes from Mexico, as do significant amounts of heroin, marijuana and (more recently) methamphetamine, while 90 percent of the weapons that fuel the escalating drug violence come from the United States. The drug trade involves a large network of operatives in both the United States and Mexico and is facilitated by corruption on both sides of the border. The drug syndicates, or cartels, are present in every state in Mexico and have drug dealers or distribution networks in approximately 230 U.S. cities and towns.

Nevertheless, until quite recently U.S. policy makers viewed the U.S.-Mexican drug trade as a Mexican responsibility. Beginning in 1986, the U.S. government certified or decertified Mexico and other drug trafficking countries on the basis of whether their governments were seen to be cooperating with the U.S. war on drugs, a process that had consequences in terms of aid and preferential trade treatment.[21] From the perspective of Mexico and other affected countries, the certification process was an intolerable arrogance from a country that was the major market for drugs and, by extension, the basic cause of the drug-related problems experienced in countries that produced or supplied drugs. Since then, U.S. policy makers have acknowledged the dual responsibility for drug trafficking, and the Obama administration as well as members of the U.S. Congress have recognized that the United States is not only the major market for drugs but is also heavily implicated in money laundering and the flow of weapons south.

Mexico has been a producer of marijuana and poppies (used for heroin) since at least the 19th century. In the state of Sinaloa, generations of families have lived on the earnings from growing poppies. Most of the marijuana and poppies were grown for personal use or sale in Mexico; some small-scale traffickers also sold drugs in the United States. It was in the mid-1980s, however, when the United States cut off the Caribbean supply routes for cocaine from Colombia to the southeastern United States, that Mexico became a major player in drug trafficking. The Colombian cartels, which at that time controlled the drug trade, switched to Mexico as a transport route for drugs to the United States, increasing the importance of the small-scale Mexican traffickers who expanded their operations and eventually formed their own cartels.[22] Mexico's status as a major conduit of drugs to the United States also coincided with the growth in poverty following the economic crisis of the 1980s, later aggravated by some of the effects of economic restructuring and the peso crisis of the mid-1990s. Many of the operatives of the drug trade are recruited among the urban and rural poor.

Another turning point occurred in the 1990s when the Colombian cartels were dismantled and the Mexican cartels took over their operations. At this time there were four major cartels in Mexico as well as several smaller ones. Three of the major cartels—the Tijuana cartel, the Juarez cartel, and the Gulf cartel, were concentrated in states along the U.S. border; the fourth, the Sinaloa cartel, was centered in the northwestern state of Sinaloa. At one point these cartels controlled 70 percent of the drugs going to the United States. Since that time the cartels have gone through a number of changes due to the death and/ or imprisonment of many of the former cartel leaders, temporary alliances between two or more cartels, and the emergence of new cartels, sometimes through splits from existing groups. The weakening of the Tijuana and Juarez cartels have left the Gulf and Sinaloa cartels as the most important in recent years, although new cartels have also appeared, such as La Familia Michoacana in the state of Michoacán, a major center for the production of marijuana and methamphetamine.

The attractions of the lucrative drug trade in the context of high levels of poverty and the absence of job opportunities have facilitated the recruitment of operatives by the cartels. For the most part, the operatives are young men ranging in age from their late teens to their early twenties, but in some impoverished districts entire families are involved. Recruitment is also facilitated by corruption, which affects government officials at all levels and from all political parties. A substantial portion of the resources from the sale of drugs goes to payoffs to police officers, prison guards, politicians, prosecutors and judges. The notoriously low wages of policemen have been traditionally supplemented through bribes; today many are on the payrolls of cartels, which expect them to protect their members or in some cases to target those of rival cartels. Osiel Cárdenas, head of the Gulf cartel, was a former police officer. Soldiers who desert are often recruited by the cartels, particularly for enforcement, in part because of their knowledge of military tactics.

Convicted drug lords run their cartels from their prison cells, and prison guards have been known to facilitate escapes by incarcerated drug lords. Government workers have been caught providing inside information to cartels, such as warning cartel members of plans for police enforcement against them. In some localities, cartels finance political campaigns, and numerous government officials are on their payroll. Cartels have taken over entirely in some towns, where they levy taxes and establish their own code of conduct. It has been estimated that cartels control 8 percent of the towns in Mexico, 32 of them in the state of Sinaloa, which has been described as the "home of the drug racket's top leaders, its most talented impresarios, and some of its dirtiest government and police officers."[23]

Those who fail to cooperate with the cartels are intimidated, resulting in a culture of silence in which the media refrains from reporting on particular cartels, police officers fail to arrest or those arrested "escape." Those who act against the cartels are murdered, sometimes quite brutally. In April, 2005, Raul Gibb Guerrero, the editor of a prize-winning newspaper in the state of Tamaulipas, was shot and killed following publication of exposés of trafficking in drugs and stolen gasoline that implicated high level officials of PEMEX. Shortly afterwards, Guadalupe García Escamilla, a radio reporter in Nuevo Laredo who received threats after investigating local corruption died after having been shot nine times when leaving the radio station. They were among seven journalists from Tamaulipas killed between 2000 and 2005, and two of some 20 journalists killed in Mexico in the six years of the Fox administration for their investigative reporting of drug trafficking and corruption.

In the same year, Alejandro Domínguez Coello was shot and killed in an ambush within six hours of taking the position of Nuevo Laredo police chief. At that time the city of Nuevo Laredo, across the border from Laredo, Texas, was the scene of escalating violence as rival cartels battled to control the lucrative crossing point for 40 percent of Mexico-U.S. trade. The previous police chief had resigned after six of his police officers were killed in the previous four months. Domínguez Coello, the owner of a printing shop, apparently came forward due to a sense of responsibility to the community when no one else dared to take the position. Of the estimated 5,000 people killed as a result of drug violence in 2008, over 500 were police officers or federal forces.

Given the circumstances, it often requires extraordinary courage simply to do one's job, and what is perhaps surprising is that there are a number of journalists who nonetheless expose drug offenders, police chiefs who arrest them, mayors and legislators who refuse to cooperate with them, and lawyers and judges that prosecute and convict them. Yudit del Rincón, a state legislator for PAN in Sinaloa, has targeted corruption among state officials connected to the drug trade. In 2008 she addressed the legislature, suggesting that all legislators be tested for drugs. They all cheered—until she then informed them that there were lab technicians in the room that were prepared to test them all then and there. She also targeted individual lawmakers associated with drug-related corruption until she received a death threat in the form of a funeral wreath with her name on it. She has subsequently been more circumspect although continues her crusade against corruption.[24]

The increase in drug-related violence, which previously focused primarily on rival cartels, dates from the late 1990s.[25] Beginning with the Zedillo administration, and especially under Fox and Calderón, the government increased arrests of cartel leaders, and contrary to prior practices, extradited many of them to the United States. This led to a backlash targeting government officials, as well as turf wars, as middle-level leaders struggle for control over the affected cartel and rival cartels attempt to take it over. In 2006, an estimated 2,500 people were killed in drug-related violence, up from 1,500 the year before. In addition to government officials and turf-war rivals, victims included innocent bystanders caught in the crossfire, particularly in border towns, such as Nuevo Laredo, where drug cartels struggled over major traffic corridors to the United States.

Shortly after taking office in December of that year, Calderón launched his military offensive, sending troops to nine states where drug production, trafficking, and/or violence were intense, while continuing practices begun under Fox, particularly the arrest and extradition of cartel leaders. Osiel Cárdenas, who had been running his drug operation from prison following his capture in 1993, was extradited to the United States in 2007. Following Calderón's crackdown, drug violence increased exponentially. Cartels also moved aggressively into other areas, including kidnapping both Mexicans and Americans for ransom—some of whom were killed—and are taking over the routes of coyotes smuggling immigrants into the United States, resulting in increased extortion of immigrants as well as a rise in the level of violence.

Another factor fueling the violence is the formation of armed militia by the cartels to enforce their control and eliminate enemies. Following the extradition of Osiel Cárdenas, the Gulf cartel formed a paramilitary group to protect its turf. It drew many of its members from the Mexican and Guatemalan military, including the Mexican Special Forces, an elite, highly trained group that took the name "Zetas." Other cartels followed suit, forming their own enforcement groups. Thousands of soldiers have deserted the army to join the cartels or paramilitary forces, which promise better salaries, food, and even medical care for their families. The emergence of paramilitary groups, particularly the Zetas, has increased not only the level of violence but also its viciousness, aimed at intimidation, through the torture, mutilation and execution of operatives who fail to carry out orders, rival cartel members, and government officials who refuse to cooperate.

The violence has been facilitated by the expiration of the U.S. ban on assault weapons in 2004 and the ease with which weapons can be obtained from retailers and gun shows in the U.S. border states, particularly Arizona and Texas.[26] Cartel "gatekeepers" on the U.S. side of the border hire "straw buyers"—generally people in need of money with a clean record—to buy weapons for them. Operatives then ship the weapons to Mexico in cars or trucks, taking advantage of the vast flow of cross-border traffic that has accelerated since NAFTA went into effect. They bribe or threaten drivers, security guards, dock loaders and sometimes owners of transport companies to carry weapons on U.S.-Mexico trips. In some cases, cartels have formed their own trucking companies or used car dealerships to facilitate the transfer of guns. The flow of an estimated 2,000 weapons daily from the United States has been likened to a "river of iron" pouring into Mexico.

While most of the weapons from the United States are conventional arms, more recently the cartels have obtained heavy weapons from Guatemala, where a 30-year civil war left a large supply of arms that are sold on the black market. The cartels have also stolen material from firms in Mexico, including 270 pounds of dynamite and hundreds of electric generators from a U.S. owned company in Durango. The arsenals of the cartels now include assault rifles, grenades and grenade launchers, and anti-tank rockets, and according to some observers are believed to equal or surpass those of the Mexican military.[27]

U.S. officials have estimated that there are as many as 450,000 people directly or indirectly employed by the cartels, including traffickers, distributors, money launderers, gunrunners and enforcers. The majority are growers. Production in Mexico has increased in recent years, and today an estimated 30 percent of

Mexico's cultivable land is in drug production, much of it in six states: Sinaloa, Sonora, Chihuahua, Durango, Michoacán, and Guerrero. Drug usage has also increased in Mexico and has included children as young as 8 or 10. According to a 2007 Mexican government report, the number of addicts doubled in the previous five years.

The increased focus of the Fox and Calderón governments on the drug trade has clearly had results. As indicated above, the arrest of drug leaders and particularly their extradition to the United States has led to a fragmentation of the cartels. Other measures by the Calderón government include the establishment of a criminal database, the professionalization of the police forces, initiatives to combat police corruption and the creation of new drug-combating forces. As of February 2009, 11,500 public employees had been sanctioned for corruption.

But some Mexican and U.S. observers have questioned the effectiveness of Calderón's tactics. Although initially very popular, the military offensive launched by Calderón is now seen as a major cause of the escalation of drug-related violence; as some put it, "Calderón took a stick and whacked a beehive," suggesting that little forethought went into the military offensive and that the Mexican police and military lack the resources to effectively combat the drug trade.[28] A survey taken following the massacre of youth in Ciudad Juárez found that half of the Mexican population believed the drug war was failing. Human rights organizations in Mexico and the United States have expressed concern regarding civil rights abuses and human rights violations committed by military troops, ranging from entering homes without warrants and illegal arrests to rape, torture and murder.[29]

With respect to some of the other initiatives of Calderón, a 2007 report by the Washington Office on Latin America pointed out that previous administrations had taken similar measures, but "new traffickers and new organizations take the place of old ones, 'clean' soldiers and police are easily corrupted, and robust supply keeps drugs flowing through Mexico and over the border into the United States."[30] In December 1996, President Zedillo appointed a military officer as drug czar and less than three months later he was found to be on the payroll of the Juarez cartel. In 2001, the corrupt Federal Judicial Police was dismantled and replaced by the Federal Investigative Agency (AFI); within the next two years, over 600 AFI agents were implicated in drug-related crimes ranging from drug trafficking to torture and murder. In 2008, several officials of SIEDO, an agency within the attorney general's office responsible for investigating organized crime, were accused of providing information, including data on U.S.-Mexico interdiction efforts, to one of the cartels. While the military has often been favorably compared to the police forces as relatively professional and less susceptible to corruption, as stated before, soldiers have deserted the army for

the cartels in droves, and highly trained officers have taken their skills and training with them to the cartels.

Drug trafficking and corruption are major challenges to efforts to establish
the rule of law in Mexico. At the same time the weakness of the judicial and
police systems undermine the efforts to combat the drug cartels. Even prior to
the expansion of drug trafficking and the explosion of drug related violence the
Mexican criminal justice system was notoriously ineffective in combating crime,
and only a fraction of those accused of committing crimes were tried and convicted. An estimated 90 percent of the victims of crime don't bother to report it
to the police.

In 2008, the Mexican legislature passed a measure to introduce greater flexibility and transparency in judicial procedures, incorporating the presumption
of innocence and changing trial procedures, which had previously been based
on written statements, to oral trials. Proceedings are public and sentencing is
based on evidence presented during the trial, similar to trials in the United
States. Many see this reform as a step in the right direction, although it is expected
to take several years to implement it at the federal level.[31]

Cooperation between the United States and Mexico on the drug war
increased during the 1990s, although distrust between the two countries also
continued, in part reflecting the fact that the United States often took unilateral
action, some of it of questionable legality, without consulting or even warning
Mexico.[32] Relations have improved since then, and in 2007 the United States
proposed an extensive program of aid to Mexico and Central America, totaling
$1.5 billion over a three-year period, to combat drugs. Modeled on Plan Colom-
bia (the program of U.S. aid which has provided $5 billion in aid to combat the
production and trafficking of drugs in Colombia), the Mérida initiative, named
for the city in Yucatán where it was announced, is heavily focused on military
aid, including helicopters and surveillance aircraft. Following protests from
Mexicans regarding the flow of weapons from the United States, the U.S. government agreed in 2008 to implement a tracking system on weapons Mexican
authorities seize from drug cartels, which will enable U.S. authorities to identify
those who sold the guns and to locate agents along the border to combat arms
trafficking.

The Obama administration has openly recognized the U.S. roles in the
Mexican drug trade as consumer, source of funding, and weapons' supplier, and
he has pledged to spend more resources on prevention and rehabilitation programs in the United States. As of early 2010, however, Obama's policies have
mainly consisted of a continuation or expansion of those of the Bush administration. The $700 million allocated from the Mérida initiative for Mexico in fis-
cal year 2009 included information technology and training for implementation
of Mexico's new legal system, but it has gone primarily to military aid. Recently

members of the United States Border Patrol and Mexican federal police began training together, sharing information and coordinating patrols in an effort to reduce the amount of drugs and the number of immigrants coming to the United States and the arms shipments and cash going into Mexico, a move that indicates an increased cooperation between the two countries.

Critics of the drug war have noted that while many of these measures are useful, the Mexico-U.S. drug trade will not be eradicated as long as there is a consumer market in the United States. History has shown that the eradication of drug crops in a given locale or elimination of specific transit routes simply results in a shift in the production of drugs elsewhere or the development of new routes.[33] In Mexico, the incorporation of the military into the drug war has led to human rights violations and in many cases corruption of the military, while measures such as the arrest and extradition of drug lords results in an escalation of violence as cartels try to take over their business.

There have been discussions in both the United States and Mexico and other Latin American countries regarding the possibility of legalizing or decriminalizing drug use. The Latin American Commission on Drugs and Democracy, headed by former presidents of Mexico, Brazil, and Colombia, called for a "paradigm shift" in dealing with the issue of drugs, including decriminalization. In Mexico, the government passed legislation in 2009 to decriminalize the possession of small amounts of drugs for personal use (five grams of marijuana, 500 mgs. of cocaine, 40 mg. of meth, or 50 mg. of heroin). The bill also encourages (but does not require) those caught with small amounts of drugs to go into rehabilitation programs. Advocates believe that decriminalization would go far to eliminate the profits in drug trafficking and the incentives for drug cartels. It has been opposed, however, by officials in Mexican border cities, who fear an influx of U.S. tourists coming to Mexico to take advantage of the new law, as well as by religious and social service representatives who fear an upsurge in drug usage by Mexican youth. According to many observers, the drug trade will require long-term solutions, including greater efforts toward prevention and rehabilitation in the United States, and in Mexico substantial legal reforms as well as greater efforts to reduce poverty and provide economic opportunities for Mexican youth.[34]

MIGRATION POLICIES IN THE UNITED STATES AND MEXICO

As discussed in Chapter 7, the migration of Mexicans to the United States has a long complex history influenced by events and conditions in both countries and the relations between them, including the development of migrant networks, transnational communities, and other transborder structures and initiatives that reinforce migration patterns. Beginning in the 1970s, immigration from Mexico grew dramatically due to such factors as the impact of globalization and neoliberalism in both countries, particularly the increasing availability of low-wage service jobs in the United States and the dislocations resulting from periodic crises, economic liberalization and the effects of NAFTA in Mexico. As of 2006 there were approximately 12 million persons of Mexican birth in the United States.[35]

Given the difficulties of obtaining visas for legal migration to the United States, much of this migration is unauthorized. Even those who are entitled to migrate, such as spouses or children of legal immigrants, must wait as long as five years before obtaining visas through provisions for family reunification, which is an additional factor in unauthorized migration as well as the presence of immigrant families in the United States in which some members may be legal and even U.S. citizens while others remain unauthorized. Today, Mexicans comprise over half of the estimated 12 million unauthorized immigrants in the United States.

The large presence of new immigrants, and particularly unauthorized immigrants, has been a controversial issue in the United States as well as other immigrant receiving countries. Government policies toward immigration have been affected by conflicting goals between those who wish to restrict immigration (and in some cases deport immigrants) and those who for various reasons favor immigration and/or are concerned regarding the treatment of immigrants in the United States. Business groups interested in recruiting people with specific skills or hiring cheap labor have generally favored immigration reform, arguing that immigrants take jobs that U.S. born workers do not want, or that there are not enough U.S. workers with the needed training and skills for certain occupations. In some cases they push for guest-worker programs that enable them to hire immigrants for limited periods of time, during which they may not be eligible for the usual labor protections and after which they must return to their home countries.

In contrast, workers have often opposed immigration, particularly unauthorized immigration, fearing it will lead to reduced jobs and lower wages for U.S.-born workers. These fears are most likely to surface in periods of economic recession when jobs are relatively scarce. However, several labor unions, as well as the AFL-CIO have come out in favor of rights of immigrants already in the country, including the legalization of unauthorized workers, since their unauthorized status and fear of deportation if they report abuses enables them to be exploited more easily. Immigrants also have become an increasingly important part of the labor force in certain industries and services and of the resurgent labor movement. Labor organizations and immigrant advocacy groups argue that any negative immigrant impact on wages and jobs can be reduced through a stronger enforcement of existing labor laws. By the same token, these groups are generally opposed to temporary guest-worker programs that create a two-tier labor market or do not permit a path to permanent status.

Since the debate around California Proposition 187 in 1994, immigrants and ethnic groups, particularly Mexicans and Mexican Americans, have become increasingly active in efforts to prevent discriminatory legislation and to promote reforms enabling unauthorized immigrants to legalize their status. Along with advocacy groups they have promoted comprehensive immigration reform that would enable unauthorized immigrants of good character to legalize their status and eventually become citizens. They are supported by the Mexican government, which has pushed for less restrictive U.S. policies when negotiating with the United States and has supported Mexican immigrants in the United States through various initiatives.

Finally, there are various restrictionist groups such as the Center for Immigration Studies, FAIR (Federation for American Immigration Reform) and Numbers U.S.A., which argue against immigration and the legalization of unauthorized immigrants on such grounds as their impact on jobs and wages, the cost of public service, and population control. Most favor the detention and/or deportation of unauthorized immigrants as well as the prevention of new immigration, and some even favor deportation of legal immigrants, or children of unauthorized immigrants born in the United States who are by definition U.S. citizens. Some of these groups include a hard core of cultural conservatives, or nativists, who are afraid of the cultural impact of immigrants and have even received funding from racist and other extremist organizations. Immigrants have also been increasingly targeted by hate groups and hate crimes, as documented in a series of reports by the Southern Poverty Law Center, which has identified some 932 hate groups in the country as of 2009, and a jump in anti-immigrant extremist groups from 173 to 309 between 2008 and 2009.[36]

Restrictionist groups have propagated a number of stereotypes and generalizations about the negative impact of immigrants, many of which have been disseminated by popular radio and television talk show hosts.[37] Partly as a result, public debates on migration often tend to be emotionally driven, with little understanding of the causes and implications of immigration. While restrictionists have emphasized costs, immigrant advocates have stressed the contributions of immigrants to the economy and to specific sectors, ranging from agriculture to information technology systems. Various academic studies have attempted to develop a nuanced and balanced perspective on the costs and benefits of immigration, although most seem to indicate that the net effect of immigration, including unauthorized immigration, has been positive. Demographic studies have also shown that, due to low birth rates and increasing life spans in the United States, only through immigration will it be possible to maintain a sufficient working-age population to provide resources for social security, Medicare, and other needs of the rapidly growing number of retired and elderly non-working population—something that is already occurring in some European countries.[38] On the Mexico side, slower population growth should reduce the numbers of emigrants in the long run, although the working-age cohort is still expanding.

U.S. government policy toward immigration has fluctuated. The 1965 Hart-Celler Act, influenced by the civil rights movement and the post-war rise in rights-based politics, marked a major shift from the highly restrictive and racist policies dating from the 19th century. Among other measures it abolished national quotas, and gave preferences to immigrants according to occupational needs and family reunification. The 1986 Immigration Reform and Control Act (IRCA) attempted to control immigration through penalizing employers who knowingly hire unauthorized immigrants. It also enabled unauthorized immigrants of good character who had been in the country since 1981 to receive amnesty, which particularly benefited Mexican immigrants. The 1990 Immigration Law, among other provisions, enabled amnestied immigrants to bring family members to the United States, and the increase in immigrants due to family reunification was an additional factor in the growth of Mexico-U.S. migration in the 1990s.

Since the California campaign for Proposition 187 in 1994, however, most U.S. immigration policy has been restrictive and even punitive, reflecting public and legislative perceptions and misperceptions about the origins of immigration and the economic and cultural impact of immigrants, as well as domestic political considerations. The Immigration Reform and Immigrant Responsibility Act of 1996 and other legislation that year responded in part to the fears of the Democratic Party and the Clinton administration that the Republicans would make immigration control a major issue in upcoming political campaigns. These measures reinforced physical barriers along the southern border with Mexico, increased penalties for illegal entry and false documents, and limited possibilities for appealing decisions regarding deportation, as well as limiting the eligibility of immigrants, both legal and unauthorized, for welfare benefits. Although since that time, legislation has been introduced in both houses of Congress for a comprehensive immigration reform that would include both enforcement measures and provisions for unauthorized immigrants to legalize their situation and eventually become citizens, comprehensive reform has been rejected in favor of enforcement, particularly after the attack on the World Trade Center and the Pentagon in September 2001. This has often been accompanied by language criminalizing unauthorized immigrants, referring to them as "illegals" and even "criminal aliens" and conflating them with drug lords and would-be terrorists.

The implementation of immigration policy in the United States was previously the domain of the Immigration and Naturalization Service, which included both enforcement of immigration legislation and the process of naturalization of new citizens. Following the creation of the Department of Homeland Security in 2002, the INS came under its jurisdiction and was divided into three agencies: the U.S. Citizenship and Immigration Services, focusing on permanent residency and citizenship; Immigration Control and Enforcement, or ICE; and U.S. Customs and Border Protection. ICE has been particularly aggressive in its efforts to target unauthorized immigrants, rounding them up in the workshops and factories where they work and even in their homes—sometimes separating families, which often include legal residents and citizens as well as unauthorized immigrants. Detained immigrants have been imprisoned in jails or detention centers, often far from their families, for months and even years.[39] Conditions in these centers, many of them privately owned with little to no government supervision, are often deplorable, and several imprisoned immigrants have died or become seriously ill due to the lack of sufficient medical care.

These policies have had devastating effects on unauthorized immigrants, who are forced deeper into the shadows, and their families, including family members in the countries of origins that are dependent on their remittances. In some cases it has also resulted in the closing of immigrant-dependent firms in the United States, which may have a ripple effect on businesses that supply the firm and the economic viability of some small towns that depend on the earnings of the employers and workers.

ICE has also encouraged local law enforcement agencies to sign an agreement through the 287(g) program that will enable them to enforce certain immigration policies. Several cities in California and other states have opposed this measure, which would undermine relations between the police force and the immigrant communities, making unauthorized immigrants reluctant to report crimes or otherwise cooperate with the police. In the case of Los Angeles, the Police Department's Special Order 40 prohibits the police from engaging in most types of immigration enforcement. In other jurisdictions, however, local enforcement agencies have been zealous in efforts to round up immigrants. One example is Sheriff Arpaio in Maricopa County, Arizona, whose zeal in pursuing immigrants allegedly led to discrimination against Latinos and a virtual neglect of other crimes and more pressing issues, as documented in a series of articles by two reporters of the East Valley Tribune, Mesa, Arizona, who received a Pulitzer prize for their coverage of this issue.[40]

In the meantime, the border patrol has been reinforced with new agents and equipment, as well as the construction of a 700-mile fence authorized by the Secure Fence Act of 2006. Apart from its negative implications for U.S.-Mexico relations, this move antagonized many municipal governments at the border, U.S. border residents whose property was taken over for fence construction, local businesses, many of which depend on cross-border Mexican shoppers, as well as environmentalists concerned about the damage to ecological systems that cross national boundaries.

At least until recently, draconian enforcement of border control had little effect in deterring cross-border migration, but it has made it considerably more costly, difficult, and dangerous. In efforts to avoid heavily guarded and fenced areas, migrants often must navigate long stretches of desert, where many have died of heat and dehydration. Others have lost their lives by asphyxiation in overcrowded trunks of cars or trucks. Thousands have died crossing the border since the mid-1990s. Another unanticipated effect of enhanced border control has been the decision of many immigrants to remain in the United States indefinitely, in some cases bringing their families, rather than returning home periodically, given the difficulties of re-entering. In this respect U.S. policies have been counterproductive, resulting in a shift from cyclical migration to permanent settlement.[41] This shift has also aggravated the pattern of significantly reducing the population of migrant-sending communities in Mexico, some of which have become virtual ghost towns.

As noted above, the Mexican government has been a strong advocate for a reduction of restrictions on Mexican immigration and for the rights of Mexicans in the United States. It is therefore ironic that it has opposed immigration across its southern border and has generally failed to protect the immigrants, mostly Central American, who cross into Mexico from Guatemala and Belize. The Mexico-Guatemalan border region consists largely of indigenous populations that share cultural and ethnic bonds and a history of cross-border migration and commercial relations. Guatemalans have crossed the border to work in Mexican coffee fields since the 19th century. With the conflicts and associated economic upheavals from the civil wars in Guatemala, El Salvador and Nicaragua in the 1970s and 1980s, there was a dramatic upsurge in migration from these countries, with some migrants crossing Mexico into the United States. Central American migration to Mexico and the United States, increasingly driven by economic conditions in the respective countries, has continued until the present. Migrants to the United States from South American countries, and even other parts of the world, also cross Mexico's southern border.

According to Mexican law, unauthorized entry into Mexico is punishable by fines, deportation and imprisonment. Migrants crossing into Mexico, and through Mexico to the United States, are also subject to frequent abuse, including extortion, robbery, assault and rape, not only by smugglers, gangs, and other criminals but also by law enforcement officers—immigration officials, police officers, and the military—some of them operating in collusion with criminal elements. There are cases in which women migrants report taking birth control pills prior to leaving home to avoid pregnancy in case they are raped. Women unable to pay off extortionists, and even children, may be sold into sex slavery.

Underlying many of these abuses is the fundamental need for measures to ensure the elimination of corruption and lawlessness and the extension of the rule of law throughout all parts of the country.

Recent Mexican initiatives to control Central American migration into Mexico emulate U.S. immigration policies in several respects. In 2002, following a visit to the United States by then Secretary of Government Santiago Creel, President Fox inaugurated Plan Sur to halt trafficking of "migrants, drugs and arms" from Central America to Mexico. Although it incorporated measures to halt abuses by authorities, it also increased the involvement of the military. In 2005, Mexico created the National Security System of Mexico, an umbrella organization incorporating the National Migration Institute (INM) as well as agencies involved in public safety. In December 2006, President Calderón established the Border State Police Force to secure the border and combat crime in the region. Mexican governments have made some efforts to prosecute officials accused of mistreating immigrants, and there are organizations, such as the Grupo Beta, an agency of the INM, which seek to protect the rights of immigrants in Mexico, but generally measures to protect immigrants and penalize those who abuse them have been inadequate and/or underfinanced.

In the United States, immigrant advocacy groups, independent think tanks and scholars, and bipartisan policy makers have issued studies and reports advocating a comprehensive immigration reform that would respond to the continuing need for both skilled and unskilled workers as well as preferences for family reunification, particularly spouses and children. Although differing on specifics, proposals for such reform would generally enable unauthorized immigrants of good character who meet certain conditions to apply for permanent residence and eventually citizenship. It would also establish a framework for future migration that focuses on labor needs for both skilled and unskilled workers and encouragement of family reunification, particularly for spouses and young children; and ensures that workers recruited temporarily are protected by labor laws, are allowed to change jobs if employers are abusive, and have the option either to apply for permanent residence or be given incentives to return to their countries of origin when their time of employment is up.

Several proposals include recommendations that immigrants receive the legal protections they are entitled to (e.g., eliminating provisions incorporated in the 1996 Immigration Reform that restrict the right of immigrants to appeal deportation decisions). With respect to enforcement, they would focus workplace enforcement on employers who knowingly hire unauthorized immigrants rather than rounding up, detaining, and deporting workers; and desist in the construction of walls and fences at the border in favor of more sophisticated intelligence and non-physical barriers, such as virtual borders, while concentrating efforts to prevent entry primarily on terrorists, drug traffickers, and other serious criminals. In several cases recommendations include reforms of administrative policies that would accelerate processes for obtaining visas, particularly for family members, some of whom must wait five years before receiving legal permission to immigrate.

Mexican legislators, scholars, as well as other civil society representatives have also called for legislative reforms addressing the treatment of Central Americans and other migrants in Mexico, such as repealing penalties for unauthorized entry, prosecuting officials as well as others guilty of human rights violations against immigrants, and other measures to ensure that immigrants coming into Mexico be treated with the same respect that Mexico demands for its migrants in the United States. In some cases, reform would entail an expansion of resources for existing initiatives and agencies, such as the Grupo Beta. At the same time, the migration of Mexicans and other immigrants to the United States is unlikely to end as long as conditions of poverty and lack of opportunity prevail in the sending countries. The issue of Mexican-U.S. migration as well as other important issues in U.S.-Mexican relations require bilateral collaboration and some have suggested regional collaboration that also incorporates the governments of Central America to address migration issues as well as the trafficking of drugs and weapons and the proliferation of gangs. Other suggestions include building on transnational ties that exist, with governments providing complimentary funding for remittances used for productive purposes, the concentration of development efforts on migrant sending areas, and the incorporation of migrant representatives in the policy advisory groups.

CONCLUSIONS

The previous overview of three major policy issues affecting U.S.-Mexico relations suggests several conclusions.

First, the United States has had a significant role in what have sometimes been seen as problems caused by Mexico. This is particularly true with respect to the drug issue, in which the emphasis has traditionally been on the role of Mexico in supplying drugs while ignoring or downplaying the fact that the United States is the major market for drugs, as well as the U.S. role in supplying weapons that have fueled the violence in the Mexican drug wars and in financing the drug trade. Unauthorized migration is blamed on immigrants, particularly Mexicans, who come to the United States seeking jobs or reunification with their families, often without taking into account the fact that this migration also responds to demands by U.S. employers for low-skilled labor. As pointed out in Chapter 4, the market reforms carried out in the 1980s, which were partly responsible for increasing inequality in Mexico, were influenced by policies pushed by the United States and international lending agencies and implemented by U.S.-trained technocrats in Mexico.

Second, unilateral and bilateral reforms undertaken to address these problems have to date been ineffective or at best insufficient to resolve these issues, and in some cases they seem to have been counter-productive. In the case of the drug issue, there has been an over-emphasis on military solutions that bring their own problems. The extensive use of the military against the drug trade in Mexico has been accompanied by an escalation of the violence in that country, as well as human rights violations on the part of military officials, and has raised fears about the militarization of Mexican society. Although the Mérida initiative addresses issues such as control of the weapons flow into Mexico, most of the funds in fact go to support for military and police forces. On his visit to Ciudad Juárez in February 2010, Calderón spoke of the need to address social problems at the root of the drug trade, but refused to move the military force of 10,000 occupying the city, and some felt that the move was largely political.

Recent efforts at immigration reform in the United States have, in effect, criminalized unauthorized immigrants, emphasizing enforcement and border restrictions, and undermining immigrant legal protections,which, which have sometimes led to human rights abuses against immigrants and even U.S. citizens. Stricter border control has increased the number of migrants who have lost their lives in attempting to cross the desert in an effort to avoid detection, and increased payments to smugglers, which has in turn attracted drug traffickers to human trafficking, and has had the unintended effect of shifting cyclical migration to more permanent migration. Flagrant human rights violations have also characterized the treatment of immigrants coming into Mexico from Central America.

Finally, there is a need for both short-term solutions and policies that will address long-term needs. The drug issue will not be resolved as long as there is a lucrative market in the United States. Some have proposed the total or partial decriminalization of drugs (e.g., beginning with marijuana), which could then be sold legally and taxed, as in the case of liquor with the repeal of prohibition, although this is probably not feasible politically, at least in the short term. Programs focusing on drug treatment, prevention and rehabilitation, exist but need to be expanded. In Mexico, initiatives addressing the low salaries and inadequate training of law enforcement officers, and thus reducing temptations for corruption, as well as more concerted efforts to identify, investigate, and penalize high-level officials involved in drug trafficking or protecting drug traffickers, are necessary although not sufficient; judicial reforms and other efforts to strengthen democratic institutions and the rule of law should be prioritized.

In the case of migration, there is a need for comprehensive reform along the lines suggested previously that will enable unauthorized migrants in the United

States to come out of the shadows and will regulate future migration flows in keeping with goals of family reunification and U.S. labor needs. Demographic trends in both the United States and Mexico, including the increased significance of immigrants in supporting an aging U.S. population, should be taken into account. In the meantime, efforts should continue to reduce abuses of immigrants in both countries; in the case of Mexico, judicial reforms and other measures to improve the rule of law could aid in preventing abuses of Central Americans and other immigrants who cross Mexico's southern border.

Many analysts see these issues as interrelated.[42] Among the most recent unauthorized immigrants have been Mexican police officers under threat by drug cartels hoping to obtain asylum in the United States. More generally, the dislocations and reduction in formal job opportunities resulting from economic restructuring in Mexico and Central America have strengthened the attraction of migrating to the United States, where economic restructuring has led to the increased availability of low-wage jobs in services. Poverty and lack of opportunity have also pushed young people in each of these countries into the lucrative drug trade. It follows that policies addressing poverty and inequality in Mexico and Central America—including initiatives to promote economic development, the creation of jobs, and educational reforms to effectively prepare the labor force for the challenges of the 21st century—are not only necessary for reducing poverty, but can contribute to reducing Mexican-U.S. migration and reducing lowering the temptations of the drug trade for impoverished and disadvantaged youth in both countries. Most analysts agree that these needs cannot be addressed by the market alone, but will require concerted government action in Mexico and continued collaboration between the United States and Mexico—and in some cases other countries, including Canada and countries in Central America—to find solutions that address the root causes of poverty, drug trafficking, and unauthorized migration.

CHAPTER 9

Mexico's Evolution: Legacies and Challenges

As Mexicans commemorate the bicentennial of independence and the centennial of the Mexican revolution in 2010, they can look back on 200 years of fundamental change that has been shaped in important ways by the legacies of prior generations. Today Mexico confronts an uncertain future, one that will continue to be influenced by history while presenting new challenges.

This Chapter summarizes Mexico's historical trajectory and contemporary developments through an examination of continuity and change among Mexico's socio-economic, political and foreign and international actors, focusing particularly on how they have affected and been affected by the economic, political and social changes over the past 30 years. It will then briefly discuss some of the major issues confronting Mexico today.

THE EVOLUTION OF SOCIO-ECONOMIC ACTORS

The concentration of economic power in Mexico can be traced to the colonial period, when a small elite of landowners, mine owners and merchants controlled much of the wealth of the colony and systems of land tenure evolved featuring vast holdings controlled by landowners and worked by different forms of coerced labor. The socio-economic elite changed over time, becoming more complex, but continuing to have a dominant role in Mexico's economy. Throughout much of the 20th century, the elite consisted of powerful economic groups combining industrial, commercial and financial resources controlled by a small number of investors or in some cases a single family. At the same time, economic growth, particularly between the 1940s and 1970s, benefitted the growth of middle groups, including small and medium business groups and farmers, managers and technicians, and a sector of the organized working class.

Beginning in the early 1980s, the debt crisis, the nationalization of private banks, and economic reforms led to a shakedown and restructuring of the economic groups. Some groups lost out, but others survived and new groups emerged, particularly with the development of an alternative financial system following the nationalization of the banks and the privatization of state-owned enterprises in the late 1980s and 1990s, which resulted in the emergence of a new class of billionaires—including Carlos Slim, one of the wealthiest men in the world—as well as private monopolies in telecommunications, banking, and mining. Some industries such as glass and cement are also controlled by monopolies or virtual monopolies, and several of these industries have substantial investments in the United States and other countries of Latin America. Today the economy is dominated by billionaires and powerful economic groups, as well as foreign corporations and banks.

Economic restructuring has had different implications for different sectors among small and medium firms. On the one hand, medium-sized firms and agricultural enterprises oriented to exports have benefited from the opening of markets. On the other hand, trade liberalization and the removal of barriers to foreign investment has led to the elimination of many small and medium firms oriented to the domestic market unable to compete with competition from trade or subsidiaries of foreign firms.

Mexican business groups continue to be represented through organizations such as the CCE, the CMHN, COPARMEX, COCAMIN, COCANACO, ABM, and CANACINTRA, to which new organizations representing stockbrokers and exporters have been added (AMIB, ANIERM). At the same time, business groups have become more active in formal politics and more directly involved in government. Support by business groups frustrated by bank nationalization was a major factor in the resurgence of PAN, one of whose members, Vicente Fox, became the first opposition president. Businesspersons have also become more active in PRI which, with the emergence of the technocrats in the 1980s and 1990s, became increasingly congenial to business interests. Aside from benefiting from privatization, business interests have been directly involved in various government initiatives, such as the NAFTA negotiations, but here as elsewhere, large private conglomerates and foreign corporations have tended to benefit at the expense of small and medium businesses.

Recent economic developments also resulted in significant changes in the Mexican working class. Workers in mining, railroads, and textiles began to organize in the late 19th and early 20th centuries. As the significance of the working class increased with the growth of industry in the post-revolutionary period, successive governments sought to channel and control labor organizations, subjecting them to a corporatist system that provided certain benefits but at the expense of labor independence. Throughout the post-war period, various unions and labor organizations struggled for union democracy and autonomy, and during the 1970s some independent unions formed in the automotive industry and among university workers, while dissident groups, calling for union democracy and autonomy, formed within existing unions, such as telecommunications and teachers.

Rural-urban migration fed the growing industrial labor force, but a substantial number of migrants were unable to find formal industrial jobs, and many of the migrants became part of the casual labor force, or informal sector, composed of vendors, workers in small workshops, and service workers (e.g., in domestic work). Even at the height of the labor movement, only about half of the workers belonged to unions.

The economic crisis of the 1980s and economic restructuring resulted in a reduction in formal sector jobs as well as a decline in wages, benefits and job security for many workers, and an increase in the informal labor sector. Ironically, it also led to an increase in the number of women working to compensate for loss of household income. Other household strategies to cope with the loss of formal sector jobs and income included migration of a family member to the United States and a combination of formal and informal work.

The loss of formal jobs and informalization of the labor force were factors in a general decline in the importance of organized labor. There was a breakdown in the three-way corporate relation between the state, labor leaders, and workers organized in the corporate sector due to the inability of labor leaders to deliver benefits to their members and more recently to the end of PRI hegemony. In some areas, notably in the maquila industries, the CTM formed "ghost unions" based on contractual agreements with employers, which has led to intense labor conflicts when workers in such industries have attempted to form independent unions. In the mobilizations following the peso crisis, an independent confederation, the UNT, was formed, drawing in some relatively independent unions and small confederations. With few exceptions, however, since the early 1980s the labor movement and rank and file workers have been on the defensive, seeking to hold on to jobs, wages, and job security, and to prevent legislation that they see as threatening their situation.

With the decline of formal unionism, the mobilization and organization of workers has also taken different forms, such as community organizations or mobilization around health and environmental issues. Workers have also engaged in cross-border networking and collaboration through particular organizations, such as the Coalition for Justice in the Maquiladoras, or around specific issues, such as NAFTA.

Dramatic changes have also occurred in the rural sector. During the post-World War II period, government emphasis on the promotion of commercial agriculture, particularly in northern Mexico, and the relative neglect of the small farms and ejidos in the central and southern part of the country, reinforced a bifurcated agricultural structure between large- and middle-sized estates in the north producing for domestic markets and exports and the small farms and peasant holdings in the south, producing for family subsistence and local consumption.

Over time, as the rural population increased, the possibilities of making a living through agriculture became increasingly difficult, particularly for those in subsistence agriculture on poorer lands, and many migrated on a cyclical basis to work on commercial estates in Mexico or the United States for part of the year, or moved permanently to urban areas. The economic crises of the 1980s and the reforms of the 1990s, particularly the 1991 amendment to Article 27 and the Agrarian Law of 1992 which ended land distribution and permitted the distribution of ejidal lands to individual holders, and the implementation of NAFTA, resulted in new disruptions to small rural producers. Although battered by trade liberalization and NAFTA, and despite expectations that it would soon be obsolete, however, the peasantry has managed to survive as a class and eke out subsistence, supplemented by income from non-agricultural activities and migrant family members.

While the traditional organizations representing workers and peasants have been weakened, these and other groups have found expression in grassroots movements—including cooperatives, community organizations, and various types of social organizations and movements—protesting human rights abuses, calling for women's rights, and demanding redress for grievances of various kinds. Many of these movements have antecedents in earlier periods: a long history of indigenous organizing preceded the emergence of the Zapatistas in Chiapas, and the mobilization of peasant ecologists in Guerrero has precedents in earlier movements, including the revolutionary army of Emiliano Zapata. Urban movements, such as the mobilization around the 1985 earthquake in Mexico City, drew upon local grassroots organizing in the 1970s and in many cases were influenced directly or indirectly by the student movement of 1968.

These movements have engaged in various tactics ranging from legal initiatives to various disruptive activities, including civil disobedience. They have also formed cross-sectoral alliances and coalitions with different movements and organizations within Mexico as well as cross-national links with counterpart groups in the United States and have received support from international human rights, environmental, labor and other groups.

They have had varying success in meeting their specific goals. In many cases, goal achievement has required some form of negotiating with the government at different levels and/or political parties and other political actors, raising the issue, for many of these groups, of maintaining their independence and resisting the clientelist practices of many government and party officials. In some instances they have had a role, direct or indirect, in political transition. Some of these movements proved to be temporary, others became more permanent or took new forms, for example civic organizations or NGOs dedicated to environmental issues, women's rights, or indigenous autonomy. While they emerge and disappear, and take various forms in different epochs, the participants may gain new skills and a sense of empowerment that can be drawn upon for future activism.

The Catholic Church has become an increasingly important social and political actor in recent years. The influence of the Church and Catholicism is, of course, a legacy of Spanish colonization; while many of its prerogatives were eliminated by the 19th century Liberal Reform and the Mexican Revolution, it continued to exercise spiritual and ideological influence. Catholics were prominent in the establishment of the PAN in 1939 and have continued to be influential within the party. Although the official Church is generally conservative in orientation, the liberalizing influence of the Second Vatican Council in the 1960s also had an impact. The emergence of Christian Base Communities radicalized some lay Catholics, and individual priests and bishops, as well as religious orders such as the Jesuits, have been involved in the formation of organizations to promote local development and the organization of indigenous groups. The Church, or groups influenced by it, was also instrumental in the formation of NGOs—an estimated two-thirds of NGOs in Mexico have religious origins.

A constitutional reform under the Salinas government in 1992 officially recognized the Church as a legal entity and eliminated some of the more onerous provisions of the Constitution (e.g., the prohibition against teaching religion in religious schools). The Church, or individual Church officials, have promoted democratization, encouraged citizen participation in the political process, and spoken out against human rights abuses. At the same time, officials have taken a conservative position on social issues, speaking out against abortion, gay marriage and other issues.

Finally, in Mexico as elsewhere, the second half of the 20th century saw the emergence of women in important social, economic and political roles. Women's mobilization and organization also have important historical precedents, but have continued to confront the deeply engrained patriarchy of Mexican society. The exclusion of women from decision-making positions in social movements, even where they were the most active members, was a factor in the formation of groups that specifically promoted the empowerment of women and mobilized around issues ranging from domestic abuse to demands for access to leadership positions. The economic crisis and restructuring forced more women into the labor force, and women whose spouses migrated were obliged to take on new obligations as the head of the household. Women have also taken an increasingly important role in the political process, generally increasing their presence in the legislature as well as other elected positions, including governors; women have also headed two of the three major political parties and have run for president. At the same time, patriarchy continues to exist, taking its most virulent form in crimes against women, notably indigenous and poor urban women.

A major new social actor has emerged in recent years—the drug cartels. Numerous factors account for their growth and significance, including the proximity of the U.S. consumer market for drugs; poverty and the lack of opportunity, particularly for youth; the absence of the rule of law; and official corruption. Although the military offensive of Calderón was initially popular, it is now being questioned by many Mexicans who believe it is at best ineffective and at worst counter-productive. Between December 2006, when the government initiated its anti-drug military campaign, and summer of 2010, some 28,000 people were killed. The cartels have in effect challenged the government monopoly of the use of force. They now control several towns and regions in Mexico, and their influence has spread to the United States.

THE GROWING HETEROGENEITY OF POLITICAL ACTORS

State formation was a major challenge confronting Mexican elites in the post-independence period. It was only in the late 19th century that the task of neutralizing regional caudillos and establishing the jurisdiction of the national government throughout Mexico was achieved. The post-revolutionary governments confronted a similar problem, which was resolved with the creation of a highly centralized state dominated by a strong executive closely linked to a hegemonic governing party. The 1917 constitution envisioned a state role in ensuring national control over natural resources and implementing social reforms; economic conditions and the challenges of industrialization also required a state role in the promotion of industrialization and modernization. The hegemony and corporatist structure of the governing party as well as the economic growth of the postwar period enabled it to provide certain benefits while maintaining control of its constituent sectors.

Even during its authoritarian phases, the Mexican state was neither monolithic or autonomous. Local governments on occasion resisted or delayed indefinitely the implementation of central government initiatives; political elites responded to direct and indirect pressures by business groups; protests by different social groups also elicited state action. The interplay of economic, social and political factors was particularly evident in the transition from an authoritarian system dominated by a hegemonic party to an electoral democracy in which several parties contest office. Populist initiatives in the 1980s, culminating in the bank nationalization of 1982, led to increased opposition by business groups, particularly by small and medium business leaders, many of whom joined the PAN, strengthening what was at that time the major opposition party. At the same time, the disruptions resulting from the economic crisis of the early 1980s and government austerity programs were factors in the growth of social protest movements among affected groups, and a split in the ruling party, with a dissident group forming the nucleus of a new political front and eventually a second opposition party, the PRD. The loss of PRI legitimacy and growing support for opposition parties was accompanied by increased activism on the part of civic action groups and the formation of the Civic Alliance, which organized election monitoring in efforts to ensure electoral transparency.

Social protest, the growth of opposition parties, and declining government legitimacy, particularly after the fraudulent presidential election of 1988, also led to efforts by the Salinas and Zedillo governments to restore legitimacy, including recognition of selected opposition victories in gubernatorial elections and a series of electoral reforms. Although these reforms were initially designed to maintain the PRI in power, the Zapatista rebellion and growing political and economic instability were factors in more meaningful reforms in 1994, including changes in the composition of the Federal Electoral Institute from predominantly PRI activists to non-partisan citizens and to permit international monitors to oversee elections. The economic crisis following the peso devaluation in 1994 led to massive social protests in the subsequent years, and the Zedillo government instituted another major reform, which ensured the independence of the electoral institutions responsible for overseeing the elections and permitted direct election for the mayor of Mexico City. The process culminated with opposition victories in the legislative and municipal elections of 1997, in which the PRI lost its majority in the legislature and opposition parties gained control of several municipalities, notably the PRD in Mexico City, and finally the election of an opposition candidate for president in 2000, ending the hegemony of the PRI and firmly establishing a pluralist party system.

The transition from a dominant party system to a pluralist system resulted in the increased heterogeneity of political actors. Access to office at various levels is now contested among three major and several smaller parties; electoral institutions ensure that elections are relatively free of fraud compared to the period of PRI hegemony; the legislature and judiciary check the power of the presidency, individual state governments and municipalities can operate with relative autonomy in relation to the federal government. Ideally, this heterogeneity provides citizen groups and social movements with multiple points of access to those who can effectively represent their interests. At the same time, old problems of clientelism and corruption have not disappeared and affect new as well as traditional political actors; electoral institutions do not always enforce the principles of free and fair elections, as was demonstrated in the 2006 elections; and the rule of law is elusive in many parts of the country.

The Mexican government also confronts major problems, including escalating crime and violence as well as endemic issues of poverty and inequality. The drug cartels, which exercise virtual control over certain areas of the country, can be seen as political as well as socio-economic actors. At the same time, the militarization of the drug war has raised questions about the increased role of the military, the corruption of military personnel, and human rights abuses reported by national and international human rights organizations.

In the process of democratic transition, socio-economic actors—neighborhood and community groups, dissident labor movements, peasant and indigenous organizations—while mobilizing around specific goals and demands, also had a role, direct or indirect, in the emergence and growth of opposition parties and the gradual opening of the political system, while civic action groups have been specifically oriented to ensuring democratic elections and government transparency. While it is not clear what form they will take, or how successful they may be, social groups, civic organizations and protest movements will undoubtedly continue to have a role in Mexico's future political life.

CHANGING EXTERNAL RELATIONS AND INTERNATIONAL ACTORS

Like other Latin American countries, Mexico's trajectory has been partly shaped by the changing global context and relations with more powerful countries. Independence did not end European efforts at intervention, notably in countries like Mexico which experienced a long period of chaos and anarchy and suffered from a series of weak governments following the wars for independence. Eventually the region fell within the sphere of influence of the United States, which sought to maintain the hemisphere free of external intervention. But Mexico became a victim of U.S. territorial expansion, as the United States successfully claimed half of Mexico's territory and created a lingering fear and distrust on the part of Mexicans of its northern neighbor.

Economically, the period of the early republics coincided with the domination of Britain as the leading world economic power, anxious to expand its relations with the former Spanish colonies as markets for its growing manufactured products and a source of agricultural and mineral commodities. An opening of trade relations was also in the interests of Latin American exporters, mine owners and those agricultural interests producing for export, often supported by the Liberals, and by the middle of the 19th century there was a general consensus among policy makers for export-oriented growth. This was reinforced by the industrial revolution in the second half of the 19th century, which resulted in increased production of industrial goods on the part of Europe and the United States and a demand for industrial minerals and agricultural products from the Latin American countries.

Following the establishment of order and the consolidation of a national government in Mexico, the modernization undertaken by the administration of Porfirio Díaz resulted in a dramatic expansion of trade as well as foreign investment, and an increased foreign presence—U.S. mining and agricultural interests, French financial groups, British electric power companies, and British and U.S. petroleum interests. European immigrants, particularly from France and Spain, established manufacturing and commercial enterprises. In the meantime, contractors hired by U.S. companies recruited Mexicans to work on railroads and in agriculture and mining in the U.S. Southwest, with Mexicans workers often working for the same company on both sides of the border.

The Porfiriato and the Mexican revolution coincided with the expansion of U.S. economic and military intervention in Latin America, notably Central America and the Caribbean. During the Mexican Revolution the United States intervened directly and indirectly (through moves to block arms transfers over the border in favor of specific revolutionary groups). In the immediate post-revolutionary period U.S. petroleum and mining interests in Mexico, supported by threats of U.S. military intervention, succeeded in blocking Mexican government initiatives to increase its control over natural resources.

The depression of the 1930s led to severe cutbacks in exports in Mexico and other Latin American countries and led to various experiments in state economic intervention in Europe and the United States. Mexican policy makers trained in Europe came back with Keynesian ideas calling for a more prominent state role in the economy, which reinforced efforts by post-revolutionary governments to rebuild the economy through such initiatives as the creation of state financial institutions and support to private banks and firms. The Cárdenas government also instituted certain policies to expand the economy, including investment in infrastructure and tariff protection and tax breaks for new and necessary industries. With the expropriation of the U.S. and British owned oil companies in 1938, it affirmed the role of the state in Mexico's economic development; state control of oil and railroads, and subsequently other key industries such as electric power and telecommunications, also provided inputs to industries at subsidized prices. At the same time, in inter-American forums, the Cárdenas government affirmed principles of national sovereignty and non-intervention specifically aimed at curbing U.S. intervention in the region.

During World War II, Mexico collaborated closely with the U.S. war effort, including launching the bracero program in which thousands of Mexicans were recruited to work in the United States, which established a pattern of migration, particularly from the west central states, that would continue to the present. The program was extended until 1964, by which time many Mexicans had found more permanent jobs and were settling in the United States, and migrant networks had been formed facilitating future migration.

During the 1970s, U.S. and other foreign banks provided extensive loans to several Latin American economies, including Mexico, which had taken advantage of growing oil prices to embark on an ambitious program to develop and exploit its oil resources. This had the ironic effect of shifting Mexico's trade profile from a growing exporter of industrial goods to a primary commodity exporter, dependent on the price of oil in the international market.

With rapid developments in transportation and in communications and information technology during the last decades of the 20th century, advanced industrial countries began to enter a post-industrialist phase in which industrial jobs were increasingly outsourced to other parts of the world to take advantage of cheaper labor and/or proximity to markets, resulting in increased concern with the opening of trade and capital markets. These changes were accompanied by an ideological shift spearheaded by the United States and Britain, from a Keynesian emphasis on state involvement in markets to a reassertion of classical liberalism, or what some would call an extreme version of liberalism, based on a market economy with little or no intervention by the state.

The economic crisis beginning in 1982 revealed the extent of Mexico's economic dependence as oil prices declined while interest rates, and thus the cost of loan repayment, increased. With the debt crisis, Mexico as well as other Latin American countries became dependent on loans from international financial institutions (IFIs), particularly the International Monetary Fund and the World Bank, which took advantage of the situation to not only foster economic stabilization but also promote the new market model, conditioning loans on structural adjustment programs that called for the privatization of state enterprises, reduction of government regulation, the elimination of all forms of trade protection, and the opening of capital markets. While this was a response to what some saw as the failure and ineffectiveness of state-led development models, at the same time it would facilitate access of transnational corporations, banks, and other economic interests to foreign—in this case, Latin American—trade and capital markets.

In the case of Mexico, these reforms were also promoted by U.S.-trained technocrats who became predominant in the PRI government during the 1980s and 1990s, facilitated by the strong presidential system. The privatization of state-owned companies drew investment from foreign companies, often as partners of domestic investors, while the creation and growth of the Mexican stock market and the issue of government bonds at high interest rates attracted portfolio investment from foreign banks and investment houses. Some of this investment was hastily withdrawn in the context of fears of devaluation in 1993–94 and particularly the series of political crises of 1994, an important factor in the peso devaluation and subsequent crisis in 1994–1995, again revealing the vulnerability of the Mexican economy to external forces.

Transnational corporations in Mexico, such as General Motors, participated in consultations leading to NAFTA that, as anticipated, attracted direct investment by foreign companies seeking the advantage of cheap labor and access to U.S. markets (chiefly from the United States but also Canada, Europe, and Asia) and was a major element in the rapid growth of the maquila industries in the 1990s. Foreign direct investment in Mexico culminated in 2001 with the opening of the banking sector to foreign investment. The opening of certain sectors previously monopolized as a result of privatization, such as telecommunications, has also brought new investment.

In the late 20th and early 21st centuries, other foreign states, notably China, a have begun to play an important role in several Latin American countries which have, in turn, sought relations with other parts of the world, notably countries of the south, in which Brazil, and more recently Venezuela under Chavez, have taken a prominent role. Given its economic relation with the United States, Mexico has been less directly involved in such initiatives, but it has negotiated free trade agreements with the EU as well as several Latin American countries. In the meantime, the increase in U.S. foreign trade agreements with other countries and the dramatic economic expansion of China and its incorporation into the World Trade Organization have virtually eliminated the initial advantages of NAFTA for Mexico as a source of cheap labor with preferential access to U.S. markets. Some investors in Mexico have shifted production to other countries where labor is cheaper; and China's export of cheap consumer goods to the United States and Mexico has undercut Mexican exports to the United States as well as production for its own domestic market. In addition, Mexico's heavy dependence on the United States, which receives 90 percent of its exports, makes it highly vulnerable to changes in the U.S. economy, as evident in the economic recession beginning in 2008.

In summary, the composition of the most relevant foreign actors in Mexico and the nature of external and international influences have changed over time. External actors have developed relations with Mexican political and socioeconomic actors which are generally asymmetrical but also fluctuate and may be conflictual or congruent, coercive or collaborative. Following Mexico's independence from the Spanish crown, the most relevant external actor has been the United States, which has on various occasions asserted its military and political hegemony. Mexico's relations with the United States are more congenial today, in part due to an increased ideological congruence and to collaboration on a variety of issues. Economic actors have ranged from corporations in extractive industries to transnational corporations in manufacturing, foreign banks, and international lending agencies. Mexico's economic dependency and vulnerability has also fluctuated over time, taking the form of excessive export dependency, especially during the oil boom, and dependence on foreign loans—ultimately culminating in the economic crises of the 1980s. The heavy dependence on port-folio capital in the 1990s was a factor in the peso crisis in 1994–95, and the dependence on exports and particularly trade with the United States has made Mexico excessively vulnerable to the current economic recession.

Mexico continues to be a source of cheap flexible labor for the United States through migration, particularly undocumented migration, which enables U.S. agricultural interests and contractors to hire workers at low wages. Migration from Mexico to the United States is in many respects a function of ongoing relations between the two countries: apart from the fact that the new border between the United States and Mexico following the Mexican American War divided Mexicans between the two countries, some of the most important episodes of Mexican-U.S. migration had their origins in direct labor recruit-ment of Mexican labor by contractors in the United States, as evident in the recruitment of Mexican workers during the Porfiriato, or the bracero program beginning in the 1940s. Subsequent migration has been prompted by condi-tions of poverty in the home country as well as the availability of employment opportunities in the neighboring country, further facilitated by migrant networks established between Mexicans in the United States and their home communities.

Mexican migrants in the United States, and to a lesser degree in other coun-tries, can to a certain extent be considered "external actors"—or more precisely, transnational actors, with social and cultural, economic and political ties on both sides of the border. They are of increasing importance for Mexico, given the significance of their remittances not only in supporting their families but also in contributing to Mexico's financial resources. Hometown associations contribute to civic projects and physical infrastructure in their home communities, which draw on government contributions but at the same time they are taking on what should be the government's role. In some cases, migrants and/or hometown associations have had a significant political role in their home communities. Hometown associations and other binational organizations have also increased institutional links between the United States and Mexico.

Finally, globalization has resulted in the increased role of international advocacy groups and other foreign NGOs, as well as the growth of cross-border links between counterpart organizations in Mexico and other countries. Inter-national solidarity organizations have supported the Zapatistas in Chiapas; coa-litions of labor, environmental and other groups have formed cross-border alliances with maquila workers and have also supported initiatives by peasants and indigenous groups to protect the environment; and human rights organiza-tions as well as women's groups have brought attention to the murder of young women in Juárez and other human rights abuses. NAFTA negotiations were an important catalyst in the establishment of cross-border alliances that linked

Canadian and U.S. environmental, labor, human rights and other groups with their counterparts in Mexico.

UNRESOLVED ISSUES AND NEW CHALLENGES

The Mexico of 2010 is far different from that of 1810 and 1910. It is in many respects a modern industrial country with a relatively large middle class; traditional social groups and classes have changed and new groups have emerged. Mexico has made a significant political transition from an authoritarian regime toward a more pluralistic and relatively democratic system, which in turn has broadened political access for formerly excluded groups of the population. Mexico's integration with the United States has become more pronounced and includes cultural, demographic and social as well as economic relations at all levels.

At the same time, Mexico confronts numerous challenges—some of them traditional problems that have taken new forms, some of them completely new. Mexico's openness to the world economy has had mixed results, and its increased integration with the United States has aggravated its dependence on the U.S. economy, which can be beneficial in periods of U.S. growth but has proved to be disastrous in times of recession. Problems of poverty and inequality have persisted over the centuries in various modes and have political, social and economic ramifications. Poverty and lack of opportunity have also been important factors in the increase in migration beginning in the 1980s and in the growing presence of drug cartels in the past two decades. Elements of clientelism, corruption, and impunity endure in spite of Mexico's shift to a more democratic system, and Mexico's judicial system suffers from an absence of due process and full respect for the rule of law. The Mexican state is less repressive than in the past, but it has not hesitated to use military force against dissident groups and protest movements, and human rights abuses often go unpunished.

Government officials at various levels, business groups, as well as foreign interests, have attempted to address some of these issues. With few exceptions, however, the solutions have been those of the elites. Those groups that have been most disadvantaged by the changes of recent years have often been excluded from the process of decision making over these policies. At the same time, through their organization and mobilization, many of these groups have demanded a response from more powerful groups and have been important catalysts, direct and indirect, in social reform and in the process of political transition. Their economic, social and political incorporation continues to be a major challenge confronting Mexico.

Notes

CHAPTER 1

1. Hundreds of indigenous cultures and civilizations had flourished throughout the Americas prior to the arrival of the Europeans, but the only other large empire at the time was that of the Inca in the Andean region of South America.

2. Although there have been numerous revolts, regional wars, military coups and revolutionary movements throughout Latin American history, there have been very few social revolutions—which involve the mobilization of subordinate groups and classes resulting in substantial change in the social and political structure of a given society. That of Mexico was the first such revolution in the twentieth century; there were three others—those of Bolivia, Cuba, and of the Sandinistas in Nicaragua.

CHAPTER 2

1. General sources on Mexican history include Bethell, *Mexico since Independence*; Joseph and Henderson, *The Mexican Reader*; Krauze, *Mexico: Biography of Power*; McLachlan and Beezley, *El Gran Pueblo*; Meyer et al, *The Course of Mexican History*, and Ruiz, *Triumphs and Tragedy*.

2. Sources on pre-Colombian Mexico include Adams, *The Origins of Mayan Civilization*; Coe, *Mexico: From the Olmecs to the Aztecs*; Díaz del Castillo, *The Conquest of New Spain*; Katz, *The Ancient American Civilizations*; Thompson, *The Rise and Fall*; and Wolf, *Sons of the Shaking Earth*.

3. Bonfil Batalla, *Mexico Profundo*, 62, xv. For examples of all three interpretations, see the excerpts from José Vasconcelos, "The Cosmic Race"; Octavio Paz, *Labyrinth of Solitude*; and Guillermo Bonfil Batalla, *México Profundo*, in Joseph and Henderson, *The Mexican Reader*, 15–32.

4. Sources on the Spanish conquest and the colonial period include, among others, Bethell, *Colonial Spanish America*; Chevalier, *Land and Society*; Díaz del Castillo, *The Conquest of New Spain*; Florescano, Orígen y desarrollo; Martínez, *Genealogical Fictions*; Prescott, *History of the Conquest*; Semo, *The History of Capitalism*; and Tutino, *From Insurrection to Resolution*.

5. See Servín et al, *Cycles of Conflict*.

6. The term *cacique* is actually from the Taino population of the Caribbean; the Spaniards brought it to New Spain. See Middlebrook, "Caciquismo and Democracy," for a discussion of the meaning of *caciquismo*.

7. Vasco de Quiroga, a bishop who worked among the Tarascans of Michocán, established communities throughout the region based on specialization in a particular craft, such as carpentry, metalworking, ceramics or textiles.

8. See Vaughan and Lewis, *The Eagle and the Virgin*.

9. See discussion in Martínez, *Genealogical Fictions*.

10. Cited in Krauze, *Biography of Power*, 112.

11. See Katz, "The Liberal Republic and the Porfiriato," and various essays in Fowler, *Gobernantes mexicanos*, tomo I.

12. On the Porfiriato, see especially various chapters in Cosio Villegas, *Historia moderna de Mexico*; other sources include Coatsworth, *Growth Against Development*; Cumberland, *Mexico: The Struggle for Modernity*; Katz "The Liberal Republic"; and Leal, *La Burguesía*.

13. On the emergence of investment groups during the Porfiriato see Hamilton, *The Limits of State Autonomy*, 46–51, 307–316. On the Monterrey group, see Saragoza, *The Monterrey Elite*.

14. There is a vast literature on the Mexican revolution; a major source is the two-volume work of Knight, *The Mexican Revolution*. See also Aguilar Camín and Meyer, *In the Shadow of the Mexican Revolution*; Gilly, *La revolución interruptida*; Joseph and Nugent, *Everyday Forms of State Formation*; Katz, *Life and Times of Pancho Vista*; Reed, *Insurgent Mexico*; Tutino, *From Insurrection to Revolution*; and Womack, "The Mexican Revolution," and *Zapata and the Mexican Revolution*. See also the 23-volume work published by the Colegio de Mexico, *Historia de la Revolución Mexicana*, which covers the period from the revolution until 1960.

15. On the Liberal party, see Cockcroft, *Intellectual Precursors*.

16. Allegedly Villa shot a man (in different versions, the son of the owner or an administrator) who had attempted to rape his sister.

17. Krauze, *Mexico: Biography of Power*, 359

18. Cited in Meyer, et al.

19. On the Cristero rebellion, see Meyer, *The Cristero Rebellion*.

20. On Mexico's negotiation with the International Bankers Committee, see Smith, *The United States and Revolutionary Nationalism*.

21. On Mexico's relations with the oil companies, see Meyer, *Mexico y los Estados Unidos*.

22. The Comintern, or Communist International, was a worldwide organization of communist parties, which at that time was under the leadership of the Russian Communist party.

23. On Mexican labor during this period, see Carr, *El movimiento obrero*, and Middlebrook, *The Paradox of Revolution*.

24. Vaughan, *Cultural Politics in Revolution*, 30.

25. See Vaughan, *Cultural Politics in Revolution*, on education during the 1920s and 1930s.

26. See Babb, *Managing Mexico*.

27. For information on the Cárdenas administration , see Anguiano, *El estado y la política obrera*; Córdova, *La política de masas del cardenismo*; Gonzalez, *Los artifices del Cardenismo* and *Los días del presidente Cárdenas*; Hamilton, *The Limits of State Autonomy*; Hernández Chavez, *La mecánica del* cardenismo; and Knight, "The Rise and Fall" and "Lázaro Cárdenas."

28. Cárdenas, *Obras: 1-Apuntes.*

29. Vaughan, *Cultural Politics in Revolution.*

30. On the oil expropriation, see Meyer, *México y los Estados Unidos.*

31. The Cárdenas government supported the republicans during the Spanish Civil War against the forces of Franco, providing military aid during the war and, when the republicans were defeated, opening Mexico to Spanish refugees; a total of 30,000 Spanish refugees came to Mexico at that time (Knight, "The Rise and Fall of Cardenismo," 284–85).

CHAPTER 3

1. The bracero program will be further discussed in Chapter 7.

2. See Bethel and Roxborough, *Latin America between the Second World War and the Cold War,* 1–32.

3. The Pax Priista, or peace of the PRI (the current incarnation of the party) is seen as parallel to the Pax Porfirista, the long period of political stability preceding the revolution.

4. Information on the elections of 1941 and their implications can be found in Hamilton, *The Limits of State Autonomy,* 254–267; Knight, "The Rise and Fall of Cardenismo," 296–302; and Medina, *Del cardenismo al avilacamachismo.*

5. On the Alemán administration, see Krauze, *Biography of Power*; Martínez, "El Modelo Económico"; and Smith, "Mexico since 1946."

6. Knight, "The Rise and Fall of Cardenismo," 315.

7. The term *charro* refers to a Mexican horseman or cowboy, characterized by a particular form of dress; *charrismo* is derived from the fact that the state-imposed leader of the railroad workers dressed as a *charro.*

8. The use of office for personal enrichment, as well as the retirement of government officials into private business, was not new; as noted in Chapter 2; the pattern was established in the immediate post-revolutionary period. However, it reached new levels during the administration of Alemán (Krauze, *Biography of Power,* 555–57).

9. Zotov, "Discovering a Land," 262. For a discussion of the government's use of media and education, see Vaughan, "Transnational Processes," 471–78; and Schmidt, "Making It Real." As in the past, cultural initiatives were oriented not only to disseminating an ideological orientation and consolidating a national consensus, but also to behavior modification. As peasants migrated from the countryside to work in the new factories, films and comic books served to acclimate them to the city.

10. Information on the Mexican political system during this period can be found in Camp, *Politics in Mexico;* Collier and Collier, *Shaping the Political Arena;* Cornelius and Craig, *The Mexican Political System in Transition;* Knight, "The Rise and Fall of Cardenismo"; Smith, "Mexico since 1946"; and Wilkie, *The Mexican Revolution.*

11. The Peruvian author, Mario Vargas Llosa, called Mexico "the perfect dictatorship." Some studies of modernization and political development in the post-war period in effect equated political stability with political development. A major proponent of this thesis, Samuel Huntington, argued that the disruptions accompanying the rapid economic modernization of developing countries could result in a high level of social mobilization and conflict, at a time when political institutions were weak and unable to channel and control political conflict (Huntington, *Political Order in Changing Societies*).

12. Hellman, *Mexican Lives*.

13. About a year before the selection, approximately three to six pre-candidates, often from the president's cabinet, became known as front-runners. Described popularly as *tapados*, meaning veiled or masked ones, they were subjects of considerable speculation and political maneuvering by those wanting to be on the good side of the incoming president. Several months prior to the election the candidate was revealed, or "unveiled" (*destapado*).

14. On the import substitution model, also referred to as inward-looking development, see Bulmer-Thomas, *Economic History,* 270–279.

15. See Bulmer-Thomas, *Economic History,* for a review of Latin American economic development since independence, especially 1–18. See Moreno-Brid and Ros, *Development and Growth in the Mexican Economy* for a historical analysis of the Mexican economy.

16. On the role of the state in late-developing countries, see Gerschenkron, *Economic Backwardness*. On the Mexican state, see Bennett and Sharpe, *Transnational Corporations*; Cypher, *State and Capital in Mexico*; Hamilton and Harding, *Modern Mexico*; Hansen, *The Politics of Mexican Development*; Hewlett and Weinert, *Brazil and Mexico;* Story, *Public Power in Mexico*; and Vernon, *Dilemma of Mexican Development* and *Private Enterprise in Mexico*.

17. Hamilton, *The Limits of State Autonomy*; Moreno-Brid and Ros, *Development and Growth*.

18. Evans and Gereffi, "Foreign Investment," 127–146.

19. On the origins and development of the Mexican automobile industry, see Bennett and Sharpe, *Transnational Corporations*.

20. On the implementation and implications of Mexico's economic miracle, see, in addition to the sources in note 16, Levy and Szekeley, *Mexico: Paradoxes*; and Graham, "Mexican and Brazilian Economic Development."

21. Levy and Székely, *Mexico: Paradoxes*, 132–138.

22. On the origins and early development of the Mexican economic groups, see Cordero and Santín, *Los grupos industriales*; Hamilton, *The Limits of State Autonomy*, and "The State and the National Bourgeoisie"; and Saragoza, *The Monterrey Elite*.

23. Meyer, "Historical Roots of the Authoritarian State," 14.

24. Smith, "Mexico since 1946," 358.

25. Middlebrook, *The Paradox of Revolution,* 214.

26. Kaufman, "Economic Orthodoxy and Political Change."

27. On labor during the post-war period, see Bizberg, *Estado y Sindicalismo;* Collier, "Popular Sector Incorporation." Middlebrook, *The Paradox of Revolution*; Roxborough, "Mexico"; and Zapata, *El Conflicto Laboral*.

28. On the development of agriculture during this period, see Barkin, *Distorted Development*; Bartra, *Agrarian Structure*; Hansen, *The Politics of Mexican Development*. On the Green Revolution in Mexico, see Hewitt de Alcántara, *La modernización de la agricultura Mexicana*.

29. On changes in Mexico's income distribution during this period, see Felix, "Income Distribution Trends."

30. On labor mobilization during the post war period, see Middlebrook, *Paradox of Revolution,* 105–55, and Roxborough, "Mexico."

31. Middlebrook, *Paradox of Revolution,* 107–55.

32. See Pellicer de Brody and Reyna, *Historia de la Revolución Mexicana*, 157–214.

33. Harvey, "The Chiapas Rebellion."

34. On the student rebellion of 1968, see Hellman, *Mexico in Crisis,* 173–186; Krause, *Biography of Power,* 694–722; and Poniatowska, *Massacre in Mexico*.

35. This article had been inserted in the penal code during the 1940s due to concerns regarding actions by Nazi and fascist movements in Mexico.

36. Poniatowska, *Massacre in Mexico*, 53.

37. Cited in Poniatowska, *Massacre in Mexico*, 54–55.

38. Jorge Aviles R., "Serious Fighting for Hours between Terrorists and Soldiers," cited in Poniatowska, *Massacre in Mexico*, 226.

39. Cited in Poniatowska, *Massacre in Mexico*, 223.

40. Ibid., 230.

41. Ibid., 238.

42. Luis Gonzalez de Alba, cited in Poniatowska, *Massacre in Mexico*, 6.

43. The "third world" referred to "less developed" or "developing" countries, generally in Asia, Africa and Latin America, to distinguish them from the "first world" of advanced capitalist countries and the "second world" of Communist countries, the Soviet Union and East Europe. In the context of the Cold War, the leadership of these countries took the position of non-alignment with either the East or the West, and in some cases promoted a "third way" distinct from both Communism and capitalism.

44. Dos Santos, "The Structure of Dependence."

45. There is a vast literature on dependency, underdevelopment, and dependent development as well as critiques of the dependency approach. Among the most well-known are Frank, *Capitalism and Underdevelopment*; and Cardoso and Faletto, *Dependency and Development*. On dependent development in Latin America, see Evans, *Dependent Development*; Evans and Gereffi, "Foreign Investment and Dependent Development"; and Gereiffi, *The Pharmaceutical Industry*.

46. The new military regimes in Latin America have been characterized as "bureaucratic authoritarian" regimes; they differed from previous military governments in terms of their institutionalization and durability and their economic development agendas as well as their extreme degree of repression. See O'Donnell, *Modernization and Bureaucratic Authoritarianism,* and Collier, *The New Authoritarianism*.

47. On the Echeverría government, see Hellman, *Mexico in Crisis*; Krause, *Mexico, Biography of Power*; and Casteñeda, *Perpetuating Power*. On economic policy, see Levy and Szekeley, *Mexico: Paradoxes*, 153–156.

48. De la Garza Toledo, "Independent Trade Unionism."

49. Efforts to modify the tax structure under Echeverría are discussed in Maxfield, *Governing Capital*.

50. Levy and Szekeley, *Mexico: Paradoxes*, 138.

51. On the economy, see Lustig, *Mexico: The Remaking of the Economy*. On CONASUPO, see Grindle, *Bureaucrats, Politicians and Peasants*.

52. The editor Julio Scherer García went on to establish the prestigious weekly news magazine *Proceso*. Several journalists, including some associated with *Excelsior*, as well as intellectuals, many of whom had initially supported Echeverría for his promises of reform, went on to establish other newspapers or journals, including the newspaper *Uno Mas Uno* (and later *La Jornada* as a result of a split in the *Uno Mas Uno* group), as well as academic journals. This marked the beginning of the breakdown of the system of media control. See Lawson, "Building the Fourth Estate."

53. On Mexico's oil policy, see Levy and Szekeley, *Mexico: Paradoxes*. The debate regarding the development and use of oil resources is discussed in Cordera and Tello, *Mexico: La disputa por la nación,* and Maxfield, *Governing Capital*.

54. On the roots of Mexico's economic crisis, see, among others, González Casanova and Aguilar Camin, *Mexico ante la crisis*; Lustig, *Mexico: The Remaking of an Economy*; and Teichman, *Policy-making in Mexico*.

55. Villarreal, "The Latin American Strategy of Import Substitution."

56. Levy and Szekely, *Mexico: Paradoxes*.

57. Bennett and Sharpe, *Transnational Corporations*, 239, 273.

58. Lustig, *Mexico: The Remaking of an Economy*.

CHAPTER 4

1. While the term globalization is often used to refer to the increase in international economic integration resulting from the rapid growth and increased scope of trade and financial transactions, it also may include other types of international transactions and influences, such as social and cultural, that have increased as a result of advances in communications and information technology.

2. Discussion of globalization and international economic integration can be found in Frieden, *Debt, Development and Democracy*; Garrett, "The Causes of Globalization"; and Stiglitz, *Globalization and Its Discontents*, among others.

3. See Babb, *Managing Mexico*, 173.

4. The term neoliberalism refers to the resemblance to classical liberalism, which was the dominant economic paradigm in Latin America in the late 19th and early 20th centuries, but neoliberalism goes much further in eliminating the role of the state in favor of the market and private enterprise.

5. Harvey, "Neoliberalism as Creative Destruction," 21–44.

6. The components of the "Washington consensus" can be found in Williamson, "What Washington Means."

7. As noted in Chapter 3, the IMF and the World Bank were established in 1946 and are part of the United Nations. The purpose of the IMF was to maintain international monetary stability and promote international trade; it provides loans to countries confronting severe balance of payments problems, generally conditioned on implementing certain reforms. The World Bank (Bank for International Construction and Development) was initially oriented to the reconstruction of Europe following World War II; subsequently it provided loans to developing countries for infrastructure and other projects.

8. Krueger, "Government Failures in Development"; Dornbusch, "The Case for Trade Liberalization."

9. Villareal, "The Latin American Strategy." For a discussion of the achievements of the Latin American countries under previous state-guided models, see Silva, "The Import Substitution Model."

10. Parallel changes occurred in the educational training of government officials in Mexico. Whereas formerly the majority of officials were trained at UNAM, those taking leading economic positions within the government were increasingly educated at private institutions, notably ITAM (Autonomous Technological Institute of Mexico) where neoclassical economic training prevailed. See Babb, *Managing Mexico*.

11. Discussion of the implications of education and advanced degrees in U.S. universities can be found in Golob, "'Making Possible What is Necessary'"; Stallings, "International Influence"; and Teichman, "The Politics of Free Markets." For information on the Mexican case, see Babb, *Managing Mexico*; Camp, "Camarillas in Mexican Politics"; Centeno,

Democracy within Reason; Centeno and Maxfield, "The Marriage of Finance and Order"; and Golob, "Beyond the Policy Frontier."

12. On the role of the state and the importance of insulation of state technocrats in economic reform, see Evans, *Embedded Autonomy*; Haggard and Kaufman, *The Political Economy*; and Kahler, "External Influence." On the case of Mexico, see Kaufman, "Economic Orthodoxy." The abstract nature of much economic theory which makes it inaccessible to the general public also facilitates the ability of economists to claim expertise and to isolate them from popular pressures, and helps them to perpetuate their position. See discussion in Babb, *Managing Mexico*, 212–219.

13. Discussion of government efforts to attract foreign and flight capital can be found in Schneider, *Business, Politics, and the State*; and Lustig, *Mexico: The Remaking of an Economy*, among others.

14. On the development of exports among private sector groups, see Heredia, "Profits, Politics and Size"; and de los Angeles Pozas, *Industrial Restructuring in Mexico*.

15. See discussion in Golob, "'Making Possible What is Necessary'"; Luna Ledesma, *Los Empresarios*; Schneider, *Business, Politics, and the State*; Thacker, *Big Business, the State, and Free Trade*; Valdez Ugalde, "Bank Nationalization to State Reform."

16. Burgess, "Loyalty Dilemmas" and "Mexican Labor at a Crossroads"; Murillo, *Labor Unions*, Zapata, "Mexican Labor in a Context of Political, Social, and Economic Change."

17. On the restructuring of the banking system, see Garrido and Puga, "Transformaciónes del empresariado mexicano," 144–145; Maxfield, "International Economic Opening," 224–225. On debt negotiations, see Lustig, *Mexico: The Remaking of an Economy*; and Schneider, *Business, Politics, and the State*.

18 On monetary stabilization, see Lustig, *Mexico: The Remaking of an Economy*, 29–30, 80–81; Pastor and Wise, "Mexican Style Neo-Liberalism," 122–123.

19. On the principles of trade liberalization, see Dornbusch, "The Case for Trade Liberalization"; and Williamson, "What Washington Means." On its implementation in Mexico, see Lustig, *Mexico: The Remaking of an Economy*; Moreno-Brid and Ros, *Development and Growth*.

20. *El Financiero International*, various issues.

21. Cited in Hellman, *Mexican Lives*.

22. On the privatization process in Mexico, see Bazdresch and Elizondro, "Privatization: The Mexican Case"; Haber et al, *Mexico Since 1980*; MacLeod, *Downsizing the State*; and Ramamurti, "The Impact of Privatization."

23. In the case of bank privatizations, the purchasers were allowed to borrow from the banks they were buying. Haber et al, *Mexico since 1980*, 105.

24. Zuñiga, "66 percent de los depósitos bancarios."

25. According to a 2002 report by the OECD, TELMEX had one of the highest phone rates in the world. As of 2006, it controlled 90 percent of fixed telephone lines and 80 percent of cellular phones in Mexico. Haber et al, *Mexico since 1980*, 89–90.

26. Thacker, *Big Business, the State, and Free Trade*.

27. Lustig, *Mexico: The Remaking of an Economy*, 108–111, 128–130; Thacker, *Big Business, the State, and Free Trade*, 125–127.

28. On the impact of economic liberalization on labor, see Bacon, *The Children of NAFTA*; Colegio de México, *Ajuste Structural, Mercados Laborales, y TLC*; La Botz, *Mask of Democracy*; de la Garza, "Manufacturing Neoliberalism"; Middlebrook, *Unions, Workers,*

and the State, and *The Paradox of Revolution*; Murillo, *Labor Unions* and Zapata, *Flexibles y Productivos?*

29. See Middlebrook, *The Paradox of Revolution*, 226–227.

30. Appendini, "Changing Agrarian Institutions"; De Grammont, *The Agricultural Sector*; Hamilton et al, "Household Welfare," 434; Cornelius and Myhre, "Introduction"; Myhre, "The Achilles' Heel of Reforms."

31. Cornelius and Myhre, "Introduction," 4–5.

32. Appendini, "Changing Agrarian Institutions," 256.

33. Tellez Kunzler, cited in De Grammont, "The Agricultural Sector," 352.

34. Cornelius and Myhre "Introduction," 4–5.

35. Barkin, "The Reconstruction of a Modern Mexican Peasantry"; De Ita, "Mexico: Impacts of Demaraction."

36 . A partial exception consists of the large ejidos, chiefly on irrigated land, which are already productive and oriented to export and consist of approximately 10 percent of the total (Cornelius and Myhre, "Introduction").

37. Appendini, "The Challenges to Rural Mexico," 258–261; Hamilton et al, "Household Welfare," 445–450; Wiggins et al, "Agricultural Policy Reform."

38. Hamilton et al, 2002, "Household Welfare," 451–2; Appedini, "The Challenges to Rural Mexico," 267–269.

39. Efforts by subsequent administrations to deal with the poverty issue will be discussed in Chapter 5.

40. Sources on NAFTA include Dussel Peters, "Industrial Policies, Regional Trends"; Golob, "Beyond the Policy Frontier"; Lustig, *Mexico: The Remaking of an Economy*; Maxfield and Shapiro, "Assessing the NAFTA Negotiations"; Studer, "Obstacles to Integration"; Thacker, *Big Business, the State, and Free Trade*; and Wise, "NAFTA, Mexico and the Western Hemisphere," and "No Turning Back."

41. Lustig, *Mexico: The Remaking of an Economy*.

42. Wise, *The Post-NAFTA Political Economy*, 10–11.

43. Golob, "Beyond the Policy Frontier," 376–378; Thacker, *Big Business, the State, and Free Trade*, 128–129.

44. During the U.S. legislative debate, a North American Development Bank was established; but its scope and funding have been limited.

45. Studer, "Obstacles to Integration"; Wise, "Unfulfilled Promise."

46. Thacker, *Big Business, the State, and Free Trade*, 143–152, 173–182.

47. Maxfield and Shapiro, "Assessing the NAFTA Negotiations," 83, 117–118.

48. Barkin, "The Reconstruction of a Modern Mexican Peasantry," 80; Appendini, "The Challenges to Rural Mexico," 266.

49. See Cook, "Regional Integration," 527–28, 536; Fox, "Assessing Binational Civil Society Coalitions"; and Wise, "The North American Free Trade Agreement." Cross-border organizing is further discussed in Chapter 6.

50. Pastor and Wise, "Mexican Style Neo-Liberalism."

51. Carrillo, "The Apparel Maquiladora Industry"; Hanson, "Industrial Organization."

52. Bennett and Sharpe, *Transnational Corporations vs. the State*, 274; Whiting, *The Political Economy of Foreign Investment*.

53. Shaiken, *Mexico in the Global Economy*.

54. Dussel Peters, "Industrial Policies," 263–265.

55. Mattar et al, "Foreign Investment in Mexico," 147.

56. Camp, *Politics in Mexico*, 190–193.

57. Lustig, *Mexico: The Remaking of an Economy*, 201–205. Pastor, "Pesos, Policies and Predictions."

58. Mattar et al, "Foreign Investment in Mexico," 153; Dussel Peters "Industrial Policies," 254, 262.

59. Pastor and Wise, "Mexican Style Neo-Liberalism," 51–56; Lustig, *Mexico: The Remaking of an Economy*.

60. Salas and Zepeda, "Employment and Wages."

61. De Grammont, "The Agricultural Sector."

62. Lustig, *Mexico: The Remaking of an Economy*, 262, n. 24; Pastor "Pesos, Policies and Predictions."

63. See Summa, "Mexico's New Super Billionaires. and MacLeod, *Downsizing the State*. Another indication that growth disproportionately benefited high income groups was that retail firms such as Sears and Price Club, normally oriented to middle income groups, openly stated that their clientele was in the top 10–15 percent of the population. According to one Price Club official, the image of a typical Price Club shopper was someone who spends $100 at a time and brings a car "to haul away the loot"—clearly excluding that half of the population that was earning two dollars a day or less. See de Palma, "Mexico's Hunger for U.S. Goods."

64. Dussel Peters, "Industrial Policies," 266.

65. Haber et al, *Mexico since 1980*, 109–110; Lustig, *Mexico: The Remaking of an Economy*, 143–154.

66. Pastor, "Pesos, Policies and Predictions," 125.

67. The Zapatista revolt will be further discussed in Chapter 6.

68. Lustig, *Mexico: The Remaking of an Economy*, 148–150.

CHAPTER 5

1. See Bezdek, "Democratic Changes in an Authoritarian System." Calvillo Unma, "A Case of Opposition Unity." The Nava case also demonstrates the contradiction inherent in PRI efforts to maintain its hegemony while presenting a democratic façade. Thus opposition victories at the local levels might be accepted under certain circumstances, particularly if the candidate in question wins (or is likely to win) by an overwhelming majority, but control of a state government by the opposition was not permitted.

2. See Aguayo Quezado, "Electoral Observation and Democracy in Mexico." Olvera, "Civil Society in Mexico at Century's End."

3. On changes in the media and the growth of the independent media, see Haber et al, *Mexico since 1984*, and Lawson, "Building the Fourth Estate."

4. This discussion of democracy and of democratic transitions in Latin America draws upon Collier, *Paths toward Democracy*; Collier and Mahoney, "Adding Collective Actors"; Haggard and Kaufman, *The Political Economy of Democratic Transitions*; Huber, Rueschemeyer, and Stephens, "The Paradoxes of Contemporary Democracy,"; Karl "Dilemmas of Democratization"; Moore, *Social Origins of Dictatorship and Democracy*; O'Donnell, "On the State, Democratization, and Some Conceptual Problems,"; O'Donnell and Schmitter, "Transitions from Authoritarian Rule"; Przeworski, "Some Problems in the Study of the Transition to Democracy"; Roberts, *Deepening Democracy?*; Rueschemeyer, Huber and Stephens, *Capitalist Development and Democracy*; and Whitehead, "Intellectual Aspects of Democracy."

5. See Przworski, "Some Problems in the Study of the Transition to Democracy."
6. Given the long tradition of military intervention in the political process in much of Latin America, some analysts add civilian control of the military as a necessary element of democracy. This has been less important in Mexico since the 1920s and 1930s, when the military was effectively brought under civilian control.
7. See Moore, Jr., *Social Origins of Dictatorship and Democracy*.
8. On the 1988 electoral campaign and the Salinas administration, see essays in Cornelius et al, *Mexico's Alternative Political Futures*; Cook et al, *The Politics of Economic Restructuring*; Randall, *Changing Structure of Mexico*; Collier, *The Contradictory Alliance*; Dresser, *Neopopulist Soluations to Neoliberal Problems*; and Russell, *Mexico Under Salinas*. On changes under the Salinas and Zedillo administrations, see Crespo, "Party Competition in Mexico"; and Gómez Tagle, "Public Institutions and Electoral Transparency in Mexico."
9. On the PAN, see Loaeza, *Partido Acción Nacional*; Mizrahi, *A New Conservative Opposition in Mexico*; and Shirk, *Mexico's New Politics*. Discussions of the PAN can also be found in Cornelius et al, *Subnational Politics and Democratization*; Rodríguez and Ward, *Opposition Government in Mexico*; and Levy and Bruhn, *Mexico: The Struggle for Democratic Development*.
10. Bruhn, *Taking on Goliath*.
11. See Aguayo Quezado, "Electoral Observation and Democracy in Mexico."
12. See Bezdek, "Democratic Changes in an Authoritarian System"; and Cavillo Umma, "A Case of Opposition Unity."
13. While the PRI representation in the Chamber of Deputies had been between 70 and 90 percent of the total in the 1970s, it was reduced to 60–70 percent in the 1980s, and was just over 50 percent in 1988. Klesner,"Realignment or Dealignment?"
14. Sources on electoral reforms include Crespo, "Party Competition in Mexico: Evolution and Prospects"; Gómez Tagle, "Public Institutions and Electoral Transparency in Mexico"; and Levy and Bruhn, *Mexico: The Struggle for Democratic Development*.
15. Dresser, Denise, *Neopopulist Solutions to Neoliberal Problems*.
16. Fox, "Assessing Binational Civil Society Coalitions."
17. Fox, "Governance and Rural Development," 19.
18. Chand, *Mexico's Political Awakening*.
19. On the banking crisis and Zedillo's economic reforms, see Nadal, "Macroeconomic Challenges"; MacLeod, *Downsizing the State*; and Haber et al, *Mexico since 1980*.
20. Nadal, "Macroeconomic Challenges."
21. On judicial reforms, see Magaloni and Zepeda, "Rule of Law in Mexico."
22. Camp, "Mexico's Armed Forces"; Camp, *Politics in Mexico*.
23. See Pastor and Wise, "Fox Administration and Politics of Economic Transition," 103–104; Dussel Peters, "Mexico's Manufacturing Sector," 250.
24. See Díaz-Cayeros, "Decentralization, Democratization and Federalism in Mexico."
25. On relations between the president and Congress during the Zedillo and Fox administrations, and the implications of divided government (opposition control of the Chamber of Deputies), see Pastor and Wise, "Fox Administration and Politics of Economic Transition," 103–104; Weldon, "Changing Patterns of Executive-Legislative Relations in Mexico"; Dresser, "Mexico: Dysfunctional Democracy"; and Levy and Bruhn, *Mexico: The Struggle for Democratic Development*.
26. On Mexico's political decentralization, see Díaz-Cayeros, "Decentralization, Democratization and Federalism in Mexico."

27. See Shaiken, "Firm Steps on Uncertain Ground," which is based on an interview with Sergio Aguayo.

28. See Haber, et al, *Mexico since 1980*.

29. Sources on anti-poverty programs include Diaz Cayeros, "Decentralization, Democratization and Federalism in Mexico"; Levy , *Progress against Poverty*; Lustig, "Salud y Desarrollo Economico," 296; Ocampo and Alexander, "Back to Basics," 2; Rapoport, "Change and Continuity in Attention to Poverty in Mexico."

30. Moreno-Brid and Ros, *Development and Growth*, 216–219.

31. Díez, "The Importance of Policy Frames." On issues of gay identity in Mexico and the emergence of groups seeking visibility and recognition of the gay community, see Laguarda, *Ser Gay en la Ciudad de México*, and Thing, *Entre Maricones, Machos y Gays."

32. Sources on the 2006 election include Dominguez et al, *Consolidating Mexico's Democracy*; Peschard, *2 de julio*; and various essays in *Latin American Perspectives*; as well as selected articles from the *Latin American Data Base* (www.ladb.unm.edu), the *Los Angeles Times*, and the *New York Times*.

33. Alonso, "Repoliticizing the Electoral Institute."

34. In an effort to pinpoint the causes of this shift, Greene finds that image, particularly perceptions regarding the relative competence of the two major candidates was a major factor ("Images and Issues"). Moreno ("Activism of Economic Voting") suggests that a shift in Calderón's campaign strategy from a focus on moral issues important to the PAN to an emphasis on the continuation of economic growth was also important in mobilizing support from those who saw the economy and their own economic situation as improving. For more on these and other assessments of the 2006 elections, see Domínguez et al, *Consolidating Mexico's Democracy*.

35. See Enríquez, "Mexico City Sit-In Has the Air of a Fiesta"; and Enríquez "Protesting along the Paseo."

36. See Articles from *Associated Press, BBC News*.

37. Klesner, "The 2006 Mexican Elections"; Camp, "Democracy Redux?"

38. Wilkinson and Ellingwood, "Mexico's public is missing in action."

39. According to one source, PEMEX was in effect a tax collection agency for the government. See Moreno-Brid and Ros, *Development and Growth*.

CHAPTER 6

1. Sources on social movements in Latin America include Brooks and Fox, *Cross-Border Dialogues;* Bruhn, *Urban Protest in Mexico and Brazil;* Eckstein, *Power and Popular Protest;* Eckstein and Wickham-Crowley, *Struggles for Social Rights* and *What Justice? Whose Justice;* Escobar and Alvarez, *Social Movements in Latin America;* Hellman, "The Riddle of New Social Movements"; Hochstettler, "Democraizing Pressures from Below" Keck and Sikkink, *Activists Beyond Borders;* Stahler Sholk et al, *Globalizing Resistance;* Yashar, *Contesting Citizenship*. On Mexico, see Bennett, *The Politics of Water*; Foweraker and Craig, *Popular Movements and Political Change;* Fox, "Assessing Binational Civil Society Coalitions"; Haber, "The Art and Implications of Political Restructuring," and *Power from Experience;* and Williams, *Social Movements and Economic Transition*.

2. Escobar and Alvarez, *Social Movements in Latin America*; Keck and Sikkink, *Activists Beyond Borders*.

3. Escobar and Alvarez, *Social Movements in Latin America*; Foweraker and Craig, *Popular Movements and Political Change in Mexico.*

4. See Hellman, "The Riddle of New Social Movements," and "Mexican Popular Movements."

5. See Yashar, *Contesting Citizenship*; Fox, "Assessing Binational Civil Society Coalitions."

6. Hochstettler, "Democratizing Processes from Below.".

7. Eckstein, "Community Mobilization for Housing in Mexico City." Davis, *Urban Leviathan.*

8. Bennett, "Evolution of Urban Popular Movements in Mexico."

9. On CONAMUP, see Bennett, "Evolution of Urban Popular Movements in Mexico" and Stephen, *Women and Social Movements in Latin America.*

10. Davis, *Urban Leviathan,* 236–7, 249–253.

11. Haber, *Urban Popular Movements in Mexico.*

12. Haber, *Urban Popular Movements in Mexico.*

13. Haber, *Urban Popular Movements in Mexico,* 194–196. Hellman, "The Riddle of New Social Movements."

14. Haber, *Urban Popular Movements in Mexico,* 199–200.

15. Davis, *Urban Leviathan,* 285–290. Haber, *Urban Popular Movements in Mexico,* 204–205.

16. The case of Miguel Ramírez, the street vendor discussed in Chapter 3, provides an example of this. Prior to 1988, the vendors' association had been affiliated with the PRI. The head of the association had decided to support the electoral campaign of Cuauhtémoc Cárdenas, and with his defeat in the fraudulent 1988 elections, the association, including Miguel, joined protests and supported the new PRD. The new Salinas government, ostensibly in response to complaints of small businesses, had the vendors moved from a prime location to a much more remote part of the city. Shortly afterward, however, the location was taken over by a new group of vendors under the direction of the PRI.

17. Haber, *Urban Popular Movements in Mexico,* 210–221.

18. Haber, *Urban Popular Movements in Mexico,* 208–209.

19. Sources on Chiapas and the Zapatista movement include Collier, *Zapatista Rebellion in Chiapas*; Harvey, *The Chiapas Rebellion*; Hernández Castillo, *Stories from Chiapas*; Ross, *Rebellion from the Roots*; Rus and Collier, "The Cases of Chamula and Zinacatan"; Rus et al, *Mayan Lives, Mayan Utopias*; and Womack, *Rebellion in Chiapas.*

20. Womack, *Rebellion in Chiapas,* 249.

21. Collier, *Zapatista Rebellion in Chiapas.*

22. Hernández Castillo, *Stories from Chiapas,* 21–26.

23. Collier, *Zapatista Rebellion in Chiapas,* 55–61.

24. Hernández Castillo, *Stories from Chiapas,* 105–107; Collier, *Zapatista Rebellion in Chiapas,* 61–63.

25. Hernández Castillo, *Stories from Chiapas*; Harvey, *The Chiapas Rebellion,* 69–76; Collier, *Zapatista Rebellion in Chiapas,* 61–64.

26. Harvey, *The Chiapas Rebellion.*

27. Harvey, *The Chiapas Rebellion,* 164–168, 194–198.

28. Otero, "Neoliberal Globalism, the State, and Civil Society." Stahler Sholk, "Resisting Neoliberal Homogenization," 50–51, 57.

29. Stephen, *Zapata Lives!* Speed, Hernández Castillo and Stephen, *Dissident Women.*

30. Womack, *Rebellion in Chiapas,* 267–268.

31. Leyva Solano, "Transformations in Las Canadas."
32. Hernández Navarro and Carlsen, "Indigenous Rights," 449.
33. Castellanos, "Marcos after the Rupture"; Stahler-Sholk. "The Zapatista Autonomy Movement."
34. Rus and Collier, "The Cases of Chamula and Zinacatan." Benítez Manout et al, "The Peace Process in Chiapas." Stahler Sholk, et al, *Globalizing Resistance.*
35. Fox, "Assessing Binational Civil Society Coalitions," 505.
36. Stephen, *Zapata Lives!*
37. On the Barzón debtors' movement, see especially Williams, *Markets and Distributive Conflict.*
38. Torres, "The *El Barzón* Debtor's Movement."; Williams, "Free Trade and Debt Bondage," 4.
39. Williams, "Fighting Banks and the State in Mexico," 4.
40. Torres, "The *El Barzón* Debtor's Movement." Williams, *Markets and Distributive Conflict in Mexico.*
41. Williams, *Markets and Distributive Conflict in Mexico.*
42. Torres, "The *El Barzón* Debtor's Movement." Williams, *Markets and Distributive Conflict.*
43. Williams, *Markets and Distributive Conflict.*
44. Torres, "The *El Barzón* Debtor's Movement." Williams, *Markets and Distributive Conflict.*
45. Paterson, "Life and Death of a Mexican Environmental Prophet."
46. Bray et al, *Community Forests of Mexico;* Boyer, "Contested Terrain"; Cienfuegos and Carlsen, "Human Rights, Ecology"; Klooster, "*Campesinos* and Mexican Forest Policy."
47. Cienfuegos and Carlsen. "Human Rights, Ecology"; Silva, "The Politics of Sustainable Development."
48. Silva, "The Politics of Sustainable Development"; Bray et al, *Community Forests of Mexico.*
49. Paterson, "Life and Death of Mexican Environmental Prophet."
50. Sources on Mexican labor include Bacon, *The Children of NAFTA*; Bensusán, "Mexican Trade Unions" and *El modelo mexicano*; Burgess, "Loyalty Dilemmas and Market Reform," ; De la Garza Toledo, "Democracia en tiempos de poscorporativismo"; Middlebrook, *The Paradox of Revolution*; Murillo, *Labor Unions, Partisan Coalitions, Market Reforms*; and Zapata, "Mexican Labor in Context of Change."
51. Burgess, "Loyalty Dilemmas and Market Reform."
52. Fox, "Assessing Binational Civil Society Coalitions," 478.
53. Hathaway, *Allies across the Border.*
54. Williams, *Mobile Capital and Transnational Labor Rights Mobilization.*
55. Cook, "Popular Sector Strategies in the NAFTA Era."
56. Carr, "Globalization from Below," 54–5.
57. Bacon, *The Children of NAFTA.*
58. Bensusán, "A New Scenario for Mexican Trade Unions."; Carr, "Globalization from Below."
59. Bacon, *The Children of NAFTA;* LaBotz, "Mexican Labor Year in Review: 2005"; Zapata, "Mexican Labor in Context of Change."
60. De la Garza Toledo, "Democracia en tiempos de poscorporativismo."
61. Middlebrook, *The Paradox of Revolution,* 296
62. Another split with the Labor Congress occurred at the end of 2004 when Elba Esther Gordillo, leader of the Mexican Teachers' Union, broke off from the Federation of Public

Service Workers Unions to form the Democratic Federation of Public Service Workers Unions.

63. LaBotz, "Mexican Labor Year in Review: 2005."

64. For information on the events of 2006 and the formation of APPO, see the CCIODH report; Esteva, "Asamblea Popular de los Pueblos de Oaxaca"; Latin American Studies Association, "Violations of Freedom of Inquiry and Expression in Oaxaca"; Rénique and Poole, "The Oaxaca Commune"; Stephen, "Reality in the Oaxaca Social Movement"; Weinberg, "Oaxaca: Backward toward Revolution"; as well as articles from the *Los Angeles Times*, the *Latin America Data Base*, *La Jonada en linea*, and the documentary film *Un poquito de tanto verdad* (A little bit of so much truth).

65. Discussion of the teachers' movement can be found in Cook, *Organizing Dissent*.

66. Sources on women in Mexico include Bennett, "Evolution of Popular Movements in Mexico"; Bennett, *The Politics of Water*; Olcott et al, *Sex in Revolution*; Rodríguez, *Women in Contemporary Mexican Politics*, and *Women's Participation in Mexican Politics*; Stephen, "Rural Women's Grassroots Activism" and *Women and Social Movements in Latin America*; and Tarrés, "The Role of Women's Nongovernmental Organizations."

67. Scholars who study women's movements in Latin America frequently distinguish between movements oriented to practical goals, stemming largely from women's traditional roles as mothers and caretakers, and those oriented to strategic goals, calling for an end of abuse and discrimination against women and gender equity.

68. Hellman, "The Riddle of New Social Movements."

69. Davis, *Urban Leviathan*; Olvera, "Civil Society in Mexico at Century's End."

70. Cook, "Popular Sector Strategies in the NAFTA Era," 527–28, 536.

71. Bacon, *The Children of NAFTA*, 91.

CHAPTER 7

1. Sánchez and Tobar, "Relatives in Mexico can only pray for miners."

2. Harris, "Hardship City."

3. Bordeaux, "The Seeds of Promise"; Sánchez and Enriquez, "A Long-Tended Dream."

4. The literature on international migration is vast. For discussions of theoretical approaches to migration, see Massey et al, "Theories of International Migration" and Portes and DeWind, ed., *Rethinking Migration: New Theoretical and Empirical Approaches*. On refugees, see Richmond, "Sociological Theories: The Case of Refugees," and Zolberg, et al, "International Factors in Refugee Movements."

5. Sources on the relationship between globalization and migration include Castles and Miller, *The Age of Migration*, and Sassen, *The Mobility of Labor and Capital*. See also references on transnationalism later in the chapter.

6. For information on assimilation, acculturation, and incorporation, see Hirschman et al, ed., *The Handbook of International Migration*; Portes, *The Economic Sociology of Migration*; and Portes and Rumbaut, *Legacies*; and journals *Ethnic and Racial Studies*, *IMF (International Migration Review*, and *Journal of Ethnic and Migration Studies*.

7. Suarez-Orozco and Qin Hilliard, *Globalization: Culture and Education in the New Millenium*.

8. On transnationalism, see Basch et al, *Nations Unbound*; Glick Schiller et al, "Towards a Transnational Perspective on Migration"; Goldring, "Power and Status in Transnational Social Fields"; Levitt, *Transnational Villagers*; Smith, "Transnational Localities," and *Mexican New York*; Smith and Guarnizo, *Transnationalism from Below*; and Stephen, *Transborder Lives*.

9. See Levitt, *Transnational Villagers* on the concept of social remittances.

10. Weber, "Historical Perspectives on Mexican Transnationalism."

11. See discussion in Fitzgerald, *A Nation of Emigrants*, pp. 15–31.

12. Stephen, *Transborder Lives.*

13. Sources on Mexican migration to the United States include Cornelius, "The Structural Embeddedness of Demand for Mexican Labor"; Cornelius and Bustamante, *Mexican Migration to the United States*; Durand and Massey, *Crossing the Border*; Hellman, *The World of Mexican Migrants*; Hondagneu-Sotelo, *Gendered Transitions*; McWilliams, *North from Mexico*; Massey et al, *Return to Aztlán*; Portes and Bach, *Latin Journey*; Smith, *Mexican New York*; and Suarez-Orozco, *Crossings*. On Mexicans and Mexican Americans in the United States see, in addition to the above, Acuña, *Anything but Mexican*, Gutierrez, "Globalization, Labor Migration, and the Demographic Revolution"; Gómez Quiñones, *Chicano Politics*; and Sánchez, *Becoming Mexican American.*

14. Like many concepts having to do with identity, that of Mexican American is a contentious one. Here it is used to refer to persons of Mexican ancestry born in the United States, while those who immigrated from Mexico (first-generation immigrants) are referred to as Mexicans. The term Latinos refers to those born in the United States of Latin American ancestry as well as immigrants from Mexico and other Latin American countries.

15. Bacon, *The Children of NAFTA*, 253.

16. U.S. citizenship did not apply to the population identified as Indian, although the border also "crossed" many indigenous groups.

17. Allen and Turner, *The Ethnic Quilt*; Moore and Vigil, "Barrios in Transition."

18. Fitzgerald, *A Nation of Emigrants*, 48–54.

19. Durand and Massey, *Crossing the Border,* pp. 8–9. On the migration of Mexican women and families, see Hondagneu-Sotelo, *Gendered Migration.*

20. See Hellman, *The World of Mexican Migrants*, pp. 45–55.

21. Sources on political activism include Acuña, *Anything but Mexican*; Bacon, *Children of NAFTA*; Gómez Quiñones, *Chicano Politics*; Gutiérrez, "Globalization, Labor Migration; and Sánchez, *Becoming Mexican American.*

22. The term Chicano is believed to be a contraction of Mexicano, but it took an explicitly political meaning in the 1960s and 1970s. It is sometimes used as synonymous with Mexican American, but not all Mexican Americans consider themselves Chicanos. Aztlán is the Aztec term for their mythical homeland; today it refers to an area roughly comprising what is now the U.S. Southwest, which was once part of Mexico.

23. The post-crisis migration is discussed in Cornelius, "*Los migrantes de la crisis*."

24. In fact, some jobs may not have existed in the absence of low-wage workers, including many in labor-intensive agriculture, some services and low-wage manufacturing jobs in areas like the garment industry, given the ease with which owners can shift production to other parts of the world. In other cases, such as the building cleaning (janitorial) industry, contractors took advantage of a pool of low-wage workers to open non-union shops in some cities, thus undercutting the wages of unionized workers. Efforts by labor unions to organize immigrants have had some success in improving wages and working conditions in these industries. Studies have also shown that immigrants, including undocumented immigrants, pay taxes, and that they use services (that they are legally entitled to) less frequently than those born in the United States (see National Immigration Law Center).

25. Larsen, "The Anti-Immigration Movement."

26. Andreas, "Politics on Edge."

27. Fox et al, "Conclusions" in *Invisible No More.*

28. Rouse, "Making Sense of Settlement"; Stephen, *Transborder Lives.*

29. Studies have shown that in contrast to men, who look forward to returning to their home country, women tend to favor remaining in the United States, where they are more likely to work outside the home and thus earn an income, giving them greater independence, and are freer from the social constraints they experience in Mexico. See Goldring, "Gendered Memory."

30. Smith, "Transnational Localities."

31. Orozco, "Transnationalism and Development", 312–320.

32. Binford suggests that in some rural communities, remittances may represent up to 90 percent of income (2006, 306).

33. Most analysts agree that those who migrate are usually not the poorest of the population, who generally lack the necessary resources to undertake the border crossing, although poorer groups may benefit from migrant networks established by earlier migrants.

34. Moctezuma Longoria et al, "Laguna Grande."

35. Sources on Mexican hometown associations include García Zamora, *Migración, remesas y desarrollo;* Goldring, "Power and Status in Transnational Social Fields," and "The Mexican State and Transmigrant Organizations"; Shannon, "Invertiendo en la Esperanza"; Smith "Transnational Localities" and *Mexican New York.*. Internal migrants in Mexico also form hometown associations; in some cases these may be more successful than external associations in providing funds for projects in the home community (Fitzgerald, *A Nation of Emigrants,* 121–124).

36. See Felix, "Posthumous Transnationalism"

37. Kraul, "Tapping generosity of immigrants."

38. Olivo and Avila, "Influence on both sides of the border."

39. Ibid.

40. The Cárdenas campaign in the United States and the Mexican government reaction is discussed in Dresser, "Exporting Conflict."

41. Fitzgerald, *A Nation of Emigrants,* 38. Dual nationality gave those Mexicans affected certain rights, such as owning property in areas off-limits to foreigners, but is not identical to dual citizenship.

42. At a meeting in Los Angeles between members of the Zacatecan State Federation of Hometown Associations and over a dozen mayors from communities in Zacatecas, for example, several mayors complained that the clubs wanted funds to go to building rodeo arenas or painting the church in communities lacking electricity or potable water. Federation representatives responded that it was projects such as refurbishing churches that prompted the migrants to organize in the first place, that if the government would support these projects, the migrants would support projects desired by the mayors, and that if the government refused to support the projects of the clubs they would withdraw from the three-for-one program. See Thompson, "Mexico's migrants profit from dollars sent home."

43. On Zacatecan migration, see Delgado Wise and Moctezuma Longoria, "Metamórfosis Migratoria"; Delgado Wise and Rodríguez Ramírez, "Los dilemmas de la migración"; Garcia Zamora, Migración, remeasa y desarrollo"; Goldring, "The Mexican State and Transmigrant Organization"; Moctezuma Longoria, *La organización de los migrantes zacatecanos;* and Moctezuma Longoria et al, *Laguna Grande.*

44. Sources on the Zacatecan clubs include Garcia Zamora, "Migración, remesas y desarrollo"; Goldring, "The Mexican State and Transnational Organizations"; and Moctezuma Longoria, "La organización de los migrantes zacatecanos" and "The Migrant Club El Remolino."

45. Amador and Infante, "El poder político de los migrantes"; Shulman, "Clubs in U.S. Spark Political Change."

46. Sources on migration from Oaxaca include Fox and Rivera-Salgado, *Indigenous Mexican Migrants*; López and Runsten, "Mixtecs and Zapotecs Working in California"; Kearney and Besserer, "Oaxacan Municipal Governance in Transition"; Maldonado and Rodríguez, "Now We Are Awake"; Rivera-Salgado, "Transnational Political Strategies"; Rivera-Salgado and Escala Rabadán, "Collective Identity and Organizational Strategies"; Stephen, "Mixtec Farmworkers in Oregon" and *Transborder Lives*; Velasco Ortiz, "Organizational Experience and Female Participation"; Velásquez C., "Migrant Communities, Gender, and Political Power."

47. Immigrants from Tlacolula began to migrate to the United States in the 1950s, forming networks that facilitated subsequent migration.

48. Durand and Massey, *Crossing the Border*; Stephen, *Transborder Lives*, 5–6.

49. See *Letters from the Other Side* for an evocative film on women and families left behind.

50. Hellman, *The World of Mexican Migrants*.

51. Goldring, "The Gender and Geography of Citizenship"; Stephen, "Mixtec Farmworkers."

CHAPTER 8

1. Attributed to Porfirio Díaz.

2. A. Martínez Camberos, *The New Invaders*, cited by Bachelor, "Toiling for the 'New Invaders.'" Generals Taylor and Scott were involved in the U.S.-Mexican war in the 1840s.]

3. The Latin American countries have also opposed the U.S. position on several other issues, among them the U.S. blockade of Cuba, the vote of Mexico and Chile in the UN Security Council in 2003 opposing UN support for the U.S. proposal to go to war in Iraq, and Latin American opposition to U.S. military bases in Colombia. A summary of some of these issues can be found in Shifter and Joyce, "No Longer Washington's Backyard."

4. The Bank of the South is a South American bank focused on scientific and technical development. UNASUR (Union of South American Nations) is an inter-governmental organization modeled on the European Union with the ultimate goal of achieving economic and political integration of member countries.

5. Pellicer in *Mexico: A Reluctant Middle Power?* argues that Mexico is, in effect, a "two-region" nation, and that this dual position has been a factor in Mexico's failure to take advantage of the opportunity to become a "middle power." At the same time, it could enable Mexico to be an "honest broker" between North and South America.

6. General sources on U.S.-Mexico relations and U.S. policy toward Mexico include Dominguez and Fernández de Castro, *The United States and Mexico*; Mazza, *Don't Disturb the Neighbors*; and Vázquez and Meyer, *Mexico frente a los Estados Unidos*. Current information can be found on several Web sites, including the Americas Program of the International Research Center (http://Americas.irc-online.org), Council on Hemispheric Affairs (www.coha.org), Latin American Data Base (www.ladb.unm.edu), and the Mexico Institute of the Woodrow Wilson Center (www.wilsoncenter.org/mexico),

as well as the *Los Angeles Times* (www.latimes.com/laplaza) and *The New York Times* (http://nytimes.com). For a summary of issues in U.S.-Mexican relations, see Selee, *More Than Neighbors*, and Starr, "A Window of Opportunity?"

7. In addition to sources indicated in note 6, see Wise, "Unfulfilled Promise" and "The North American Free Trade Agreement"; Studer, "Obstacles to Integration"; and Dussel Peters, "Foreign Direct Investment in Mexico." Sources of statistical information include the Secretaría de Economía (Mexico), the U.S. State Department, and UNC-TAD's *World Investment Report* for 2008.

8. Studer, "Obstacles to Integration," 62.

9. Gereffi and Martínez, "Mexico's Economic Transformation under NAFTA."

10. Wise, "The North American Free Trade Agreement," 140.

11. Dussel-Peters, *The Impact of Foreign Direct Investment*, 6–8.

12. Secretaria de Economía. "Exportaciones totales de México."

13. U.S. Department of State, *Background Note: Mexico.*

14. See Cornelius, "Impacts of NAFTA on Mexico-to-U.S. Migration."

15. Moreno-Brid and Ros, *Development and Growth*, 197–199.

16. See Yúnez-Naude and Barceinas, "The Reshaping of Agricultural Policy," 221–223.

17. Wilkinson, "Mexico agricultural subsidies are going astray."

18. Ellingwood, "'No apparent motive.'"

19. Sources on the drug issue include Biettel, *Mexico's Drug-Related Violence*; Cook, *Mexico's Drug Cartels*; Freeman and Sierra, "Mexico: The Militarization Trap"; Meyer, *At a Crossroads*; and Verini, "Arming the Drug Wars," as well as the series "Mexico under Siege" in the *Los Angeles Times.*

20. An estimated $15 to $25 billion flows into Mexico from the United States annually from the drug trade. See Biettel, *Mexico's Drug-Related Violence*, 8. For a history of drug trafficking to the United States and a discussion of the Mexican cartels, see Biettel, *Mexico's Drug-Related Violence* and Cook, *Mexico's Drug Cartels.*

21. See Domínguez and Fernández de Castro, *The United States and Mexico,* 41–49.

22. Freeman and Sierra, "Mexico: The Militarization Trap," 270–271.

23. Wilkinson, "Where 'the monster' roams freely."

24. Ibid.

25. On drug-related violence, see Biettel, *Mexico's Drug-Related Violence.*

26. This process is described in Verini, "Arming the Drug Wars."

27. Ellingwood, "Drug gangs are winning the arms race."

28. A controversial book published in Mexico by former officials in the Fox government, Ruben Aguilar and Jorge Casteñeda, is strongly critical of the Calderón military initiative, arguing that the focus should be on the United States and should include decriminalization as well as measures to reduce kidnappings, corruption, and violence in Mexico. See Ellingwood, "Book slams Mexico's campaign."

29. On the issue of torture, see also Fainaru and Booth, "Mexico accused of torture in the drug war."

30. Meyer et al, *At a Crossroads,* 1.

31. Several of these changes had been introduced in the state of Chihuahua in 2004, but do not include drug-related crimes, which are under federal jurisdiction.

32. One example was "Operation Casablanca," a covert action conducted by the U.S. DEA (Drug Enforcement Administration) in the mid-1990s, involving the arrest of 22 bank employees at 10 Mexican banks, without informing the Mexican government until after the fact (Domínguez and Fernández de Castro, 48).

33. Mexican drug traffickers have already expanded their presence in Central America, particularly Guatemala, seeking new maritime routes following an upsurge in marine patrols around Mexico; storing drugs, weapons and drug money in Guatemalan hideouts; and building airstrips for transporting cocaine from South America and then north to points in Mexico (Ellingwood, "Mexico's Drug War Is Pushing Gangs into Guatemala"). They are also financing small farmers to grow poppies. As in the case of Mexico, the cartels have infiltrated the Guatemalan police forces and drawn in a range of collaborators, including high-level officials as well as poor Guatemalans unable to resist the massive sums the cartels offer for cooperation. The increased presence of the Mexican cartels has contributed to an upsurge of violence in the affected countries, notably Guatemala, already suffering from high levels of poverty, crime and insecurity in the aftermath of a 30-year civil war. A struggle between the Zetas and other Mexican cartels as well as Guatemalan gangs to control sales in Guatemala has led to bloody conflicts and vicious killings in several provinces of Guatemala.

34. Freeman and Sierra, "Mexico: The Militarization Trap," 294–296.

35. Sources on U.S. migration policy and policy recommendations, in addition to sources cited above, include Cornelius, "Controlling 'unwanted' immigration"; the Council on Foreign Relations, *US Immigration Policy*; Dresser, *U.S.-Mexico Relations*; Escobar Latapí and Martin, *Mexico-U.S. Migration Management*; Hagan and Phillips, "Border Blunders"; the Immigration Policy Center, *The Economics of Immigration Reform*; Jonas and Tactaquin, "Latino Immigrant Rights"; Lowenthal, "Moving the Debate Forward"; Myers, *Immigrants and Boomers*; Pastor and Alba, "Guest Workers and the New Transnationalism"; and the Unity Blueprint for Immigration Reform, (http://www.unityblueprint.org). On Mexico's southern border, see the Johnson, *The Forgotten Border*; and Castillo, *Mexico: Caught between the United States and Central America*.

36. See Potok, "Rage on the Right."

37. On media distortions of the immigration issue, see Suro, *Promoting Misconceptions*.

38. See Myers, *Immigrants and Boomers*.

39. Barry, *ICE Detention Reforms Hide Abusive Practices*. For more on the private prison complex and conditions in detention centers, see series by Tom Barry in *Americas Program of the Center for International Research*, (http://Americas.irc-online.org).

40. See Giblin and Gabrielson, "Reasonable Doubt." Following the denunciation of the Sheriff's actions by local officials, including the Phoenix police department and mayor of Phoenix, as well as by religious, human rights and advocacy groups, the federal government opened an investigation of the Sheriff for civil rights abuses including discrimination and unconstitutional searches and seizures.

41. Durand and Massey, *Crossing the Border*, 12. The number of Mexicans coming to the United States, as well as the number of undocumented immigrants in the United States, has declined since 2008, although it is not clear to what extent this is due to stricter enforcement or to the U.S. recession and lack of job opportunities.

42. See for example Portes and Hoffman, "Latin American Class Structures."

Bibliography

Acuña, Rodolfo F. *Anything but Mexican: Chicanos in Contemporary Los Angeles*. London: Verso, 1996.

Adams, Richard. *The Ancient American Civilizations*. New York: Praeger, 1974.

Adams, Richard E. W., ed., *The Origins of Maya Civilization*. Albuquerque, New Mexico: University of New Mexico Press, 1977.

Aguayo Quezada, Sergio. "Electoral Observation and Democracy in Mexico," in *Electoral Observation and Democratic Transitions in Latin America*. Edited by Kevin J. Middlebrook. La Jolla: Center for U.S.-Mexican Studies, University of California, San Diego, 1998.

Aguilar Camín, Hector and Lorenzo Meyer. *In the Shadow of the Mexican Revolution: Contemporary Mexican History, 1910–1989*. Austin: University of Texas Press, 1993.

Ainslee, Ricardo C. "Cultural Mourning, Immigration and Engagement: Vignettes from the Mexican Experience," in *Crossings: Mexican Immigration in Interdisciplinary Perspectives*. Edited by Marcelo M. Suarez-Orozco. Cambridge, MA: David Rockefeller Center for Latin American Studies, Harvard University, 1998.

Allen, James P. and Eugene Turner. *The Ethnic Quilt: Population Diversity in Southern California*. Northridge: The Center for Geographical Studies, California State University, 1997.

Alonso, Jorge. "Repoliticizing the Election Institute: A Severe Setback for Mexican Democracy." *Envio Digital*. April 2004. <http://www.envio.org.hi/articulo/2105/>

Amador, Lucero and Victoria Infante. "El poder político de los migrantes," *La Opinion* (May 25), 1B–2B.

Americas Program of the Center for International Research. <http:Americas.irc-online.org>

Andreas, Peter. "Politics on Edge: Managing the U.S.-Mexican Border," *Current History*, 105 (688), February, 2006.

Anguiano, Arturo. *El estado y la política obrera del cardenismo*. Mexico: Ediciones Era, 1975.

Appendini, Kirsten. "The Challenges to Rural Mexico in an Open Economy." *Mexico's Politics and Society in Transition*. Edited by Joséph S. Tulchin and Andrew D. Selee. Boulder: Lynne Rienner Publishers, Inc., 2003.

———. "Changing Agrarian Institutions: Interpreting the Contradictions." *The Transformation of Rural Mexico*. Edited by Wayne Cornelius and David Myhre. La Jolla: Center for U.S.-Mexican Studies, University of California, San Diego, 1998.

Babb, Sarah, *Managing Mexico: Economists from Nationalism to Neoliberalism*. Princeton: Princeton University Press, 2001.

Bachelor, Stephen J. "Toiling for the 'New Invaders': Autoworkers, Transnational Corporations, and Working Class Culture in Mexico City, 1955–1968." In *Fragments of a Golden Age: The Politics of Culture in Mexico since 1940*. Edited by Gilbert M. Joseph, Anne Rubenstein, and Eric Zotov. Durham: Duke University Press, 2001.

Bacon, David. *The Children of NAFTA: Labor Wars on the U.S./Mexican Border*. Berkeley: University of California Press, 2004.

Barkin, David. *Distorted Development: Mexico in the World Economy*. Boulder, CO: Westview Press, 1990.

———. "The Reconstruction of a Modern Mexican Peasantry." *Journal of Peasant Studies*. 30.1 (October 2002): 73–90.

Barry, Tom. *ICE Detention Reforms Hide Abusive Prices*. Americas Program of the Center for International Research. <http:Americas.irc-online.org>

Bartra, Roger. *Agrarian Structure and Political Power in Mexico*. Baltimore: The Johns Hopkins Press, 1993.

Basch, Linda, Nina Glick Schiller, and Christina Szanton Blanc. *Nations Unbound: Transnational Projects, Postcolonial Predicaments, and Deterritorialized Nation States*. Amsterdam: Gordon and Breach, 1994.

Bazdresch, Carlos and Carlos Elizondo. "Privatization: The Mexican Case." Paper presented at Latin America 2000 Conference, University of Illinois at Urbana-Champaign (Texas Papers on Latin America) 1992.

Benítez Manaut, Raul, Andrew Selee and Cynthia J. Arnson. "Frozen Negotiations: The Peace Process in Chiapas." *Mexican Studies/Estudios Mexicanos*. Winter 2006: 1, 22.

Bennett, Douglas and Kenneth E, Sharpe. "The State as Banker and Entrepreneur: The Last Resort Character of the Mexican State's Economic Intervention." *Brazil and Mexico: Patterns in Late Development*. Edited by Sylvia Ann Hewlett and Richard S. Weinert. Philadelphia: Institute for the Study of Human Issues, 1982.

———. *Transnational Corporations versus the State: The Political Economy of the Mexican Auto Industry*. Princeton: Princeton University Press, 1985.

Bennett, Vivienne. "The Evolution of Urban Popular Movements in Mexico between 1968 and 1988." *The Making of Social Movements in Latin America: Identity, Strategy, and Democracy*. Edited by Arturo Escobar and Sonia E. Alvarez. Boulder, CO: Westview, 1992.

———. *The Politics of Water: Urban Protest, Gender, and Power in Monterrey, Mexico*. Pittsburgh: University of Pittsburgh Press, 1995.

Bensusán, Graciela. *El modelo mexicano de regulación laboral*. Mexico: Universidad Autónoma Metropolitana-Xochimilco, 2000.

———. "A New Scenario for Mexican Trade Unions: Changes in the Structure of Political and Economic Opportunities." *Dilemmas of Political Change in Mexico*. Edited by Kevin J. Middlebrook. London and La Jolla: Institute of Latin American Studies and Center for U.S.-Mexican Studies, 2004.

Bethell, Leslie, ed. *Colonial Spanish America*. Cambridge: Cambridge University Press, 1987.

———. *Mexico since Independence*. Cambridge: Cambridge University Press, 1991.

Bethell, Leslie and Ian Roxborough, eds. *Latin America between the Second World War and the Cold War: 1944–1948*. Cambridge: Cambridge University Press, 1992.

Bezdek, Robert R. "Democratic Changes in an Authoritarian System: *Navismo* and Opposition Development in San Luís Potosí," in *Opposition Government in Mexico*. Edited by Victoria E. Rodríguez and Peter M. Ward. Albuquerque, New Mexico: University of New Mexico Press, 1995.

Biettel, June S. *Mexico's Drug-Related Violence*. CRS Report for Congress. Washington, D.C.: Congressional Research Service, May 27, 2009.

Binford, Leigh. 2002. "Migrant Renittances and (Under)Development in Mexico," *Critique of Anthropology*, 23, 3.

Bizberg, Ilán. *Estado y Sindicalismo en México*. Mexico: El Colegio de México, 1990.

Bonfil Batalla, Guillermo. *Mexico Profundo: Reclaiming a Civilization*. Austin: University of Texas Press, 1996.

Bourdeaux, Richard. 2006. "The Seeds of Promise," *Los Angeles Times* (April 16): A1, A12–14.

Boyer, Christopher R. "Contested Terrain: Forestry Regimes and Community Responses in Northeastern Michocán," in *The Community Forests of Mexico: Managing for Sustainable Landscapes*. Edited by David Barton Bray, Leticia Moreno-Pérez and Deborah Barry. Austin: University of Texas Press, 2005.

Bray, David Barton , Leticia Moreno-Pérez, and Deborah Barry, ed. *The Community Forests of Mexico: Managing for Sustainable Landscapes*. Austin: University of Texas Press, 2005.

Brooks, David and Jonathan A. Fox. *Cross-Border Dialogues: U.S.-Mexico Social Movement Networking*. La Jolla, CA: Center for U.S.-Mexican Studies, University of California, San Diego, 2002.

Bruhn, Kathleen. *Taking on Goliath: The Experience of a New Left Party and the Struggle for Democracy in Mexico*. University Park, Pennsylvania: The Pennsylvania State University Press, 1997.

———. *Urban Protest in Mexico and Brazil*. Cambridge: Cambridge University Press, 2008.

Bulmer-Thomas, Victor. *The Economic History of Latin America since Independence*. Second edition. Cambridge: Cambridge University Press, 2003.

Burgess, Katrina, "Loyalty Dilemmas and Market Reform: Party-Union Alliances under Stress in Mexico, Spain and Venezuela." *World Politics*, 52, October, 1999.

———. "Mexican Labor at a Crossroads." *Mexico's Politics and Society in Transition*. Edited by Joseph S. Tuchin and Andrew D. Selee. Boulder: Lynne Rienner, 2002.

Calvillo Unma, Tomas. "A Case of Opposition Unity: The San Luis Potosí Democratic Coalition of 1991," in *Subnational Politics and Democratization in Mexico*. Edited by Wayne A. Cornelius, Todd A. Eisenstadt and Jane Hindley. La Jolla: Center for U.S.-Mexican Studies, University of California, San Diego, 1999.

Camp, Roderic A. "Camarillas in Mexican Politics: The Case of the Salinas Cabinet." *Mexican Studies/Estudios Mexicanos*. 6.1 (Winter 1991).

———. "Democracy Redux? Mexico's Voters and the 2006 Presidential Race" in *Consolidating Mexico's Democracy: The 2006 Presidential Campaign in Comparative Perspective*. Edited by Jorge I. Domínguez, Chappell Lawson and Alejandro Moreno. Baltimore: Johns Hopkins Press, 2009.

———. "Mexico's Armed Forces: Marching to a Democratic Tune?" in *Dilemmas of Political Change in Mexico*. Edited by in Kevin J. Middlebrook. La Jolla: Center for U.S.-Mexican Studies, University of California, San Diego, 2004.

————. *Politics in Mexico: The Democratic Transition* (fifth edition). Oxford: Oxford University Press, 2007.

Cárdenas, Lázaro. *Obras: 1-Apuntes: 1913–1940.* Mexico: Universidad Nacional Autónoma de México, 1972.

Cardoso, Fernando Henrique and Enzo Faletto. *Dependency and Development in Latin America.* Berkeley: University of California Press, 1979.

Carr, Barry. "Globalization from below: labour internationalism under NAFTA," *International Social Science Journal,* 159, March 1999.

————. *El movimiento obrero y la política en Mexico: 1910–1929.* Mexico: Sep-Setentas, 1976.

Carrillo, Jorge. "The Apparel Maquiladora Industry at the Mexican Border." *Global Production: The Apparel Industry in the Pacific Rim.* Edited by Edna Bonacich et al. Philadelphia: Temple University Press, 1994.

Castellanos, Laura. "Learning, Surviving: Marcos after the Rupture." *NACLA Report on the Americas.* May–June 2008: 3, 41.

Casteñeda, Jorge G. *Perpetuating Power: How Mexican Presidents Were Chosen.* New York: The New Press, 2000.

Castillo, Manuel Angel. "Mexico: Caught between the United States and Central America." *Migration Information Source.* Migration Policy Institute: April 1, 2006.

Castles, Stephen and Mark J. Miller. *The Age of Migration: International Populatio Movements in the Modern World* (third edition). New York: Guilford Press, 2003

CCIODH (*Comisión Civil Internacional de Observación por los Derechos Humanos*). 2007. <http://cciodh.pangea.org/quinta/informefinal/informesinmarcas.pdf>

Centeño, Miguel Angel. *Democracy within Reason: Technocratic Revolution in Mexico.* University Park, Pennsylvania: Penn State Press, 1994.

Centeño, Miguel Angel and Sylvia Maxfield. "The Marriage of Finance and Order: Origins and Implications of Change in the Mexican Political Elite." Paper presented at Conference "Mexico: Contrasting Visions," sponsored by Columbia University and the New York University Consortium, 1989.

Chambers, Edward J. and Peter H. Smith, ed. *NAFTA in the New Millennium.* La Jolla, CA: Center for U.S.-Mexican Studies, University of San Diego, 2002.

Chand, Vikram K. *Mexico's Political Awakening.* Notre Dame: University of Notre Dame Press, 2001.

Chevalier, Francois. *Land and Society in Colonial Mexico.* Berkeley: University of California Press, 1963.

Cienfuegos, Enrique and Laura Carlsen, "Human Rights, Ecology, and Economic Integration: The Peasant Ecologists of Guerrero" in *Confronting Globalization: Economic Integration and Popular Resistance in Mexico,* ed. by Timothy A. Wise, Hilda Salazar, and Laura Carlsen. Bloomfield, CT: Kumarian Press, 2003.

Coatsworth, John. *Growth Against Development. The Economic Impact of Railroads in Porfirian Mexico.* Northern Illinois University Press, 1981.

Cockcroft, James D. *Intellectual Precursors of the Mexican Revolution, 1900-1913.* Austin: University of Texas Press, 1968.

————. *Mexico's Hope: An Encounter with Politics and History.* New York: Monthly Review Press, 1998.

Coe, Michael D. *Mexico: From the Olmecs to the Aztecs.* New York: Thames and Hudson, 1994.

Colegio de México, *Ajuste Estructural, Mercados Laborales, y TLC.* Mexico: El Colegio de México, 1992.

Collier, David, ed. *The New Authoritarianism in Latin America.* Princeton: Princeton University Press, 1979.

Collier, David and Ruth Berins Collier. *Shaping the Political Arena.* Princeton: Princeton University Press, 1991.

Collier, George A. with Elizabeth Lowery Quaratiello. *Basta! Land and the Zapatista Rebellion in Chiapas (Revised edition).* Oakland, CA: Food First Books, 1999.

Collier, Ruth Berins. *The Contradictory Alliance: State-Labor Relations and Regime Change in Mexico.* Research Series no. 83. Berkeley: International and Area Studies, University of California, 1992.

———. *Paths toward Democracy: The Working Class and Elites in Western Europe and South America.* Cambridge: Cambridge University Press, 1999.

———. "Popular Sector Incorporation and Political Supremacy: Regime Evolution in Brazil and Mexico." *Brazil and Mexico: Patterns in Late Development.* Edited by Sylvia Ann Hewlett and Richard S. Weinert. Philadelphia: Institute for the Study of Human Issues, 1981.

Collier, Ruth Berins and James Mahoney. "Adding Collective Actors to Collective Outcomes: Labor and Recent Democratization in South America and Southern Europe." *Comparative Politics.* (April 1997)

Cook, Colleen W. *Mexico's Drug Cartels.* CRS Report for Congress. Washington, D.C.: Congressional Research Service, October 16, 2007.

Cook, Maria Lorena. *Organizing Dissent: Unions, the State, and the Democratic Teachers' Movement in Mexico.* University Park, Pennsylvania: The Pennsylvania State University Press, 1996.

———. "Regional Integration and Transnational Politics: Popular Sector Strategies in the NAFTA Era." *The New Politics of Inequality in Latin America: Rethinking Participation and Representation.* Edited by Douglas A. Chalmers et al. Oxford: Oxford University Press, 1997.

Cook, Maria Lorena, Kevin Middlebrook, and Juan Molinar Horcasitas, ed. *The Politics of Economic Restructuring: State-Society Relations and Regime Change in Mexico.* La Jolla: Center for U.S.-Mexican Studies, University of California, San Diego, 1994.

Cordera, Rolando and Carlos Tello. *Mexico: La disputa por la nación.* Mexico: Siglo XXI, 1981.

Cordero, Salvador and Rafael Santín. *Los grupos industriales: una nueva organización económica en Mexico.* Cuadernos de l CES 23: Colegio de Mexico, 1977.

Córdova, Arnaldo. *La política de masas del cardenismo,* Mexico: Ediciones Era, 1974.

Cornelius, Wayne A. "Controlling 'unwanted' immigration: lessons from the United States, 1993–2004." *Journal of Ethnic and Migration Studies* 31 (July 2005).

———. "Impacts of NAFTA on Mexico-to-U.S. Migration," in *NAFTA in the New Millennium.* Edited by Edward J. Chambers and Peter H. Smith. La Jolla, California: Center for U.S.-Mexican Studies, University of California, San Diego, 2002.

———. "*Los migrantes de la crisis*: The Changing Profile of Mexican Migrants to the United States," in *Social Responses to Mexico's Economic Crisis of the 1980s.* Edited by Mercedes González de la Rocha and Agustín Escobar Latapí. La Jolla: Center for U.S.-Mexican Studies, University of California, San Diego, 1991

———. "The Structural Embeddedness of Demand for Mexican Immigrant Labor: New Evidence from California," in *Crossings: Mexican Immigration in Interdisciplinary Perspectives.* Edited by Marcelo M. Suarez-Orozco. Cambridge, MA: David Rockefeller Center for Latin American Studies, Harvard University, 1998.

Cornelius, Wayne and Jorge Bustamante, eds. *Mexican Migration to the United States: Origins, Consequences and Policy Options*. La Jolla: Center for U.S.-Mexican Studies, University of California, San Diego, 1989.

Cornelius, Wayne and Ann L. Craig. *The Mexican Political System in Transition*. La Jolla: Center for U.S.-Mexican Studies, University of California, San Diego, 1988.

Cornelius, Wayne, Judith Gentleman, and Peter H. Smith, ed. *Mexico's Alternative Political Futures*. La Jolla: Center for U.S.-Mexican Studies, University of California, San Diego, 1989.

Cornelius, Wayne and David Myhre. "Introduction." *The Transformation of Rural Mexico*. Edited by Wayne Cornelius and David Myhre. La Jolla: Center for U.S.-Mexican Studies, University of California, San Diego, 1988.

Cornelius, Wayne, Philip A. Martin and James F. Hallifield, eds. *Controlling Immigration: A Global Perspective*. Stanford: Stanford University Press, 2004.

Cosio Villegas, Daniel. *Historia moderna de Mexico: El Porfiriato*. Mexico: Editorial Hermes, 1965.

Council on Foreign Relations. *U.S. Immigration Policy*. Independent Task Force Report No. 63. 2009.

Council on Hemispheric Affairs (COHA). <http://www.coha.org/>

Crespo, Antonio. "Party Competition in Mexico: Opportunities and Prospects," in *Dilemmas of Political Change in Mexico*. Edited by Kevin J. Middlebrook. London: Institute of Latin American Studies, University of London, 2004.

Cumberland, Charles C. *Mexico: The Struggle for Modernity*. London: Oxford University Press, 1968.

Cypher, James M. *State and Capital in Mexico: Development Policy since 1940*. Boulder, CO: Westview Press, 1990.

Davis, Diane. *Urban Leviathan: Mexico City in the Twentieth Century*. Philadelphia: Temple University Press, 1994.

De Grammont, Hubert C. "The Agricultural Sector and Rural Development in Mexico: Consequences of Economic Globalization." *Confronting Development: Assessing Mexico's Economic and Social Policy Challenges*. Edited by Kevin J. Middlebrook and Eduardo Zepeda. Stanford/La Jolla: Stanford University Press/Center for U.S.-Mexican Studies, University of California, San Diego, 2003.

De Ita, Ana. "Mexico: Impacts of Demarcation and Titling by PROCEDE on Agrarian Conflicts and Land Concentration." *Centro de Estudios para el Cambio en el Campo Mexicano*. Mexico: 2003.

De la Garza Toledo, Enrique. "La democracia en tiempos del poscorporativismo: el caso del Sindicato de Telefonistas de la República Mexicana." *Democracia y Cambio Sindical en México*. Coordinated by Enrique de la Garza. Mexico: Friedrich Ebert Stiftung and Centro Americano para la Solidaridad Sindical Internacional, 2001.

———. "Independent Trade Unionism in Mexico: Past Development and Future Perspectives." *Unions, Workers and the State in Mexico*. Edited by Kevin J. Middlebrook. La Jolla: Center for U.S.-Mexican Studies, University of California, San Diego, 1991.

———. "Manufacturing Neoliberalism: Industrial Relations, Trade Union Corporatism and Politics." *Mexico in Transition: Neoliberal Globalism, the State, and Civil Society*. Edited by Gerardo Otero. London: Zed Books, 2003.

De los Angeles Pozas, Maria. *Industrial Restructuring in Mexico: Corporate Adaptation, Technological Innovation, and Changing Patterns of Industrial Relations in Monterrey*. La Jolla: Center for U.S.-Mexico Studies, University of California, San Diego, 1993.

De Palma, Anthony. "Mexico's Hunger for U.S. Goods Is Helping to Sell Trade Pact." *The New York Times*, November 7, 1993, Section 4.

Delgado Wise, Raul and Hector Rodríguez Ramírez. 2005. "Los dilemas de la migración y el desarrollo de Zacatecas: el caso de la region de alta migración internacional," in *Contribuciones al análisis de la migración internacional y el desarrollo regional en Mexico*. Edited by Raul Delgado Wise and Beatrice Knerr. Zacatecas, Mexico: Universidad Autónoma de Zacatecas, 2005.

Delgado Wise, Raul and Miguel Moctezuma Longoria. "Metamórfosis Migratoria y Evolución de la Estructura Productiva de Zacatecas (1983-1950)," *Regiones* (Mexico), 1, 1 (April-June, 1993).

Díaz del Castillo, Bernal. *The Conquest of New Spain*. Baltimore: Penguin Books, 1963. Translation by J.M. Cohen.

Díaz-Cayeros, Alberto. "Decentralization, Democratization and Federalism in Mexico," in *Dilemmas of Political Change in Mexico*. Edited by Kevin J. Middlebrook. La Jolla: Center for U.S.-Mexican Studies, University of California, San Diego, 2004.

———. "An Opportunity for Mexico's Poor." *San Diego Union*. 15 January 2009.

Díez, Jodi. "The Importance of Policy Frames in Contentious Politics: Mexico's National Antihomophobia Campaign," in *Latin American Research Review*, 45, 1, 2010.

Domínguez, Jorge I. and Rafael Fernández de Castro. *The United States and Mexico: Between Partnership and Conflict*. New York: Routledge, 2001.

Domínguez, Jorge I., Chappell Lawson and Alejandro Moreno, eds. *Consolidating Mexico's Democracy: The 2006 Presidential Campaign in Comparative Perspective*. Baltimore: Johns Hopkins Press, 2009.

Dornbusch, Rudiger. "The Case for Trade Liberalization in Developing Countries." *Modern Political Economy and Latin America: Theory and Policy*. Edited by Jeffry Frieden et al. Boulder: Westview, 2000.

Dos Santos, Theotonio. "The Structure of Dependence." *American Economic Review*. LX (May 1970): 2.

Dresser, Denise. "Exporting Conflict: Transboundary Consequences of Mexican Politics," in *The California-Mexico Connection*. Edited by Abraham Lowenthal and Katrina Burgess. Stanford: Stanford University Press, 1993.

———. "Mexico: Dysfunctional Democracy," in *Constructing Democracy in Latin America*, 3rd edition. Edited by Jorge I. Domínguez and Michael Shifter. Baltimore: Johns Hopkins Press, 2008.

———. *Neopopulist Solutions to Neoliberal Problems: Mexico's National Solidarity Program*. La Jolla: Center for U.S.–Mexican Studies, University of California, San Diego, 1991.

———. *U.S.-Mexico Relations: Permeable Borders, Transnational Communities*. Pacific Council on International Policy: 2006.

Durand, Jorge and Douglas S. Massey. *Crossing the Border: The Mexican Migration Project*. New York: Russell Sage Foundation, 2004.

Dussel Peters, Enrique. *The Impact of Foreign Direct Investment in Mexico*. Discussion Paper DP11. *Working Group on Development and Environment in the Americas*, April 2008.

——— "Industrial Policies, Regional Trends, and Structural Change in Mexico's Manufacturing Sector." *Confronting Development: Assessing Mexico's Economic and Social Policy Challenges*. Edited by Kevin J. Middlebrook and Eduardo Zepeda. Stanford/La Jolla: Stanford University Press/Center for U.S.-Mexican Studies, University of California, San Diego, 2003.

————. *Polarizing Mexico: The Impact of Liberalization Strategy.* Boulder: Lynne Rienner Publishers, 2000.

Eckstein, Susan. "Poor People vs. the State and Capital: Anatomy of a Successful Community Mobilization for Housing in Mexico City." *Power and Popular Protest: Latin American Social Movements.* Edited by Susan Eckstein. Berkeley: University of California Press, 2001.

————. ed. *Power and Popular Protest: Latin American Social Movements.* Berkeley: University of California Press, 2001.

Eckstein, Susan Eva and Wickham-Crowley, Timothy P., ed. *Struggles for Social Rights in Latin America.* New York: Routledge, 2003.

Eckstein, Susan Eva and Wickham-Crowley, Timothy P., ed. *What Justice? Whose Justice? Fighting for Fairness in Latin America.* Berkeley: University of California Press, 2003.

El Colegio de México. *Historia de la revolución Mexicana* (23 volumes). Mexico City: El Colegio de México, Various dates.

Ellingwood, Ken. "Book slams Mexico's campaign against drug cartels." *Los Angeles Times,* January 1, 2010.

————. "Drug gangs are winning the arms race." *Los Angeles Times,* March 15, 2009, A1, A16.

————. "Mexico's drug war is pushing gangs into Guatemala." *Los Angeles Times,* June 4 2009, A1.

————. "'No apparent motive' in shooting of teens." *Los Angeles Times,* February 2, 2010.

Enríquez, Sam. "Mexico City Sit-In Has the Air of a Fiesta." *Los Angeles Times.* 5 August 2006: A5.

————. "Protesting along the Paseo." *Los Angeles Times.* 31 July 2006: A4.

Escobar Latapí, Agustín and Susan F. Martin, ed. *Mexico-U.S. Migration Management: A Binational Approach.* Latham, Maryland: Lexington Books, 2008.

Escobar, Arturo and Sonia E. Alvarez, ed. *The Making of Social Movements in Latin America: Identity, Strategy, and Democracy.* Boulder, CO: Westview, 1992.

Esteva, Gustavo. "The Asamblea Popular de los Pueblos de Oaxaca: A Chronicle of Radical Democracy." *Latin American Perspectives.* January 2007: 1, 34.

Evans, Peter. *Dependent Development: The Alliance of Multinational, State and Local Capital in Brazil.* Princeton: Princeton University Press, 1979.

————. *Embedded Autonomy: States and Industrial Transformation.* Princeton: Princeton University Press, 1995.

Evans, Peter and Gary Gereffi. "Foreign Investment and Dependent Development: Comparing Brazil and Mexico." *Brazil and Mexico: Patterns in Late Development.* Edited by Sylvia Ann Hewlett and Richard S. Weinert. Philadelphia: Institute for the Study of Human Issues, 1982.

Fainaru, Steve and William Booth. "Mexico accused of torture in the drug war." *Washington Post,* July 9, 2009.

Felix, Adrian. "Posthumous Transnationalism: Postmortem Repatriation from the United States and Mexico." Unpublished manuscript, n.d.

Felix, David. "Income Distribution Trends in Mexico and the Kuznets Curve." *Brazil and Mexico: Patterns in Late Development.* Edited by Sylvia Ann Hewlett and Richard S. Weinert. Philadelphia: Institute for the Study of Human Issues, 1982.

Fitzgerald, David. *A Nation of Emigrants: How Mexico Manages Its Migration.* Berkeley: University of California Press, 2009.

Florescano, Enrique. *Orígen y desarrollo de los problemas agrarias de México, 1500-1821.* Mexico: Ediciones Era, 1971.

Foner, Nancy, Rubén G. Rumbaut, and Steven J. Gold, eds. *Immigration Research for a New Century: Multidisciplinary Perspectives*. New York: Russell Sage Foundation, 2000.

Foweraker, Joe and Ann Craig, ed. *Popular Movements and Political Change in Mexico*. Boulder, CO: Lynne Reinner: 1990.

Fowler, Will, ed. *Gobernantes Mexicanos*, tomos I and II. Mexico: Fondo de Cultura Económica, 2004.

Fox, Jonathan. "Assessing Binational Civil Society Coalitions: Lessons from the U.S.-Mexican Experience." *Dilemmas of Political Change in Mexico*. Edited by Kevin J. Middlebrook. London and San Diego: Institute of Latin American Studies and Center for U.S.-Mexican Studies, 2004.

———. "Governance and Rural Development in Mexico: State Intervention and Public Accountability," in *Journal of Development Studies*. 32 (October 1995): 1.

Fox, Jonathan and Gaspar Rivera-Salgado, ed. *Indigenous Mexican Migrants in the United States*. La Jolla: Center for U.S.-Mexican Studies and Center for Comparative Immigration Studies, University of California, San Diego, 2004.

Fox, Jonathan Andrew Selee, and Xóchitl Bada. "Conclusions" in Bada et al, ed. *Invisible No More: Mexican Migrant Civic Participation in the United States*. Washington, D.C.: Woodrow Wilson International Center for Scholars, 2006.

Frank, Andre Gunder. *Capitalism and Underdevelopment in Latin America: Historical Studies of Chile and Brazil*. New York: Monthly Review Press, 1967.

Freeman, Laurie and Jorge Luis Sierra. "Mexico: The Militarization Trap," in *Drugs and Democracy in Latin America: The Impact of U.S. Policy*. Edited by Coletta A. Youngers and Eileen Rosin. Boulder: Lynne Reinner Publishers, 2004.

Frieden, Jeffry A. *Debt, Development and Democracy: Modern Political Economy in Latin America: 1965-1985*. Princeton: Princeton University Press, 1991.

Garcia Zamora, Rodolfo. *Migración, remesas y desarrollo. Los retos de las organizaciones migrantes mexicanas en Estados Unidos*. Zacatecas, Mexico 2005.

Garrett, Geoffrey. "The Causes of Globalization." *Comparative Political Studies*. 33.6/7 (August-December 2000) 941–991.

Garrido, Celso and Cristina Puga. "Transformaciones del empresariado mexicano en la década de los ochenta." *Los empresarios mexicanos, ayer y hoy*. Edited by Cristina Puga and Ricardo Tirado. Mexico: Ediciones El Caballito, 1992.

Gereiffi, Gary. *The Pharmaceutical Industry and Dependency in the Third World*. Princeton: Princeton University Press, 1983.

Gereffi, Gary and Martha A. Martínez. "Mexico's Economic Transformation under NAFTA," in *Mexico's Democracy at Work: Politics and Economic Dynamics*. Edited by Russell Crandall, Guadalupe Paz, and Riordan Roett. Boulder: Lynne Rienner, 2003.

Gerschenkron, Alexander. *Economic Backwardness in Historical Perspective*. Harvard University Press, 1962.

Gilly, Adolfo. *La revolución interrumpida: Mexico, 1910–1920, una guerra campesina por la tierra y el poder*. Mexico: Ediciones "El Caballito," 1975.

Giblin, Paul and Ryan Gobrielson. "Reasonable Doubt," *East Valley Tribune* (Mesa, Arizona), July 9-13, 2009

Glick, Schiller, Nina, Linda Basch, and Christina Szanton Blanc. "Towards a Transnational Perspective on Migration: Race, Class, Ethnicity and Nationalism Reconsidered," *Annals of the New York Academy of Sciences*, 645, 1992.

Goldring, Luin. "The Gender and Geography of Citizenship in Mexico-U.S. Transnational Spaces," *Identities*, 7, 4 (January, 2001).

————. "Gendered Memory: Constructions of Rurality among Mexican Transnational Migrants" in *Creating the Countryside: The Politics of Rural and Environmental Discourse*. Edited by E. Melanie Du Puis and Peter Vandergeest. Philadelphia: Temple University Press, 2001.

————. "The Mexican State and Transmigrant Organizations: Negotiating the Boundaries of Membership and Participation," *Latin American Research Review*, 37, 3, 2003

————. "Power and Status in Transnational Social Fields," in *Transnationalism from Below*. Edited by Smith, Michael Peter and Luis Eduardo Guarnizo. Transaction Publishers, 1998.

Golob, Stephanie R.. "Beyond the Policy Frontier: Canada, Mexico and the Ideological Origins of NAFTA." *World Politics*. 55.3 (April 2003).

————. "'Making Possible What is Necessary,': Pedro Aspe, the Salinas Team, and the Next Mexican Miracle." *Technopols: Freeing Politics and Markets in Latin America in the 1990s*. Edited by Jorge I. Dominguez. University Park: Penn State Press. 1997.

Gómez Quiñones, Juan. *Chicano Politics: Reality and Promise, 1940–1990*. Albuquerque: University of New Mexico Press, 1990.

Gómez Tagle, Silvia. "Public Institutions and Electoral Transparency in Mexico," in *Dilemmas of Political Change in Mexico*. Edited by Kevin J. Middlebrook. London: Institute of Latin American Studies, University of London, 2004.

González Casanova, Pablo, ed. *La clase obrera en la historia Mexicana*. Mexico City: Siglo Veintiuno Editores, 1980.

González Casanova, Pablo and Hector Aguilar Camín, ed. *Mexico ante la crisis: El context internacional y la crisis económica*. Mexico: Siglo Ventiuno, 1985.

González, Luis. *Los artífices del cardenismo, Historia de la Revolución Mexicana, Periodo 1934–1940*, t. XIV. Mexico: El Colegio de México, 1979.

————. *Los días del president Cárdenas, Historia de la Revolución Mexicana, Periodo 1934-1940*, t. XV. Mexico: El Colegio de México, 1981.

Graham, Douglas H. "Mexican and Brazilian Economic Development: Legacies, Pattens and Performance." *Brazil and Mexico: Patterns in Late Development*. Edited by Sylvia Ann Hewlett and Richard S. Weinert. Philadelphia: Institute for the Study of Human Issues, 1982.

Greene, Kenneth F. "Images and Issues in Mexico's 2006 Presidential Elections" in *Consolidating Mexico's Demcracy: The 2006 Presidential Campaign in Comparative Perspective*. Edited by Jorge I. Domínguez, Chappell Lawson and Alejandro Moreno. Baltimore: The Johns Hopkins Press, 2009.

Grindle, Merilee Serrill. *Bureaucrats, Politicians and Peasants in Mexico: A Case Study in Public Policy*. Berkeley, University of California Press, 1977.

Gutiérrez, David G. "Globalization, Labor Migration, and the Demographic Revolution: Ethnic Mexicans in the Late Twentieth Century," in *The Columbia History of Latinos in the United States since 1960*. Edited by David G. Gutierrez. New York: Columbia University Press: 2004

Haber, Paul Lawrence. "The Art and Implications of Political Restructuring in Mexico: The Case of Urban Popular Movements." *The Politics of Economic Restructuring: State-Society Relations and Regime Change in Mexico*. Edited by Maria Lorena Cook, Kevin J. Middlebrook and Juan Molinar Horcasitas. La Jolla: Center for U.S.-Mexican Studies at the University of California, San Diego, 1994.

————. *Power from Experience: Urban Popular Movements in Late Twentieth Century Mexico*. University Park, Pennsylvania: The Pennsylvania State University Press, 2006.

Haber, Stephen, Herbert S. Klein, Noel Maurer and Kevin J. Middlebrook. *Mexico since 1980.* Cambridge: Cambridge University Press, 2008.

Hagan, Jacqueline and Scott Phillips. "Border Blunders: The Unanticipated Human and Economic Costs of the U.S. Approach to Immigration Control, 1986–2007." *Criminology and Public Policy.* 7 (2008): 1.

Haggard, Stephan and Robert R. Kaufman. *The Political Economy of Democratic Transitions.* Princeton: Princeton University Press, 1994.

Hamilton, Nora. *The Limits of State Autonomy: Post-Revolutionary Mexico.* Princeton: Princeton University Press, 1982A.

———. "State-Class Alliances and Conflicts: Issues and Actors in the Mexican Economic Crisis." *Latin American Perspectives,* 12, 4 (Fall 1983).

———. "The State and the National Bourgeoisie in Post-Revolutionary Mexico: 1920–1940." *Latin American Perspectives,* 11, 4 (Fall 1982).

Hamilton, Nora and Timothy F. Harding, ed. *Modern Mexico: State, Economy and Social Conflict.* Bevery Hills: Sage Publications, 1986.

Hamilton, Sarah, Billie R. DeWalt, and David Barkin. 2003. "Household Welfare in Four Rural Mexican Communities: The Economic and Social Dynamics of Surviving National Crises," *Mexican Studies/Estudios Mexicanos,* 19, 2 (Summer): 433–462.

Hansen, Roger D. *The Politics of Mexican Development.* Baltimore: The Johns Hopkins University Press, 1971.

Hanson, Gordon H. "Industrial Organization and Mexico-U.S. Free Trade: Evidence from the Mexican Garment Industry." *Global Production: The Apparel Industry in the Pacific Rim.* Edited by Edna Bonacich et al. Philadelphia: Temple University Press, 1994.

Harris, Scott Duke. "Hardship City," *Los Angeles Times Magazine* (October 30, 2005: pp. 18–21).

Harvey, David. "Neoliberalism as Creative Destruction." *Annals of the American Academy of Political and Social Science.* 610.1 (2007) 21–44.

Harvey, Neil. *The Chiapas Rebellion: The Struggle for Land and Democracy.* Durham, North Carolina: Duke University Press, 1998.

Hathaway, Dale. *Allies across the Border: Mexico's 'Authentic Labor Front' and Global Solidarity.* Cambridge, MA: South End Press, 2000.

Hellman, Judith Adler. *Mexico in Crisis.* Second Edition. New York: Holmes and Meier, 1983.

———. *Mexican Lives.* New York: The New Press, 1994.

———. "Mexican Popular Movements, Clientelism, and the Struggle for Democratization." *Latin American Perspectives.* 21, 2, Spring 1994.

———. "The Riddle of New Social Movements: Who They Are and What They Do." *Capital, Power, and Inequality in Latin America.* Edited by Sandor Halebsky and Richard L. Harris. Boulder, CO: Westview Press, 1995.

———. *The World of Mexican Migrants: The Rock and the Hard Place.* New York: The New Press, 2008.

Heredia, Blanca. "Profits, Politics and Size: The Political Transformation of Mexican Business." *The Right and Democracy in Latin America.* Edited by Douglas Chalmers et al. New York: Praeger, 1992.

Hernández Castillo, R. Aida. *Histories and Stories from Chiapas: Border Identities in Southern Mexico.* Austin: University of Texas, 2001.

Hernández Chavez, Alicia. *La mecánica cardenista, Historia de la Revolución Mexicana, Periodo 1934–1940,* t. XVI. Mexico: El Colegio de México, 1978.

Hernández Navarro, Luis and Laura Carlsen. "Indigenous Rights: The Battle for Constitutional Reform in Mexico." *Dilemmas of Political Change in Mexico*. Edited by Kevin J. Middlebrook. La Jolla: Center for U.S.-Mexican Studies at the University of California, San Diego, 2004.

Hewitt de Alcantará, Cynthia. *La modernización de la agricultura Mexicana: 1940–1970*. Mexico: Siglo XXI, 1978.

Hewlett, Sylvia Ann and Richard S. Weinert, ed. *Brazil and Mexico: Patterns in Late Development*. Philadelphia: Institute for the Study of Human Issues, 1982.

Hirschman, Charles, Philip Kasinitz, and Josh deWind, ed. *The Handbook of International Migration: The American Experience*. New York: Russell Sage Foundation, 1999.

Hochstettler, Kathryn. "Democratizing Pressures from Below? Social Movements in the New Brazilian Democracy." *Democratic Brazil: Actors, Institutions and Processes*. Edited by Peter R. Kingstone and Timothy J. Power. Pittsburgh, Pennsylvania: University of Pittsburgh Press, 2000.

Hondagneu-Sotelo, Pierrette. *Gendered Transitions: Mexican Experience of Immigration*. Berkeley: University of California Press, 1994.

Huber, Evelyne, Dietrich Rueschemeyer and John D. Stephens. "The Paradoxes of Contemporary Democracy: Formal, Participatory, and Social Democracy" in *Comparative Politics*. (April 1997)

Huntington, Samuel. *Political Order in Changing Societies*. New Haven, CT: Yale University Press, 1968.

Immigration Policy Center. *The Economics of Immigration Reform: What Legalizing Undocumented Immigrants Would Mean for the U.S. Economy*. Washington, D.C.: April 2009.

Johnson, Jennifer, *The Forgotten Border: Migration and Human Rights at Mexico's Southern Border*. Latin America Working Group Education Fund, Washington, D.C., January 2009.

Jonas, Susanne and Catherine Tactaqui. "Latino Immigrant Rights in the Shadow of the National Security State: Responses to Domestic Preemptive Strikes." *Social Justice*. Spring-Summer 2004.

Joseph, Gilbert M. and Daniel Nugent, eds. *Everyday Forms of State Formation: Revolution and the Negotiation of Rule in Modern Mexico*. Durham: Duke University Press, 1994.

Joseph, Gilbert M. and Timothy J. Henderson, eds. *The Mexico Reader: History, Culture, Politics*. Durham: Duke University Press, 2002.

Kahler, Miles. "External Influence, Conditionality, and the Politics of Adjustment." *The Politics of Economic Adjustment: International Conflicts and the State*. Edited by Stephan Haggard and Robert R. Kaufman. Princeton: Princeton University Press, 1992.

Karl, Terry. "Dilemmas of Democratization in Latin America" *Comparative Politics*. 25, 1 (October 1990).

Katz, Friedrich. "The Liberal Republic and the Porfiriato: 1867–1910." *Mexico since Independence*. Edited by Leslie Bethel. Cambridge: Cambridge University Press. 1991.

———. *The Life and Times of Pancho Villa*. Stanford: Stanford University Press, 1998.

Kaufman, Robert. "Economic Orthodoxy and Political Change in Mexico: The Stabilization and Adjustment Policies of the de la Madrid Administration." *Debt and Democracy in Latin America*. Edited by Barbara Stallings and Robert Kaufman. Boulder: Westview Press, 1989.

Kearney Michael and Federico Besserer. "Oaxacan Municipal Governance in Transnational Context," *Indigenous Mexican Migrants in the United States*. Edited by in Fox, Jonathan and Gaspar Rivera-Salgado. La Jolla: Center for U.S.-Mexican Studies and Center for Comparative Immigration Studies, University of California, San Diego, 2004.

Keck, Margaret E. and Kathryn Sikkink. *Activists Beyond Borders: Advocacy Networks in International Politics*. Ithaca, New York: Cornell University Press, 1998.

Klesner, Joseph L. "The 2006 Mexican Elections: Manifestations of a Divided Society?" *P.S.: Political Science and Politics*. 40, 1, 2007.

———. "Institutionalizing Mexico's New Democracy," in *Changing Structure of Mexico: Political, Social and Economic Prospects*. Second edition Edited by Laura Randall. Amonk, New York: M. E. Sharpe, 2006.

———. "Realignment or Dealignment? Consequences of Economic Crisis and Restructuring for the Mexican Party System" in *The Politics of Economic Restructuring: State Society Relations and Regime Change in Mexico*. Edited by Maria Lorena Cook, Kevin J. Middlebrook and Juan Molinar Horcsitas. La Jolla: Center for U.S.-Mexican Studies, University of California, San Diego, 1994.

Klooster, Dan. "*Campesinos* and Mexican Forest Policy during the Twentieth Century." *Latin American Research Review*. 38, 2, 2003.

Knight, Alan. "Lázaro Cárdenas." *Gobernantes mexicanos*, t. II. Edited by Will Fowler. Mexico: Fondo de Cultura Económica, 2004.

———. *The Mexican Revolution*, Volumes 1 and 2. Lincoln: University of Nebraska Press, 1986.

———. "The Rise and Fall of Cardenismo." *Mexico since Independence*. Edited by Leslie Bethel. Cambridge: Cambridge University Press, 1991.

Kraul, Chris. "Tapping Generosity of Immigrants," *Los Angeles Times* (June 8, 2000), A1, A10.

Krause, Enrique. *Mexico, Biography of Power: A History of Modern Mexico*. New York: Harper Collins, 1997.

Krueger, Anne O. "Government Failures in Development." *Modern Political Economy and LatinAmerica: Theory and Policy*. Edited by Jeffry Frieden et al. Boulder: Westview, 2000.

La Botz, Dan. *Mask of Democracy: Labor Suppression in Mexico Today*. Boston: South End Press, 1992.

———. "Mexican Labor Year in Review: 2005." *Mexican Labor News and Analysis*. 11, 1 (January 2006) (www.ueinternational.org/Mexico_info/mlna.php.)

La Jornada en linea <http//www.jornada.unam/mx/ultimas>

Laguarda Ruíz, Rodrigo. *Ser Gay en la Ciudad de Mexico: Lucha de Representaciones y Apropiacción de Identidad, 1968–1982*. Tesis para optar al grado del doctorado en Antropología, Centro de Investigaciones y Estudios Superiores en Anthropología Social (CIESAS), Cd. de México, México, 2007.

Larsen, Solana. "The Anti-Immigration Movement: From Shovels to Suits," *NACLA Report on the Americas*, 40, 3 (May–June, 2007).

Latin America Data Base. Various issues, 2006. <http://www.ladb.unm.edu>

Latin American Perspectives. *The Mexican Presidency, 2006–2012: Neoliberalism, Social Movements and Electoral Politics*. 33, 2, March 2006.

Latin American Studies Association. *Violations against Freedoms of Inquiry and Expression in Oaxaca de Juárez*. Report from the LASA Fact-Finding Delegation to Oaxaca. 2008. <http://lasa.international.pitt.edunews/oaxacareport.html>

Lawson, Chappell. "Building the Fourth Estate: Media Opening and Democratization in Mexico" in *Dilemmas of Political Change in Mexico*. Edited by Kevin J. Middlebrook. London: Institute of Latin American Studies, University of London. 2004.

Leal, Juan Felipe. *La burguesía y el Estado mexicano*. Mexico: Ediciones "El Caballito," 1974.

Letters from the Other Side, film by Heather Courtney. New Day Films. (www.letters fromtheotherside.com).

Levitt, Peggy *The Transnational Villagers*. Berkeley: University of California Press, 2001.

Levy, Daniel and Gabriel Székely. *Mexico: Paradoxes of Stability and Change*. Second Edition. Boulder, Colorado: Westview Press, 1987.

Levy, Daniel C. and Kathleen Bruhn, with Emilio Zebadúa. *Mexico: The Struggle for Democratic Development*. Berkeley: University of California Press.

Levy, Santiago. *Progress against Poverty: Sustaining Mexico's PROGRESA-OPORTUNIDADES Program*. Washington, D.C.: Brookings Institution Press, 2006.

Leyva Solano, Xochitl. "Regional, Organizational and Communal Transformations in Las Canadas." *Mayan Lives, Mayan Utopias: The Indigenous Peoples of Chiapas and the Zapatista Rebellion*. Edited by Jan Rus, Rosalva Aida Hernández Castillo, and Shannan L. Mattace. Bloomfield, CT: Rowman and Littlefield, 2003.

Loaeza, Soledad. *Partido Acción Nacional: La larga marcha, oposición leal y partido de protesta*. Mexico: Fondo de Cultura Económica, 1999.

López, Felipe H. and David Runsten. "Mixtecs and Zapotecs Working in California: Rural and Urban Experiences," in *Indigenous Mexican Migrants in the United States*. Edited by Jonathan Fox and Gaspar Rivera-Salgado. La Jolla: Center for U.S.-Mexican Studies and Center for Comparative Immigration Studies, University of California, San Diego, 2004.

Los Angeles Times. 2005–2009 <http://latimes.com/>

Lowenthal, Abraham F. "Moving the Debate Forward: What California Can Teach Us." *Americas Quarterly* (Summer 2008).

Luna Ledesma, Matilde. *Los Empresarios y el Cambio Político: Mexico 1970–1987*. Mexico: Ediciones Era, 1992.

Lustig, Nora. *Mexico: The Remaking of an Economy*. 2nd edition Washington, D.C.: The Brookings Institution, 1998.

———. "Salud y Desarrollo Económico" in *El Trimestre Económico*. 74 (October-December 2007): 296.

MacLeod, Dag. *Downsizing the State: Privatization and the Limits of Neoliberal Reform in Mexico*. Penn State Press, 2004.

Magaloni, Beatriz and Guillermo Zepeda. "Democratization, Judicial and Law Enforcement Agencies, and the Rule of Law in Mexico" in *Dilemmas of Political Change in Mexico*. Edited by in Kevin J. Middlebrook. London: Institute of Latin American Studies, University of London, 2004.

Maldonado, Centolia and Patricia Artia Rodríguez. "'Now We Are Awake': Women's Political Participation in the Oaxacan Indigenous Binational Front," in *Indigenous Mexican Migrants in the United States*. Edited by Jonathan Fox and Gaspar Rivera-Salgado. La Jolla: Center for U.S.-Mexican Studies and Center for Comparative Immigration Studies, University of California, San Diego, 2004.

Mártinez, Maria Antonia. "El modelo económico de la presidencia de Miguel Alemán." *Gobernantes mexicanos*, Tomo II. Edited by Will Fowler. Mexico: Fondo de Cultura Económica, 2008.

Martínez, Maria Elena. *Genealogical Fictions: Limpieza de Sangre, Religion, and Gender in Colonial Mexico*. Stanford, CA: Stanford University Press, 2008.

Massey, Douglas et al. "Theories of International Migration," *Population and Development Review*, 19, 3 1993.

Massey, Douglas et al. *Return to Aztlan: The Social Process of International Migration from Western Mexico*. Berkeley: University of California Press, 1987.

Mattar, Jorge, Juan Carlos Moreno-Bird, and Wilson Peres. "Foreign Investment in Mexico after Economic Reform." *Confronting Development: Assessing Mexico's Economic and Social Policy Challenges*. Edited by in Kevin J. Middlebrook and Eduardo Zepeda. Stanford/La Jolla/Stanford University Press/Center for U.S.-Mexican Studies, University of California, San Diego, 2003.

Maxfield, Sylvia. *Governing Capital: International and Mexican Politics*. Ithaca: Cornell University Press, 1990.

———. "International Economic Opening and Government Business Relations." *Mexico's Alternative Political Futures*. Edited by Wayne Cornelius et al. La Jolla: Center for U.S.-Mexico Studies, University of California, San Diego, 1989.

———. "The International Political Economy of Bank Nationalization: Mexico in Comparative Perspective." *Latin American Research Review*. 27.1 (1992)

Maxfield, Sylvia and Adam Shapiro. "Assessing the NAFTA Negotiations: U.S.-Mexican Debate and Compromise on Tariff and Non-Tariff Issues." *The Post-NAFTA Political Economy: Mexico and the Western Hemisphere*. Edited by Carol Wise. University Park: Pennsylvania State University Press, 1998.

Mazza, Jacqueline, *Don't Disturb the Neighbors: The United States and Democracy in Mexico, 1980–1995*. New York: Routledge, 2001.

McLachlan, Colin and William H. Beezley. *El Gran Pueblo: A History of Greater Mexico*. Englewood Cliffs, N.J.: Prentice Hall, 1994.

McWilliams, Carey. *North from Mexico: The Spanish-Speaking People of the United States*. New York: Greenwood Publishers ,1968.

Mexico: Cámara de Diputadoes. "Composición por tipo de eleccion y Grupo Parlamentario." (http://www.diputados.gov.mx/).

Mexico Institute, Woodrow Wilson Center (www.wilsoncenter.org/mexico).

"Mexico: Remittances, Jobs, Economy." *Migration News*, 14, 3 (July, 2007). (http://migration.ucdavis.edu/).

Meyer, Jean. *The Cristero Rebellion: The Mexican People between Church and State*. Cambridge: Cambridge University Press, 1976.

Meyer, Lorenzo. "Historical Roots of the Authoritarian State in Mexico." *Authoritarianism in Mexico*. Edited by José Luis Reyna and Richard Weinert. Philadelphia: Institute for the Study of Human Issues, 1977.

———. *México y los Estados Unidos en el conflicto petroleo (1917–1942)*. Mexico: El Colegio de México, 1972.

Meyer, Maureen, with Coletta Youngers and Dave Bewley-Taylor. *At a Crossroads: Drug Trafficking, Violence, and the Mexican State*. Washington, D.C.: Washington Office on Latin America, The Beckley Foundation Drug Policy Programme, Briefing Paper 13 (November 2007).

Meyer, Michael C., William L. Sherman, and Susan M. Deeds. *The Course of Mexican History*. Seventh edition. New York/Oxford: Oxford University Press, 2003.

Middlebrook, Kevin J. "Caciquismo and Democracy: Mexico and Beyond." *Bulletin of Latin American Research*. 28.3 (July 2009).

———. *The Paradox of Revolution: Labor, the State, and Authoritarianism in Mexico*. Baltimore: Johns Hopkins Press, 1995.

———, ed. *Unions, Workers, and the State in Mexico*. La Jolla: Center for U.S.-Mexican Studies, University of California, San Diego, 1991.

Mizrahi, Yemile. *A New Conservative Opposition in Mexico: The Politics of Entrepreneurs of Chihuahua*. Berkeley: University of California Press, 1994.

Moctezuma Longoria, Miguel. "The Migrant Club El Remolino: A Binational Community Experience," in *Confronting Globalization: Economic Integration and Popular Resistance in Mexico*. Edited by Timothy Wise, et al. Bloomfield, Connecticut: Kumarian Press, 2003.

———. *La organizacióno de los migrantes zacatecanos en los Estados Unidos*. Zacatecas, Mexico: Universidad Autónomia de Zacatecas, n.d.

———. et al. *"Laguna Grande: Un Circuito Social Transnacional de Sistema Madura*, Proyecto de Investigacion Comunidades Transnacionales Mexico-Estados Unidos, Universidad Autónoma de Zacatecas, Mexico (August 22, 2005).

Moore, Barrington, Jr. *Social Origins of Dictatorship and Democracy: Lord and Peasant in the Making of the Modern World*. Boston: Beacon Press, 1966.

Moore, Joan and James Diego Vigil. "Barrios in Transition," in *In the Barrios: Latinos and the Underclass Debate*. Edited by Joan Moore and Raquel Pinderhughes. New York: Russell Sage Foundation, 1993.

Moreno, Alejandro. "The Activation of Economic Voting in the 2006 Campaign" in *Consolidating Mexico's Democracy: The 2006 Presidential Campaign in Comparative Perspective*. Edited by Jorge I. Domínguez, Chappell Lawson and Alejandro Moreno. Baltimore: The Johns Hopkins Press, 2009.

Moreno-Brid, Juan Carlos and Jaime Ros. *Development and Growth in the Mexican Economy: A Historical Perspective*. Oxford: Oxford University Press, 2009.

Murillo, Maria Victoria. *Labor Unions, Partisans Coalitions, and Market Reforms in Latin America*. Cambridge: Cambridge University Press, 2001.

Myers, Dowell. *Immigrants and Boomers: Forging a New Social Contract for the Future of America*. Russell Sage Foundation, 2007.

Myhre, David. "The Achilles' Heel of the Reforms: The Rural Finance System." *The Transformation of Rural Mexico*. Edited by Wayne Cornelius and David Myhre. La Jolla: Center for U.S.-Mexican Studies, University of California, San Diego, 1998.

National Immigration Law Center. http:www.nilc.org.

O'Donnell, Guillermo. *Modernization and Bureaucratic Authoritarianism in Latin America: Studies in South American Politics*. Berkeley: Institute of International Studies, University of California.

———. "On the State, Democratization, and Some Conceptual Problems." *World Development*. (August 1993)

O'Donnell, Guillermo and Philippe Schmitter. *Transitions from Authoritarian Rule: Tentative Conclusions about Uncertain Democracies*. Baltimore: The Johns Hopkins Press, 1986.

Ocampo, José Antonio and Kjirsten Alexander. "Back to Basics." *American Quarterly*. 2 (Spring 2008): 2.

Olcott, Jocelyn, Mary Kay Vaughan, and Gabriela Cano, ed. *Sex in Revolution: Gender, Politics and Power in Modern Mexico*. Durham: Duke University Press, 2006.

Olivo, Antonio and Oscar Avila. "Influence on both sides of the border," *Chicago Tribune* (April 6, 2007).

Olvera, Alberto. "Civic Alliance: Pro-Democratic Social Movements, Civil Society, and the Public Sphere." *Project of Civil Society and Governance in Mexico*. Institute for Development Studies, 2000.

———. "Civil Society in Mexico at Century's End" in *Dilemmas of Political Change in Mexico*. Edited by Kevin J. Middlebrook. London: Institute of Latin American Studies, University of London, 2004.

Orozco, Manuel. "Transnationalism and Development: Trends and Opportunities in Latin America" in *Remittances: Development Impact and Future Prospects*. Edited by Samuel Munzele and Dilip Ratner. World Bank, Washington, D.C., 2005. (www.ladialog.org/publications/2005/fall/part_sic.pdf).

Otero, Gerardo. "Neoliberal Globalism, the State, and Civil Society in Mexico," in *Mexico in Transition: Neoliberal Globalism, the State, and Civil Society*. London and New York: Zed Books, 2004.

Pastor, Manuel. "Pesos, Policies and Predictions: Why the Crisis, Why the Surprise, and Why the Recovery?" *The Post-NAFTA Political Economy: Mexico and the Western Hemisphere*. Edited by Carol Wise. University Park: Pennsylvania State Press, 1998.

Pastor, Manuel and Carol Wise. "State Policy, Distribution, and Neoliberal Reform in Mexico." *Journal of Latin American Studies*. 29.2 (1997)

———. "Mexican Style Neo-Liberalism." *The Post-NAFTA Political Economy: Mexico and the Western Hemisphere*. Edited by Carol Wise. University Park: Penn State Press, 1998.

———. "The Fox Administration and the Politics of Economic Transition" in *Mexico's Democracy at Work: Politics and Economic Dynamics*. Edited by Russell Crandall, Guadalupe Paz, and Riordan Roett. Boulder: Lynne Rienner, 2005.

Pastor, Manuel and Susan Alva. "Guest Workers and the New Transnationalism: Possibilities and Realities in an Age of Repression." *Social Justice* 31 (2004): 1–2.

Paterson, Kent. "The Life and Death of a Mexican Environmental Prophet." *Americas Program Report*. Washington, D.C.: Center for International Policy. (23 September 2009).

Paz, Octavio. *The Labyrinth of Solitude: Life and Thought in Mexico*. New York: Grove Press, 1961.

Pellicer, Olga. *Mexico: A Reluctant Middle Power?* FES Briefing Paper. Mexico: Friedrich Ebert Stiftung, 2006.

Peschard, Jacqueline, ed. *2 de Julio: Reflexiones y alternaivas*. Mexico: Universidad Nacional Autónoma de México, 2007.

Poniatowska, Elena. *Massacre in Mexico*. Columbia: University of Missouri Press, 1975.

Portes, Alejandro, ed. *The Economic Sociology of Immigration: Essays on Networks, Ethnicity, and Entrepreneurship*. New York: Russell Sage Foundation, 1995.

Portes, Alejandro and Josh deWind, ed. *Rethinking Migration: New Theoretical and Empirical Perspectives*. New York: Berghahn Books, 2007.

Portes, Alejandro and Kelly Hoffman. "Latin American Class Structures: Their Composition and Change during the Neoliberal Era." *Latin American Research Review* 38, 1 (2003).

Portes, Alejandro and Ruben G. Rumbaut. *Immigrant America: A Portrait* (second edition). Berkeley: University of California Press, 2006.

Portes, Alejandro and Ruben G. Rumbaut. *Legacies: The Story behind the Immigrant Second Generation*. Berkeley: University of California Press, 2001.

Potok, Mark. "Rage on the Right: The Year in Hate and Extremism," *Intelligence Report*. Southern Poverty Law Center, 137, Spring 2010.

Prescott, William H. *History of the Conquest of Mexico*. Chicago: Bantam Books, 1967.

Przeworski, Adam. "Some Problems in the Study of the Transition to Democracy" in *Transitions from Authoritarian Rule: Comparative Perspectives*. Edited by Guillermo O'Donnell, Philippe C. Schmitter and Lawrence Whitehead. Baltimore: The Johns Hopkins Press, 1985.

Quiñones, Sam. "Mexican Hometown Clubs Vote for L.A. Politics," *Los Angeles Times* (March 5, 2005): B1.

Ramamurti. Ravi. "The Impact of Privatization on the Latin American Debt Problem." *Journal of Interamerican Studies and World Affairs,* 34, 2, Summer 1992.

Randall, Laura, ed. *Changing Structure of Mexico: Political, Social and Economic Prospects.* Second edition. Armonk, New York: M.E. Sharpe, 2006.

Rapoport, Sara Gordon. "Change and Continuity in Attention to Poverty in Mexico" in *Changing Structure of Mexico: Political, Social and Economic Prospects* (Second Edition). Edited by Laura Randall. Amonk, N. Y.: M. E. Sharpe, 2006.

Reed, John. *Insurgent Mexico.* New York: International Publishers, 1969.

Rénique, Gerardo and Deborah Poole. "The Oaxaca Commune: Struggling for Autonomy and Dignity." *NAFTA Report on the Americas.* 41, 3, May-June 2008.

Reyna, José Luis and Richard S. Weinert, ed. *Authoritarianism in Mexico.* Philadelphia: Institute for the Study of Human Issues, 1977.

Reynolds, Clark. *The Mexican Economy: Twentieth Century Structure and Growth.* New Haven: Yale University Press, 1970.

Richmond, Anthony H. "Sociological Theories of International Migration: The Case of Refugees," *Current Sociology,* 36, 2, 1986.

Rivera-Salgado, Gaspar. "Transnational Political Strategies: The Case of Mexican Indigenous Migrants," in *Immigration Research for a New Century: Multidisciplinary Perspectives.* Edited by Nancy Foner et al. New York: Russell Sage Foundation, 2000.

Rivera-Salgado, Gaspar and Luis Escala Rabadan. "Collective Identity and Organizational Strategies of Indigenous and Mestizo Mexican Migrants," in *Indigenous Mexican Migrants in the United States.* Edited by Jonathan Fox and Gaspar Rivera-Salgado. La Jolla: Center for U.S.-Mexican Studies and Center for Comparative Immigration Studies, University of California, San Diego, 2004.

Roberts, Kenneth M. *Deepening Democracy? The Modern Left and Social Movements in Chile and Peru.* Stanford: Stanford University Press, 1998.

Rodríguez, Victoria E. *Women in Contemporary Mexican Politics.* Austin: The University of Texas Press, 2003.

———. ed. *Women's Participation in Mexican Political Life.* Boulder, CO: Westview Press.

Rodríguez, Victoria E. and Peter M. Ward, ed. *Opposition Government in Mexico.* Albuquerque, New Mexico: University of New Mexico Press, 1995.

Rosenberg, Tina. "A Payoff Out of Poverty?" *The New York Times.* (21 December 2008).

Ross, John. *Rebellion from the Roots: Indian Uprising in Chiapas.* Monroe, Maine: Common Courage Press, 1995.

Rouse, Roger. "Making Sense of Settlement: Class Transformation, Cultural Struggle, Transnationalism among Mexican Migrants in the United States 1992" in *Towards a Transnational Perspective on Migration: Race, Class, Ethnicity and Nationalism Reconsidered.* Edited by Nina Glick Schiller, Linda Basch, and Christina Szanton Blanc. *Annals of the New York Academy of Sciences,* 645 (1992).

Roxborough, Ian. "Mexico." *Latin America between the Second World War and the Cold War: 1944–1948.* Edited by Leslie Bethel and Ian Roxborough. Cambridge: Cambridge University Press, 1992.

Rueschemeyer, Dietrich, Evelyn H. Stephens and John D. Stephens. *Capitalist Development and Democracy.* Chicago: University of Chicago Press, 1992.

Ruiz, Ramón Eduardo. *Triumphs and Tragedy: A History of the Mexican People.* New York: W.W.Norton & Company, 1992.

Rus, Jan and George A. Collier. "A Generation of Crisis in the Central Highlands of Chiapas: The Cases of Chamula and Zinacantan, 1974–2000." *Mayan Lives, Mayan Utopias: The Indigenous Peoples of Chiapas and the Zapatista Rebellion.* Edited by Jan Rus, Rosalva Aida Hernández Castillo, and Shannan L. Mattace. Bloomfield, CT: Rowman and Littlefield, 2003.

Rus, Jan, Rosalva Aida Hernández Castillo, and Shannan L. Mattace, ed. *Mayan Lives, Mayan Utopias: The Indigenous Peoples of Chiapas and the Zapatista Rebellion.* Bloomfield, CT: Rowman and Littlefield, 2003.

Russell, Philip L. *Mexico under Salinas.* Austin: Mexico Resource Center, 1994.

Salas, Carlos and Eduardo Zepeda. "Employment and Wages: Enduring the Costs of Liberalization and Economic Reform." *Confronting Development: Assessing Mexico's Economic and Social Policy Challenges.* Edited by Kevin J. Middlebrook and Eduardo Zepeda. Stanford/La Jolla: Stanford University Press/Center for U.S.-Mexican Studies, University of California, San Diego. 2003.

Sánchez, Celia and Hector Tobar. "Relatives in Mexico can only pray for miners," *Los Angeles Times* (August 16, 2007): A4.

Sánchez, Celia and Sam Enriquez. "A Long-Tended Dream is Open for Business," *Los Angeles Times* (May 25, 2007): A8.

Sánchez, George J. *Becoming Mexican American: Ethnicity, Culture and Identity in Chicano Los Angeles, 1900–1945.* New York: Oxford University Press, 1993.

Saragoza, Alex M. *The Monterrey Elite and the Mexican State, 1880–1940.* Austin: University of Texas Press, 1988.

Schiller, Nina Glick, Linda Basch, and Cristina Blanc-Szanton. *Towards a Transnational Perspective on Migration: Race, Class, Ethnicity and Nationalism Reconsidered.* New York: Annals of the New York Academy of Sciences, Vol. 646 (1992).

Schmidt, Arthur. "Making It Real Compared to What? Reconceptualizing Mexican History since 1940." *Fragments of a Golden Age: The Politics of Culture in Mexico since 1940.* Edited by Joseph, Gilbert M., Anne Rubenstein, and Eric Zotov. Durham: Duke University Press, 2001.

Schneider, Ben. *Business, Politics and the State in 20th Century Latin America.* Cambridge: Cambridge University Press, 1997.

Secretaría de Economía, Mexico. "Exportaciones totales de México." <http://www.economia-snci.gob.mx/sphp_pages/estadisticas/cuad_resumen/expmx_e.htm>

Selee, Andrew. N.d. *More than Neighbors: An Overview of Mexico and U.S.-Mexico Relations.* Washington, D.C.: Mexico Institute, Woodrow Wilson Center for Scholars, 2008. <http://www.wilsoncenter.org/mexico/>

Selee, Andrew and Katis Putnam. *Mexico's 2009 Midterm Elections: Winners and Losers.* Washington, D.C.: Mexico Institute, Woodrow Wilson International Center, 2009.

Semo, Enrique. *The History of Capitalism in Mexico: Its Origins.* Austin: University of Texas Press, 1993.

Servín, Elisa, Leticia Reina, and John Tutino, ed. *Cycles of Conflict, Centuries of Change: Crisis, Reform and Revolution in Mexico.* Durham: Duke University Press, 2007.

Shaiken, Harley. "Firm Steps on Uncertain Ground," in *Berkeley Review of Latin American Studies,* Fall 2007.

———. *Mexico in the Global Economy: High Technology and Work Organization in Export Industries.* La Jolla: Center for U.S.-Mexican Studies, University of California/San Diego, 1990.

Shannon, Amy. "Invirtiendo en la Esperanza: Comunidades Transnacionales como Emprendedores Sociales y Políticos" *enlacesAmerica*. 10 (October, 2005) (www. enlacesAmerica.org).

Shifter, Michael and Daniel Joyce. "No Longer Washington's Backyard," *Current History* (February 2009).

Shirk, David. *Mexico's New Politics: The PAN and Democratic Change*. Boulder: Lynne Rienner Publisher, 2005.

Shulman, Robin. "Clubs in U.S. Spark Political Change in Mexico," *Los Angeles Times* (August 27, 2001). B5.

Silva, Eduardo. "The Import Substitution Model: Chile in Comparative Perspective," *Latin American Perspectives*, 34, 3 (May 2007).

———. "The Politics of Sustainable Development: Native Forest Policy in Chile, Venezuela, Costa Rica and Mexico," *Journal of Latin American Studies*, 29, 2, May 1997.

Smith, Geri. "Election Lessons from Mexico." *BusinessWeek*. (2 November 2004) <http:// www.businessweek.com/>

Smith, James F. "Job Programs Aim to Curb Migrant Flow," *Los Angeles Times* (August 20, 2001). A1, A15.

Smith, Michael Peter and Luis Eduardo Guarnizo, ed. *Transnationalism from Below*. Transaction Publishers, 1998.

Smith, Peter H. "Mexico since 1946: Dynamics of an authoritarian regime." *Mexico since Independence*. Edited by Leslie Bethel. Cambridge: Cambridge University Press. 1991.

Smith, Robert Courtney. *Mexican New York: Transnational Lives of New Immigrants*. Berkeley: University of California Press, 2006.

Smith, Robert. "Transnational Localities: Community, Technology and the Politics of Membership within the Context of Mexico and U.S. Migration." in *Transnationalism from Below*. Edited by Michael Peter Smith and Luis Eduardo Guarnizo. Transaction Publishers, 1998.

Smith, Robert Freeman. *The United States and Revolutionary Nationalism in Mexico*. Chicago: University of Chicago Press, 1973.

Speed, Shannon, Rosalva Aida Hernández Castillo, and Lynn M. Stephen. *Dissident Women: Gender and Cultural Politics in Chiapas*. Edited by Austin: University of Texas Press, 2006.

Stahler Sholk, Richard. "Resisting Neoliberal Homoginization: The Zapatista Autonomy Movement," in *Latin American Perspectives*, 34, 2, March 2007.

Stahler Sholk, Richard, Harry E. Vanden, and Glen David Kuecker, ed. *Globalizing Resistance: The New Politics of Social Movements in Latin America*, in *Latin American Perspectives*, 34, 2, March 2007.

Stallings, Barbara. "International Influence on Economic Policy: Debt, Stabilization and Structural Reform." *The Politics of Economic Adjustment: International Constraints, Distributive Conflicts, and the State*. Edited by Stephan Haggard and Robert R. Kaufman. Princeton: Princeton University Press, 1992.

Starr, Pamela. "Mexico and the United States: A Window of Opportunity?" *Special Report*. Los Angeles: Pacific Council on International Policy, 2009.

Stephen, Lynn. "Mixtec Farmworkers in Oregon: Linking Labor and Ethnicity through Farmworker Unions and Hometown Associations," in *Indigenous Mexican Migrants in the United States*. Edited by Jonathan Fox and Gaspar Rivera-Salgado. La Jolla: Center for U.S.-Mexican Studies and Center for Comparative Immigration Studies, University of California, San Diego, 2004.

———. "Reality in the 2006 Oaxaca Social Movement." *Americas Policy Program, CIP.* (17 July 2008)

———. "Rural Women's Grassroots Activism: 1980–2000: Reframing the Nation from Below." *Sex in Revolution: Gender, Politics and Power in Modern Mexico.* Edited by Jocelyn Olcott, Mary Kay Vaughan and Gabriela Cano. Durham, N.C.: Duke University Press, 2006.

———. *Transborder Lives: Indigenous Oaxacans in Mexico, California, and Oregon.* Durham: Duke University Press, 2007.

———. *Women and Social Movements in Latin America: Power from Below.* Austin: University of Texas Press, 1997.

———. *Zapata Lives! Histories and Cultural Politics in Southern Mexico.* Berkeley: University of California Press, 2002.

Stiglitz, Joséph E. *Globalization and Its Discontents.* New York: W.W. Norton and Company, 2002.

Story, Dale. *Industry, the State, and Public Power in Mexico.* Austin: University of Texas Press, 1986.

Studer, Isabel. "Obstacles to Integration: NAFTA's Institutional Weakness." *Requiem or Revival? The Promise of North American Integration.* Edited by Isabel Studer and Carol Wise. Washington, D.C.: The Brookings Institution, 2007.

Suarez-Orozco, Marcelo M., ed. *Crossings: Mexican Immigration in Interdisciplinary Perspectives.* Cambridge: Harvard University Press, 1998.

Suarez-Orozco, Marcelo M. and Desirée Baolian Qin Hilliard, *Globalization: Culture and Education in the New Millennium.* Berkeley: University of California Press, 2004.

Summa, John. "Mexico's New Superbillionaires," *Multinational Monitor* (www.multinationalmonitor.org/hyper/issues/1994/11/mm1194_09.html).

Suro, Roberto. *Promoting Misconceptions: News Media of Immigration.* Los Angeles: Center for the Study of Immigrant Integration, University of Southern California, December 2009.

Tarrés, Maria Luisa, "The Role of Women's Nongovernmental Organizations in Mexican Political Life," in *Women's Participation in Mexican Political Life.* Edited by Victoria E. Rodríguez. Boulder, CO: Westview Press, 1998.

Teichman, Judith. *Policy-Making in Mexico: From Boom to Crisis.* Boston: Allen and Unwin, 1988.

———. *The Politics of Freeing Markets in Latin America: Chile, Argentina, and Mexico.* Chapel Hill: The University of North Carolina Press, 2001.

Thacker, Strom C. *Big Business, the State, and Free Trade: Constructing Coalitions in Mexico.* Cambridge: Cambridge University Press, 2000.

The New York Times. 2007–2009. <http://www.nyt.com>

Thing, James. *Entre Maricones, Machos, y Gays: Globalization and the Construction of Sexual Identities among Queer Mexicanos.* A Dissertation in Partial Fulfillment of the Requirements for the Degree of Doctor in Philosophy (Sociology), Faculty of the Graduate School, University of Southern California, Los Angeles, 2009.

Thompson, Ginger. "Mexico's Migrants Profit from Dollars Sent Home," *The New York Times* (February 23, 2005): A1.

Thompson, J. Eric. *The Rise and Fall of Maya Civilization.* Norman: University of Oklahoma Press, 1966.

Torres, Gabriel. "The *El Barzón* Debtor's Movement: From the Local to the National in Protest Politics." *Subnational Politics and Democratization in Mexico.* Edited by Wayne

A. Cornelius, Todd A. Eisenstadt and Jane Hindley. La Jolla: Center for U.S.-Mexican Studies, University of California, San Diego, 1999.

Tutino, John. *From Insurrection to Revolution in Mexico: Social Bases of Agrarian Violence, 1750–1940*. Princeton: Princeton University Press, 1986.

U.S. Department of State. *Background Note: Mexico*. <http://www.state.gov/r/pa/ei/bgn/35749.htm/>

UNCTAD (UN Commission for Trade and Development). *World Investment Report.* 2008.

Unity Blueprint for Immigration Reform. 2007. <http://www.unityblueprint.org/>

Valdez Ugalde, Francisco. "From Bank Nationalization to State Reform: Business and the New Mexican Order." *The Politics of Economic Restructuring: State-Society Relations and Regime Change in Mexico*. Edited by Maria Lorena Cook, Kevin J. Middlebrook, and Juan Molinar Horcasitas. La Jolla: Center for U.S.-Mexican Studies, University of California, San Diego, 1994.

Vasconcelos, José. *The Cosmic Race: A Bilingual Edition*. Baltimore: Johns Hopkins University Press, 1997.

Vaughan, Mary K. *Cultural Politics in Revolution: Teachers, Peasants and Schools in Mexico, 1930-1940*. Tuscon: The University of Arizona Press, 1997.

———. "Transnational Processes and the Rise and Fall of the Mexican Cultural State: Notes from the Past." *Fragments of a Golden Age: The Politics of Culture in Mexico since 1940*. Edited by Gilbert M. Joseph, Anne Rubenstein, and Eric Zotov. Durham: Duke University Press, 2001.

Vaughan, Mary Kay and Stephen E. Lewis, ed. *The Eagle and the Virgin: Nation and Cultural Revolution in Mexico, 1920–1940*. Durham: Duke University Press, 2006.

Vázquez, Josefina Zoraida and Lorenzo Meyer. *México frente a los Estados Unidos (un ensayo historic, 1776–1993*. Mexico: Fondo de Cultura Económica, 1994.

Velasco Ortiz, Laura. 2004. "Organizational Experiences and Female Participation among Indigenous Oaxaquenos in Baja California," *Indigenous Mexican Migrants in the United States*. Edited by Jonathan Fox and Gaspar Rivera-Salgado. La Jolla: Center for U.S.-Mexican Studies and Center for Comparative Immigration Studies, University of California, San Diego, 2004.

Velazquez C., Maria Cristina. 2004. "Migrant Communities, Gender, and Political Power in Oaxaca," *Indigenous Mexican Migrants in the United States*. Edited by Jonathan Fox and Gaspar Rivera-Salgado. La Jolla: Center for U.S.-Mexican Studies and Center for Comparative Immigration Studies, University of California, San Diego, 2004.

Verini, James. "Arming the Drug Wars." *International Business News*, July 2008.

Vernon, Raymond. *The Dilemma of Mexican Development: The Roles of the Public and Private Sectors*. Cambridge: Harvard University Press, 1963.

———. *Public Policy and Private Enterprise in Mexico*. Cambridge: Harvard University Press, 1964.

Villareal, René. "The Latin American Strategy of Import Substitution: Failure or Paradigm for the Region?" *Manufacturing Miracles*. Edited by Gary Gereffi and Donald Wyman. Princeton: Princeton University Press, 1990.

Waldinger, Roger. *Between Here and There: How Attached Do Latino Immigrants Remain to Their Native Country?* Report of the Pew Hispanic Center, University of California, Los Angeles, 2007.

Weber, Devra. "Historical Perspectives on Mexican Transnationalism: With Notes from Angumacutiro," *Social Justice*, 26, 3 (Fall, 1999).

Weinberg, Bill. "Oaxaca: Backward toward Revolution." *Working U.S.A.: The Journal of Labor and Society.* Vol. 10 (December 2007)

Weldon, Jeffrey A. "Changing Patterns of Executive-Legislative Relations in Mexico." *Dilemmas of Political Change in Mexico.* Edited by in Kevin J. Middlebrook. London: Institute of Latin American Studies, University of London, 2004.

Whitehead, Lawrence. "International Aspects of Democratization." *Transitions from Authoritarian Rule: Comparative Perspectives.* Edited by Guillermo O'Donnell, Philippe C. Schmitter and Lawrence Whitehead. Baltimore: The Johns Hopkins Press, 1985.

Whiting, Van R., Jr. *The Political Economy of Foreign Investment in Mexico: Nationalism, Liberalism, and Constraints on Choice.* Baltimore: Johns Hopkins, 1992.

Wiggins, Steve., et al. "Agricultural Policy Reform and Rural Livelihoods in Central Mexico. Discussion." *Journal of Development Studies.* 38.4 (April 2002): 179–202.

Wilkie, James W. *The Mexican Revolution: Federal Expenditures and Social Change since 1910.* Revised edition. Berkeley: University of California Press, 1970.

Wilkinson, Tracy. "Calderón visits Juárez." *Los Angeles Times,* February 12, 2010.

———. "Mexico agricultural subsidies are going astray," *Los Angeles Times,* March 7, 2010.

———. "A tipping point for Mexico?" *Los Angeles Times,* February 20, 2010.

———. "Where 'the monster' roams freely." *Los Angeles Times,* December 28, 2008, AI, A10.

Wilkinson, Tracy and Ken Ellingwood. "Mexico's public is missing in action," *Los Angeles Times,* December 30, 2009, A1.

Wilkinson, Tracy and Richard Marosi. "Mexico shifts tactics in the drug war." *Los Angeles Times,* August 23, 2009, A21.

Williams, Heather L. "Mobile Capital and Transborder Labor Rights Mobilization, *Politics and Society,* 27, 1, March 1999.

———. "Of Free Trade and Debt Bondage: Fighting Banks and the State in Mexico." *Latin American Perspectives.* 28, 4, July 2001.

———. *Social Movements and Economic Transition: Markets and Distributive Conflict in Mexico.* London: Cambridge University Press, 2001.

Williamson, John. "What Washington Means by Policy Reform." *Modern Political Economy and Latin America: Theory and Policy.* Edited by Jeffry Frieden et al. Boulder: Westview, 2000.

Wise, Carol. "NAFTA, Mexico and the Western Hemisphere." *The Post-NAFTA Political Economy: Mexico and the Western Hemisphere.* Edited by Carol Wise. University Park, Pennsylvania: Pennsylvania State University Press, 1998.

———. "No Turning Back: Trade Integration and the New Development Mandate." *Requium or Revival? The Promise of North American Integration.* Edited by Isabel Studer and Carol Wise. Washington, D.C.: The Brookings Institution, 2007

———. "The North American Free Trade Agreement," *New Political Economy,* 14, 1 (March 2009).

———. *The Post-NAFTA Political Economy: Mexico and the Western Hemisphere.* University Park, Pennsylvania: Pennsylvania State University Press, 1998.

———. "Unfulfilled Promise: Economic Convergence under NAFTA." *Requium or Revival? The Promise of North American Integration.* Edited by Isabel Studer and Carol Wise. Washington, D.C.: The Brookings Institution, 2007.

Woldenberg, José. "Lo Bueno, lo Malo y lo Peor." *2 de Julio: Reflexiones y Perspectivas.* Edited by in Jacqueline Peschard. Mexico: Universidad Nacional Autónoma de México, 2007.

Wolf, Eric R. *Sons of the Shaking Earth: The People of Mexico and Guatemala – Their Land, History and Culture.* Chicago: The University of Chicago Press, 1959.

Womack, John, Jr. "The Mexican Revolution: 1910–1920." *Mexico since Independence.* Edited by Leslie Bethel. Cambridge: Cambridge University Press, 1991.

————. *Rebellion in Chiapas: An Historical Reader.* New York: The New Press, 1999.

————. *Zapata and the Mexican Revolution.* New York: Vintage, 1968.

World Bank Group. "World Development Indicators." *WDI Online.* http://ddp-ext.world-bank.org.libproxy.usc.edu/ext/DDPQQ/member.do?method=getMembers&userid=1&queryId=6

Yashar, Deborah J. *Contesting Citizenship in Latin America: The Rise of Indigenous Movements and the Postliberal Challenge.* Cambridge: Cambridge University Press, 2005.

Yúñez-Naude, Antonio and Fernando Barceinas Paredes. "The Reshaping of Agricultural Policy in Mexico," in *Changing Structure of Mexico: Political, Social and Economic Prospects*, Second edition. Edited by Laura Randall. Armonk, New York: M.E. Sharpe, 2006.

Zapata, Francisco. *El conflicto syndical en América Latina.* Mexico: El Colegio de México, 1986.

————. ed. *Flexibles y Productivos? Estudios sobre flexibilidad laboral en México*, Mexico: El Colegio de México, 1998.

————. "Mexican Labor in a Context of Political, Social and Economic Change," in *Changing Structure of Mexico: Political, Social and Economic Prospects*, Second edition. Edited by Laura Randall. Armonk, New York: M. E. Sharpe.

Zolberg, Aristide R., Astri Suhrke and Sergio Aguayo. "International Factors in the Formation of Refugee Movements," *International Migration Review*, 20, 2 (1986).

Zotov, Eric. "Discovering a Land 'Mysterious and Obvious': Renarratavizing Post-Revolutionary Mexico." *Fragments of a Golden Age: The Politics of Culture in Mexico since 1940.* Edited by Joseph, Gilbert M., Anne Rubenstein, and Eric Zotov. Durham: Duke University Press, 2001.

Zuñiga, Juan Antonio. 1993. "El 66% de los depósitos bancarios se concentra en tres grupos," *La Jornada* (Mexico) (July 13).

CREDITS

Maps
1-1: Hamilton, Nora; *The Limits of State Autonomy.* © 1982 Princeton University Press. Adapted by permission of Princeton University Press.
2-1: *Mexico since Independence.* Edited by Leslie Bethell. Copyright © 1991 Cambridge University Press. Adapted with permission.

Images
2-1: Mexico City, 1926 (mural) by Jóse Clemente Orozco (1883–1949), Escuela Nacional Preparatoria San Ildefonso. © Schalkwijk/Art Resource, NY.
3-1: Mexico City, 1942 (tempera on masonite) by Juan O'Gorman (1905–1982) Museo de Arte Moderno, Mexico City, Mexico/Index/The Bridgeman Art Library Nationality/copyright status: Mexican/in copyright until 2058.
3-2: © Bettmann/CORBIS.
5-1: AP Images/Victor R. Caivano.
6-1: *Marcha de APPO.* Asamblea de Artistas Revolucionarios de Oaxaca (ASARO), Fowler Museum, University of California, Los Angeles.
7-1: AP Images.
8-1: *No Pais sin Maiz.* Asamblea de Artistas Revolucinarios de Oaxaca (ASARO), Boeckmann Center for Iberian and Latin American Studies, Special Collections, USC Libraries, University of Southern California, Los Angeles.

Poem
p. 255: Steven J. Bachelor, "Toiling for the 'New Invaders': Autoworkers, Transnational Corporations, and Working-Class Culture in Mexico City, 1955-1968," the epigraph poem by A. Martinez Comberos, "The New Invaders," 1947, in *Fragments of a Golden Age*, Gilbert M. Joseph, Anne Rubenstein, Eric Zolov, Eds., pp. 273-326. Copyright 2001, Duke University Press. All rights reserved. Reprinted by permission of the publisher.

Index

Small and medium firms, 52, 77, 104, 114,
124, 130–31, 135, 181–82
and debtors' revolt, 191, 214
impact of trade liberalization on, 116,
119
and PAN, 146, 286
SME (Mexican Electrical Workers' Union),
169–70
SNTE (National Union of Education
Workers), 85, 202
See also teachers
"social liberalism," 151–52
social movements
achievements of, 216–17
autonomy of, 178, 214
and consciousness raising, 178
continuity and change in, 174, 213–14
definition of, 175
and democracy, 174–75, 178, 215, 217
emergence of, 137
environmental, 176
heterogeneity of, 214
impact of, 217
indigenous, 176
in Latin America, 214
local issues in, 212
origins of, 212–13
participation of middle class groups in,
214
perspectives on, 175–79
relation of, with political parties, 177,
215
tactics of, 178, 215
trajectory of, 178–79
and women, 176, 207–12
See also protest movements
Sonora, 15
Sosa, Flavio, 207
South America
democratization in, 142, 177
increased autonomy of, 256
Mexican trade relations with, 96
military dictatorships in, 95, 99, 176
Southern Poverty Law Center, 273
South Korea, 93, 94
Soviet Union
collapse of, 123
industrialization of, 48
Spain, 1, 94
and colonial period in Mexico, 14–24,
225, 241, 250
and conquest of the Americas, 14–17
investments of, in Mexico, 259
migration from, 30–31, 289
refugees from, 297 n.31

Spanish American war, 29
STPRM (Union of Petroleum Workers of
the Mexican Republic), 43–44, 47,
49, 55
See also oil workers
student movement of 1968, 87–93
demands of, 87–89
demonstration of, in Tlatelolco Plaza, 90
and direct democracy, 88
divisions within, 88–89
Marxist groups within, 89
National Strike Committee (CNH) of,
88–89
origins of, 87–88
repression of, 90–93
silent demonstration of, 89–90
support for, 89–90
Superbarrio, 182
Supreme Court, 41, 55–56
increased independence of, 10, 160
reform of, 157, 171
SVREP (Southwest Voter Registration and
Education Project), 230

Tabasco, 30
Taiwan, 93
Tamaulipis, 44, 266
Tampico, 49
Tarahumara indigenous community, 195
Taxco, 19
taxes, 29, 41, 181, 185, 266, 279
in colonial period, 19–20, 23
and concessions to business, 30, 105,
109–10, 174–75, 289
on foreign companies, 41, 49, 55
and redistribution, 140, 159
reform of, 79, 97, 169
as source of government revenues, 42,
55, 77, 79, 83
value added, 162, 216
teachers
dissident movements of, 203
and Local, 22, 201
in Oaxaca, 201–03, 206
radicalization of, 48–49
role of, in rural mobilization, 53
and rural education, 46
techno-bureaucracy, 109, 112–13, 115, 135
See also technocrats
technocrats, 110, 112, 115, 150, 152, 279,
282, 290, 301 n.12
tecnicos, 10, 70, 110
Tejeda, Adalberto, 45
telephone workers, 84, 200. *See also* Union
of Telephone Workers

Printed in the USA
CPSIA information can be obtained
at www.ICGtesting.com
CBHW050917241123
2082CB00006B/181